Japan's Territory under International Law

Legal History Library

VOLUME 69

Studies in the History of International Law

VOLUME 25

The titles published in this series are listed at *brill.com/shil*

Japan's Territory under International Law

Edited by

Masaharu Yanagihara and Atsuko Kanehara

BRILL | NIJHOFF

LEIDEN | BOSTON

公益財団法人日本国際問題研究所
The Japan Institute of International Affairs

This book's research and publication were made possible thanks to funding from the Japan Institute of International Affairs (JIIA).

Cover illustration: Close-up of globe with the focus on Japan and surrounding countries. Credit: abzee, through iStockphoto.com.

Library of Congress Cataloging-in-Publication Data

Names: Yanagihara, Masaharu, 1952- editor. | Kanehara, Atsuko. editor.
Title: Japan's territory under international law / edited by Masaharu Yanagihara and Atsuko Kanehara.
Other titles: Kokusaihō kara mita ryōdo to Nihon. English
Description: Leiden ; Boston : Brill/Nijhoff, 2024. | Series: Studies in the history of international law; volume 25 | Includes index.
Identifiers: LCCN 2024036190 (print) | LCCN 2024036191 (ebook) | ISBN 9789004706354 (hardback) | ISBN 9789004706361 (ebook)
Subjects: LCSH: Japan–Boundaries. | Japan–Territorial questions.
Classification: LCC KZ3684.5.J3 K6513 2024 (print) | LCC KZ3684.5.J3 (ebook) | DDC 341.4/20952–dc23/eng/20240807
LC record available at https://lccn.loc.gov/2024036190
LC ebook record available at https://lccn.loc.gov/2024036191

Typeface for the Latin, Greek, and Cyrillic scripts: "Brill". See and download: brill.com/brill-typeface.

ISSN 1874-1793
ISBN 978-90-04-70635-4 (hardback)
ISBN 978-90-04-70636-1 (e-book)
DOI 10.1163/9789004706361

This book is printed on acid-free paper and produced in a sustainable manner.

Contents

Foreword

This book publishes research results from the "Territory and Sovereignty Working Group" for the "Territory, Sovereignty, and History Research Project" launched by the Japan Institute of International Affairs (JIIA) in 2017. This book is the outcome of the joint work undertaken by all of the authors under said research framework.

The situation surrounding the territory of Japan continues to be severe, and in recent years, it seems that the severity of the situation has increased. Since the 1990s, there have been a variety of attempts to find a solution for the Northern Territories (for example, the Kawana Proposal of April 1998). Since the border between Etorofu Island and Urup Island was delimited in Article 2 of the Treaty of Commerce, Navigation and Delimitation between Japan and Russia (also known as the Treaty of Shimoda) in 1855, the Government of Japan has asserted that the four northern islands (Etorofu Island, Kunashiri Island, Shikotan Island, and the Habomai Islands) are the "inherent territory" of Japan, that the islands have never been foreign territory, and that the islands were not included in the Kurile Islands that were renounced under Article 2(c) of the 1951 San Francisco Peace Treaty.

However, a peace treaty, which is a prerequisite for the "handover" of the Habomai Islands and Shikotan Island to Japan as stipulated in Article 9 of the 1956 Japan-Soviet Joint Declaration, has yet to be concluded between Japan and Russia. If anything, in recent years, there have been occasional statements by Russian leaders that seem to indicate a return to the position once held by the former Soviet Union, that "there is no territorial dispute over the Northern Territories in the first place." In addition, Article 67 of the Russian Constitution, revised in July 2020, clearly states that ceding Russian territory is prohibited. On March 21, 2022, Russia announced the unilateral termination of negotiations on the Japan-Russia Peace Treaty.

As for Takeshima, the Republic of Korea (ROK) consistently takes the position that no territorial dispute exists in the first place. In January 1905, the Government of Japan reaffirmed via a Cabinet decision that Takeshima was Japanese territory, and, in Article 2(a) of the San Francisco Peace Treaty, "Korea, including the islands of Quelpart, Port Hamilton and Dagelet" were renounced, but Takeshima was not included in this renunciation. To date, the Government of Japan has formally proposed to the Government of the ROK three times, in 1954, 1962, and 2012, to settle the dispute at the International Court of Justice. However, the ROK's basic position is that it will not respond to such proposals and that it will not respond to diplomatic negotiations as long as there is no dispute over Dokdo/Takeshima. On the other hand, as Takeshima is considered to have been under the effective control of the ROK since 1954 (an "illegal occupation" from Japan's point of view) it has seemed prudent for the ROK to adopt a "quiet diplomacy" policy, but the ROK has also been vociferously asserting the legitimacy of its possession over Takeshima at every opportunity (for example, protesting the map of Japan at the 2021 Tokyo Olympic Games torch relay course).

Furthermore, with regard to the Senkaku Islands, the People's Republic of China (PRC) began officially to claim sovereignty over the islands in 1971, and, particularly since 2008, it has dispatched official vessels to frequently enter and intrude into the contiguous zone and territorial waters of the Senkaku Islands, and appears to be attempting to change the status quo by force. The Japan Coast Guard website provides daily data on the number of China Coast Guard ships that have entered the contiguous zone around the Senkaku Islands and that are intruding into Japan's territorial waters, and the number of such ships has rapidly increased, especially since September 2012. With regard to these actions, the Government of Japan has consistently taken the position that the Senkaku Islands are the inherent territory of Japan and that there is no territorial dispute over the islands, as the Government of Japan declared, in January 1895, the islands to be *terra nullius*, and, since their incorporation into Japan under international law, the islands have never been foreign territory. In the November 7, 2014 document titled "Regarding Discussions toward Improving Japan-China Relations," which indicates an agreement between Japan and the PRC, while confirming that Japan and the PRC have differing views on the recent tensions in the waters of the East China Sea, including those around the Senkaku Islands, the Government of Japan maintained its position that there is no territorial dispute over the Senkaku Islands, because this document refers to the waters, not to the land itself.

Both the ROK and the PRC have mobilized researchers, not only from their own countries but also from other countries, and have ramped up their efforts to communicate their legitimacy to the international community. Moreover, in addition to spreading information through their websites, they are also employing a variety of other methods, such as international symposia, the publication of papers in academic journals, and the publication of specialized books.

This book does not aim to underpin the position of the Government of Japan or any government on the Northern Territories, Takeshima, or the Senkaku Islands, by closely analyzing their various historical backgrounds and legal issues and then presenting concrete and feasible solutions for each from the perspective of international law, or by presenting newly discovered primary materials that would be advantageous to Japan. Rather, this book is focused on two questions from a historical and theoretical perspective: 1) the historical evolution of the concept of "territory" and 2) methods for resolving territorial disputes.

Under modern international law, a State has citizens who are nationals of that State, and the territory of a State consisting of such citizens is delimited by national borders. "Defined territory" is one of the requirements for statehood, and all States under modern international law are territorial States.

It may be understood that the legal basis for such territories has been shown by the concept of "territorial title" – specifically, the five titles of occupation, accretion, cession, prescription, and conquest. However, while territorial title does indeed refer to the fact that a certain area is claimed as a territory, it is a concept that has only been used when there is a change of territory among Western countries or when a non-Western area is to be incorporated into the territory of a Western country. The legal basis for the existing territory of a Western country or for the territory of a new State itself would have to be explained by something other than these territorial titles.

There is another limitation to the concept of territorial title. Territorial disputes between States often arise when the facts are extremely complex and varied. If one of the territorial titles clearly applies and the facts satisfy the requirements, then there should be no dispute in the first place. In reality, however, it is often extremely difficult to determine the facts, such as whether a territory is truly *terra nullius* or whether it is actually the territory of another State, and which State has been in effective possession of the land, which is a requisite for occupation. That is to say, territorial disputes cannot always be resolved simply by applying one of the territorial titles.

This book's first question, the historical evolution of the concept of "territory," is based on the concept of how territory in modern international law, as described above, was established and changed. It then examines East Asian views on the concept of territory and the actual situation of the spatial order in East Asia before the establishment of modern international law relations, and lays out a discussion of the issues in relation to Japan's contemporary territorial issues.

In the East Asian world, there were a variety of intrinsic territorial concepts such as "*shioki* (control)," "*fuyō* (dependency)," "*hankoku* (domain State)," "*hanpō* (domain territory)," "*zokkoku* (subject State)," "*ryōzoku* (dual client State)," "*kyōiki* (territory)," "*hanto* (territory)," "*hōdo* (domain)," and "*ikokusakai* (the area next to a foreign country)." It is therefore required to analyze how the process of determining territory in the East Asian world was conducted using the concept of territory under modern international law, and, furthermore, what kinds of spaces were considered to be extensions of land that was regarded as territory, such as "overseas territory" and "leased territory." This analysis covers various issues that include Japan bringing Ezo (the lands to the north of the main Japanese island of Honshu) under direct control, the delimitation of borders with Russia (the Kurile Islands and Karafuto (also known as Sakhalin)), the status of the Ryūkyū Kingdom (modern-day Okinawa), and the attribution of remote islands such as the Ogasawara islands (uninhabited islands), the Senkaku Islands, and Takeshima.

The four chapters in Part 1 "Defining the Territory of Modern Japan" and in Part 2 "Territorial Extensions in Modern Japan" were written from this point of view.

Part 1, Chapter 1, "Incorporation of Remote Islands into the Territory of Japan: Focusing on Iō-tō and Minami-Tori-shima" (Masaharu YANAGIHARA) presents ten major examples (including the Senkaku Islands and Takeshima) of the incorporation of remote islands into modern Japan, with the case of Iō-tō clearly showing that there are two methods of incorporation: the occupation of *terra nullius* and the reconfirmation of the fact that a certain area of land is Japanese territory (reconfirmation of the intent of possession). It concludes that in the case of Minami-Tori-shima, the method of incorporation was, without any doubt, occupation. Part 1, Chapter 2, "Ryūkū Attribution Issue and Ernest Satow: Assessment of the Newspapers Debate between Japan and Qing and Its Background " (Tadashi MORI) analyzes Ernest Satow's February 13, 1880 memorandum on the Ryūkyū attribution issue and makes it clear that Sato supported Japan's claim to Ryūkyū based on his assessment of the modern international legal order, but without delving too deeply into historical factual disputes, the significance of tribute, or the dual affiliation theory.

Part 2, Chapter 3, "Acquisition of 'Colony' and Legal System of Japan" (Tetsuya YAMADA) examines how Japan perceived the concept of territory when it acquired so-called "overseas territory" and how this perception affected the legal system, focusing on the point that, while this was a theoretical issue, there were also political aspects to the issue of constitutional application, such as parliamentary tactics and factional disputes within the government. Part 2, Chapter 4, "The Concept of Leaseholds from the Perspective of Modern Japan" (Yuichi SASAKI) argues that, in contrast to Europe and the United States, where, after World War I, leased territory went from being viewed as a disguised or perverted form of cession to being understood to be not the same as cession, in modern Japan, the non-cession theory prevailed over the disguised cession theory from the beginning. Furthermore, it analyzes the facts and circumstances surrounding Japan's leased territory that were behind the prevalence of the non-cession theory.

The second question addressed in this book, on methods for resolving territorial disputes, looks at the latest developments in international jurisprudence and other territorial dispute resolution cases as well as at changes in the usage and significance of international law concepts that are related to territory, taking up existing articles and commentaries on judicial precedents and, in particular, examining their points with Japan's territorial issues in mind.

Since the 1980s, there has been an overwhelming increase in the number of cases that deal with territorial disputes, including issues of maritime delimitation, which are being handled not only by the International Court of Justice, but also by the International Tribunal for the Law of the Sea and other courts and tribunals. In these international courts and tribunals, the conclusions are not reached based on any one of the territorial titles; rather the actual territorial disputes are resolved through the use of various legal theories such as the acquiescence, recognition, and protest of the countries involved, "continuous and peaceful display of territorial sovereignty," "*effectivités*," and the theory of critical date and intertemporal law. Additionally, the international courts and tribunals are also addressing questions of how to evaluate the connection or disconnection between the traditional concept of "territory" in pre-modern European and non-European regions and the concept of "territory" in modern international law.

With Japan's territorial disputes in mind, the five papers in Part 3 "Intent and Time in Territorial Disputes" and in Part 4 "Territorial Disputes in International Courts and Tribunals" analyze these various attempts by international courts and tribunals.

Part 3, Chapter 5, "The Arguments Based on 'Law' in Territorial Disputes" (Atsuko KANEHARA) looks at law-related assertions and claims, focusing on how laws incorporate those assertions and claims into the legal world, considering, in order, "historic rights" as a claim relating to law, intent and time as the main factors involved in determining the relationship to law, and the factor of "operational intent" in territorial disputes, before finally proposing an integrated position for Japan, as a Sovereign State, on the issue of the Senkaku Islands. Part 3, Chapter 6, "Significance of Silence in Territorial Disputes: Toward Legal Construction on "75 Years of Silence" regarding the Senkaku Islands (Pinnacle Islands)" (Tomofumi KITAMURA) examines, with the goal of exploring the implications for the Senkaku Islands issue, pre-war judicial precedents and theories regarding acquiescence, estoppel, and prescription, etc., along with early judicial precedents from the International Court of Justice and related theories, and then attempts to unravel these entangled concepts and understand their existence and content. Part 3, Chapter 7, "Temporal Elements and Their Regulation in Determining

Territorial Disputes: Practical Application to Territorial Disputes of Japan" (Hironobu SAKAI) first summarizes the respective roles in territorial disputes of the principles of critical date and intertemporal law, then considers how these two principles function in judicial practice, and from there examines their specific application to Japan's territorial disputes based on the practical role of the two principles that is obtained.

Part 4, Chapter 8, "Application and Evaluation of "Premodern/Non-European Territorial Control" in International Courts and Tribunals" (Tomoko FUKAMACHI) examines ten judicial precedents involving pre-modern European and non-European territorial dominion and ascertains how the courts have dealt with the intents or aims of the parties and the concepts of title that were used, that is, it reviews how pre-modern and non-European territorial dominion and legal evaluations were conducted and considers the factors that guided such treatment. Part 4, Chapter 9, "Recognition of the Existence of Territorial Sovereignty Disputes in International Courts and Tribunals: The Use of the Coastal State Litigation before the Annex VII Arbitration of the UN Convention on the Law of the Sea" (Dai TAMADA) contains a detailed analysis of "Coastal State Litigation" in the UNCLOS Annex VII Arbitration Tribunal – the Chagos Marine Protected Area Arbitration and the Dispute Concerning Coastal State Rights – and, by utilizing the Chagos Method A and the Crimean Method presented therein, shows that it is possible to obtain recognition of the existence of a territorial sovereignty dispute over, for example, Takeshima.

I would also like to briefly explain here the two terms "territory" and "territorial land." "Territory" is divided into three parts and consists of "territorial land" for terrestrial areas, "territorial waters" for maritime areas (consisting of "inland waters" such as ports and the "territorial seas" outside of "inland waters") and "territorial airspace" for aerial areas. Among them, territorial land is determined first, followed next by territorial waters of the surrounding maritime areas, and then territorial airspace above the territorial land and territorial waters. Territorial land is positioned at the center of the idea of territory, with territorial waters and territorial airspace are determined by territorial land. As such, the term "territorial land" is also used to refer to the entirety of the territory. This book also uses the two terms "territory" and "territorial land" in that sense.

The main purpose of this book is to shed light on Japan's territorial situation from a different and unique perspective by analyzing the historical evolution of the concept of "territory" and by analyzing the various legal theories on resolving territorial disputes. Although this book does not have any chapters that directly address the facts and legal issues of the Northern Territories, Takeshima, and the Senkaku Islands in detail, each of the chapters in this book presents multiple points of view that can provide significant insight into the resolution of these issues, and I am convinced that they will be of useful reference to practitioners, researchers, and even members of the general public who are interested in territorial issues.

This book is an English version of YANAGIHARA Masaharu and KANEHARA Atsuko (eds.), *Kokusaihō kara Mita Ryōdo to Nihon* 国際法からみた領土と日本 [Japan's Territory under International Law] (Tokyo: University of Tokyo Press, 2022) in Japanese. The translation was done by Urban Connections and checked by each author. I would like to express my very deep gratitude for JIIA's strong support for the publication.

I would like to express my sincere admiration and deep appreciation for the efforts of Mr. Yamada Hideki of University of Tokyo Press, who completely understood and wholeheartedly supported the goals of this book in Japanese in his editing of it. There was a collaborative effort between Mr. Yamada and the authors. I would also obviously like to express gratitude to University of Tokyo Press for taking on the task of publishing the original version of this book despite the difficult publication conditions. The hard work provided by the members of JIIA to support the smooth functioning of the two study groups created mutual and cross-cutting connections among the individual and independent papers, thus enabling this book to amount to more than just the sum of its parts. JIIA provided a variety of assistance in relation to the actual publishing of this book as well. I would like to express deep gratitude for this support.

Masaharu YANAGIHARA

Figures

Notes on Contributors

Tomoko FUKAMACHI
(born in 1969) is Professor of public international law at Fukuoka Women's University. She obtained her M.L. from Kyushu University in 1994. Her recent publications are as follows: "Ryōiki ni kansuru Genshi Kengen: Ryōiki Kengen Ron wa nani o dokomade atsukaunoka [Original Title to Territory: To What and To What Extent Is the Legal Framework of Title to Territory Applied]," *Hōgaku Seminā* 765 (2018) (in Japanese), which is translated into English and published in *Japan Review* 6 (1) (2023).

Atsuko KANEHARA
a graduate from the University of Tokyo, is Research Director for the Canon Institute for Global Studies, and Senior Fellow for the Sasakawa Peace Foundation. She is an expert on public international law. Her main publications are as follows: "Reassessment of the Acts of the State in the Law of State Responsibility: A Proposal of an Integrative Theoretical Framework of the Law of State Responsibility to Effectively Cope with the Internationally Harmful Acts of Non-state Actors," *Recueil des cours* 399 (2019); "Refining Japan's Integrative Position on the Territorial Sovereignty of the Senkaku Islands," *International Law Studies* 97 (2021).

Tomofumi KITAMURA
(born in 1979) is Associate Professor of public international law at the University of Tokyo. He obtained his Ph.D. from the University of Tokyo. His main publications are as follows: "Kokusaihō ni okeru Jijō Henkō Gensoku no Hōteki Konkyo [Legal Basis of the rebus sic stantibus Principle in International Law]," *Kokusai Kankeiron Kenkyū* 27 (2008) (in Japanese); "Kokusaihō jō no Kinkyūhinan ni kansuru Ichi Kōsatsu [A Study of Necessity in International Law]," *Hōgakkai Zasshi* 55 (2)–56 (2) (2015–2016) (in Japanese).

Tadashi MORI
(born in 1970) is Professor of public international law at the University of Tokyo. He obtained his Ph.D. from the University of Tokyo in 2008. His main publications are as follows: *Origins of the Right of Self-Defence in International Law: From the Caroline Incident to the United Nations Charter* (Brill, 2018); "Collective Self-Defence in International Law and in the New Japanese Legislation for Peace and Security (2015)," *Japanese Yearbook of International Law* 60 (2018); "Decisions in Japan to Use Military Force or to Participate in

Multinational Peacekeeping Operations," in Curtis A. Bradley (ed.), *Oxford Handbook of Comparative Foreign Relations Law* (Oxford University Press, 2019).

Hironobu SAKAI
(born in 1963) is Professor of international economic law at Waseda University and Emeritus Professor at Kyoto University. He obtained his M.L. from Kyoto University. His main publications are as follows: "*La bonne administration de la justice* in the Incidental Proceedings of the International Court of Justice," *Japanese Yearbook of International Law* 55 (2012); "The Quest for a Win-Win Solution in the Delimitation of Continental Shelf in the East China Sea: An Irreconcilable Conflict between China and Japan?" in James Kraska, Ronan Long, and Myron H. Nordquist (eds.), *Peaceful Maritime Engagement in East Asia and the Pacific Region* (Brill, 2022).

Yuichi SASAKI
(born in 1987) is Associate Professor of Japanese political and diplomatic history at Meiji Gakuin University. He obtained his Ph.D. from the University of Tokyo in 2016. His main publications are as follows: *Teikoku Nihon no Gaikō, 1894–1922: Naze Hanto wa Kakudai shitanoka* [Japanese Diplomacy and the Dynamics of Imperial Expansion, 1894–1922] (University of Tokyo Press, 2017) (in Japanese); *Kindai Nihon Gaikō-shi* [Japanese Diplomatic History, 1853–1945] (Chūō Kōron Shinsha, 2022) (in Japanese); "Reception and Practice of Diplomacy in Modern Japan: Power, Interests, and Norms," *International Relations of the Asia-Pacific* 22 (2) (2022).

Dai TAMADA
(born in 1974) is Professor of public international law at Kyoto University. He obtained his Ph.D. from Kyoto University in 2014. His main publications are as follows: *Kokusai Saiban no Hanketsukō Ron* [Legal Effects of Judgments of International Courts and Tribunals] (Yūhikaku, 2012) (in Japanese); *Whaling in the Antarctic: Significance and Implications of the ICJ Judgment* (co-edited, Brill/Nijhoff, 2016); *Theory and Practice of Export Control: Balancing International Security and International Economic Relations* (co-edited, Springer, 2017); *Implementation of the United Nations Convention on the Law of the Sea: State Practice of China and Japan* (co-edited, Springer, 2021).

Tetsuya YAMADA
(born in 1965) is Professor of public international law at Nanzan University. He obtained his Ph.D. from Kyushu University. His main publications are as follows: *Kokuren ga Tsukuru Chitsujo: Ryōiki Kanri to Kokusai Soshikihō* [Does

the UN Create Order?: International Territorial Administration and the Law of International Organizations] (University of Tokyo Press, 2010) (in Japanese); *Kokusai Kikō Nyūmon Dainihan* [Introduction to International Organizations 2nd ed.] (University of Tokyo Press, 2023) (in Japanese).

Masaharu YANAGIHARA
(born in 1952) is Professor of public international law at the Open University of Japan and Emeritus Professor at Kyushu University. He obtained his Ph.D. from the University of Tokyo in 1981. His main publications are as follows: *Vorufu no Kokusaihō Riron* [The Theory of Christian Wolff] (Yūhikaku, 1998) (in Japanese); "Significance of the History of the Law of Nations in Europe and East Asia," *Recueil des cours* 371 (2015); *Teikoku Nihon to Fusenjōyaku: Gaikōkan ga mita Kokusaihō no Genkai to Kibō* (Japan's Engagement with Briand-Kellogg Pact) (NHK Publishing, 2022) (in Japanese).

PART 1

Defining the Territory of Modern Japan

CHAPTER 1

Incorporation of Remote Islands into the Territory of Japan

Focusing on Iō-tō and Minami-Tori-shima

Masaharu Yanagihara

1 Introduction

The notion that Japan gave no consideration whatsoever to modern international law during the Edo Era (1603–1867), not even in the Era's final years, and that it only established foreign relations based on modern international law and accurately determined its territories in the Meiji period (1868–1912), is unlikely to be an accurate reflection of the facts. At the end of Edo Era, the ruling Tokugawa shogunate was in a situation where it had no choice but to be conscious of "(modern) States," "borders," and "territories" in the modern international legal sense. This can be seen in examples such as when the shogunate made Ezo (the historic term for lands to the north of the main Japanese island of Honshu, such as modern-day Hokkaido) into a directly controlled territory, delimited borders with Russia (the Kurile Islands and Karafuto (also known as Sakhalin)), dealt with the Ryūkyū affiliation issue, and determined the attribution of the Ogasawara Islands or Bonin Islands (*Mu-nin-jima* or *Bu-nin-jima*, meaning uninhabited islands).

However, such attempts by the shogunate were still largely unsatisfactory, and it cannot be said that there was sufficient knowledge of modern international law at that time. At first, the Meiji Government also lacked sufficient knowledge of international law and was at times faced with confusing situations. However, before long, the Meiji Government was actively working to define Japan's territories while also basing its foreign policy on revisions of the unequal treaties previously concluded by the shogunate. Some representative examples include the renaming of Ezo to Hokkaido, the Ryūkyū disposition, and the incorporation of remote islands. During the Franko-Prussian War of 1870 and the Chishima-Ravenna collision incident of 1892, the definition and extent of "territorial seas" also became an issue.[1]

1 Refer to Yanagihara Masaharu 柳原正治, "Nihon ni Okeru Ryōkai no Han-i ni Kansuru Senrei -Gaimushō Jyōyakukyoku Hen "Kokusaihō Senrei Ishū (7) Ryōkai no Han-i" o Sozai

 | DOI:10.1163/9789004706361_002

The incorporation of remote islands in modern Japan includes the Ogasawara Islands, which had been recognized as a serious boundary problem since the end of the Edo Era, Minami-Daitō-jima and Kita-Daitō-jima in 1885, Iō-tō in 1891, Uotsuri-jima and Kuba-jima [and Kumeaka-shima (Taisho-jima). The Senkaku Islands] in 1895, Tori-shima in 1897, Minami-Tori-shima in 1898, Oki-Daitō-jima in 1900, Takeshima in 1905, Nakano-Tori-shima in 1908, and then, after the beginning of the Showa Era (1926–1989), Okino-Tori-shima in 1931. Of these, this chapter focuses on the two cases of Iō-tō and Minami-Tori-shima, which are regarded as seminal points in terms of the legal position of measures for incorporation into Japanese territory.

According to the theory of modern international law, there are two ways to incorporate a remote island into a territory: through the occupation of "*terra nullius*" and through the reaffirmation of territory (reaffirmation of territorial intent). "Occupation" is a territorial title that has been claimed in place of "discovery" since the 17th century, and is a theory that is modeled after "*occupatio*," a method of acquiring property rights under ancient Roman law.[2] In the latter half of the 19th century, *terra nullius* was considered to refer not only to areas uninhabited by humans, but also to areas inhabited by indigenous peoples that had a certain degree of social and political organization but had not yet reached a stage analogous to that of Western civilization. If a State effectively occupied such *terra nullius* with the intention of claiming it, then the State could incorporate the *terra nullius* into its own territory.

Reaffirmation of territory is an incorporation method in which an island that is considered to have originally been the territory of a State is reaffirmed as such, and the competent authorities and a name are determined. The basis for reaffirming that an island was originally territory is either that it was occupied at some point before the incorporation measures, or that it could be territory from before – it is often not specified when from – by some method other than occupation.

to Shite" 日本における領海の範囲に関する先例－外務省条約局編『国際法先例彙輯（7）領海ノ範囲』を素材として [Precedents Concerning the Scope of Territorial Sea in Japan: Based on 'Precedents in International Law Concerning the Scope of Territorial Sea' Edited by the Treaty Bureau in the Ministry of Foreign Affairs], Yanagihara Masaharu et al. (eds.), *Kokusaihō Chitsujo to Gurōbaru Keizai – Mamiya Isamu Sensei Tsuitō* 国際法秩序とグローバル経済－間宮勇先生追悼 (Tokyo: Shinzansha, 2021), 5–32.

2 However, "occupation of owner-less property" under ancient Roman law relates to the ownership of movable property, not to land. For example, refer to R. Lesaffer, "Argument from Roman Law in Current International Law: Occupation and Acquisitive Prescription," *European Journal of International Law*, vol. 16, no. 1 (2005): 40–41.

The case of Iō-tō clearly demonstrated the existence of these two methods, while in the case of Minami-Tori-shima the occupation method was clearly adopted. In the following sections, this chapter will examine the incorporation process and the legal aspects of these two cases.

2 Iō-tō

2.1 *The Incorporation Process*

Iō-tō is one island in a volcanic archipelago (with the other islands being Kita-Iō-tō and Minami-Iō-tō) and is now a part of the Ogasawara Islands. The incorporation of Iō-tō involved an extremely interesting process.

The existence of Iō-tō was known to Europeans in the 16th century, but it was an isolated island in the middle of the ocean and remained uninhabited for many years. According to Tokyo Prefecture Documents, now held by the Tokyo Metropolitan Archives, the following is an account of the development of Iō-tō by the Japanese. In November 1887, Tokyo Prefectural Governor Takasaki Goroku embarked on the ship *Meiji Maru* to survey and develop Iō-tō and Tori-shima. Yokoo Tōsaku was in charge of surveying Iō-tō, but at the time, it was determined that there were no prospects for colonization.[3] Subsequently, in June 1889, Tanaka Eijirō, Yorioka Shōzō, and other private persons sailed there on the *Nanyō Maru*, discovered a sulfur mine, left behind eight laborers, and began mining sulfur and fishing. On November 30, an agreement was exchanged between the entrepreneur Tanaka Eijirō and the labor representative Arai Yoshikuni, and six more voyages were made until July 1890, during which time 3,300 bags of sulfur were mined. During this period, on March 24, 1890, Tanaka petitioned Governor Takasaki for a 50-year lease free of rent for sulfur mining and fishing. In response to this request, the General Affairs Division of the Tokyo Prefectural Government prepared a letter, "Request for Lease of Island" from Governor Hachisuka Mochiaki to the Minister of Home Affairs Saigō Jūdō (prepared on April 5 and delivered on July 21; No. 4941). It stated, "The island is uninhabited, and its location is completely recognized as being within the Empire's territory."[4]

---

3 Refer to Tokyo Metropolitan Government (ed.), *Tōkyō Shishikō Shigaihen Dai 72* 東京市史稿市街編 第 72 [The History of Tokyo City, Town Edition, vol. 72] (Tokyo: Tokyo Metropolitan Government, 1981), 643–648. When citing this document below, it will be referred to as "*The History of Tokyo City, Town Edition*" with the volume number and year of publication added.

4 Tokyo Prefecture Documents (Tokyo Metropolitan Archives Collection) 619.C2.19: Nr.7: 45(1)–48, 63; 619.C2.19: Nr.10: 168; 619.C6.02: Nr.6: 160(1)–162, 215(1). The reason it took more than three months from preparation by the General Affairs Division to delivery to the Minister of

However, due to Tanaka's death on July 25, 1890, mining was suspended in August. Tanaka's remaining family, Omita Toshiyoshi, Arai Yoshikuni, and others argued over the mining rights, and petitions were filed by numerous people (including by Tanaka Eijirō's heir, Tanaka Shunsaku). On October 31, Governor Hachisuka submitted the "Request for Approval Regarding the Affiliation of Islands" (No. 6940) to the Minister of Home Affairs Saigō. In it, he wrote that,

> The island's previous affiliation is unknown. … Originally, this island was uninhabited, and its location shows that it is considered to be within the boundaries of the Imperial territory. Moreover, there is no evidence of foreign possession. Therefore, I request that it be determined that the island is affiliated with the Ogasawara Islands under the jurisdiction of this Prefecture.[5]

Afterwards, in response to a July 4, 1891 letter from Minister of Home Affairs Shinagawa Yajirō to Minister for Foreign Affairs Enomoto Takeaki that stated "A proposal of the name and affiliation of the island will be now submitted to the Cabinet. However, as there is the possibility that this is a matter of international relations, I would like to hold, for the sake of caution, deliberations with you" (Hibetsu Kō No. 257). Enomoto responded in a July 8 letter (Shinten Sō No. 534)[6] that he had no objections. Therefore, on August 6, the Minister of Home Affairs submitted the document "Matter Concerning Island Names" (Hibetsu Kō No. 257) to Prime Minister Matsukata Masayoshi and requested a Cabinet Decision with an Imperial Decree draft.[7] However, an August 13 opinion from

---

Home Affairs is presumed to be that it took time to coordinate within the Tokyo Prefectural Government, including the opinion by the Agriculture and Commerce Division. When citing documents from the Tokyo Prefecture Documents, only the classification number, binding number, and page number will be noted. For types, titles, and departments in charge, refer to Tokyo Metropolitan Archives (ed.), *Tōkyōto Kōbunshokan Shozō Mokuroku 1* (*Tōkyōhu Bunsho – Meiji*) 東京都公文書館所蔵目録1（東京府文書－明治） [Tokyo Metropolitan Archives Collection Catalog 1 (Tokyo Prefecture Documents – Meiji)] (Tokyo: Tokyo Metropolitan Archives, 2000). Refer also to the information retrieval system for the Tokyo Metropolitan Archives (https://www.archives.metro.tokyo.lg.jp/).

5 Japan Center for Asian Historical Records (JACAR) Ref. A15112383800 (from the 4th image), *Kōbun Ruishū* 公文類聚 [Public Documents Collection] Part 15, 1891, vol. 38 (National Archives of Japan); Ref. B03041152400 (7th image), *Teikoku Hanto Kankei Zakken* 帝国版図関係雑件 [Miscellaneous Matters Related to the Territory of the Empire of Japan] (1.4.1.7) (Diplomatic Archives of the Ministry of Foreign Affairs); *Tōkyōhu Bunsho* 東京府文書 [Tokyo Prefecture Documents] 619.A8.02: Nr.9: 245–246.

6 JACAR: B03041152400 (from the 3rd image).

7 JACAR: A15112383800 (from the 2nd image); B03041152400 (5th image).

the Legislation Bureau stating "The Bureau believes that the request should of course be approved" was accompanied by a note from Minister of Agriculture and Commerce Mutsu Munemitsu dated August 14. The note stated,

> Although it is clear that these three islands are actually uninhabited islands with no known affiliation, there is no need to publicly announce that they are affiliated with the Ogasawara Islands, as there is currently no party with whom there would be a dispute about them. If anything, it would be extremely injudicious if such a thing were to be publicly announced by an Imperial Decree. Rather, from the beginning, these islands have been regarded as being affiliated with the Ogasawara Islands, and I therefore believe that it would be better for the Tokyo Prefectural Governor to make a request to the Minister of Home Affairs to name the islands, following the cases of Daitō-jima and Uokagi-jima [Uotsuri-jima] in 1885, the affiliation of which had not yet been decided and which were deemed to be affiliated with the Okinawa Islands.[8]

Despite Minister Mutsu's opinion, the Cabinet Decision on August 19 stated,

> In the case of Daitō-jima and one other island,[9] which were dealt with in 1885 by being deemed to be affiliated with the Okinawa Islands, at the time, a field survey of the islands, which already had the names of 'Daitō-jima' and so on, was made and the Minister of Home Affairs provided a detailed report to the Grand Minister of State. However, the point of the attached request from the Minister of Home Affairs is as follows. The islands have until now been uninhabited, and there has therefore been no administrative problem without their affiliation and names. However, the number of people from mainland Japan who are traveling to the islands to engage in fishing and mining, etc., has been increasing, and it has therefore become necessary, for administrative purposes, to determine the islands' affiliation and name, in which case, the example of the Daitō-jima survey report cannot be used as a precedent. Therefore, it is recognized that the affiliation and name may be determined by an Imperial Decree as requested by the Minister of Home Affairs.

8 JACAR: A15112383800 (from the 9th image). This note has Gotō Shōjirō's seal on it, so it is assumed that Gotō agreed with Mutsu's opinion (see Gotō's note below).

9 "Daitō-jima and one other island" is understood to refer to two islands, Minami-Daitō-jima and Kita-Daitō-jima.

There are three distinct notes attached to this Cabinet Decision, one of which is by Minister for Foreign Affairs Enomoto Takeaki, expressing his support for the original proposal by the Minister of Home Affairs. On the other hand, the note from Minister of Posts and Telecommunications Gotō Shōjirō reads,

> First, I expressed my agreement with the opinion of the Minister of Agriculture and Commerce, which I believe now to be appropriate. Furthermore, I believe that, in terms of the order of official work, it is not appropriate for the Secretary of the Legislation Bureau to so hastily refute the opinion of the Minister of Agriculture and Commerce, despite the Ministers of Finance, the Navy, and Justice having yet to disclose their opinions on the proposal.

It cannot be determined which Minister wrote the third note, but it says, "I also agree with the note by the Minister of Posts and Telecommunications about the order of official work. Nevertheless, I concur with the view of the Minister for Foreign Affairs that the request from the Minister of Home Affairs is appropriate."[10]

Following this Cabinet Decision, Imperial Decree No. 190 was issued on September 9, stating "The three islands spread between 24 degrees 0 minutes north latitude and 25 degrees 30 minutes north and between 141 degrees 0 minutes east longitude and 141 degrees 30 minutes east latitude off the south-southwest coast of the Ogasawara Islands under the jurisdiction of Tokyo Prefecture are affiliated with the Ogasawara Islands, with the one in the center being called 'Iō-tō,' the one to the south being called 'Minami-Iō-tō,' and the one to the north being called 'Kita-Iō-tō.'"[11]

---

10 JACAR: A15112383800 (from the 11th image). Gotō's note is signed by Mutsu Munemitsu.

11 JACAR: A15112383800 (from the 3rd image); B03041152400 (8th image); *Kanpō* 官報 [Official Gazette] vol. 2461, September 10, 1891, 97. On September 14, five days after the promulgation of the Imperial Decree, Tokyo Prefectural Governor Tomita Tetsunosuke issued an order to Chief of the Ogasawara Islands Kuwahara Kaihei to "investigate the situation on the island and state your opinion" (no. 4634), and the result of the investigation was the "Iō-tō Inspection Report" dated November 21, 1891. Tokyo Prefecture Documents 619.A2.08: Nr.35: 285–295. Also refer to "*The History of Tokyo City, Town Edition, vol. 82*" (1991), 259–267. In addition, see the "Inquiry into the Situation of the Two Islands Around Iō-tō" from September 15 that was addressed by the Tokyo Prefecture Director of the Bureau of Home Affairs [First Director Ginbayashi Mitsuo] to Chief of the Ogasawara Islands Kuwahara. Tokyo Prefecture Documents 619.C6.02: Nr.6: 157(1)–158.

However, Minister Mutsu did not relent. On November 5, he submitted "Reservations Regarding the Promulgation of the Affiliation and Name of Iō-tō" (Kanbō Kō No. 81) to Prime Minister Matsukata Masayoshi. It stated,

> I have reservations about the affiliation and name of Iō-tō that were promulgated by Imperial Decree No. 190 in September of this year.
> A: These islands have traditionally been islands affiliated with Japan. The Imperial Decree merely established their jurisdiction and named them.
> B: These islands were not previously affiliated with Japan. Only after the Imperial Decree was issued did they become affiliated with Japan.
> At the time that the Imperial Decree was issued, I believed that the primary purpose of the Cabinet Decision was based on the explanation in A. However, I have received applications for the operation of a mine on the island. The handling [of these applications] under the Mining Law differs depending on whether reading A or reading B is used, and it is therefore necessary, on this occasion, to clarify the Cabinet's official opinion on this matter. I hereby request an immediate Cabinet meeting.[12]

Although a record of the discussions amongst Ministers about Minister Mutsu's reservations cannot be found, on November 16, about 10 days after Minister Mutsu submitted his reservations, a new Cabinet Decision was made, "Addressing Reservations from the Ministry of Agriculture and Commerce Regarding the Promulgation of the Affiliation and Name of Iō-tō," which reads,

> In light of the principles of the law of nations and of a review of the island's history, the islands have until now been affiliated with the Empire, and it is not the case that they only became part of the Empire following Imperial Decree No. 190 of this year. As the competent authorities and the name of the islands were somewhat unclear, it is clearly the case that the decision to promulgate Imperial Decree No. 190 was made merely for that reason.

In other words, Imperial Decree No. 190 was not occupation, but rather a measure to reaffirm that the islands had always been "islands affiliated with

12 JACAR Ref. A15112383900 (from the 1st image), *Kōbun Ruishū* 公文類聚 [Public Documents Collection] Part 15, 1891, vol. 38 (National Archives of Japan).

Japan" and to establish the competent authorities and name the islands. The Ministry of Agriculture and Commerce was then notified of this decision on December 3.[13]

Thereafter, the Ministry of Agriculture and Commerce conducted an inquiry, including for applications that had temporarily been sent back to their petitioners,[14] and finally, on May 19, the Minister of Agriculture and Commerce issued an order in response to the application for sulfur prospecting by Inoue Hisashi, the agent of Tanaka Shunsaku.[15]

2.2 *Legal Issues*

2.2.1 Reasons Why It Has Been Regarded as a Case of Occupation

As for the measures to incorporate Iō-tō that followed the above process, two points will be discussed here. The first point is that in *Island Occupation* (*Collection of Precedents in International Law,* 2), October 1933, which was edited by the Treaty Bureau of the Ministry of Foreign Affairs, six examples, the Ogasawara Islands, Iō-tō, Kumeaka-shima/Kuba-jima/Uotsuri-jima, Minami-Tori-shima, Oki-Daitō-jima, and Nakano-Tori-shima, are listed as "Cases of Islands Occupied by the Empire," which raises the question of why Iō-tō is also listed as a case of occupation. *Island Occupation* mentions the Cabinet Decision on August 19, 1891 and Imperial Decree No. 190 from September 9, but does not mention the November 16 Cabinet Decision at all.[16]

Where primary historical materials were archived offers perhaps the strongest reason for this classification. Minister Mutsu's reservations expressed on November 5, the Cabinet Decision of November 16 (stamped with the seal of Minister for Foreign Affairs Enomoto), and the August 13 opinion from the Legislation Bureau with the attached note from Minister Mutsu are all held only at the National Archives of Japan and not at the Diplomatic Archives of the Ministry of Foreign Affairs. It can be speculated that *Island Occupation* regarded Iō-tō as a case of occupation because it was written based on primary

13 JACAR: A15112383900 (from the 3rd image).

14 Refer to "Notification of Application for Lease of Land" on January 23, 1892 from Chief Kuwahara to Governor Tomita (Sō no. 83). Refer also to the December 21, 1891 letter addressed to Governor Tomita by the Secretary of Home Affairs (in Shin no. 486). Tokyo Prefecture Documents 619.C6.02: Nr.6: 228.

15 Tokyo Prefecture Documents 619.C2.19: Nr.8: 74.

16 Ministry of Foreign Affairs Treaty Bureau (ed.), *Tōsho Sensen* (*Kokusaihō Senrei Ishū,* 2) 島嶼先占（国際法先例彙輯，2） [Island Occupation (Collection of Precedents in International Law, 2)] (October 1933), 35. However, the date of the Cabinet Decision is not listed. Refer also to Ministry of Foreign Affairs (ed.), *Nihon Gaikō Bunsho Dai 24 Kan* 日本外交文書 第24巻 [Diplomatic Documents of Japan], vol. 24, 515–518.

historical materials that were held by the Ministry of Foreign Affairs. Certainly, if one were to rely solely on the Cabinet Decision on August 19, 1891 and on Imperial Decree No. 190 from September 19, then it is not surprising that one would regard it as a case of occupation.[17]

In the materials at the Tokyo Metropolitan Archives, as well as in the materials at the Diplomatic Archives of the Ministry of Foreign Affairs, Imperial Decree No. 190 from September 9, 1891 can be found, but none of the other documents can be found. Only Imperial Decree No. 190 is mentioned in a document (Sō No. 83) sent from Chief of the Ogasawara Islands Kuwahara Kaihei to Governor Tomita Tsunosuke on January 23, 1892, and in a report sent by Governor Tomita to Minister of Agriculture and Commerce Kōno Toshikama on March 16.[18]

2.2.2 Criteria for Distinguishing Occupation from Reaffirmation of Territory

The second point is that, although it was clearly stated in Mutsu's reservations on November 5 that there are two methods, occupation and reaffirmation of territory, the question is whether the criteria for distinguishing between them were clearly indicated at the time. Looking at primary historical materials from 1890 to 1891, there are both documents stating that Iō-tō has been part of Japan's territory (*hanto*) for a long time and documents stating that Iō-tō could not be said to be within Japan's territory.

---

17 The July 4th Cabinet submission is stored in the Diplomatic Archives of the Ministry of Foreign Affairs, but the August 19th Cabinet Decision itself is not. Akiyama Masanosuke and Kurachi Tetsukichi, former officials of the Ministry of Foreign Affairs, also mentioned Iō-tō as an example of occupation, but made no mention of the November Cabinet Decision. Akiyama Masanosuke 秋山雅之介, *Kokusai Kōhō* 国際公法 [Public International Law] (Tokyo: Tōkyō Senmon Gakkō, 1893), 43; Kurachi Tetsukichi 倉知鉄吉, *Kokusai Kōhō* 国際公法 [Public International Law] (Tokyo: Nihon Hōritsu Gakkō, 1899), 88. (The works of these two authors were mentioned by Professor Sasaki Yūichi at a study group on the historical transition of the concept of "territory.") Furthermore, Tachi Sakutarō, who was in practice an international legal advisor to the Ministry of Foreign Affairs, also mentioned the Ogasawara Islands, Minami-Tori-shima, and Iō-tō in his 1933 paper as an example of Japan's recent annexation (occupation) of islands. As for Iō-tō, he only mentions the August 6 Cabinet request and Imperial Decree no. 190. Tachi Sakutarō 立作太郎, "Mushu no Tōsho no Sensen no Hōri to Senrei" 無主の島嶼の先占の法理と先例 [The Legal Principles and Precedents for the Occupation of Ownerless Islands]. *Kokusaihō Gaikō Zasshi* 国際法外交雑誌, vol. 32, no. 8 (1933): 47. In addition, Momose Takashi 百瀬孝, *Shiryō Kenshō Nihon no Ryōdo* 史料検証日本の領土 [Survey of Historical Materials: The Territory of Japan] (Tokyo: Kawade Shobō Shinsha, 2010), 63, accurately describes the November Cabinet Decision.

18 Tokyo Prefecture Documents 619.C2.19: Nr.10: 118; 619.C6.02: Nr.6: 242.

In terms of documents that state, "The island is uninhabited, and its location is completely recognized as being within the Empire's territory," these include the "Request for Lease of Island" (No. 4941),[19] which was created in Tokyo Prefecture at the request of Tanaka Eijirō on March 24, 1890 and was sent by Governor Hachisuka to Minister of Home Affairs Saigō on July 21, the "Request for Approval Regarding the Affiliation of Islands" (No. 6940),[20] which was sent by Governor Hachisuka to Minister of Home Affairs Saigō on October 31, and, additionally, "Submission of Application for Sulfur Exploration" (No. 7454),[21] which was sent by Governor Hachisuka to Minister of Agriculture and Commerce Mutsu on November 25.

On the other hand, as for those stating that Iō-tō is not within Japan's territory, the February 1, 1890 reply by an official from the Mining Bureau in the Ministry of Agriculture and Commerce, in response to an application by Kawani Rijūrō to lease an area, stated that, "It is difficult to inquire into the matter as the affiliation [of the island] is unclear."[22] Furthermore, a draft proposal (that was discarded), dated July 29, 1890, and addressed to Chief of the Ogasawara Islands Akagawa Kōsuke from Ginbayashi Tsunao, the First Department Director of the Tokyo Prefectural Government, stated that, "There is no definite place in the Imperial map [for the island]. Furthermore, we are currently only engaged in partial development, and there has been insufficient activity for occupation."[23]

Furthermore, Iō-tō was said to be an uninhabited island with an undetermined territory and an undetermined affiliation in the May 5, 1891 response from Chief of the Ogasawara Islands Kuwahara Kaihei to Tanaka Eijirō's union request for travel to Iō-tō,[24] in the October 8, 1891 request from Chief of the Ogasawara Islands Kuwahara to Governor of Tokyo Prefecture Tomita Tetsunosuke titled "Request for Approval for Scheduled Boat to Iō-tō in November" (Sō No. 574),[25] in the March 16, 1892 report from Governor Tomita to Minister of Agriculture and Commerce Kōno,[26] and, finally, in the May 2,

19 Tokyo Prefecture Documents 619.C6.02: Nr.6: 161(1), 215(1).

20 JACAR: A15112383800 (from the 4th image); B03041152400 (7th image); Tokyo Prefecture Documents 619.A8.02: Nr.9: 245–246.

21 Tokyo Prefecture Documents 618.B5.13: Nr.1: 4.

22 Tokyo Prefecture Documents 619.C2.19: Nr.10: 214.

23 Tokyo Prefecture Documents 619.C6.02: Nr.6: 216. The February 4 document was also similar. Tokyo Prefecture Documents 619.C6.02: Nr.6: 222.

24 Tokyo Prefecture Documents 619.C2.19: Nr.7: 41.

25 Tokyo Prefecture Documents 619.A2.08: Nr.35: 296.

26 Tokyo Prefecture Documents 619.C6.02: Nr.6: 242.

1892 "Report on Date for Commencing Sulfur Mining in Ogasawara Island and Iō-tō" from Tanaka Shunsaku and others.[27]

As per the above, the documents that describe Iō-tō as being part of Japan's territory are limited to those dated November 1890 or earlier. However, in the July 27, 1890 opinion from the First Department Director of the Tokyo Prefectural Government, which was quoted above, Iō-tō was said to not be within Japan's territory (although this draft was later discarded), so even at the time, there was not a unanimous opinion within Tokyo Prefecture.[28]

The November 16, 1891 Cabinet Decision stated only "In light of the principles of the law of nations and of a review of the islands' history."[29] It is presumed that the theory that Iō-tō is not *terra nullius* was formulated by examining the facts of the expedition/survey from four years prior (1887) and the sulfur mining from two years prior (1889) based upon "the principles of the law of nations." Additionally, on March 23, 1892, the year after the Cabinet Decision, Minister for Foreign Affairs Enomoto Takeaki sent a (confidential) letter to Nomura Yasushi, the Japanese Minister to France, which stated, "A few years ago, the *Meiji Maru* was dispatched to explore the area, and since then, our people have continued to live there."[30] It is a fact that inhabitants were present there.

Incidentally, the "handling ... under the Mining Law" that is referred to in Minister Mutsu's November 5 Reservations is understood to be the attribution of sulfur mining rights.[31] In other words, if occupation was adopted as the basis for the affiliation of Iō-tō and the mining rights on that island, then there were fears that all mining activities conducted prior to the measure of occupation would be considered to be legally meaningless.

The January 23, 1892 letter sent to Governor Tomita by Chief of the Ogasawara Islands Kuwahara (Sō No. 83) is noteworthy when it comes to this point. It stated, "Due to the unclear jurisdiction over Iō-tō at the time, the document was temporarily returned, but, as it was determined during September

27 Tokyo Prefecture Documents 619.C2.19: Nr.7: 39 (2).

28 Refer also to the Tokyo Prefecture Documents "Notification of Sulfur Prospecting by Omita Toshiyoshi," (Hei no. 124). Tokyo Prefecture Documents 618.B5.13: Nr.1: 6; 619.C2.19: Nr.12: 248.

29 JACAR: A15112383900 (4th image).

30 JACAR: B03041152400 (19th image).

31 The November 21, 1891 "Iō-tō Inspection Report" (Sō no. 697) to Governor Tomita from Chief of the Ogasawara Islands Kuwahara stated that "I certify that, besides the business of collecting sulfur, this is not an island where the promotion of new industry should be planned." Tokyo Prefecture Documents 619.A2.08: Nr.35: 289. Refer also to "*The History of Tokyo City, Town Edition, vol. 82*" (1991), 261.

last year that Iō-tō is affiliated with the Ogasawara Islands, I would like you to consider this matter for the time and date it was originally submitted."[32] Additionally, there was also a letter to Minister of Agriculture and Commerce Mutsu Munemitsu from Kawani Rijuro and others, which was entitled "Supplementary Application for Leasing an Area of Iō-tō" and stated, "Japan's Mining Law controls the mining industry within Japanese territory, but shall not be construed as controlling Japanese citizens. Therefore, if it is not confirmed that Iō-tō is Japanese territory, then it shall not be subject to the sanctions of the Mining Law."[33]

From the above historical materials, it can be considered that the issue of sulfur mining rights, which were under the jurisdiction of the Minister of Agriculture and Commerce, was the reason for Minister Mutsu's insistence on reaffirmation of Iō-tō as Japanese territory rather than on Iō-tō becoming Japanese territory through occupation.

However, as far as the historical materials of the time are concerned, it is difficult to say that there is a clear indication of the criteria for distinguishing between occupation and reaffirmation of territory. For the reaffirmation of territory, it is necessary to clarify when Iō-tō became a territory and on what kind of facts – such as "effective control" – that claim is based on, but historical materials with that information have not been found. The July 21, 1890 document from Governor Hachisuka (No. 4941) only stated that Iō-tō's location "is completely recognized as being within the Empire's territory."[34] This is an assertion that Iō-tō "geographically, can naturally be said to be Japanese territory." In addition to Iō-tō, similar logic was used in the cases of Tori-shima[35] and Okino-Tori-shima.[36] However, it is not clear what exactly these criteria are. It is clear from the case of Okino-Tori-shima that they are not solely an island's proximity to mainland Japan. That the physical proximity of an island – that

32 Tokyo Prefecture Documents 619.C2.19: Nr.10: 118.

33 Tokyo Prefecture Documents 619.C2.19: Nr.10: 213. Refer also to the December 15, 1891 "Report on Request for Sulfur Prospecting on Iō-tō and the Ogasawara Islands" to Mutsu from Yorioka, etc. Tokyo Prefecture Documents 619.C2.19: Nr.10: 165.

34 Tokyo Prefecture Documents 619.C6.02: Nr.6: 161(1), 215(1).

35 JACAR Ref. A15113117100 (from the 9th image), *Kōbun Ruishū* 公文類聚 [Public Documents Collection] Part 21, 1897, vol. 2 (National Archives of Japan); Tokyo Prefecture Documents 622.D2.06: Nr.6: 62–64(1).

36 JACAR Ref. A14100246500 (from the 3rd image), *Kōbun Ruishū* 公文類聚 [Public Documents Collection] Part 55, 1931, vol. 1 (National Archives of Japan); Ref. B02031163800 (2nd image), *Honpō Tōsho Ryōyū Kankei Zakken* 本邦島嶼領有関係雑件 [Miscellaneous Matters Related to the Island Territory of Japan] (A.4.1.0.3) (Diplomatic Archives of the Ministry of Foreign Affairs).

is, being a "nearby island" – did not amount to the necessary grounds under international law had already been conveyed by British Minister Parkes at the time of the decision to incorporate the Ogasawara Islands into the territory of Japan in 1875.[37]

As has already been stated above, the "island's history" recorded in the Cabinet Decision on November 16, 1891 refers to the expedition and surveys conducted four years earlier, to the fact of sulfur mining two years earlier, and to the presence of inhabitants. If being a "nearby island" is not the basis for Iō-tō to be Japanese territory, then all that remains is the fact of such expeditions, surveys, sulfur mining, and the presence of inhabitants. If that is the case, it is possible to argue that Iō-tō was Japanese territory from four years before, in 1887. Looking at the historical materials from the time, there is no evidence that this point was thoroughly discussed.

There are also questions about the extent to which Minister Mutsu had knowledge of the theory of occupation. There is no evidence to suggest that he, say, referred to literature on international law or consulted with experts in international law – for example foreign specialists employed by the Japanese Government such as Henry Willard Denison and Alessandro Paternostro, or officials in the Ministry of Foreign Affairs – when he made his proposal on November 5, 1891. Additionally, a note from August 14, 1891 stated that although Iō-tō is an "uninhabited island with no known affiliation," "there is currently no party with whom there would be a dispute … It would be extremely injudicious if such a thing were to be publicly announced by an Imperial Decree. Rather, from the beginning, these islands have been regarded as being affiliated with the Ogasawara Islands." However, no rationale is given as to why Iō-tō can be regarded as being affiliated with the Ogasawara Islands.[38] Furthermore, the recommendation[39] to follow the example from 1885, in which the islands of Daitō-jima and Uokagi-jima (whose affiliation was unknown) were deemed to

37 Dialogue with Minister for Foreign Affairs Terashima Munenori on November 5, 1875. *Dai Nihon Gaikō Bunsho* 大日本外交文書 [Diplomatic Documents of Greater Japan], vol. 8, 362–363.

38 In a note attached to the August 19 Cabinet Decision, Minister for Foreign Affairs Enomoto Takeaki explains, "The Minister of Agriculture and Commerce's assertion that it would be 'injudicious' is likely a sentiment in reference to foreign countries. If that is so, I consider it to be an unwarranted concern" (JACAR: A15112383800 [12th image]). However, it is not clear what he means specifically.

39 JACAR: A15112383800 (10th image).

belong to Okinawa Prefecture, is inaccurate and unclear from both a factual and legal standpoint.[40]

3 Minami-Tori-Shima

3.1 *The Incorporation Process*

In Japan's Meiji Era, the theory of occupation was first discussed in a concrete case during the so-called "Taiwan Expedition" in 1874. It was Charles E. De Long, the US Minister to Japan, and Charles William Le Gendre, a French-born American, who "instructed" the Meiji Government on this theory. On September 23, 1873, in a dialogue with Minister for Foreign Affairs Soejima Taneomi, De Long stated that, "Even if China insists to have jurisdiction over it, unless China's orders are actually carried out there, said jurisdiction is essentially groundless, and it becomes the possession of whoever has taken it."[41] Le Gendre was a foreign specialist employed by the Japanese Government through De Long's introduction, and in the first memorandum that Le Gendre submitted to the Japanese Government, in 1872, he wrote that, according to "universal laws of all nations" in uncivilized lands such as Australia, New Zealand, and California in the United States, "There is the right to make an area one's territory if one exercises jurisdiction over said area by deciding on laws and establishing systems."[42]

Referencing these opinions, and with Gustave Emile Boissonade de Fontarabie as a direct advisor, during the negotiations with the Qing between August and October 1874, the Japanese Government (Yanagiwara Sakimitsu and Ōkubo Toshimichi) developed the argument that Taiwan was considered an "unoccupied and uncivilized land," that Qing sovereignty did not extend to Taiwan, and that Taiwan could not be considered a part of Qing territory.[43]

---

40 As of 1885, decisions over jurisdiction and the erecting of national markers for Uokagi-jima (which is considered to be Uotsuri-jima), as well as for Kuba-jima and Kumeaka-shima, were postponed.

41 *Dai Nihon Gaikō Bunsho* 大日本外交文書 [Diplomatic Documents of Greater Japan], vol. 7, 5.

42 Waseda University Institute of Social Sciences 早稲田大学社会科学研究所 (ed.), *Ōkuma Bunsho Dai 1 Kan* 大隈文書 第 1 巻 [Ōkuma Documents vol. 1] (Tokyo: Waseda University Institute of Social Sciences, 1958), 20. Refer also to Tachi Yoshinori 立嘉度 (trans.), *Banchi Shozoku Ron Ge* 蕃地所属論 下 [Affiliation Theory for Uncivilized Lands, Part 2], (ed.) Honda Masatatsu 本多政辰 (Tokyo: Sanyūsha, 1874), 6.

43 Refer to the "Excerpt of Public Laws," a note attached to the "Rebuttal to the Reply from the Qing Prime Minister Yamen" from Ōkubo to Qing Prime Minister Yamen, *Dai Nihon Gaikō Bunsho* 大日本外交文書 [Diplomatic Documents of Greater Japan], vol. 7, 245.

However, large questions remain as to how much this theory of "occupation" was subsequently shared within the Japanese Government, and how much it could be said to have been used in the process of incorporating remote islands. In the case of Iō-tō, which was examined in the previous section, as well as in the cases of Minami-Daitō-jima, the Senkaku Islands, and Tori-shima, it is difficult to say that incorporation measures were taken with a sufficient understanding of the occupation method under modern international law. Minami-Tori-shima in 1898 was the first case in which this point was directly addressed.

Minami-Tori-shima (also known as Marcus Island or Wikks Island) was discovered by the Spaniard Bernardo de la Torre in 1543, but there are no records of subsequent visits to the island until 1864 by an American ship. In June 1889, Andrew Rosehill, the captain of an American ship, landed on the island. Recognizing the value of the uninhabited island as a source of palm oil and guano (bird droppings), he raised the American flag on a palm tree, returned to Honolulu (then the Kingdom of Hawaii), and made an application for collecting guano to the US State Department through the US Minister to Hawaii who was stationed in Honolulu. However, the application was not handled as an official procedure and was only kept on record in the US State Department.[44]

Mizutani Shinroku (1850–1921) is considered to be the first Japanese person to try and settle on Minami-Tori-shima. He landed on the island on December 3, 1896 and submitted an island discovery notification to Minister of Home Affairs Kabayama Sukenori and Tokyo Prefectural Governor Koga Michitsune on April 5. Mizutani wrote, "On December 3, 1896, I scraped the bark off a tree and carved the characters 'December 3, Meiji 29 (1896), Japanese, Mizutani' into the tree. This island is unaffiliated with any other country, is completely one of the Ogasawara Islands, and I believe it should belong to the territory of the Empire of Japan."[45] In response to this report, the Tokyo Prefectural

---

Ōkubo Yasuo 大久保泰甫, *Bowasonādo to Kokusaihō – Taiwan Shuppei Jiken no Tōshizu* ボワソナードと国際法－台湾出兵事件の透視図 [Boissonade and International Law: Perspectives on the Taiwan Expedition] (Tokyo: Iwanami Shoten, 2016), 129–259 analyzes, in detail, *Bosshi Shushi Sho*, which includes the original French texts of 19 memoranda submitted to Ōkubo by Boissonade (held by the National Archives of Japan).

44 Refer to B. Welsch, "Was Marcus Island Discovered by Bernardo de la Torre in 1543?," *Journal of Pacific History*, vol. 39, no. 1 (2004): 109–122. For the list of surveys and studies on Minami-Tori-shima, even though the information is a little old, refer to Hiraoka Akitoshi 平岡昭利, "Minamitorishima no Ryōyū to Keiei – Ahōdori kara Chōfun, Rinkō Saishu e" 南鳥島の領有と経営－アホウドリから鳥糞，リン鉱採取へ [Territory and Management of Minami-Tori-shima: From Short-Tailed Albatrosses to Guano and Phosphate Mining]. *Rekishi Chirigaku* 歴史地理学, vol. 45, no. 4 (2003): 1.

45 JACAR Ref. B03041152600 (from the 7th image), Teikoku Hanto Kankei Zakken (1.4.1.7) (Diplomatic Archives of the Ministry of Foreign Affairs); Ref. C06091185100 (from the

Government and the Ministry of Home Affairs proceeded with a review of the island's affiliation.

The first issue that was discussed within the Ministry of Home Affairs was whether the island that Mizutani claimed to have discovered was the same as the Marcus Island on the nautical charts held by the Hydrographic Office in the Navy. A document (Tōkō No. 70) prepared on June 5, 1897 by Ogata Koreaki, Prefectural Division Chief in the Ministry of Home Affairs, stated that a field survey should be conducted to determine the island's affiliation.[46] Therefore, Mizutani visited the island again on June 25, took detailed astronomical observations, created a rough map, and, on September 13, submitted an "Application to Lease an Island" to Minister of Home Affairs Kabayama, claiming that the island was the same as Marcus Island.[47]

In response to this, on October 8, the Minister of Home Affairs prepared the "Cabinet Submission on the Affiliation of Marcus Island."[48] The subsequent incorporation process was complicated, going through three stages within the Japanese Government, and finally, on July 1 of the following year, a Cabinet Decision was made to incorporate the island into Japanese territory based on the theory of occupation. (The details of these three stages are discussed in the next subsection.) Additionally, on December 10, 1898, Tokyo Prefectural Governor Senge Takatomi gave Mizutani approval for a business plan for Minami-Tori-shima (2 Hei No. 2313), but the process leading up to this decision was also quite complicated.[49]

Four years after the Cabinet Decision was made, the so-called "Minami-Tori-shima Incident" occurred from July to August 1902. The aforementioned Captain Andrew Rosehill visited the island in 1902, 13 years after his first visit in June 1889. Captain Rosehill's visit was done in accordance with the August 18, 1856 "Guano Islands Act," which granted Americans the right to collect guano. Japan dispatched a cruiser, demanded that Captain Rosehill leave, and, after some exchanges, he left.[50]

24th image), 1898, Kōbun Bikō [Public Documents Remarks], Doboku [Civil Engineering], 2nd, vol. 22 (National Institute for Defense Studies, Ministry of Defense); Tokyo Prefecture Documents 625.D4.19: Nr.22: 452. Refer to the hand-drawn figure that accompanies this chapter, Figure 1.1.

46 JACAR: C06091185100 (42nd image).

47 JACAR: C06091185100 (from the 18th image); Tokyo Prefecture Documents 625. D4.19: Nr.22: 398(1)–399(1).

48 JACAR: B03041152600 (from the 1st image); C06091185100 (from the 3rd image); Tokyo Prefecture Documents 625.D4.19: Nr.22: 432–433.

49 Refer to the documents in Tokyo Prefecture Documents 625.D4.19.

50 Refer to Ishii Kenji 石井建次 (Official in the Ministry of Foreign Affairs, South Seas Bureau), "Minamitorishima ni Tsuite – Kakureta Teikoku Gaikōshi no Ichi Pēji" 南鳥島に

During the incident, in a cable (No. 54) from Takahira Kogorō, Japanese Minister to the US, to Minister for Foreign Affairs Komura Jutarō, he expressed concerns that "the US Government may claim the right of discovery by the US ship captain." However, the US Government never made such a claim.[51]

Immediately afterwards, Professor Takahashi Sakuye of Tokyo Imperial University took up this incident in a seminar on international law at Tokyo Imperial University, and the results of the student debate were published in *Kokka Gakkai Zasshi* [*The Journal of the Association of Political and Social Science*].[52] One of the students, Kijimoto Tokizō (Professor at Kyoto Imperial University from 1908), examined the occupation method in detail. He argued that even if the United States had taken possession of the island by the fact that Captain Rosehill had raised the American flag, there was no continuation

ついて一隠れた帝国外交史の１頁 [Minami-Tori-shima: A Hidden History of Imperial Diplomacy]. *Gaikō Hyōron* 外交評論 April Issue (1942) [JACAR Ref. B02031163700 (from the 9th image), Honpō Tōsho Ryōyū Kankei Zakken (A.4.1.0.3) (Diplomatic Archives of the Ministry of Foreign Affairs)]. Captain Rosehill stated that, through the US Government, he would sue for damages over the failure of his bird-catching plan, but the "Incorporation of Minami-Tori-shima into the Jurisdiction of Tokyo Prefecture" records (June 20, 1931) state that there are no records of the details after that. JACAR: B02031163700 (from the 2nd image). W. A. Bryan, *A Monograph of Marcus Island: An Account of its Physical Features and Geology, with Descriptions of the Fauna and Flora* (Honolulu: Bishop Museum Press, 1903) describes how Bryan went to the island on Rosehill's ship, stayed there for a week, and conducted a survey of animals, plants, and fish, including of the sooty tern, despite interference from Japanese soldiers. The book contains a photograph of a wooden sign that is said to have been placed on the beach on the south side of the island by the Japanese Government in 1899 (81). The tree that Mizutani carved and wrote his name in 1894 is on the west side of the island, so it is clearly different from this wooden marker. It is unknown how the wooden sign was installed.

51 JACAR Ref. B03041152800 (images 12 to 13), Teikoku Hanto Kankei Zakken (1.4.1.7) (Diplomatic Archives of the Ministry of Foreign Affairs). It should be noted that the US Government's favorable attitude toward Japan's measures on this issue may be attributed to the moderate Japanese claims in the Japan-US negotiations over the Midway Islands from 1899 to 1901 and Wake Island in 1902, as stated by the Ministry of Foreign Affairs of Japan. Treaty Bureau, *supra* note 16, 63. Refer also to endnote 73.

52 "Minamitorishima Jiken" 南鳥嶋事件 [The Minami-Tori-shima Incident]. *Kokka Gakkai Zasshi* 国家学会雑誌, vol. 16, no. 188 (1902): 96–107; Shimizu Ken-ichirō 清水賢一郎, "Minamitorishima Jiken" 南鳥嶋事件 [The Minami-Tori-shima Incident]. *Ibid.*, 107–117; Kijimoto Tokizō 雉本朗造, "Minamitorishima Jiken (Kokusai Kōhō Enshū Hōkoku)" 南鳥嶋事件（国際公法演習報告） [The Minami-Tori-shima Incident (Public International Law Seminar Report)]. *Kokka Gakkai Zasshi* 国家学会雑誌, vol. 16, no. 189 (1902): 88–118. Refer also to Tezuka Yutaka 手塚豊, "Minamitorishima Sensen Zengo no Ichi Kōsatsu" 南鳥島先占前後の一考察 [A Study of before and after the Minami-Tori-shima Precedent]. *Hōgaku Kenkyū* 法学研究, vol. 36, no. 1 (1963): 34–35, for a report on this exercise and Takahashi's opinion.

of the possession thereafter, and concluded that, although it must be said that Japan's possession was flawed because there was no notice of the fact, it was made effective via tacit approval by other nations.[53]

Professor Takahashi himself also published a statement in the Yomiuri Shimbun newspaper, stating that the acquisition of land should be based on "possession" rather than on "discovery," and deemed that the United States lacked the legal grounds to protest Japan's territorial sovereignty.[54]

3.2 *Legal Issues*

3.2.1 Legal Basis for Incorporation – Three Stages

There are a variety of legal issues surrounding the incorporation of Minami-Tori-shima, but the following two points will be focused on. The first legal issue is the grounds for the island being affiliated with Japan. Mizutani himself, given the location of the island, naturally regarded it as part of Japan's territory, as shown in his "Application to Lease an Island" that was addressed to the Minister of Home Affairs on September 13, 1897.[55]

The August 7, 1895 "Declaration of the Delimitation of Borders between Japan and Spain" was the first piece of evidence brought forth to support this geographical position. In response to the cession of Taiwan to Japan under the Treaty of Shimonoseki that was signed on April 17, 1895, this was a declaration made between Japan and Spain to prevent future disputes in the area around Taiwan and the Philippines.[56] Article 2 of the Declaration stipulates that "The Government of Spain declares that it shall not consider islands to the north and northeast of said demarcation line to be its own," and Article 3 stipulates that "The Government of Japan declares that it shall not consider islands to the south and southeast of said demarcation line to be its own." In other words, it was a joint declaration that the Bashi Channel, located at 21 degrees 25 minutes

53 Kijimoto, *supra* note 52, 113–116.

54 "Minamitorishima no Senryōken (Takahashi Hōgaku Hakase no Iken)" 南鳥島の占領権（高橋法学博士の意見） [Minami-Tori-shima Possession Rights (Opinion from Professor Takahashi)], *Yomiuri Shimbun* 読売新聞, October 4, 1902. In a book published in 1901, Takahashi further elaborated on this theory of occupation as the "source" of territorial sovereignty. Takahashi Sakuye 高橋作衛, *Heiji Kokusai Kōhō* 平時国際公法 [Public International Law in Times of Peace] (Tokyo: Nihon Hōritsu Gakkō, 1903), 367–378.

55 JACAR: C06091185100 (19th image); Tokyo Prefecture Documents 625.D4.19: Nr.22: 398(1).

56 Refer to the Privy Council's "Inspection Report," (July 26, 1895). JACAR Ref. A03033941100 (5th image), Sūmitsuin Ketsugi 1 [Privy Council Resolution 1], Minami Taiheiyō Chū ni aru Nichisei Ryōkoku Hanto no Kyōkai ni kansuru Sengensyo [Declaration Concerning the Boundaries of Japan and Spain in the Western Pacific], Resolution of July 30, 1896 (National Archives of Japan).

north latitude, would be used as a demarcation line to separate Japanese and Spanish territories. Extending this demarcation line to the east, Marcus Island (Minami-Tori-shima) is located at 24 degrees 17 minutes 12 seconds north latitude, about 170 *ri* (668 km) north of the demarcation line, so it is Japanese territory. (Refer to the attached diagram hand-drawn by an official of the Japanese Ministry of Foreign Affairs, p. 35, Figure 1.1.)[57]

In a June 5, 1897 document (Tōkō No. 70) issued by the Chief of the Prefectural Department of the Ministry of Home Affairs, this rationale is introduced as the opinion of Major Arikawa Sadahiro, the Chief of the Hydrographic Office in the Ministry of the Navy.[58] Then, the "Cabinet Submission on the Affiliation of Marcus Island" by Minister of Home Affairs Kabayama on October 8, 1897 stated, with a similar rationale,

> The location of the island is also within the bearing stipulated in Article 2 of the Declaration of the Delimitation of Borders between Japan and Spain, so there is no question that the island is affiliated with Japan. However, although the island was previously uninhabited and therefore not placed under the jurisdiction of any authorities, a person has now applied for a lease of said island. Thus, it is necessary to affirm the affiliation of the island, and it should therefore henceforth be affiliated with Tokyo Prefecture and be placed under the jurisdiction of the Chief of the Ogasawara Islands.[59]

Additionally, the October 14 opinion from Tanaka Zui, First Department Director of the Internal Affairs Division in the Tokyo Prefectural Government, also stated, as the opinion for the Tokyo Prefectural Government and based on the Japan-Spain Joint Declaration, that there is no doubt that Minami-Tori-shima

57 JACAR: B03041152600 (4th image). Refer also to JACAR: C06091185100 (10th image).

58 JACAR: C06091185100 (43rd image). Arikawa was also of the opinion that, "Even if Marcus Island is taken as a special island, if we look at it from its general location, then it is only natural that it belongs to Japan." Arikawa began working in the Hydrographic Office in the Navy around 1893, and on October 26, 1897, he became captain of the *Tenryū*. Given his background, he does not appear to have been particularly familiar with international law. Refer to, for example, Hikone Shōzō 彦根正三 (ed.), *Kaisei Kan-inroku Kō Meiji 26 Nen 1 Gatsu* 改正官員録甲明治 26 年 1 月 [Revised Official Records Part 1, January 1893] (Tokyo: Hakkō Shoin, 1893), 87; Society for the Preservation of Naval History 海軍歴史保存会 (ed.), *Shōkan Rireki Jō (Nihon Kaigunshi Dai 9 Kan)* 将官履歴 上（日本海軍史第 9 巻）[History of Generals and Admirals Part 1 (History of the Japanese Navy, vol. 9)] (Tokyo: Kaigun Rekishi Hozonkai, 1995), 618.

59 JACAR: B03041152600 (3rd image); C06091185100 (5th image); Tokyo Prefecture Documents 625.D4.19: Nr.22: 432–433.

is an island affiliated with Japan. However, it stated that the issue of Minami-Tori-shima's affiliation under international law should be decided by the Ministry of Home Affairs, not by the Tokyo Prefectural Government.[60]

That being said, the Japan-Spain Joint Declaration was originally a joint declaration to establish the demarcation line between Taiwan, which became Japanese territory, and the Philippines, which was Spanish territory. It would therefore obviously be unreasonable to apply it to Minami-Tori-shima, more than 3,000 kilometers away.

On March 14, 1898, Minister of Home Affairs Yoshikawa Akimasa submitted a proposal to the Cabinet (Tōkō No. 140) for Prime Minister Itō Hirobumi that showed a different view. Although he recognized that "it is indisputable that Minami-Tori-shima is geographically affiliated with Japan," without mentioning the Japan-Spain Joint Declaration, he noted that Mizutani had made a round trip voyage to the island, had explored the island, and had submitted an application to lease the island, and that it had become necessary to determine the island's affiliation, and proposed changing the island's name from "Marcus Island" to "Mizutani Island"[61] and affiliating it with Tokyo Prefecture from now on.[62]

While geographical factors remained in this proposal, the July 1 Cabinet Decision completely denied such factors. The Cabinet Decision begins by referring to the submission by the Minister of Home Affairs, in that "it is indisputable that Minami-Tori-shima is a location which is geographically affiliated with Japan" and then continues,

> However, upon examination, the island in question ... is an isolated island, so distant from the Ogasawara Islands that it is difficult to recognize it as a part of them. Moreover, there is an unaffiliated island called 'Grampus'[63] between it and the Ogasawara Islands. Therefore, it seems

60 Tokyo Prefecture Documents 625.D4.19: Nr.22: 431.

61 On May 20, 1898, Tokyo Governor Okabe Nagamoto sent a letter to Director Arakawa of the Prefectural Government Bureau in the Ministry of Home Affairs (1 Hatsu no.541), proposing that the name Minami-Tori-shima was appropriate because it was located to the south (*minami* in Japanese) of Tori-shima, and later the island's name was changed to Minami-Tori-shima. Tokyo Prefecture Documents 625.D4.19: Nr.22: 428–429.

62 JACAR Ref. A15113186700 (from the 4th image), *Kōbun Ruishū* 公文類聚 [Public Documents Collection] Part 22, 1898, vol. 2 (National Archives of Japan).

63 Grampus Island is said to have been discovered by the *Ferris* (Captain: John Meares) in 1788, with Japanese and American nationals continuing to explore it from 1888. In 1900, a survey by the *Kongō* of the Japanese Navy confirmed that it did not exist, and it was removed from nautical charts. Refer to Hasegawa Ryōichi 長谷川亮一, *Chizu kara Kieta Shimajima – Maboroshi no Nihonryō to Nanyō Tankenkatachi* 地図から消え

> groundless to say that 'Marcus Island' belongs to Japan as a matter of geography. Nevertheless, besides there being no evidence of foreign possession, according to reference books provided by an official from the Minister of Home Affairs, a Japanese citizen named Mizutani Shinroku has moved inhabitants to the island since December 1896, has built houses, has engaged in the capture of birds and fish and the cultivation of land, and is expected to be remarkably successful. As such, there exist the facts of so-called possession under international law, and there are no problems with the island being affiliated with Japan and being under the jurisdiction of the Chief of the Ogasawara Islands in Tokyo Prefecture.[64]

In other words, after clearly confirming that the geographical location of Minami-Tori-shima is not valid as a basis for it being affiliated with the Ogasawara Islands, the fact that there had been no possession by other countries, and that Mizutani had moved inhabitants to the island, built houses, and engaged in the capture of birds and fish and the cultivation of land were recognized as the "facts of so-called possession under international law," and so affiliated the island with Japan. This is deemed to be a determination of Japanese affiliation based on the occupation method.

No records could be found that show what discussions took place in the Home Office or in the Legislation Bureau 1) during the five months from Minister of Home Affairs Kabayama's preparation of the Cabinet submission on October 8, 1897 with the Japan-Spain Joint Declaration as the basis for affiliation, until the Cabinet submission by Minister of Home Affairs Yoshikawa on March 14, 1898, and 2) in the following four months until the Cabinet Decision on July 1. Although it is true that the Cabinet was different at each of the three stages (the second Matsukata Cabinet, the third Itō Cabinet, and the first Ōkuma Cabinet), there is no record that the intentions of the respective Prime Ministers or the respective Ministers of Home Affairs (Kabayama Sukenori, Yoshikawa Akimasa, and Itagaki Taisuke) were reflected.

た島々ー幻の日本領と南洋探検家たち [Islands Disappearing from Maps: Phantom Japanese Territory and South Sea Explorers] (Tokyo: Yoshikawa Kōbunkan, 2011), 72–75, 142–145, 158–159.

64 The decision was made on July 14 and then the Ministry of Home Affairs was notified. JACAR: A15113186700 (from the 1st image); Ref. A15113320500 (from the 3rd image), *Kōbun Ruishū* 公文類聚 [Public Documents Collection] Part 24, 1898, vol. 3 (National Archives of Japan). The same document is also published in JACAR Ref. A15113659900, *Kōbun Ruishū* 公文類聚 [Public Documents Collection] Part 32, 1909, vol. 1 (National Archives of Japan) as "Legislation Bureau Opinions, July 1898."

It was confirmed that on May 19, 1898 Mizutani made a detailed report to the Tokyo Prefectural Government on the colonization of the island, which was then passed on to the Legislation Bureau.[65] While Mizutani's colonization was mentioned in the document dated March 14, the report dated May 19 gave a more detailed account of the colonization. Additionally, in a May 24 letter from Arakawa Kunizō, the Director of the Prefectural Government Bureau in the Ministry of Home Affairs, to Ume Kenjirō, the Director of the Legislation Affairs Bureau (in Kentō No. 4), the geographic location of Minami-Tori-shima is described in detail, and the name "Minami-Tori-shima" is considered to be appropriate because it is located to the south of Tori-shima.[66]

The Legislation Bureau (Shibata Kamon, Kanokogi Kogorō, and other Counselors in the Legislation Bureau) probably referred to this information and kept in close contact with the Ministry of Home Affairs (Arakawa became the head of the Prefectural Government Bureau from January 21, 1898,[67] while Inoue Yūichi became the head of the Prefectural Division of the Prefectural Government Bureau from September 1897), and it is presumed that they abandoned the rationale of being "geographically affiliated with Japan" and changed to a basis that emphasized the facts of Mizutani's colonization, that is, a basis premised on "occupation."

This idea based on occupation is reflected in both the Minister of Home Affairs Directive from July 19 (Kun No. 653) and the Tokyo Prefectural Public Notice from July 24 (Tokyo Prefectural Public Notice No. 58), which state, "from now on affiliated with that Prefecture" and "from now on affiliated with this Prefecture."[68]

Incidentally, officials from the Ministry of Foreign Affairs were completely left out of the third and final stage. The Cabinet submission on October 8, 1897 was accepted by the Ministry of Foreign Affairs on October 29.[69] On March 14,

---

65 JACAR: A15113186700 (images 7 to 12).

66 JACAR: A15113186700 (images 3 to 4).

67 After working for the Ministry of Home Affairs, Arakawa Kunizō served as the Governor of Fukui Prefecture from 1892 to 1897, and on January 21, 1898, he was appointed as the Director of the Prefectural Government Bureau. When he was younger, Arakawa co-translated a textbook on international law by August Wilhelm Heffter, and it is surmised that he had sufficient knowledge of both national and international law. (August Wilhelm Heffter, *Kaishi Bankoku Kōhō* 海氏万国公法 [Heffter's Law of Nations] (trans.) Arakawa Kunizō 荒川邦蔵 and Kinoshita Shūichi 木下周一 (Ministry of Justice, 1877)).

68 Tokyo Prefecture Documents 302.D3.17: Nr.35: 68; 302.D3.17: Nr.34: 67. The July 24 announcement by Tokyo Prefecture was published in the *Yomiuri Shimbun* and the *Miyako Shimbun* on the same day.

69 Refer to the note attached to the Cabinet submission. JACAR: B03041152600 (2nd image).

1898, Minister of Home Affairs Yoshikawa issued an advance notice (note in Tōkō No. 140) to Minister for Foreign Affairs Nishi Tokujirō that he would make a Cabinet submission for the incorporation of "Mizutani Island."[70] However, after the July 1 Cabinet Decision, on October 5, Vice Minister for Foreign Affairs Hatoyama Kazuo sent a letter (Sō No. 288) to Vice Minister of Home Affairs Suzuki Mitsuyoshi that requested confirmation that the "Minami-Tori-shima" in the July 24 notice from Tokyo Prefecture was indeed the same island as Mizutani Island because "the names are different."[71] In response to a telephone request from the Ministry of Foreign Affairs, the Tokyo Prefectural Government had sent this July 24 notice to the Ministry of Foreign Affairs on October 1.[72] This means that the Ministry of Home Affairs did not notify the Ministry of Foreign Affairs of the July 1 Cabinet Decision either in advance or afterwards. The Diplomatic Archives of the Ministry of Foreign Affairs hold the October 8, 1897 Cabinet submission, but not the March 14, 1898 Cabinet submission, nor the July 1, 1898 Cabinet Decision.

Because the Ministry of Home Affairs was in charge of the issue of incorporating remote islands, and since the island was not considered to be the subject of dispute with other countries due to its position as *terra nullius*, it can be speculated that the Ministry of Foreign Affairs was not approached at all. As mentioned above, however, the Minami-Tori-shima incident occurred four years later, which put the Japanese diplomatic authorities into a rather difficult and confusing situation.[73]

---

70 JACAR Ref. B03041152700 (1st image), Teikoku Hanto Kankei Zakken (1.4.1.7) (Diplomatic Archives of the Ministry of Foreign Affairs).

71 JACAR: B03041152700 (from the 11th image).

72 JACAR: B03041152700 (from the 10th image).

73 A July 21 document prepared by Major Sanada Tsurumaru, a member of the First Section of the Military Affairs Bureau in the Ministry of the Navy, stated that, "It became purely Imperial territory," but the legal basis for this is not clearly stated. However, the document denies any right of discovery that the United States may claim, stating that Japanese have resided in the area since 1898, and that "It can be positively declared that this is Japanese territory, and I believe that no one in the world can dispute this." However, it also notes that, "At that time, it would have been appropriate to publicly announce to the world that the island will be incorporated into Japanese territory. (This was the case with Iō-tō, which is associated with the Ogasawara Islands.) The announcement in Tokyo Prefecture alone cannot be said to be an announcement to the world." JACAR: B03041152800 (16th image). This clearly shows dissatisfaction with the measures taken by the Government of Japan in 1898.

3.2.2 The Concept of the "Facts of So-Called Possession under International Law"

3.2.2.1 *Occupation as an Act of the State*

The second issue is the "facts of so-called possession under international law" described in the July 1 Cabinet Decision. Two points need to be argued about this concept. The first is whether the acts of private persons, who have not been mandated by the State, fulfill the occupation requirement that occupation must be an act of a State.

At the end of the 19th century, there was no dispute about the fact that the subject of occupation had to be the State. As typified by Emer de Vattel's book in 1758, the basic view was that, even if voyagers in the "Age of Discovery" set out on an expedition, with or without a sovereign mandate, and encountered and occupied an island or other uninhabited land, sovereignty over that island or land could not be recognized without "*possession réelle*" ("real possession") by the State.[74]

However, in a paper published in 1902 at the time of the Minami-Tori-shima Incident, Shimizu Ken-ichirō argued that "possession" requires an act of the State, distinguishing between the acts of an official appointed for the purpose of occupying an island and the acts of colonists, and that in the latter case, the act must be "ratified by the State," with this idea being said to be based on Walker.[75] The work referred to here is considered to be Thomas Alfred Walker's 1895 work.[76] Takahashi Sakuye noted that, in addition to Walker, Friedrich von Martens also expressed similar ideas.[77] Kijimoto Tokizō also cites Holzendorff.[78]

---

74 E. de Vattel, *Le droit des gens, ou principes de la loi naturelle, appliqués à la conduite & aux affaires des nations & des souverains* (Londres: Apud Liberos Tutior, 1758), Liv.1. Chap. 18. § 207.

75 Shimizu, *supra* note 52, 109–110.

76 Th. A. Walker, *A Manual of Public International Law* (Cambridge: University Press, 1895), 27. Westlake also notes the need for timely ratification before other countries intervene. J. Westlake, *International Law: Part 1: Peace* (Cambridge: University Press, 1904), 99.

77 Takahashi, *supra* note 54, 371. Friedrich von Martens, *Kokusaihō Jōkan* 国際法上巻 [International Law vol. 1], (trans.) Nakamura Shingo 中村進午 (Tokyo: Tōkyō Senmon Gakkō Press, 1900), 567; F. v. Martens, *Völkerrecht. Das internationale Recht der civilisirten Nationen, systematisch dargestellt. Deutsche Ausgabe von Carl Bergbohm* (Berlin: Weidman, 1883), Bd.1, 352. (The original Russian version was published in 1882.)

78 Kijimoto, *supra* note 52, 96. Holzendorff argues that when a State assumes a private law title that was acquired by a subject via *terra nullius*, the State can be found to have "public law recognition, *ex post facto* approval, or ratification in the sense that the former private law relationship is transferred into the domain of public law (*öffentlich rechtliche Genehmigung oder nachträgliche Anerkennung, oder eine Ratification*)." F. v. Holzendorff, "Neuntes Stück. Das Landgebiet der Staaten," *Id.* (Hrsg.), *Handbuch des Völkerrechts. Auf*

A similar idea can be found in William Edward Hall. Hall distinguishes between "possession" by a person who has been "furnished with a general or specific authority" and "possession" by a person who has not been furnished with such authority, and states that in order for "occupation," which is an act of the State, to be established, the latter requires the State's ratification of the act of possession and other acts such as colonization.[79]

As stated above, even if it is not possible to determine the extent to which the idea of "ratification" was common at the time, there is no doubt that it was advocated for by many influential scholars.

3.2.2.2 What Does "*Possession Réelle*" Refer to, and Does It Differ Depending on the Area in Question?

Another point to be discussed regarding the concept of "facts of so-called possession under international law" concerns "*possession réelle*" itself as a requirement for "occupation" to be established. Whether it is the act of an authorized official or of a private person who has not been furnished with such authority, the question is the extent to which, if any, "real" possession actually exists, and whether it has been considered to vary depending on the era or on the area in question (e.g., whether it is an isolated island in the middle of the sea).

According to the International Declaration Regarding Occupation of Territories by the Institute of International Law, which was adopted on September 7, 1888, "Taking possession is accomplished by the establishment of a responsible local power (*pouvoir local responsable*), provided with sufficient means to maintain order and assure the regular exercise of its authority within the limits of the occupied territory. These means may be taken over from the institutions existing within the occupied territory."[80]

Grundlage europäischer Staatspraxis. Zweites Band: Die völkerrechtliche Verfassung und Grundordnung der auswärtigen Staatsbeziehungen (Hamburg: J. F. Richter, 1887), 258.

79 W. E. Hall, *Hōru Shi Kokusai Kōhō* ホール氏国際公法 [Hall's Public International Law], (trans.) Tachi Sakutarō 立作太郎 (Tokyo: Tōkyō Hōgakuin, 1899), 150–151. This is a translation of W. E. Hall, *A Treatise on International Law* (4th ed., Oxford: Clarendon Press, 1895), 109–110. The first edition of the book was published in 1880 and has a slightly different title, but the wording in the relevant passage is the same. W. E. Hall, *International Law* (Oxford: Clarendon Press, 1880), 87–88, 90.

80 *Annuaire de l'Institut de droit international*, tome 10 (1888/89), 201–204. Refer also to M. Hébié, "The Acquisition of Original Titles of Territorial Sovereignty in the Law and Practice of European Colonial Expansion," M. G. Kohen and M. Hébié (eds.), *Research Handbook on Territorial Disputes in International Law* (Cheltenham: Edward Elgar, 2018), 81–85; Taijudō Kanae 太壽堂鼎, *Ryōdo Kizoku no Kokusaihō* 領土帰属の国際法 [Title to Territory in International Law] (Tokyo: Tōshindō, 1998), 62–65. It should be noted that Article 35 of the General Act of the Berlin Conference, which required "the establishment

Thus, if the "establishment of a responsible local power" is a condition of *possession réelle*, then, even if one adopts the aforementioned concept of "ratification," the act of ratification does not mean the completion of "occupation" as a territorial title through the simple *ex post facto* approval of acts performed by private persons. Unless one takes it to mean that the State has engaged in the "establishment of a responsible local power" based on the actions of private persons such as colonization and emigration, then it is impossible to establish occupation through the acts of private persons. However, the theorists who developed this logic of "ratification" never clearly stated that this was what they meant by ratification.

That being the case, before the aforementioned International Declaration in 1888, what kind of facts did theories deem "*possession réelle*" to refer to? An examination of the five scholars[81] cited in Memorandum No. 5 of Boissonade's "*Bosshi Shushi Sho*," i.e., Emer de Vattel,[82] Georg Friedrich von Martens,[83] Henry Wheaton,[84] August Wilhelm Heffter,[85] and Johann Kaspar Bluntschli,[86] shows that they mostly agree that the fact that an island is discovered and visited is not enough, and that the fact that an island is under one's "actual and *de facto*" authority is necessary. However, none of them specifically referred to the "establishment of a responsible local power."[87]

---

of authority (*l'existence d'une autorité* [in German: *Vorhandensein einer Obrigkeit*]) … sufficient to protect existing rights, and, as the case may be, freedom of trade and of transit under the conditions agreed upon," was limited to a particular region, namely "the coasts of the African continent." Refer also to A. Fitzmaurice, *Sovereignty, Property and Empire, 1500–2000* (Cambridge: Cambridge University Press, 2014), 276–290.

81 Four individuals other than Wheaton are featured in "Excerpt of Public Laws" (September 27, 1874). *Dai Nihon Gaikō Bunsho* 大日本外交文書 [Diplomatic Documents of Greater Japan], vol. 7, 245. Refer also to note 43 in this chapter.

82 Vattel, *supra* note 74, Liv.1. Chap. 18. §§ 207–208.

83 G. F. v. Martens, *Précis du droit des gens moderne de l'Europe fondé sur les traités et l'usage* (2e éd., Gottingue: Librairie de Dieterich, 1801), Liv.2. Chap.1. § 37. The corresponding section is not in the first edition from 1789.

84 H. Wheaton, *Elements of International Law: With a Sketch of the History of the Science* (Philadelphia: Carey, Lea & Blanchard, 1836), Part 2. Chap.4. § 5, 138.

85 A. W. Heffter, *Das europäische Völkerrecht der Gegenwart* (Berlin: E. H. Schroeder, 1844), 125–126.

86 J. C. Bluntschli, *Das moderne Völkerrecht der civilisirten Staten als Rechtsbuch dargestellt* (3.Aufl., Nördlingen: Beck, 1878), 170–171.

87 Refer also to E. Ortolan, *Des moyens d'acquérir le domaine international ou propriété d'État entre les nations, d'après le droit des gens public, comparés aux moyens d'acquérir le propriété entre particuliers, d'après le droit privé; et suivis de l'examen des principes de l'équilibre politique* (Paris: Amyot, 1851), 45–46.

After 1885, a new tendency emerged to "exact that more solid grounds of title shall be shown than used to be accepted as sufficient,"[88] and there were some works stating that the establishment of "authority" as had been stipulated at the Berlin Conference had become necessary.[89] However, the notion that "the establishment of authority ... sufficient to protect ... freedom of trade and of transit," or the "establishment of a responsible local power" unconditionally established *possession réelle* did not necessarily immediately become commonplace.[90]

What about the point that "*possession réelle*" may have been regarded differently depending on the area in question? In an 1896 work, the French professor of public law Gaston Jèze wrote that scholars of international law of the late 18th and 19th centuries were unanimous in their opinion that "*possession réelle*" meant "actual possession" (*posséder réellement*).[91] Jèze further considers that this "actual possession" depends on the nature of the area in question. In the case of barren islets, for example the island of Perim (a volcanic island at the entrance to the Red Sea), the deployment of a garrison constituted effective control, while in the case of Aden for Britain or Obock for France, the establishment of a coal storage station was sufficient, and the mining of guano

88 W. E. Hall, *A Treatise on International Law* (3rd ed., Oxford: Clarendon Press, 1890), 116–117.

89 J. Westlake, *Chapters on the Principles of International Law* (Cambridge: University Press, 1894), 139. However, in the narrative that follows, Westlake stated that "we should certainly be going too far if we said that authority must always be present when its action is required," and that the need for "authority" depends on the nature and rapidity of the stream of emigration or enterprise (165–166). Takahashi Sakuye argues that "occupation must be effectively established," and although there are different theories as to what kinds of acts constitute occupation, he agrees with Westlake's theory that "in general, it is sufficient if there is a latent ability to maintain order." Takahashi, *supra* note 54, 374–378. Takahashi is citing Westlake, *Kokusaihō Yōron* 国際法要論 [Compendium of International Law], (supplementary trans.) Fukai Eigorō 深井英五郎 (Tokyo: Minyūsha, 1901), 280, but the relevant part of the above work in the original (165) is quite different from Fukai's translation.

90 In his 1904 work, Westlake examined in detail Articles 34 and 35 of the General Act of the Conference of Berlin, and in conclusion, the 1894 work, with its limitations, is presented almost verbatim. Westlake, *supra* note 76, 108–109. (The then-most current consensus of opinion is the International Declaration of 1888, 110–111.) The second edition from 1910 has the same description. J. Westlake, *International Law: Part 1: Peace* (2nd ed., Cambridge: University Press, 1910), 110–113. Refer also to Holzendorff, *supra* note 78, 258; Walker, *supra* note 76, 27, etc. However, Oppenheim's 1905 work lists possession and administration (establishment of a responsible authority) as requirements for effective occupation. L. Oppenheim, *International Law: A Treatise. vol.1: Peace* (London: Longmans, Green, 1905), 276–277.

91 G. Jèze, *Étude théorique et pratique sur l'occupation comme mode d'acquérir les territoires en droit international* (Paris: V. Giard & E. Brière, 1896), 229–230.

formations would also constitute actual possession. In the case of Senegambia and the Congo Basin, on the other hand, the establishment of a "responsible local power" was necessary, and the permanent presence of missionaries was considered insufficient.[92]

Similar ideas were expressed in Salomon's work, which was published seven years before Jèze's. Salomon argues that "effectiveness" ("*effectivité*") can vary greatly from case to case, and that actions such as building a lighthouse on an isolated rock in the ocean, setting up a coal depot on an island along a busy shipping route, mining guano formations (see the Guano Islands Act passed by the US Congress on August 18, 1856), and so on constituted actual, rather than feigned, possession.[93]

The examples given by Salomon and Jèze – the establishment of a coal depot, the mining of guano formations, the construction of a lighthouse, and the stationing of missionaries, etc. – suggest that the "establishment of a responsible local power" may not always be required in cases such as isolated islands, and that, in some cases, even actions by private persons may fall under *possession réelle*.[94]

3.2.2.3 *What Kind of Concept Is the "Facts of So-Called Possession under International Law"?*

Considering all of the above points about theories from the time, the following five possibilities can be envisioned for the relationship between "*possession*

92 *Ibid.*, 237–238.

93 Ch. Salomon, *L'occupation des territoires sans maître: Étude de droit international* (Paris: A. Giard, 1889), 307–310, 317–319.

94 Jèze, *supra* note 91, 237–238, 382–384; Salomon, *supra* note 93, 318–319. In addition, in a work by Senga Tsurutarō in 1903, five years after the Minami-Tori-shima measures were taken, he clearly stated that, "For an uninhabited island or a small island with a few villages, even if only a single lighthouse is set up, it can be considered to have already been occupied." Senga Tsurutarō 千賀鶴太郎 (lecture), *Kokusai Kōhō* (*Kyōto Hōsei Daigaku Dai 1 Ki 2 Gakunen Kōgiroku*) 国際公法(京都法政大学第 1 期 2 学年講義録) [Public International Law (Record of a lecture at Kyōto Hōsei University during the 1st term for 2nd year students)] (Kyoto: Kyōto Hōsei University, 1903), 291–292. Sometime later, an article by Tachi Sakutarō that was published in 1933, similarly to the Clipperton case judgement on January 28, 1931, stated that, "It must be said that to hold that the conditions of *possession réelle* are not required for uninhabited islands in practice is contrary to existing theory and customary practice," but, regarding the occupation of uninhabited islands, noted that it is not always necessary to establish a "local power to administer and maintain order," and that ultimately, "it is sufficient in each case that the power of the occupying country prevails on the land to be occupied." Tachi, *supra* note 17, 13, 16, 28.

réelle" and the State/private persons. (This does not necessarily mean that scholars or States at the time were actually advocating these possibilities.)

a) Facts that fall under *possession réelle* must be performed by the State itself. In no case can the acts of private persons satisfy the requirements of occupation.

b) Facts that fall under *possession réelle* must also be performed by the State itself, but, based on acts such as colonization and emigration that are performed by private persons, the State itself ratifies those acts of private persons *ex post facto* in the sense of the "establishment of a responsible local power" or the "establishment of power (national rights)."

c) The acts of private persons are not sufficient for the mere act of taking possession, and there is a need for "something more than the mere act of taking possession" by private persons, specifically, colonization, and, further, there must be a declaration by the private person that the colonized land belongs to their home country. Then, the State's "simple adoption" of such acts by private persons satisfies the two requirements necessary for occupation: the "fact of possession" and the expression of the intent to possess.[95]

d) Acts falling under *possession réelle* – not "establishment of a responsible local power," but mediated facts, for example, emigration, building houses, capturing birds and fish, and cultivating the land, etc., may be conducted by private persons, and then the State merely "approves" ("ratifies") such actions by private persons *ex post facto* to complete its "occupation" as a territorial title.

e) The occupation requirement for effective prior possession is satisfied by a private person conducting acts that fall under *possession réelle* – the aforementioned mediated acts. Based on the fact that these are the acts of private persons, a Cabinet Decision is made, and a directive is issued to express that State's territorial intent. In other words, a State "occupies" islands that are *terra nullius* by satisfying the two requirements of "*possession réelle*" through the actions of private persons and the State's issuance of a "declaration of territorial intent," after which the islands are incorporated into the State's territory.

There are no documents to support that officials in the Legislation Bureau and the Ministry of Home Affairs examined in detail these possibilities for the incorporation of Minami-Tori-shima and worked out the legal grounds

---

95 Hall, *supra* note 79 [1880], 90. It is understood that Hall regarded this "simple adoption" as "ratification." There is room for different interpretations as to whether Hall regarded the declaration of a private person as a requirement for occupation.

for the "facts of so-called possession under international law." However, if the incorporation of Minami-Tori-shima could be evaluated as not illegal in light of international legal theories of the time, then either option d) or e) could be considered. (For more on this notion, refer also to "4 Conclusion.")

4 Conclusion

Needless to say, even in the early Showa Era, the concepts of exclusive economic zones and continental shelves did not exist, and the substantive benefits of incorporating remote islands far from the Japanese mainland were that of emigration where the environment was habitable (depending upon land size, the possibility of crop cultivation, the existence of drinking water, and easy access via ship, etc.; islands such as the Ogasawara Islands and Minami-Daitō-jima/Kita-Daitō-jima are those cases.), and otherwise the main economic value was in albatross feathers, guano, fishery resources, and minerals such as sulfur and phosphate ore. Although there are cases (uninhabited islands in the waters near Okinawa Prefecture) where it is possible that there were national defense factors that required crackdowns on a State's own "territory" amidst heightened tensions between States, as can be inferred via the confidential orders from Minister of Home Affairs Minister Yamagata Aritomo in 1885,[96] it was only in the case of Okino-Tori-shima in 1931 that military interests were clearly brought to the forefront.[97] As examined in this chapter, economic benefits were the main factors for Iō-tō and Minami-Tori-shima.[98]

96 Refer to "Inquiry Concerning Patrol Interrogation Procedures on Daitō-jima" by Deputy of Okinawa Prefectural Governor Nishimura Sutezō and Okinawa Prefecture Grand Secretary Mori Nagayoshi. *Daitōjima Torishirabesho* 大東島取調書 [Daitō-jima Research Report] (held by Naha City Museum of History), 66–68.

97 The June 23 Cabinet Decision includes the expression, "As the island is of great military and fishery importance, it is now confirmed that the area is affiliated with Japan." JACAR: A14100246500 (from the 3rd image).

98 From January to February 1892, various newspapers in Spain and the Philippines (under Spanish rule at the time) reported that the incorporation of Iō-tō would further promote "Viscount Enomoto's colonialism," and successive articles concerned about the impact on the Mariana islands were published. In response to this, a March 23 letter from Minister for Foreign Affairs Enomoto Takeaki to Nomura Yasushi, the Japanese Minister to France, stated that, "It has never been an aggression on foreign territory as by the incorporation the administrative jurisdiction is decided and the name is defined." Regarding this matter, there are no documents indicating that the Spanish Government made a formal protest to the Japanese Government. JACAR: B03041152400 (from the 9th image); Ref. C10125184600 (from the 1st image), 1892, Kōbun Zasshū [Public Record Collection], vol. 10 Tochi [Land] (National Institute for Defense Studies, Ministry of Defense).

However, with regard to Minami-Tori-shima, Foreign Secretary Ishii Kikujirō's August 1902 "Minami-Tori-shima Dispatch Trip Report" will also be touched on here. It notes that "The Pacific Ocean will become the center of the international view of the world, and the action and drama of the new century will play out on this grand stage," but also that "So-called acquisitions are no less than empty words on a piece of paper, and we will find that there are few islands that leave traces of a human presence or keep ships sailing on the sea." Moreover, it notes that Japan should promote a policy of occupying these islands not just "on paper" – in other words, to occupy them "effectively" – by making "acquisition" equivalent to "occupation" and incorporating them into its own territory, and Foreign Secretary Ishii proposed that, "With the Ogasawara Islands as our base for management of the South Seas, we will make Minami-Tori-shima our first satellite location, from there advancing to the south in a steady stream and dispatching warships from time to time to provide convenience and protection to our emigrees so that our management of this area can be realized in the near future."[99]

This chapter examined the two cases of Iō-tō and Minami-Tori-shima, which are regarded as seminal, albeit inadequate, in terms of the legal status of Japan's measures incorporating them into its territory. The analysis of the implications of such considerations for the legal status of the Senkaku Islands, Takeshima, and the Northern Territories will be left to future works. The two cases of Iō-tō and of Minami-tori-shima are important for the analysis. As for the Senkaku Islands, the point is whether the Japanese Government took into consideration the case of Iō-tō, which makes it clear that a distinction should be made between islands that were previously affiliated with Japan and islands that were not previously affiliated with Japan and only became so by the issuance of an Imperial Decree. As for Takeshima, which "referenced" the case of Minami-Tori-shima, which is considered an example of occupation, is the current position of the Japanese Government, which considers the Takeshima case as one of reaffirmation of territory rather than of occupation, legally feasible and desirable from a policy standpoint?[100] In discussing these points, it

99 JACAR Ref. B03041152900 (from the 29th image), Teikoku Hanto Kankei Zakken (1.4.1.7) (Diplomatic Archives of the Ministry of Foreign Affairs).

100 For a discussion on this point, refer to, for example, Park Bae-geun 朴培根, "Nihon ni Yoru Tōsho Sensen no Shosenrei – Takeshima Dokudo ni Taisuru Ryōiki Kengen o Chūshin to Shite" 日本による島嶼先占の諸先例―竹島／独島に対する領域権原を中心として [Some Observations on the Territorial Incorporation of Islands by Japan with Special Reference to the Territorial Title over Liancourt (Takeshima/Dokdo)]. *Kokusaihō Gaikō Zasshi* 国際法外交雑誌, vol. 105, no. 2 (2006): 38–47.

will be necessary to proceed with a more detailed examination of the various relevant primary historical sources.

On the latter issue, there is one last thing that should be confirmed here. The case of Minami-Tori-shima was referenced not only for Takeshima, but also for the cases of Oki-Daitō-jima and Nakano-Tori-shima. For Takeshima, Nakai Yōzaburō "moved to the island and engaged in fishing,"[101] while for Nakano-Tori-shima, Yamada Teizaburō "discovered the island and conducted field surveys … and engaged in the business of mining phosphate ores and capturing birds," which were regarded as "facts of possession under international law."[102] As for Oki-Daitō-jima, although the term "facts of (so-called) possession under international law" is not used by the Government of Japan, the fact that Nakamura Jissaku "circumnavigated the island in question and explored the island's interior" was taken as the basis.[103] For Takeshima, Oki-Daitō-jima, and Nakano-Tori-shima, the legal basis for incorporation was based on the concept of "the facts of (so-called) possession under international law" with regard to the acts of private persons, following the example of Minami-Tori-shima.

However, the Cabinet Decision documents not just for Minami-Tori-shima, but also for Takeshima and Nakano-Torishima, are not held in the Diplomatic Archives of the Ministry of Foreign Affairs.[104] *Island Occupation* (*Collection of Precedents in International Law,* 2) was compiled by the Treaty Bureau in the Ministry of Foreign Affairs in 1933, and explains the cases of Minami-Tori-shima and Nakano-Tori-shima, but does not refer to the respective Cabinet Decisions at all, and there is no explanation for the concept of the "facts of (so-called) possession under international law." Neither Shimizu, Kijimoto, nor Takahashi, who published papers on the Minami-Tori-shima case, made any evaluation of the "facts of so-called possession under international law." The cases of Minami-Tori-shima and Nakano-Tori-shima are taken up in a paper by Tachi Sakutarō in 1933,[105] and the same is true there. It is speculated that he did not know about the concept in the first place.

---

101 JACAR Ref. A01200222600 (from the 1st image), *Kōbun Ruishū* 公文類聚 [Public Documents Collection] Part 29, 1905, vol. 1 (National Archives of Japan).

102 JACAR: A15113659900 (from the 2nd image).

103 JACAR: A15113320500 (from the 1st image).

104 While the Minister for Foreign Affairs was concurrently serving as the Prime Minister when the Cabinet Decision was made on Minami-Tori-shima (Ōkuma Shigenobu), it does not mean that the Ministry of Foreign Affairs was opposed to the respective Cabinet Decisions on Takeshima and Nakano-Tori-shima because the Cabinet documents on these islands bear the seal of the Ministers for Foreign Affairs (Komura Jutarō and Terauchi Masatake).

105 Tachi, *supra* note 17, 44–48.

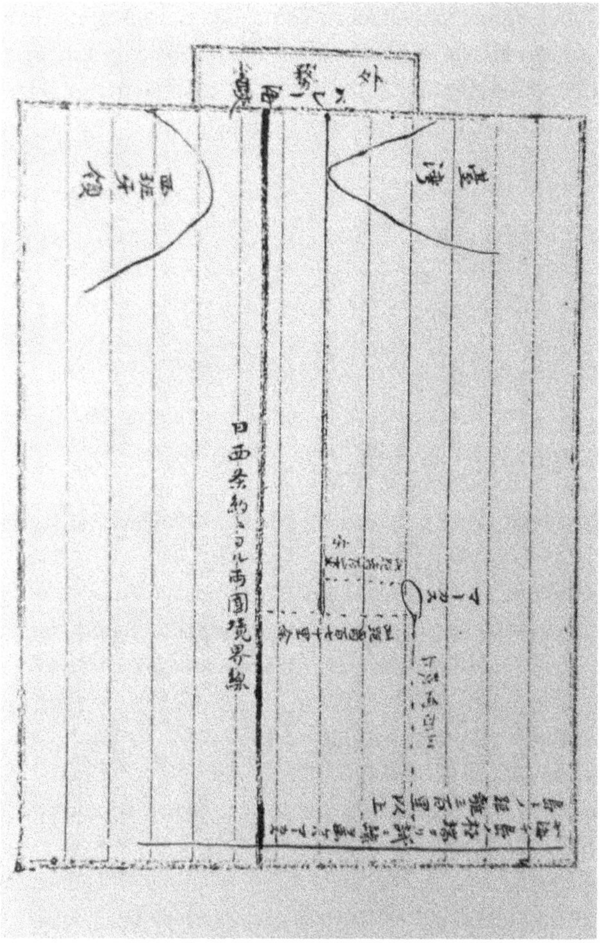

FIGURE 1.1 Location of the bilateral demarcation line and Marcus Island according to the 1895 declaration of the delimitation of borders between Japan and Spain. Japan center for Asian historical records (JACAR), Ref. B03041152600 (4th image). Teikoku Hanto Kankei Zakken (1.4.1.7)
DIPLOMATIC ARCHIVES OF THE MINISTRY OF FOREIGN AFFAIRS OF JAPAN

Minami-Tori-shima in 1898 was the first case in which incorporation measures were addressed head-on based on an understanding of the method of occupation under modern international law, and the case was undoubtedly used as a reference in the subsequent cases of Oki-Daitō-jima, Takeshima, and Nakano-Tori-shima. However, it is not clear to what extent the rationale for deeming the acts of private persons to be "facts of (so-called) possession under international law" was supported by the international legal theories of the time, and furthermore, it cannot be said that the leading scholars of international law in Japan, either at the time or later, had knowledge of such grounds.[106]

Bibliography

Primary Sources

Japanese

Hikone, Shōzō 彦根正三, ed. *Kaisei Kan-inroku Kō Meiji 26 Nen 1 Gatsu* 改正官員録 甲 明治 26 年 1 月 [Revised Official Records Part 1, January 1893]. Tokyo: Hakkō Shoin, 1893.

Japan Center for Asian Historical Records (JACAR). (1) National Archives of Japan, A01200222600; A03033941100; A14100246500; A15112383800; A15112383900; A15113117100; A15113186700; A15113659900. (2) Diplomatic Archives of the Ministry of Foreign Affairs, B02031163700; B03041152400; B03041152600; B03041152700; B03041152800; B03041152900. (3) National Institute for Defense Studies, Ministry of Defense, C06091185100; C10125184600.

Kanpō 官報 [Official Gazette]. No. 2461, September 10, 1891.

Ministry of Foreign Affairs of Japan, ed. *Dai Nihon Gaikō Bunsho* 大日本外交文書 [Diplomatic Documents of Greater Japan], vols. 7, 8. Tokyo: Nihon Kokusai Kyōkai, 1939, 1940.

Ministry of Foreign Affairs of Japan, ed. *Nihon Gaikō Bunsho* 日本外交文書 [Diplomatic Documents of Japan], vol. 24. Tokyo: United Nations Association of Japan, 1952.

Ministry of Foreign Affairs Treaty Bureau, ed. *Tōsho Sensen* (*Kokusaihō Senrei Ishū, 2*) 島嶼先占(国際法先例彙輯, 2) [Island Occupation (Collection of Precedents in International Law, 2)]. Tokyo, 1933.

106 Akiyama Masanosuke cites "facts of ownership," "facts of possession," and "*de facto* possession" as requirements for occupation. Akiyama, *supra* note 17, 42; *Id.*, *Kokusaihō Kōgi Heiji* (*Meiji Hōritsu Gakkō 33 Nendo 3 Gakunen Kōgiroku*) 国際公法講義 平時(明治法律学校 33 年度 3 学年講義録) [Lectures on Public International Law: Peacetime (Record of a lecture at Meiji Law School for Class of 1900, 3rd year students)] (Tokyo: Meiji Hōritsu Gakkō Kōhōkai, 1900), 139, 142–143; *Id.*, *Kokusai Kōhō Jōkan Heiji* 国際公法 上巻 平時 [Public International Law vol. 1: Peacetime] (Tokyo: Wafutsu Hōritsu Gakkō / Shoshi Meihōdō, 1902), 214, 224–225. In his 1903 book, Takahashi Sakuye also cites "the fact of occupation" as a requirement for occupation. Takahashi, *supra* note 54, 374. However, it is doubtful whether Akiyama's concept of "facts of ownership (possession)" or Takahashi's concept of "facts of occupation" was based on Minami-Tori-shima's "facts of so-called possession under international law."

Nishimura, Sutezō 西村捨三, and Mori, Nagayoshi 森長義. "Daitōjima Junshi Torishirabe Yōryō no Gi ni Tsuki Ukagai" 大東島巡視取調要領之儀ニ付伺 [Inquiry Concerning Patrol Interrogation Procedures on Daitō-jima]. In *Daitōjima Torishirabesho* 大東島取調書 [Daitō-jima Research Report]. Okinawa: 1903.

Society for the Preservation of Naval History 海軍歴史保存会, ed. *Shōkan Rireki Jō (Nihon Kaigunshi Dai 9 Kan)* 将官履歴 上（日本海軍史 第 9 巻）[History of Generals and Admirals Part 1 (History of the Japanese Navy, vol. 9)]. Tokyo: Kaigun Rekishi Hozonkai, 1995.

Tokyo Metropolitan Government, ed. *Tōkyō Shishikō Shigaihen Dai 72, Dai 82* 東京市史稿 市街編 第72、第82 [The History of Tokyo City, Town Edition, vols. 72, 82]. Tokyo: Tokyo Metropolitan Government, 1981, 1991.

Tokyo Prefecture Documents (Tokyo Metropolitan Archives Collection). 302.D3.17; 618.B5.13; 619.A2.08; 619.A8.02; 619.C2.19; 619.C6.02; 622.D2.06; 625.D4.19.

Western Language

The Institute of International Law. "Projet de déclaration internationale relative aux occupations de territoires, adopté par l'Institut à Lausannne." *Annuaire de l'Institut de droit international*, tome 10 (1888/89): 201–204.

Secondary Sources

Japanese

Akiyama, Masanosuke 秋山雅之介. *Kokusai Kōhō* 国際公法 [Public International Law]. Tokyo: Tōkyō Senmon Gakkō, 1893.

Akiyama, Masanosuke 秋山雅之介. *Kokusai Kōhō Jōkan Heiji* 国際公法 上巻 平時 [Public International Law vol. 1: Peacetime]. Tokyo: Wafutsu Hōritsu Gakkō / Shoshi Meihōdō, 1902.

Akiyama, Masanosuke 秋山雅之介. *Kokusaihō Kōgi Heiji (Meiji Hōritsu Gakkō 33 Nendo 3 Gakunen Kōgiroku)* 国際公法講義平時（明治法律学校 33 年度 3 学年講義録）[Lectures on Public International Law: Peacetime (Record of a lecture at Meiji Law School for Class of 1900, 3rd year students)]. Tokyo: Meiji Hōritsu Gakkō Kōhōkai, 1900.

Hall, William Edward. *Hōru Shi Kokusai Kōhō* ホール氏国際公法 [Hall's Public International Law]. Translated by Tachi Sakutarō 立作太郎. Tokyo: Tōkyō Hōgakuin, 1899.

Hasegawa, Ryōichi 長谷川亮一. *Chizu kara Kieta Shimajima – Maboroshi no Nihonryō to Nanyō Tankenkatachi* 地図から消えた島々 – 幻の日本領と南洋探検家たち [Islands Disappearing from Maps: Phantom Japanese Territory and South Sea Explorers]. Tokyo: Yoshikawa Kōbunkan, 2011.

Heffter, August Wilhelm. *Kaishi Bankoku Kōhō* 海氏万国公法 [Heffter's Law of Nations]. Translated by Arakawa Kunizō 荒川邦蔵 and Kinoshita Shūichi 木下周一. Tokyo: Ministry of Justice, 1877.

Hiraoka, Akitoshi 平岡昭利. “Minamitorishima no Ryōyū to Keiei – Ahōdori kara Chōfun, Rinkō Saishu e” 南鳥島の領有と経営 – アホウドリから鳥糞，リン鉱採取へ [Territory and Management of Minami-Tori-shima: From Short-Tailed Albatrosses to Guano and Phosphate Mining]. *Rekishi Chirigaku* 歴史地理学 45, no. 4 (2003): 1–14.

Kijimoto Tokizō 雉本朗造. “Minamitorishima Jiken (Kokusai Kōhō Enshū Hōkoku)” 南鳥嶋事件（国際公法演習報告） [The Minami-Tori-shima Incident (Public International Law Seminar Report)]. *Kokka Gakkai Zasshi* 国家学会雑誌 16, no. 189 (1902): 88–118.

Kurachi, Tetsukichi 倉知鉄吉. *Kokusai Kōhō* 国際公法 [Public International Law]. Tokyo: Nihon Hōritsu Gakkō, 1899.

Martens, Friedrich von. *Kokusaihō Jōkan* 国際法 上巻 [International Law vol. 1]. Translated by Nakamura Shingo 中村進午. Tokyo: Tōkyō Senmon Gakkō Press, 1900.

Momose, Takashi 百瀬孝. *Shiryō Kenshō Nihon no Ryōdo* 史料検証 日本の領土 [Survey of Historical Materials: The Territory of Japan]. Tokyo: Kawade Shobō Shinsha, 2010.

Ōkubo, Yasuo 大久保泰甫. *Bowasonādo to Kokusaihō – Taiwan Shuppei Jiken no Tōshizu* ボワソナードと国際法－台湾出兵事件の透視図 [Boissonade and International Law: Perspectives on the Taiwan Expedition]. Tokyo: Iwanami Shoten, 2016.

Park, Bae-geun 朴培根. “Nihon ni Yoru Tōsho Sensen no Shosenrei – Takeshima Dokudo ni Taisuru Ryōiki Kengen o Chūshin to Shite” 日本による島嶼先占の諸先例 – 竹島／独島に対する領域権原を中心として [Some Observations on the Territorial Incorporation of Islands by Japan with Special Reference to the Territorial Title over Liancourt (Takeshima/Dokdo)]. *Kokusaihō Gaikō Zasshi* 国際法外交雑誌 105, no. 2 (2006): 32–47.

Senga, Tsurutarō 千賀鶴太郎. *Kokusai Kōhō (Kyōto Hōsei Daigaku Dai 1 Ki 2 Gakunen Kōgiroku)* 国際公法（京都法政大学第 1 期 2 学年講義録）[Public International Law (Record of a lecture at Kyōto Hōsei University during the 1st term for 2nd year students)]. Kyoto: Kyōto Hōsei University, 1903.

Shimizu Ken-ichirō 清水賢一郎. “Minamitorishima Jiken” 南鳥嶋事件 [The Minami-Tori-shima Incident]. *Kokka Gakkai Zasshi* 国家学会雑誌 16, no. 188 (1902): 107–117.

Tachi Yoshinori 立嘉度 (trans.). *Banchi Shozoku Ron Ge* 蕃地所属論 下 [Affiliation Theory for Uncivilized Lands, Part 2]. Edited by Honda Masatatsu 本多政辰. Tokyo: Sanyūsha, 1874.

Tachi, Sakutarō 立作太郎. “Mushu no Tōsho no Sensen no Hōri to Senrei” 無主の島嶼の先占の法理と先例 [The Legal Principles and Precedents for the Occupation of Ownerless Islands]. *Kokusaihō Gaikō Zasshi* 国際法外交雑誌 32, no. 8 (1933): 15–62.

Taijudō, Kanae 太壽堂鼎. *Ryōdo Kizoku no Kokusaihō* 領土帰属の国際法 [Title to Territory in International Law]. Tokyo: Tōshindō, 1998.

Takahashi, Sakuye 高橋作衛. *Heiji Kokusai Kōhō* 平時国際公法 [Public International Law in Times of Peace]. Tokyo: Nihon Hōritsu Gakkō, 1903.

Takahashi, Sakuye 高橋作衛. "Minamitorishima Jiken" 南鳥嶋事件 [The Minami-Torishima Incident]. *Kokka Gakkai Zasshi* 国家学会雑誌 16, no. 188 (1902): 96–107.

Takahashi, Sakuye 高橋作衛. "Minamitorishima no Senryōken (Takahashi Hōgaku Hakase no Iken)" 南鳥島の占領権(高橋法学博士の意見) [Minami-Tori-shima Possession Rights (Opinion from Professor Takahashi)]. *Yomiuri Shimbun* 読売新聞, October 4, 1902.

Tezuka, Yutaka 手塚豊. "Minamitorishima Sensen Zengo no Ichi Kōsatsu" 南鳥島先占前後の一考察 [A Study of before and after the Minami-Tori-shima Precedent]. *Hōgaku Kenkyū* 法学研究 36, no. 1 (1963): 5–39.

Waseda University Institute of Social Sciences 早稲田大学社会科学研究所, ed. *Ōkuma Bunsho Dai 1 Kan* 大隈文書 第 1 巻 [Ōkuma Documents vol. 1]. Tokyo: Waseda University Institute of Social Sciences, 1958.

Westlake, John. *Kokusaihō Yōron* 国際法要論 [Compendium of International Law]. Supplementary translated by Fukai Eigorō 深井英五郎. Tokyo: Min-yūsha, 1901.

Yanagihara, Masaharu 柳原正治. "Nihon ni Okeru Ryōkai no Han-i ni Kansuru Senrei – Gaimushō Jyōyakukyoku Hen "Kokusaihō Senrei Ishū (7) Ryōkai no Han-i" o Sozai to Shite" 日本における領海の範囲に関する先例 – 外務省条約局編『国際法先例彙輯(7)領海ノ範囲』を素材として [Precedents Concerning the Scope of Territorial Sea in Japan: Based on 'Precedents in International Law Concerning the Scope of Territorial Sea' Edited by the Treaty Bureau in the Ministry of Foreign Affairs]. In *Kokusaihō Chitsujo to Gurōbaru Keizai – Mamiya Isamu Sensei Tsuitō* 国際法秩序とグローバル経済 – 間宮勇先生追悼 [International Legal Order and Global Economy: In Memory of Professor Isamu Mamiya], edited by Yanagihara Masaharu et al. Tokyo: Shinzansha, 2021: 5–32.

Western Languages

Bluntschli, Johann Caspar. *Das moderne Völkerrecht der civilisirten Staten als Rechtsbuch dargestellt*, 3.Aufl. Nördlingen: Beck, 1878.

Bryan, William Alanson. *A Monograph of Marcus Island: An Account of its Physical Features and Geology, with Descriptions of the Fauna and Flora.* Honolulu: Bishop Museum Press, 1903.

Fitzmaurice, Andrew. *Sovereignty, Property and Empire, 1500–2000.* Cambridge: Cambridge University Press, 2014.

Hall, William Edward. *A Treatise on International Law*, 3rd ed. Oxford: Clarendon Press, 1890.

Hall, William Edward. *International Law.* Oxford: Clarendon Press, 1880.

Hébié, Mamadou. "The Acquisition of Original Titles of Territorial Sovereignty in the Law and Practice of European Colonial Expansion." In *Research Handbook on Territorial Disputes in International Law*, edited by Marcelo G. Kohen and Mamadou Hébié. Cheltenham: Edward Elgar, 2018: 36–86.

Heffter, August Wilhelm. *Das europäische Völkerrecht der Gegenwart*. Berlin: E. H. Schroeder, 1844.

Holzendorff, Franz von. "Neuntes Stück. Das Landgebiet der Staaten." In *Handbuch des Völkerrechts. Auf Grundlage europäischer Staatspraxis*. Zweites Band: Die völkerrechtliche Verfassung und Grundordnung der auswärtigen Staatsbeziehungen, edited by Franz von Holzendorff. Hamburg: J. F. Richter, 1887: 223–276.

Jèze, Gaston. *Étude théorique et pratique sur l'occupation comme mode d'acquérir les territoires en droit international*. Paris: V. Giard & E. Brière, 1896.

Lesaffer, Randall. "Argument from Roman Law in Current International Law: Occupation and Acquisitive Prescription." *European Journal of International Law* 16, no. 1 (2005): 25–58.

Martens, Friedrich von. *Völkerrecht. Das internationale Recht der civilisirten Nationen, systematisch dargestellt. Deutsche Ausgabe von Carl Bergbohm*. Bd.1. Berlin: Weidman, 1883.

Martens, Georg Friedrich von. *Précis du droit des gens moderne de l'Europe fondé sur les traités et l'usage*, 2e éd. Gottingue: Librairie de Dieterich, 1801.

Oppenheim, Lassa. *International Law: A Treatise. vol.1: Peace*. London: Longmans, Green, 1905.

Ortolan, Eugène. *Des moyens d'acquérir le domaine international ou propriété d'État entre les nations, d'après le droit des gens public, comparés aux moyens d'acquérir le propriété entre particuliers, d'après le droit privé; et suivis de l'examen des principes de l'équilibre politique*. Paris: Amyot, 1851.

Salomon, Charles. *L'occupation des territoires sans maître: Étude de droit international*. Paris: A. Giard, 1889.

Vattel, Emer de. *Le droit des gens, ou principes de la loi naturelle, appliqués à la conduite & aux affaires des nations & des souverains*. Londres: Apud Liberos Tutior, 1758.

Walker, Thomas Alfred. *A Manual of Public International Law*. Cambridge: University Press, 1895.

Welsch, Bernhard. "Was Marcus Island Discovered by Bernardo de la Torre in 1543?" *Journal of Pacific History* 39, no. 1 (2004): 109–122.

Westlake, John. *Chapters on the Principles of International Law*. Cambridge: University Press, 1894.

Westlake, John. *International Law: Part 1: Peace*. Cambridge: University Press, 1904.

Westlake, John. *International Law: Part 1: Peace*, 2nd ed. Cambridge: University Press, 1910.

Wheaton, Henry. *Elements of International Law: With a Sketch of the History of the Science*. Philadelphia: Carey, Lea & Blanchard, 1836.

CHAPTER 2

Ryūkyū Attribution Issue and Ernest Satow

Assessment of the Newspapers Debate between Japan and Qing and Its Background

Tadashi Mori

1 Introduction

At the end of March 1879, tensions between Japan and China's Qing Dynasty heightened following the Government of Japan's abolishment of the Ryūkyū Domain and establishment of Okinawa Prefecture ("Ryūkyū Disposition"). The Qing Government demanded that Japan withdraw its disposition because the Ryūkyū Kingdom was a tributary state of China, leading to increased tension between both countries over the attribution of the Ryūkyū Kingdom ("Ryūkyū Attribution Issue").

In May 1879 and thereafter, there were two inquiries and replies between the Qing Government and the Government of Japan, where the claims of each party were reciprocated, and running parallel to this, mediation[1] was carried out by former US President Ulysses S. Grant. Both Qing and Japan responded to this mediation and explored a venue for direct negotiations, with preliminary negotiations commencing in March 1880 and official negotiations taking place between August 18 and October 21, 1880. These resulted in an agreement[2] in

1 There are documents that position Grant's involvement as "good offices." However, good offices and mediation are more or less the same in the sense that they are non-binding on the parties to the dispute, and it has been pointed out "the two are often used interchangeably in positive law" (Yamamoto Sōji 山本草二, *Kokusaihō* 国際法 [International Law] (Tokyo: Yūhikaku, 1994 (New Edition)), 681). In the latter half of the 19th century, negotiations between the parties to the dispute, mediation that is non-binding on the parties to the dispute, and arbitration that binds the parties to the dispute were commonly mentioned when discussing dispute resolution procedures. (William Edward Hall, *International Law* (Oxford: Clarendon Press, 1880), 306 provides one example of discussion that is largely in the same era as Grant's involvement.) In this chapter, the author follows the original text when quoting, but generally uses the word "mediation."

2 This agreement was originally scheduled to be signed 10 days after the conclusion of the agreement with the approval of the Emperor of the Qing Dynasty. However, the Qing side later withdrew its agreement to the signing. On March 5 of the following year, 1881, the Qing side issued an imperial order to renegotiate, and rescinded the draft amendment to partition

 | DOI:10.1163/9789004706361_003

which the main island of Okinawa and all islands north of it were designated as Japanese territory, while Miyako Islands and the Yaeyama Islands were designated as Qing territory, and the Sino-Japanese Amity Treaty was effectively revised.

How was the Ryūkyū Attribution Issue perceived under international law by Japan, China and the Western powers that had entered the region?

This question concerns the "acceptance of international law"[3] by Japan and Qing, but it also goes beyond that. From the 1860s to 1870s, Japan not only accepted international law in its relations with Western powers, but also attempted to apply it to its relations with the countries of East Asia. Meanwhile, it has been pointed out that Qing had also begun using international law in its relations with Western powers, but instead of applying this

the islands. For the Ryūkyū Disposition, including the development leading up to it, see Watanabe Miki 渡辺美季, "'Ryūkyū Shobun' to Ryūkyū Bunkatsu Kōshō – Nisshin Kankei no Tenki" 『琉球処分』と琉球分割交渉ー日清関係の転機 [Ryūkyū Disposition and Negotiation on Ryūkyū Partitioning: Turning Point of Japan–Qing Relations] in *Handobukku Kindai Chūgoku Gaikōshi* ハンドブック近代中国外交史 [Handbook of Modern Chinese Diplomatic History], Okamoto Takashi 岡本隆司 and Hakoda Keiko 箱田恵子 (eds.) (Kyoto: Minerva Shobō, 2019), 90–91; Nishizato Kikō 西里喜行, *Shinmatsu Chū Ryū Nichi Kankeishi no Kenkyū* 清末中琉日関係史の研究 [A Study of Relations between China, Ryukyu and Japan in Late Qing Period] (Kyoto: Kyoto University Press, 2005), 282–392; and Hakoda Keiko 箱田恵子, "Ryūkyū Shobun o Meguru Nisshin Kōshō to Chūsai Saiban Seido" 琉球処分をめぐる日清交渉と仲裁裁判制度 [The Arbitration System and the Sino-Japanese Negotiation over the Annexation of Ryūkyū], *Shisō* 史窓, no. 77 (2020), 17–22. As for the legal positioning of the Ryūkyū Disposition, see Yanagihara Masaharu, "Some Thoughts on the Concept of Territory in the Late Edo and Early Meiji Periods," https://www.jiia-jic.jp/en/resourcelibrary/pdf/Shioki_Fuyo_Zokkoku_and_Sovereignty.pdf, 20–22; Yanagihara Masaharu, "Shioki, Fuyō, Zokkoku and Sovereignty," https://www.jiia-jic.jp/en/resourcelibrary/pdf/Shioki_Fuyo_Zokkoku_and_Sovereignty.pdf, 17–24; and Matsui Yoshirō 松井芳郎, *Kokusaihō gakusha ga Yomu Senkaku Mondai* 国際法学者がよむ尖閣問題 [The Senkaku Issue as Read by International Law Scholars] (Tokyo: Nippon Hyōronsha, 2014), 33–36.

3 There is much literature on the subject. For leading Japanese works in the field of international law, see Yanagihara Masaharu, "Significance of the History of the Law of Nations in Europe and East Asia," *Recueil des Cours de l'Academie de droit international de la Haye*, vol. 371 (2015), 317–349; and Hamamoto Shōtarō, "International Law, Regional Developments: East Asia," in *The Max Planck Encyclopedia of Public International Law*, Rüdiger Wolfrum (ed.) (Oxford: Oxford University Press, 2012), vol. 5, 907–926; for diplomatic history, see *Higashi Ajia Kindaishi* 東アジア近代史, vol. 2 (March 1999), and *Higashi Ajia Kindaishi* 東アジア近代史, vol. 3 (March 2000). For a work that addresses questions concerning the expression "acceptance of international law," see Toyota Tetsuya 豊田哲也, "19 Seiki Higashi Ajia to Kindaikokusaihō no Kokkachūshinshugi no Keisei" 19世紀東アジアと近代国際法の国家中心主義の形成 [19th-century East Asia and the Formation of State-Centrism in Modern International Law], *Kokusaihō Gaikō Zasshi* 国際法外交雑誌, vol. 116, no. 4 (2018), 2–3. Note that the above references are not discussions of simple "acceptance."

to its relations with Asian countries, Qing maintained its traditional stance of handling these relations as issues of the East Asian order.[4] Taking into consideration this inconsistency, the abovementioned question also concerns, amid the dispute over the attribution of Ryūkyū, the perceptions of Qing and Japan regarding the application of international law to their bilateral relations, as well as the perceptions of Western powers regarding how international law applied to Japan–Qing relations.[5]

The relationship between acceptance of international law and the traditional East Asian order has conventionally been described in formulaic terms, with the arrival of European powers in East Asia bringing a view of order based on modern international law to the region, which collided with the traditional East Asian order, and Qing's loss during the Sino-Japanese War paving the way for its collapse.[6] This perception is likely an appropriate one, but as this discussion seems to have emerged, connecting several major points over the course of time, it has created room for a more detailed analysis of this process of change.

For example, until the 1860s, Western powers demanded and established their relations with Japan and Qing respectively based on international law, but in the 1870s, they "began to pay attention to the relationships between Qing and the vassal states surrounding the Chinese Empire."[7] In this context, the questions of what, at a certain point in time, Western powers thought about the norms applicable to Japan–Qing relations or the order underlying them, and how such perceptions evolved over time, together with the perceptions of Asian countries, including Japan and Qing, are expected to provide important clues for elucidating how the view of order in this region changed.[8]

4 Kawashima Shin 川島真, *Chūgoku Kindai Gaikō no Keisei* 中国近代外交の形成 [Formation of Modern Chinese Diplomacy] (Nagoya: Nagoya University Press, 2004), 17; Nishizato, *supra* note 2, 284.

5 Suzuki Shōgo argued, regarding attribution issues of Ryūkyū, that "the abolition of the Ryūkyū Kingdom and the subsequent dispute between China and Japan are the early clashes of two disparate international systems," (Suzuki Shōgo, *Civilization and Empire: China and Japan's Encounter with European International Society* (London: Routledge, 2009), 161).

6 See Ōnuma Yasuaki, "When was the Law of International Society Born? – An Inquiry of the History of International Law from an Intercivilizational Perspective," *Journal of the History of International Law*, vol. 2 (2000), 1–66, esp., 30–32, 51–54; Suzuki, *supra* note 5, 175.

7 Motegi Toshio 茂木敏夫, "Chūkateikoku no 'Kindai' teki Saihen to Nihon" 中華帝国の『近代』的再編と日本 [The Modern Reorganization of the Chinese Empire and Japan], in *Iwanami Kōza Kindai Nihon to Shokuminchi 1 Shokuminchi Teikoku Nihon* 岩波講座近代日本と植民地1植民地帝国日本 [Iwanami Lectures Modern Japan and Colonies vol. 1 Colonial Empire Japan], Ōe Shinbu 大江志乃夫 et al. (eds.) (Tokyo: Iwanami Shoten, 1992), 63.

8 Matsui hints at many discussions on this topic. See Matsui, *supra* note 2, 113 *et seq.*

The differences in the perceptions of international law between Japan and China, as well as how the Western powers, especially Britain, which played a leading part, were aware of and involved in them, have been examined in detail in relation to the dispatch of military forces to Taiwan prior to the "Ryūkyū Disposition" and the related negotiations between Japan and Qing. These previous studies point out that Qing was opposed to Japan advocating the application of international law, that Japan did not consistently give its view based on international law, and that the British Minister to Qing Thomas Francis Wade, who mediated the negotiations, ultimately prioritized a solution based on the traditional East Asian view of order.[9]

In contrast, there are not very many papers or discussions focusing on international law regarding the Ryūkyū Attribution Issue.[10] In addition, except

9 On these points, see Aoyama Harutoshi 青山治世, "Taiwan Shuppei Jiken" 台湾出兵事件 [Taiwan Expedition Incident], in Okamoto and Hakoda (eds.), *supra* note 2, 88–89; Kobayashi Takao 小林隆夫, 19 Seiki Igirisu Gaikō to Higashi Ajia 19世紀イギリス外交と東アジア [19th Century British Diplomacy and East Asia] (Tokyo: Sairyūsha, 2012), 38–63; Kobayashi Takao 小林隆夫, Taiwan Jiken to Ryūkyū Shobun – Rujandoru no Yakuwari Saikō – (2) 台湾事件と琉球処分ールジャンドルの役割再考ー(2) [Taiwan Incident and Ryūkyū Disposition: Reconsidering the role of Le Gendre (2)], *Seiji Keizai Shigaku* 政治経済史学, no. 341 (1994), 17–28; Ōkubo Yasuo 大久保泰甫, *Bowasonādo to Kokusaihō – Taiwan Shuppeijiken no Tōshizu* ボワソナードと国際法ー台湾出兵事件の透視図 [Boissonade and International Law: Perspective of the Taiwan Expedition] (Tokyo: Iwanami Shoten, 2016); Kurihara Jun 栗原純, "Taiwan Jiken (1871–1874 Nen) – Ryūkyū Seisaku no Tenki to Shiteno Taiwan Shuppei" 台湾事件(1871–1874年)ー琉球政策の転機としての台湾出兵 [Taiwan Incident (1871–1874): Dispatch of troops to Taiwan as a turning point in Ryūkyū policy], *Shigaku Zasshi* 史学雑誌 vol. 87, no. 9 (1978), 61–64; Robert Eskildsen, "Meiji 7 Nen Taiwan Shuppei no Shokuminchiteki Sokumen" 明治7年台湾出兵の植民地的側面 [Colonial Aspects of the 1874 Taiwan Expedition], in *Meiji Ishin to Ajia* 明治維新とアジア [Meiji Restoration and Asia], Meiji Ishin shigakukai (ed.) (Tokyo: Yoshikawa Kōbunkan, 2001), 61–76; Ichinose Norie 一瀬啓恵, Meiji Shoki ni okeru Taiwan Shuppei Seisaku to Kokusaihō no Tekiyō 明治初期における台湾出兵政策と国際法の適用 [Taiwan Expedition Policy and Application of International Law in the Early Meiji Era], *Hokudaishigaku* 北大史学, no. 35 (1995), 23–43; Zhang Chixiong 張啓雄, Nisshin Gokan Jyōyaku ni Oite Ryūkyū no Kizoku wa Kettei Saretaka? 日清互換條約において琉球の帰屬は決定されたか [Did the Sino-Japanese Treaty Determine the Attribution of Ryūkyū?] *Okinawa Bunka Kenkyū* 沖縄文化研究, no. 19 (1992), 100–107.

10 In addition to Ueda Toshio 植田捷雄, Ryūkyū no Kizoku o Meguru Nisshin Kōshō 琉球の帰属を繞る日清交渉 [Sino-Japanese Negotiations Concerning the Ryūkyū Attribution], *Tōyō Bunka Kenkyūsyo Kiyō* 東洋文化研究所紀要, no. 2 (1951), 151–201, prominent examples of more recent literature include Hakoda, *supra* note 2, 1–23, which focuses on how the arbitration tribunal was perceived in the same negotiation process, and Zhang Tian-en 張天恩, Ryūkyū Mondai o Meguru Nisshin Kōshō to Kokusaihō 琉球問題をめぐる日清交渉と国際法 [Sino-Japanese Negotiations and International Law over the Ryūkyū Issue], *Socio-science* ソシオサイエンス, no. 26 (2020), 18–39, which illustrates the difference in understanding of international law between Japan and Qing.

for the personal mediation by Grant that was touched upon earlier, perhaps because of the lack of major involvement of Western powers, there has been almost no review of their perceptions of international law as far as the author is aware. However, that is not to say that Western powers such as Britain had no interest in this issue; rather they were proactive in gathering information on this subject.[11] Within this context, it is of particular interest that, over the period from January 1879 to February 1880, the assessment of this issue within the British Legation in Japan changed a great deal.

Prior to the Ryūkyū Disposition, at a meeting with Minister of Internal Affairs Terashima Munenori, held on January 13, 1879, British Minister to Japan Harry Smith Parkes pointed out, "Generally speaking, the Ryūkyū Islands are believed to belong to both Japan and Qing." In response, Terashima said, "The islands do not belong to both countries. Ryūkyū has merely dispatched missions to present gifts to the Qing Emperor on occasion and does not pay taxes to Qing." However, Parkes added, "As long as tribute is paid to Qing, the Ryūkyū Islands will be considered to belong to Qing." Terashima replied by again pointing out that no taxes had been levied by Qing and stated that the Taiwan Expedition made clear that Ryūkyū did not belong to Qing. Parkes responded that he had seen the provisions exchanged between Japan and Qing during the Taiwan Expedition, and that it contained no such text.[12]

---

11 Britain had compiled a booklet of "confidential" information from letters and public telegraphs between its ministers to Japan and Qing and its Foreign Secretary (*Confidential Print: Correspondence respecting the LOOCHOO ISLANDS. 1879–82. Printed for the use of the Foreign Office. February 1883* (The National Archives (UK), FO881/4718)), which indicates that Britain had great interest in the matter. In addition, as will be mentioned later, the Japanese Government also actively provided information to the British Minister and Acting Minister to Japan (see *infra* notes 27, 90 and corresponding text to *infra* notes 91, 93, 95, 97).

12 "Meiji 12 Nen 1 Gatsu 13 Nichi Eikoku Kōshi Raishō Gaimukyō tono Taiwa Ryakki (Ryūkyūhan Ikken)" 明治 12年 1月 13日英国公使来省外務卿との対話略記(琉球藩一件) [Abridged Dialogue between the British Minister and the Japanese Minister for Foreign Affairs on January 13, 1879 (On the Case of Ryūkyū Domain)] in *Ryūkyū Shobun Ge* 琉球処分・下 [Ryūkyū Disposition Part 2], Matsuda Michiyuki 松田道之, in *Ryūkyū Shozoku Mondai Kankei Shiryō* 琉球所属問題関係資料 [Ryūkyū Attribution Issue Related Documents] vol. 4, Yokoyama Manabu 横山学 (ed.) (Tokyo: Honpō Shoseki, 1980)), 132–138. See Namihira Tsuneo 波平恒男, *Kindai Higashi Ajiashi no Nakano Ryūkyū Heigō – Chūka Sekai Chitsujo kara Shokuminchi Teikoku Nihon e* 近代東アジア史のなかの琉球併合ー中華世界秩序から植民地帝国日本へ [The Disposition of Ryūkyū in the History of Modern East Asia: From the Chinese World Order to the Colonial Empire of Japan] (Tokyo: Iwanami Shoten, 2014), 298–299. Parkes said in a note to Wade dated September 3, 1879 (FO881/4718/16(ii) (FO46/247, no. 161(ii))) that the consolation money stated in the provisions exchanged between Japan and Qing at the time of the Taiwan Expedition did not form the basis of attribution of Ryūkyū to Japan.

In a letter to the Foreign Secretary, the 3rd Marquess of Salisbury, dated August 1, 1879, Parkes pointed out that Ryūkyū had paid tribute to both Japan and China, had a national identity and autonomy as an independent nation, and was recently annexed by Japan.[13] In a memorandum prepared on July 6, 1879 attached to this letter, Ernest Mason Satow, a secretary at the British Legation in Japan, also provided an overview of the Ryūkyū Disposition from 1871 onwards, and pointed out that the fact that in October 1872, the Ministry of Foreign Affairs had jurisdiction over the Ryūkyū Domain when King Shōtai of the Ryūkyū Kingdom was made a vassal and said domain was established "seems to indicate that the [Ryūkyū] islands were not yet regarded as an integral part of the Japanese Empire."[14] In a letter to the Foreign Secretary, the 3rd Marquess of Salisbury, dated September 18, 1879, too, Parkes criticized Japan's claims of sovereignty, pointing out that Japan had not explained the reason it had permitted tributes from the Ryūkyū Kingdom to Qing.[15] In any case, he took a negative view of Japan's claims. It is believed that, because he touched upon the dual affiliation and imperial tributes, Parkes seems to have assumed a traditional East Asian view of order.[16]

This critical stance towards Japan undergoes a reversal in a memorandum by Satow[17] (hereinafter "the Satow Memorandum") that was attached to a letter[18] sent to the Foreign Secretary, the 3rd Marquess of Salisbury, by Acting British Minister to Japan John G. Kennedy, dated February 13, 1880. Kennedy, who sent the memorandum, viewed it in a positive light.[19] This memorandum

13 FO881/4718/5 (FO46/247, no. 140).

14 FO881/4718/5(iv) (FO46/247, no. 140(iv); Ian Nish (ed.), *British Documents on Foreign Affairs: Reports and Papers from the Foreign Office Confidential Print, Part I, From the Mid-Nineteenth Century to the First World War, Series E, Asia, 1860–1914, vol. 2, Korea, the Ryūkyū Islands, and North-East Asia, 1875–1888* (Federick: University Publications of America, 1989) (hereinafter, BDFA2), 62–68). *See also*, Suzuki, *supra* note 5, 157.

15 FO881/4718/13 (FO46/247, no. 163).

16 For the concept of tribute and dual affiliation in the traditional East Asian view of the world order, see Motegi, *supra* note 7, 61–65; for the plurality of such views of order, see Arano Yasunori 荒野泰典, *Kinsei Nihon to Higashi Ajia* 近世日本と東アジア [Modern Japan and East Asia] (Tokyo: University of Tokyo Press, 1988), 29–65; Suzuki, *supra* note 5, 34–55; Hamamoto, *supra* note 3, 909–911; for "the basis of ambiguity in international relations" in East Asia, see Mitani Hiroshi 三谷博, *Nihonshi no Naka no 'Fuhen'* 日本史のなかの「普遍」 [Searching for Generalities in Japanese History] (Tokyo: University of Tokyo Press, 2020), 196 198.

17 FO881/4718/50(i) (FO46/256, no. 26(i); *BDFA2, supra* note 14, 70–74).

18 FO881/4718/50 (FO46/256, no. 26; *BDFA2, supra* note 14, 69–70).

19 See text corresponding to *infra* note 22.

introduced the de facto dispute[20] over the Ryūkyū issue between Japan and Qing that played out in newspapers between November 1879 and February 1880 (newspapers debate between Japan and Qing) and supported Japan's claims concerning its exercise of sovereignty. Regarding China, the memorandum stated, "The country has never exercised any authority in any way over the [Ryūkyū] islands," and emphasized that it was not the case that Qing had claimed sovereignty over the Ryūkyū Kingdom in the first place.[21] It appears that the memorandum viewed the matter in terms of sovereignty and authority based on the modern international legal order perspective, rather than dual affiliation and imperial tributes based on the traditional East Asian view of order.

What are the implications of these changes in the British Legation in Japan? Can this mean that Britain's basis for assessing Sino-Japanese relations shifted from the traditional East Asian view of the world order to the view of order based on modern international law? Or should it be viewed as a change based on some more specific background? Regarding the Satow Memorandum, Kennedy pointed out that "Mr. Satow, after stating the views of each writer, proceeds to weigh the evidence, and pronounces in favour of the arguments adduced on behalf of Japan,"[22] but what, in the first place, was asserted in the "de facto dispute between Japan and China" that triggered the memorandum and what did Satow place importance on in reaching the above conclusion?

This chapter will first elucidate the scope of the Satow Memorandum, which has not received much attention to date, and, after organizing the arguments therein, shed light on how Satow summarized the views of each author and what exactly Satow focused on in arriving at his conclusion. Based on that, it will explore the background of this evaluation and touch upon the significance thereof.

---

20 It was not the official opinion of both countries that was published in the newspapers. Nevertheless, since the articles were written by the government affiliates of each country, this was described as a "de facto dispute between Japan and Qing." See *infra* notes 23, 24, 26.

21 FO881/4718/50(i) (FO46/256, no. 26(i); *BDFA2, supra* note 14, 70–74).

22 FO881/4718/50 (FO46/256, no. 26; *BDFA2, supra* note 14, 69–70).

2 Scope of the Satow Memorandum and Debate on Newspapers between Japan and Qing

2.1 *Scope of the Satow Memorandum*

According to the Satow Memorandum and Kennedy's letter concerning it, the Satow Memorandum examined the debate that played out across an article entitled *Audi Alteram Partem* (*Listen to the Voices of Others*), which was believed to be representative of China's position, appearing in the *Japan Gazette* between November and December 1879,[23] and a rebuttal article[24] entitled *Rebuttal* published in *Tokyo Nichi Nichi Shimbun* from the end of January to the beginning of February 1880.[25] Although not mentioned in the Satow Memorandum and Kennedy's letter, the article itself published in *Japan Gazette* was intended to refute the "official position of the Japanese Government" published in the *Tokio Times* on October 11, 1879.[26] Therefore, arranged chronologically, there is

---

23 Published in parts across November 29, 1879, December 6, 1879, December 20, 1879, and January 10, 1880. The author referred to "Audi Alteram Partem – A Critique, The Japan Gazette, 1879," in *The Demise of the Ryūkyū Kingdom: Western Accounts and Controversy*, Yamaguchi Eitetsu and Arakawa Yūkō (eds.) (Ginowan: Yōjushorin, 2002), 27–61 (hereinafter, "Audi Alteram Partem") as a summary of these. According to the Satow Memorandum and Kennedy's letters on this topic, the article is believed to have been written by an American interpreter (Dr. McCartee) working at the Chinese Legation in Japan.

24 Published in parts on January 28, 29, 31 and February 9, 1880. A rough draft written by Inoue Kowashi at the request of Itō Hirobumi remains ("*Yokohama Shimbun Bakuron Sōkō*" 横浜新聞駁論草稿 [Rebuttal Draft to the Article in a Newspaper Published in Yokohama], in *Inoue Kowashi den. Shiryō hen* no. 5 井上毅傳 史料編第5 [Life of Kowashi Inoue, Historical Materials, vol. 5], Inoue Kowashi Denki Hensan Iinkai 井上毅傳記編纂委員會 (eds.) (Tokyo: Kokugakuin University Library, 1975), 506–514). See Yamashita Shigekazu 山下重一, "'Japan Gazetto' Ronsetsu no Ryūkyū Shobun Hihan to Inoue Kowashi no Hanron" 『ジャパン・ガゼット』論説の琉球処分批判と井上毅の反論 [Criticism of the Ryūkyū Disposition in the Japan Gazette Article and Kowashi Inoue's Counterargument], *Kokugakuin Hōgaku* 國學院法學, vol. 40, no. 1 (2002), 54. The same article is also included in Yamashita Shigekazu 山下重一, *Zoku Ryūkyū Okinawashi Kenkyū Josetsu* 続琉球・沖縄史研究序説 [Continued Introduction to Ryūkyū and Okinawan History Research] (Tokyo: Ochanomizu Shobō, 2004), 221–261 with "slight amendments" (266).

25 FO881/4718/50 (FO46/256, no. 26; *BDFA2*, *supra* note 14, 70); FO881/4718/50(i) (FO46/256, no. 26(i); *BDFA2*, *supra* note 14, 70–71).

26 "Audi Alteram Partem," *supra* note 23, 27. The article published in *Tokio Times* is included as "Japan and Ryūkyū, The Tokio Times, 1879" (hereinafter, "Japan and Ryūkyū") in Yamaguchi and Arakawa (eds.), *supra* note 23, 12–26. While the expression "the official statement of the Japanese Government" is seen in the article published in *Japan Gazette*, the article published in *Tokio Times* is in fact almost identical to *Memorandum upon the Claim of Japan to the Absolute and Undivided Sovereignty of the Riu Kiu Islands, with Reference to the Opposing Claims of the Government of China* (*July 1879*) (FO881/4718/20(ii)

first the view of the Japanese Government published in *Tokio Times*, then the rebuttal by the Qing Government (Chinese Legation in Japan) published in *Japan Gazette*, and then the Japanese Government's surrebuttal published in *Tokyo Nichi Nichi Shimbun*. It is unclear[27] whether Satow read the first article published in *Tokio Times*, but this chapter will also review it so as to understand the objections of the Qing side published in *Japan Gazette*, and set out Satow's assessment of the latter two articles.[28]

2.2 *Debate on Newspapers between Japan and Qing*

The views of the Japanese Government in *Tokio Times* consist of I. Ancient and Medieval History, II. Geographical Relations, III. Language, Religion, Race, and Customs, IV. Medieval and Early Modern History, and a section without a heading (Summary).[29] The Qing rebuttal published in *Japan Gazette* has a

(FO46/248, no. 187(ii)) published by the Japanese Government (hereinafter, "Japanese Government memorandum"). The same memorandum is a translation of "Shina Seifu no Kōron ni Taishite Waga Nihon ni Ryūkyūtō o Senryōsuru no Syuken Aru no Oboegaki" 支那政府ノ抗論ニ対シテ我日本ニ琉球島ヲ専領スルノ主権アルノ覚書 [Notes regarding sovereignty over the Ryūkyū Islands to Japan in response to the objection of the Chinese Government] in *Ryūkyū Shozoku Mondai 1* 琉球所属問題1 [Ryūkyū Attribution Issue 1], Ministry of Foreign Affairs of Japan (ed.) in Yokoyama (ed.), *supra* note 12, vol. 8, 329–352, hereinafter "Japanese Government notes"), the contents of which are the same as those of the first review by the Japanese side dated July 16, 1879 (FO881/4718/13(ii) (FO46/247, no. 163(ii))).

27 The aforementioned "Japanese Government memorandum" note 26, which is almost identical to the article, was passed from the Japanese Government (Minister of Home Affairs Itō Hirobumi) to the British Legation in Japan (Acting Minister Kennedy), (FO881/4718/20 (FO46/248, no. 187)), with Satow being in a position where he may have come across it.

28 For an examination of the abovementioned *Tokio Times* article, *Japan Gazette* article, and Inoue Kowashi's draft of the *Tokyo Nichi Nichi Shimbun* article, see Yamashita, *supra* note 24. The same work, as will be described later, suggested that "in terms of debate over historical facts, the author of the *Gazette* article has by far the stronger argument" (*ibid.*, 89). This chapter does not delve into "historical disputes," but rather focuses on Satow's assessment with regard to the debate. Meanwhile, Satow's assessment is also introduced in Zhang, *supra* note 10, 23. However, said article does not discuss in detail the debate in the news articles nor Satow's assessment thereof. This chapter, however, does focus on these points.

29 Here, it is described as a "summary," but as will be seen later, it was not simply a summary of the preceding assertions; rather, it also touched on the relationship between the assessment of Ryūkyū's dual affiliation, the Sino-Japanese Treaty of Amity, and the dispatch of troops to Taiwan. The volume of the summary in the *Tokio Times* article is comparable to the total of I to IV excluding the reference material section.

similar structure,[30] refuting the Japanese Government's views in detail.[31] In response, Japan's surrebuttal published in *Tokyo Nichi Nichi Shimbun* touches only upon I and IV and a part of the summary. Below, the author will summarize the claims made by both countries by theme. Note that the numbering of (1) to (15) below were added by the author to make it easier to understand the points of debate.

2.2.1 Ancient and Medieval History

In relation to ancient history, the *Tokio Times* article pointed out that (1) Ryūkyū was called "Minami-shima" (written with the same characters (南島) as Nantō below) or "Okinawa" and (2) there was a historical relationship between the islanders of Minami-shima and the Japanese Imperial Court.[32] Regarding medieval history, (3) the Ryūkyū King claimed to be a descendant of Minamoto no Tametomo, a direct descendant of the Japanese Imperial family.[33]

In response, the article published in *Japan Gazette* first pointed out that (1) the name "Ryūkyū" or "Okinawa" had been used since China discovered the islands in 608, and that "Nantō" (written with the same characters 南島 as Minami-shima above) means "southern islands," which had been used to include all islands located south of Kyushu (including Macau and Luzon). On the other hand, (2) with regard to the relationship between the islanders of Minami-shima and the Japanese Imperial Court, which the Japanese side claimed, the article argued that Minami-shima referred to the present-day Ōsumi Islands (Yakushima, Tanegashima, etc.) and the Tokara Islands, not

30 I. (Reexamination of History), II. (Geographical Relationship), III. (Language, Religion, Race, Customs), IV. (Early Modern History), V. (Shimazu Iehisa's Ordinance), Summary. Parts I to IV comprises over 90% of the total, while the Summary makes up less than 10%.

31 The *Tokio Times* article, as laid out in Yamaguchi and Arakawa, *supra* note 23, comprises 60 lines for I, 16 lines for II, 43 lines for III, 58 lines for IV, plus 102 lines for reference materials (Shimazu Iehisa's Ordinance, Oath of Shou Ning, Oath of the Council of Three), and 187 lines for summary. The *Japan Gazette* article, following the same layout, comprises 321 lines for I, 34 lines for II, 286 lines for III, 296 lines for IV, 51 lines for V, and 94 lines for summary. The latter is 2.3 times as long as the former with the reference materials included; if reference materials are excluded for the former, the latter is about 3 times the volume of the former.

32 "Japan and Ryūkyū," *supra* note 26, 12–13. There are records of rank conferment in 707, arrival of islanders from Minami-shima and other islands at the Japanese Imperial Court in 715, dispatch of the Dazai-shi (Chief of the Dazaifu local government office) to Minami-shima and erection of a stone monument with inscription of the island's name in 735, and the words "Minami-shima is under the jurisdiction of Dazaifu" in the *Engishiki* (a Japanese corpus of laws and regulations compiled in 927).

33 *Ibid.*, 13. The son of Minamoto no Tametomo (Sonton) named himself Shuntennō and became the first Ryūkyū king. The lineage ended for a time but was later revived.

Ryūkyū or Okinawa. Regarding medieval history, it also (3) rejected Japan's claim that the King of the Ryūkyū Kingdom was a descendant of Minamoto no Tametomo as nothing more than a myth, and claimed that he was descended from a prince of the Yuan Dynasty.[34]

In response to these objections from the Qing side, the "Rebuttal" first (1) examined in detail what Minami-shima refers to under the heading "Okinawa and Minami-shima Names," and concluded that "Shikaki is the current Ishigaki, while Kumi is also known as Kume-yama," and that Minami-shima "is without a doubt the name that collectively refers to present-day Ryūkyū and the Satsuma Islands."[35] Next, (2) under the heading "Imperial Tributes of the Minami-shima Islands," it emphasized that, regardless of whether Ryūkyū was discovered by the Chinese or given its name by the Chinese, the Ryūkyū people were not submissive to China during the Sui, Tang, Song, and Yuan dynasties, and that they had been making imperial tributes to Japan since that time.[36] Furthermore, (3) under the heading "Considerations of Ryūkyū as Descendants of Tametomo," the Rebuttal asserted the validity of the legend of Minamoto no Tametomo while citing historical works, and refuted the Chinese claim associated with the Yuan Dynasty.[37]

2.2.2 Geographical Relations As Well As Language, Religion, Race and Customs, etc.

(4) Each of the two countries' claims on geographical relations were brief.[38] (5) With regard to its claims regarding language, religion, race, customs, etc., Japan only made a simple note that each of them had a strong connection with Japan.[39] The Qing side refuted these issues in more detail, but also recognized that examining these points did not approach the "main issue."[40] There was no refutation of this in the "Rebuttal."

---

34 "Audi Alteram Partem," *supra* note 23, 27–37.

35 "Bakugi Dai 1 Pen" 駁議第一編 [Rebuttal Part 1], *Tokyo Nichi Nichi Shimbun* 東京日日新聞, January 28, 1880. Kumi is understood to be present-day Kume-jima, and this understanding is mentioned in "Bakugi Dai 2 Hen" 駁議第二編 [Rebuttal Part 2], *Tokyo Nichi Nichi Shimbun* 東京日日新聞, January 29, 1880.

36 "Bakugi Dai 2 Hen" 駁議第二編 [Rebuttal Part 2], *Tokyo Nichi Nichi Shimbun* 東京日日新聞, January 29, 1880.

37 "Bakugi Dai 3 Pen" 駁議第三編 [Rebuttal Part 3], *Tokyo Nichi Nichi Shimbun* 東京日日新聞, January 31, 1880.

38 For Japan's claim, see "Japan and Ryūkyū," *supra* note 26, 14. For China's claim, see "Audi Alteram Partem," *supra* note 23, 37–38.

39 "Japan and Ryūkyū," *supra* note 26, 14–15.

40 "Audi Alteram Partem," *supra* note 23, 38–47. Early modern history, which will be reviewed next, is part of the "main issue" (*ibid.*, 47).

2.2.3 Medieval and Early Modern History

Japan's claims regarding medieval and early modern history focused on (6) the fact that in 1441 (the first year of Kakitsu) the Ryūkyū Islands were bestowed to Shimazu Tadakuni by Ashikaga Yoshinori, became a dependency (Kakitsu Dependency), and belonged to Satsuma since then. As part of this, Japan stated that (7) as punishment for the failure of the Ryūkyū King to pay tribute to Satsuma during the Sengoku Era, Tokugawa Ieyasu ordered Shimazu Iehisa to dispatch an expeditionary force to Ryūkyū (i.e., to conquer it) and that Ryūkyū belonged to Satsuma. It also pointed out that Shimazu Iehisa dispatched vassals to establish a tax collection system and issued a proclamation of 15 articles, and that Shōnei along with the Council of Three took an oath to obey the proclamation.[41]

Regarding these points, the Chinese side first pointed out that, on the one hand, regarding (6) the Kakitsu Dependency, some historical sources improperly equated Nantō with Ryūkyū, and, on the other hand, also that there was no mention of this matter in other historical sources or that it could not access the historical sources on which Japan relied. Additionally, (7) regarding the abovementioned order by Tokugawa Ieyasu to dispatch an expeditionary force to Ryūkyū, the Chinese side pointed out that Shimazu Tadatsune (Iehisa) asked Tokugawa Ieyasu for permission to dispatch military forces, Ryūkyū was invaded by Satsuma soldiers in 1609, and the Amami Islands were placed under Satsuma control. Meanwhile, it also pointed out that tribute to the Ming Dynasty began during this period. The Chinese side also argued that there were problems with Japan's translation of Shimazu Iehisa's proclamation, and that the oaths taken by Shōnei and the Council of Three were the product of barbaric times and did not constitute evidence of rule.[42]

In response to the point that the historical materials relied on by the Japanese side regarding the Kakitsu Dependency could not be accessed, the Rebuttal pointed out, under the heading (6) "Consideration of Ryūkyū Affiliation with Satsuma during the Time of the Ashikaga Clan," that this was an ancient record handed down by Satsuma. Developments after that were only very briefly touched upon.[43]

---

41 "Japan and Ryūkyū," *supra* note 26, 16–17. The proclamation and oath are included afterwards (*ibid.*, 17–21).

42 "Audi Alteram Partem," *supra* note 23, 51–58.

43 "Bakugi Dai 4 Pen" 駁議第四編 [Rebuttal Part 4], *Tokyo Nichi Nichi Shimbun* 東京日日新聞, February 5, 1880.

2.2.4 Summary

Based on the above points, the article in *Tokio Times* stated that "there is no room to doubt the fact that Ryūkyū has always been a dependency of Japan," and proceeded to point out that (8) the abolition of Ryūkyū and establishment of a prefecture was only a part of the administrative system arrangement following the Meiji Restoration and that (9) regarding the notion that Ryūkyū paid tribute to China's dynasties, the latter had been deceived by the former. Furthermore, it stated that, (10) with regard to the claim that the disposition of Ryūkyū violated the Sino-Japanese Treaty of Amity, in light of the facts that had heretofore been stated, namely the submission of Ryūkyū to the military power of Japan and the fact that the rulers of Japan protected and ruled the Ryūkyū people and created laws and taxed them, the claim that Ryūkyū was Chinese territory "needs no argumentative refutation," and the above historical description was sufficient. (11) In response to the claim that Ryūkyū belonged to both Japan and China, the article stated that the claim of "dual affiliation" was not common, and pointed out again that the Chinese side had been deceived. It pointed out that China had only given purely nominal protection to Ryūkyū, while Japan had exercised de facto sovereignty from time immemorial and had clarified its authority[44] by military force. The article emphasized that Japan conquered Ryūkyū, gave it its laws and a constitution, and bound its rulers. (12) The article also rejected the claim that Ryūkyū was a semi-independent country, noting that Japan had never granted such independence to Ryūkyū, and it pointed out that such claims were incompatible with the territorial ownership that the Sino-Japanese Articles of Amity was premised upon. In addition, touching upon recent developments, the article concluded the discussion by (13) pointing out that during the Taiwan Expedition, the right to dispatch military forces to punish the massacre of the people of Ryūkyū by local people was not contested and was clearly permitted by the Qing Government, and finally, (14) emphasizing the importance of friendly relations between Japan and Qing.[45]

Meanwhile, the article in *Japan Gazette* first strongly condemned the suggestion that (9) China had been deceived by Ryūkyū as a conspiracy by Satsuma. (11) It also refuted the claim that China was merely providing nominal protection to Ryūkyū by citing the tribute from Ryūkyū. Furthermore, it asserted that (15) (also related to (2)) "If there is something like a 'right to discovery,' … that right belongs to China. If there is something like a right of conquest, …

44 It is described as "sovereignty" in the Japanese Government notes ("Japanese Government notes" *supra* note 26, 347).

45 "Japan and Ryūkyū," *supra* note 26, 21–26.

that right also belongs to China." (10) The article rejected Japan's claim that it created the laws of Ryūkyū on the grounds that no evidence thereof had been presented. (11) In response to the assertion that the claim of "dual affiliation" was not common, it pointed out that such a relationship was also mentioned in the historical documents of Japan, and (14) concluded the discussion by noting that it was unusual to issue such a refutation in a newspaper but emphasizing the need to nevertheless do so.[46]

In the "Rebuttal" published in response, what can be called a "summary" was very brief. It only quoted and affirmed a passage from Xie Zhaozhe's *Wuzazu* that Ryūkyū was a small country that could not maintain its independence, that it was awarded official status by China but also obeyed Japan, and that it could be easily attacked by Japan because of its proximity but China could assist it from across the ocean.[47]

3 Assessment of the Debate on Newspapers between Japan and Qing

The next issue is how Satow assessed the debate on newspapers between Japan and Qing. Before considering this point, the author would like to go on a slight tangent and present an overview of the assessment of this debate by Yamashita Shigekazu, a contemporary historian. This will make the significance of Satow's assessment clearer.

3.1 *Assessment by Yamashita Shigekazu*

In an essay published in 2002, Yamashita Shigekazu examined the debate between Japan and Qing, and considered that "in terms of the debate over historical facts, the author of the *Gazette* article has by far the stronger argument."[48] In reaching this conclusion, Yamashita, in addition to a preliminary consideration, examined the basic structure of the debate by dividing the whole into "ancient and medieval history," "geography, language, religion, race, and customs," and "early modern and modern history theory," following the same basic structure as the debate. "Early modern and modern history" corresponds to the history and summary of the medieval and early modern periods in Section 2 of this chapter.

46 "Audi Alteram Partem," *supra* note 23, 58–61.

47 "Bakugi Dai 4 Pen" 駁議第四編 [Rebuttal Part 4], *Tokyo Nichi Nichi Shimbun* 東京日日新聞, February 5, 1880.

48 Yamashita, *supra* note 24, 89. Also see *supra* note 28.

Regarding "ancient and medieval history," Yamashita first summarized the *Japan Gazette* article and Inoue Kowashi's rebuttal, and stated that the latter did not address at all the fact that the former "pointed out that tribute to the Imperial Court from some islands of Nantō does not imply Japan's possession of the entirety of Ryūkyū" ((2) in Section 2.2 above). Moreover, he noted that "neither the '[Japanese Government] notes'[49] nor Inoue's rebuttal[50] claimed in particular that payments of tribute from Ryūkyū in ancient Japan were a basis for Japan's sovereignty over Ryūkyū; rather, they mainly emphasized the legend that King Shun of Ryūkyū was the son of Minamoto no Tametomo ((3) of the same section). He then stated that Inoue's refute "must be considered to be extremely incomplete as a rebuttal," and concluded that "at present, there are no historians who consider the legend around Tametomo to be historical fact."[51]

Next, regarding "geography, language, religion, race, and customs" ((4) and (5) of the same section), Yamashita pointed out that, in response to the "[Japanese Government] notes," which only "provide a very brief description" of these topics, the *Japan Gazette* article "provided a rebuttal from multiple angles, but Inoue Kowashi's draft of the article did not respond to this at all."[52] In this regard, Yamashita pointed out that in the background was "the dispute between the Chinese side, which insisted that the traditional tributary relationship with Ryūkyū was one to be persistently maintained, and the Japan side, which insisted that the tributary system was merely a formal and ceremonial relationship," and that Inoue Kowashi, who was well aware of this, "deliberately did not delve into this issue, but emphasized only the substantive control of Ryūkyū since the conquest by Satsuma."[53]

Finally, with regard to "early modern and modern history," he first summarized the debate on the Kakitsu Dependency ((6) of the same section) and asserted that "from the current level of research, the Gazette's article pointed out that the Kakitsu Dependency was not a historical fact, and that the Satsuma-Ryūkyū relationship had long been friendly and equal, which was far more plausible than Inoue's rebuttal, which relied solely on the ancient records of Satsuma."[54]

---

49 See *supra* note 26.

50 This refers to "Yokohama Shimbun Rebuttal Draft" by Inoue Kowashi, *supra* note 24.

51 Yamashita, *supra* note 24, 65–70.

52 *Ibid.*, 72. This point is not mentioned in the "Rebuttal" published in *Tokyo Nichi Nichi Shimbun*.

53 *Ibid.*, 72–75.

54 *Ibid.*, 76–80.

Next, he pointed out that "the harshest criticism of the Japanese Government's claim was actually in the part (regarding (5) of the same section) that Inoue did not answer," and pointed out that the Chinese rebuttal contained "pointed findings" and "an extremely powerful rebuttal," and that Inoue Kowashi's draft "Rebuttal" "showed how inaccurate the Meiji Government leadership at the time was in its perception of the history and current state of Okinawa."[55]

Based on these considerations, Yamashita concluded at the end of his paper that "it must be said that, in terms of the debate over historical facts, the author of the *Gazette* article has by far the stronger argument."[56] Without the need to reaffirm all the points, it can be said that Yamashita viewed the debate between Japan and China as "a debate over historical facts."

3.2 *Outline of the Satow Memorandum and Its Assessment*

What was Satow's assessment of the debate between Japan and Qing, compared with that of the contemporary historian Yamashita Shigekazu? First, the author would like to review the Satow Memorandum and then consider its assessment.

3.2.1 Overview of the Satow Memorandum and Summary by Satow

The Satow Memorandum was originally handwritten and spanned 31 pages.[57] Here, the author would like to refer to the printed version published in BDFA2 for ease of review.[58] In the memorandum, the summary of the article in *Japan Gazette* was very brief, while the introduction and summary of Japan's claims in the *Tokyo Nichi Nichi Shimbun* were more than three times the length. The assessment thereof was of almost the same length as the latter.[59]

At the beginning, the memorandum introduced the *Japan Gazette* article and enumerated the following five points which the article's author had aimed to make: (i) the Chinese origin of "Ryūkyū" was older than the Japanese origin of "Okinawa," and that Nantō in ancient Japanese history books did not refer to

55 *Ibid.*, 80–86.

56 *Ibid.*, 89. Yamashita proceeded with his argument based on the premise that Inoue Kowashi's draft was not published (*ibid.*, 86–93). However, as stated above, it was published in *Tokyo Nichi Nichi Shimbun* (see *supra* note 24).

57 FO46/256, no. 26(i).

58 BDFA2, *supra* note 14, 70–74 (see *supra* note 18). The same notes span four pages in appearance.

59 The former was 28 lines, the latter was 97 lines. It is reasonable to assume that the difference was due to the latter being written in Japanese. The assessment section was 99 lines long.

the Ryūkyū Islands ((1) and (2) of Section 2.2); (ii) the ancestors of the Ryūkyū kings were not descendants of Minamoto no Tametomo, but a prince of the Yuan Dynasty ((3) of the same section), (iii) the language, religion, race, and customs of Ryūkyū were not very similar to those of Japan ((5) of the same section), (iv) the Kakitsu Dependency was not a historical fact ((6) of the same section); and (v) Japan's opposition to Ryūkyū's submission to China was not made until 1872 ((9) and (11) of the same section).[60]

Furthermore, the purpose of the article's author was to show that the "right to discovery" and the "right of conquest," if any, belonged to China ((15) of the same section), that China had exercised more than nominal protection of Ryūkyū ((11) of the same section), and that Japan's claim that it created the laws of Ryūkyū was not supported by evidence ((10) of the same section).[61]

Meanwhile, the part corresponding to (i) above covered most of the summary of Japan's claims, accounting for about two-thirds of the total. Next, Japan's rebuttal related to (ii) and (iv) was summarized, and the summary concluded by referring to a passage from Xie Zhaozhe's *Wuzazu*.[62] The summary generally reflected Japan's claims appropriately.

3.2.2 Assessment by the Satow Memorandum

Satow's assessment based on this summary followed the structure of (i) to (v) above.

First, regarding (i), Satow stated at the beginning of his assessment that the authors of the Japanese side, "is successful in proving that the islands belonging to the Loochoo group did in ancient times recognize the supremacy of Japan, and also that the latter country possessed some slight degree of authority in those islands as far as the erection of signposts goes." He proceeded to state that, considering the reference to Ishigaki Island in the "Rebuttal," it would not be unfair to think that the people of Ryūkyū had respect for the Japanese Imperial Court. On the other hand, however, the interactions between Ryūkyū and the Japanese Imperial Court did not last very long, and in medieval times, the people of Ryūkyū were able to maintain a more independent position. In contrast, the true authority of the Satsuma people over Ryūkyū seemed to have begun with their invasion in the early 17th century, when they annexed the five islands under the control of the Ryūkyū King.[63]

---

60 *BDFA2*, *supra* note 14, 70–71 (FO881/4718/50(i); FO46/256, no. 26(i)).
61 *Ibid.*, 71.
62 *Ibid.*, 71–72.
63 *Ibid.*, 72–73.

Next, regarding (ii), after summarizing the arguments of both Japan and China, Satow concluded, "But whether the actual King of Loochoo be descended from [Minamoto no Tametomo or a prince of the Yuan Dynasty] can be of little practical importance in the determination of the present dispute."[64]

As for (iii) language, religion, race, and customs, Satow pointed out the closeness with Japan in a balanced manner, while considering the objections by Qing.[65]

(iv) With regard to doubts about the credibility of the assertions in the article in *Japan Gazette* on the Kakitsu Dependency, Satow found that the Qing side's debate prevailed in this respect.[66]

As for (v), Satow pointed out, regarding the lack of any points of refute in the "Rebuttal," that "none is possible [in terms of refute]."[67]

Based on his review of these individual discussions, Satow summarized the debate as follows:

> It seems worth while to observe that the attitude of China in this question has been constantly misunderstood and misrepresented. She is frequently spoken of as laying a claim to sovereignty to Loochoo, and as disputing with Japan about proprietary rights. To exhibit the matter in this light is no doubt of great service to Japan, as the Chinese Government [has] never exercised any authority over the [Ryūkyū] islands. The real position [of China] is that the Loochooans, finding their autonomy threatened by Japan, … turned to China and besought her to use her influence to preserve them from being deprived of their independence. The justification for China's interference … was the specific paternal relation, … and China has simply supported their claim. The Loochooans, when ordered by Japan to break off their long-standing relations with China, refused to become guilty of what they considered would be base ingratitude [by severing ties], but offered to submit to incorporation in the Japanese Empire, if the Japanese Government would obtain by negotiation with that of China their release from the obligation.[68]

64 *Ibid.*, 73.

65 *Ibid.* On this note, it is recalled that Satow had published the discussion of "Note on Loochoo" in 1874 in *Transactions of the Asiatic Society of Japan*, vol. 1, 1–9 (the same study was published in Patrick Beillevaire (ed.), *Ryūkyū Studies Since 1854*, vol. 2 (London: Curzon Press, and Tokyo: Edition Synapse, 2002)).

66 BDFA2, *supra* note 14, 73 (FO881/4718/50(i); FO46/256, no. 26(i)).

67 *Ibid.*

68 *Ibid.*, 73–74. For Ryūkyū's position, see Satow Memorandum dated July 6, 1879 (FO881/4718/5(iv); FO46/247, no. 140(iv); BDFA2, *supra* note 14, 66).

After summarizing the dispute as described above, Satow concluded the memorandum by stating that, in his opinion, the two countries would not resort to the use of force over Ryūkyū, and that "there is little doubt if left to themselves, [Japan and China] will effect an amicable arrangement of this question."[69]

3.2.3 Key Aspects of the Assessment in the Satow Memorandum

The following points can be presented as the key aspects of Satow's assessment.

First, he clearly stated the superiority of Japan's claims concerning the issue of sovereignty over Ryūkyū.[70] This contrasts with the negative stance taken toward Japan's claims by the British Legation in Japan mentioned in Section 1 above.

Second, one of the factors that led to this assessment can be said to be a somewhat indifferent stance toward the "debate over historical facts." This is evident from the point about the debate over the ancestry of the Ryūkyū kings ((ii) above), whereby Satow denied its very significance, stating that it "can be of little practical importance in the determination of the present dispute."

This stance can also be seen in (i) above regarding ancient and medieval history. It can be said that Satow supported Japan's claims on the relationship between Ryūkyū and the Japanese Imperial Court in ancient times, but that itself did not lead to his assessment of Japan's claim of sovereignty. The exchanges seen in ancient times did not continue through to the Middle Ages, especially the Sengoku Era, and Satow acknowledged that Ryūkyū was able to maintain a more independent position. On the other hand, about the Kakitsu Dependency ((iv) above), he considered the Qing side to have won the debate on this point, but that did not lead to his assessment of the overall claim by Qing. It can be said that Satow drew no conclusions from the debate over historical facts from ancient times and the Middle Ages.[71] Rather than starting from there, he focused on Satsuma's rule over Ryūkyū since the early modern period, whereby Satsuma's true authority over Ryūkyū began with the invasion in the early 17th century.

Third, in relation to the preceding point, it can be noted that, with regard to Japan's claim of sovereignty, Satow emphasized the exercise of authority.

---

69 *BDFA2*, *supra* note 14, 74 (FO881/4718/50(i); FO46/256, no. 26(i)).

70 Satow stated, "To exhibit the matter in … light [of sovereignty] is no doubt of great service to Japan." (See text corresponding to *supra* note 68.) See text corresponding to *supra* note 22 for Kennedy's evaluation of this point.

71 Regarding the dispute over language, religion, race and customs ((iii) above), while Satow noted closeness to Japan, that did not lead to his assessment of Japan's claims (*BDFA2*, *supra* note 14, 73 (FO881/4718/50(i); FO46/256, no. 26(i))).

When emphasizing Satsuma's rule over Ryūkyū since the early modern period, he focused particularly on the exercise of authority.[72] In relation to ancient history, too, Satow pointed out that Japan had some slight degree of authority over the Ryūkyū Islands, as evidenced by its erection of a stone monument[73] ((i) above). Furthermore, at the end of the assessment, Satow pointed out that the Chinese Government had never exercised any authority over the Ryūkyū Islands, and in relation to this point, that China did not dispute sovereignty or proprietary rights over the Ryūkyū Islands in the first place.

Fourth, again related to the same point, it is considered that Satow, while having taken due account of the traditional East Asian view of the world order, "proclaimed the superiority"[74] of Japan's claims in terms of "asserting sovereignty." In the last part of the assessment, Satow pointed out that China and Ryūkyū maintained their traditional East Asian view of the world order, and that China did not make claims based on the view of the order under modern international law, such as "asserting sovereignty."

Section 1 of this chapter stated that Parkes' view of the attribution of Ryūkyū up to September 1879 was premised on a traditional East Asian view of the world order.[75] In contrast, Satow, in his memorandum, while considering not only the existence of such a view of order, but also the fact that China and Ryūkyū held said view, nevertheless "proclaimed the superiority"[76] of Japan's claims based on the criteria of "sovereignty," "proprietary rights," and "authority," or in other words, based on the order based on modern international law.

4 Background to the Assessment by the Satow Memorandum

As discussed above, Satow's assessment of the issue of the attribution of Ryūkyū had several key aspects and it differed greatly from the assessment presented by the British Legation in Japan up to September 1879, including

72 However, Satow did not go into the details of Satsuma's rule of Ryūkyū since the early modern period. As Yanagihara pointed out in *supra* note 2 ("Shioki, Fuyō, Zokkoku and Sovereignty"), 5, the positioning of Ryūkyū in the early modern period can be thought of as "a very ambiguous situation, when viewed from present perspectives, ..., which cannot be grasped from the perspective of modern law and modern international law." It seems that Satow also suggested a disconnect between the modern period and the Meiji Era in the memorandum created on July 6, 1879. (See text corresponding to *supra* note 14).

73 See *supra* note 32.

74 See *supra* note 70.

75 See text corresponding to *supra* note 16.

76 See *supra* note 70.

Satow's own assessment in a July 1879 memorandum, which was based on dual affiliation and imperial tributes. This assessment may have been influenced by the nature of the "de facto dispute between Japan and China." In the debate, however, Qing frequently developed its claims from the standpoint of the traditional East Asian view of the world order, while Japan generally did so from the standpoint of the order based on modern international law, and Satow can be thought to have made his assessment from the latter standpoint. If that was indeed the case, Satow's assessment, or his shift to such an assessment, may have been due to some other background factor.

As such a background factor, one might imagine that there was some ordinance from Britain that indicated or instructed a change in the basis of assessment, but the text of *Confidential Print: Correspondence respecting the LOOCHOO ISLANDS 1879–82* mentioned in *supra* note 11 did not contain any instructions or otherwise to that effect.[77] Said text also included exchanges between the Minister to Japan and the Minister to Qing, but even then, there was no exchange of views related to the basis for assessing Japan–Qing relations.

With that being the case, it is conceivable that the assessment in the Satow Memorandum or the shift to such an assessment was based on some specific factor within the British Legation in Japan, especially in close proximity to Satow. Several such factors are conceivable,[78] but actually it is rather difficult

---

77 Of the documents on which this booklet (FO881/4718) was based, the author has not been able to comprehensively examine the documents sent from Japan to the Legation in Japan (FO262) and those addressed to the Legation in Qing (FO228), and intends to address this in future works. As for items addressed to Japan from the Legation in Japan and the Legation in Qing (FO17 and FO46), the author has conducted a comprehensive examination of the items for the period covered by FO881/4718 and included all items that deemed to be important.

78 For example, one of the reasons could be the fact that Kennedy served as the Acting Minister while Minister Parkes was back in Britain in February 1880. (See Frederick Victor Dickens (Takanashi Kenkichi 高梨健吉 (trans.), *Pākusu Den – Nihon Chūzai no Hibi* パークス伝－日本駐在の日々 [The Life of Sir Harry Parkes: Minister Plenipotentiary to Japan]) (Tokyo: Heibonsha, 1984), 364.) However, it was not the case that any further letters critical of Japan were written upon Parkes' return to his post.

Another reason could have been that the danger of a war between Japan and Qing had been avoided between the end of 1879 and the beginning of 1880. In the letter to which the Satow Memorandum was attached, Kennedy showed agreement with Satow's view that there was almost no doubt that Japan and Qing would resolve this issue peacefully, and requested the Foreign Secretary to especially consider this point (FO881/4718/50 (FO46/256, no. 26; *BDFA2*, *supra* note 14, 70)). At the time, the avoidance of war or armed conflict in the region was important for Britain from the standpoint of maintaining its trade with China. As such, it is conceivable that Britain's viewpoint changed from a time of crisis (or when one was perceived) and a time when the crisis had been averted.

to identify them. Nevertheless, as will be explained below, it can be said that this issue, which relates also to a shift in the view of order, came to be positioned within the framework of international dispute resolution procedures under the order based on modern international law, which was prompted by the involvement of former US President Grant, and that the British Legation in Japan was also aware of this development.

4.1 *Ryūkyū Attribution Issue within International Dispute Resolution Procedures*

4.1.1 Grant's Mediation and International Dispute Resolution Procedures

As mentioned in Section 1, after the "Ryūkyū Disposition" at the end of March 1879, Grant mediated the dispute settlement between the two countries at the request of the Qing side, almost at the same time as the exchange of claims by letter (inquiry and reply) that began in May between the Meiji and Qing Governments. When Grant visited China, the Qing Government requested a "public review" (公評),[79] but Grant, understanding this as meaning

79 The meaning of 公評 (gōng píng) itself was a major source of debate. At this time, it had been used as a translation for "arbitration." However, originally, "公評 had the meaning of impartially reaching a conclusion as well as holding public deliberations among a large number of people" (Hakoda Keiko 箱田恵子, "Shinmatu Chūgoku ni Okeru Chūsaisaibankan – 1860, 70 Nendai o Chūshin ni" 清末中国における仲裁裁判観－1860、70年代を中心に [The Understanding of Arbitration in Late Qing: Focusing on the Decades of the 1860s and 70s], *Kyōto Joshi Daigaku Daigakuin Bungaku Kenkyūka Kenkyūkiyō Shigakuhen* 京都女子大学大学院文学研究科研究紀要 史学編, vol. 17 (2018), 18). The latter definition would imply something other than arbitration. The words 公評 (public review) and 公評是非 (public judgment) also became problematic at the time of Taiwan Expedition. It was pointed out that Zongli Yamen used it to mean public deliberations by a large number of people, while Wade took it to mean arbitration (FO17/676, no. 222; Ian Nish (ed.), *British Documents on Foreign Affairs: Reports and Papers from the Foreign Office Confidential Print, Part I, From the Mid-Nineteenth Century to the First World War, Series E, Asia, 1860–1914, vol. 21, Treaty Revision and Sino-Japanese Dispute over Taiwan, 1868–1876* (Federick, University Publications of America, 1989), 248; See Hakoda, *supra* note 79, 23–27; Ōkubo, *supra* note 9, 204–206). It has also been suggested that 公評 meant "an attempt to put pressure on Japan with the critical voices of other countries" (Hakoda, *supra* note 79, 26), and also, "clearly different from the peaceful dispute resolution in Western international law, a way of thinking deeply rooted in Chinese society traditionally as a method of resolving conflicts, where an observing third party (in this case, third-party countries) stated a judgement finding for or against without taking sufficient steps to hear the claims of both countries involved in the dispute" (Ōkubo, *supra* note 9, 206).

"arbitration," refused the request and promised "good offices" or "mediation,"[80] which is also what Grant is considered to have indeed engaged in.

Grant subsequently sent a letter dated August 13, when he was in Japan, to Yixin (Prince Kung) and Iwakura Tomomi, proposing that commissioners from both sides be sent to negotiate directly, and that if an agreement could not be reached through negotiation, the matter should be referred to arbitration.[81] It is reasonable to assume that the commissioners referred to here means "commissioners employed for special objects, such as the settlement of frontiers, supervision of the execution of a treaty, etc."[82] which is cited as one form of "agents of a state in its international relations" in Hall's *International Law* published in 1880. In this way, Grant's proposal was for a dispute resolution procedure[83] within the framework of international law.

Upon receipt of this, the Zongli Yamen (Office for the General Management of Affairs Concerning the Various Countries) replied in a letter to Foreign Minister Inoue Kaoru dated September 20 that Japan and China should follow Grant's advice and send out members to negotiate the Ryūkyū issue.[84] The Japanese Government responded in a letter from Foreign Minister Inoue to the Zongli Yamen dated October 22 that it would accept the holding of negotiations.[85]

80 Hakoda, *supra* note 2, 5–8. See *supra* note 1 regarding "good offices" and "mediation."

81 "August 13, 1879: To Prince Kung and Iwakura Tomomi," in John Y. Simon (ed.), *The Papers of Ulysses S. Grant, vol. 29: October 1, 1878-September 30, 1880* (Carbondale: Southern Illinois University Press, 2008), 213–215. See Hakoda, *supra* note 2, 5–6.

82 Hall, *supra* note 1, 251.

83 See *supra* note 1.

84 "'Ryūkyū Shozoku ni Kanshi Nisshin Ryōkoku Fungi Ikken' 104 (1879 Nen) 9 Gatsu 20 Ka Shinkoku Sōri Kakkoku Jimu Ō Daijin yori Gaimushō Ate (Ryūkyū Anken Kaishō ni Kansuru Ken)" 「琉球所属に関し日清両国紛議一件」104（1879年）9月 20日清国総理各国事務王大臣より外務省宛（琉球案件会商に関する件）[Dispute between Japan and Qing regarding the affiliation of Ryūkyū 104, September 20 (1879) Zongli Yamen to the Ministry of Foreign Affairs (Regarding Ryūkyū affairs)], Ministry of Foreign Affairs of Japan (ed.), *Nihon Gaikō Bunsho* 日本外交文書 [Documents on Japanese Foreign Policy], vol. 12 (Tokyo: UN Association of Japan, 1949), 187–188. See Hakoda, *supra* note 2, 6.

85 "'Ryūkyū Shozoku ni Kanshi Nisshin Ryōkoku Fungi Ikken' 107 (1879 Nen) 10 Gatsu 22 Nichi Inoue Gaimukyō yori Shinkoku Sōri Kakkoku Jimu Ō Daijin Ate (Ryūkyū Anken Kaishō ni Kansuru Mōshide ni Taishi Kaitō no Ken)" 「琉球所属に関し日清両国紛議一件」107（1879年）10月 22日井上外務卿より清国総理各国事務王大臣宛（琉球案件会商に関する申出に対し回答の件）[Dispute between Japan and Qing regarding the affiliation of Ryūkyū 107, October 22 (1879) Minister for Foreign Affairs Inoue addressed to Zongli Yamen (Response to a request regarding Ryūkyū affairs)], *ibid.*, 200–201. See Hakoda, *supra* note 2, 6. See 5–6 and 11–16 of the same article for developments afterwards.

Thus, Grant's mediation is considered to have been positioned within the framework of international dispute resolution procedures under the order based on modern international law. Grant himself understood the Qing request within such a framework, undertook mediation rather than arbitration, and proposed direct negotiations by commissioners and an arbitration in the case that no agreement were to be reached by the negotiations. Japan also seems to have understood Grant's mediation within that framework. For Japan, whether it was mediation or an attempt at arbitration by Grant was a matter of great concern.[86] On the other hand, although it is not clear what the Qing Government specifically intended when it requested Grant to conduct a "public review,"[87] by accepting Grant's subsequent proposal, it is thought to have at least outwardly accepted the placement of the issue of the attribution of Ryūkyū within the framework of international dispute resolution procedures.

4.1.2 Perception of the British Legation in Japan

Reflecting these developments, the British Legation in Japan also came to perceive that the issue of the attribution of Ryūkyū was positioned within the framework of international dispute resolution procedures.

Grant's actions were also mentioned in Parkes' September 9, 1879 letter to Wade,[88] where the word "mediation" is also found. Subsequently, the letter from Kennedy to the Foreign Secretary, the 3rd Marquess of Salisbury, dated October 31 of the same year made clear mention of the relationship with dispute resolution procedures, reporting, for example, that "both parties [have] agreed to appoint Commissioners with a 'view of coming to some settlement'" and that "the Chinese Government act upon the advice conveyed to them by General Grant, to whose mediation they had submitted the Loochoo dispute during the General's visit to China."[89] In the same letter, Kennedy also reported that he had received, from the Foreign Minister of the Japanese Government, copies of a letter from the Zongli Yamen to Foreign Minister Inoue dated September 20 and a letter from Foreign Minister Inoue to the Zongli Yamen dated October 22, and attached translations thereof.[90] As mentioned above,

86 For the Japanese Government's longstanding wariness about arbitration by Grant, see Hakoda, *supra* note 2, 7–8, 11–16.

87 See *supra* note 79 for the ambiguity of 公評.

88 FO881/4718/16(iii) (FO46/247, no. 161(iii)).

89 FO881/4718/19 (FO46/248, no. 194; *BDFA2*, *supra* note 14, 26).

90 FO881/4718/19(i)(ii) (FO46/248, no. 194(i)(ii)). However, the former is dated September 22 and the latter is dated October 20. In addition, the Japanese Government passed important exchanges with Qing concerning this matter along to Britain, including the letter from the Qing Minister in Japan to Japanese Foreign Minister Terashima dated October 7, 1878,

it was in the exchange of these letters that both countries agreed to negotiate with commissioners.

In addition, a letter from Kennedy to the Foreign Secretary, the 3rd Marquess of Salisbury, dated December 19, 1879 stated that Foreign Minister Inoue, who had visited Kennedy the day before (18th), had told him that the rumor that the US Government offered to mediate the Ryūkyū issue was unfounded, and that Japan had no intention of referring the matter to another country. The letter communicated that, in any case, no offer of mediation or arbitration had been made to Japan.[91]

Furthermore, after the Satow Memorandum, the subject of this chapter, was written, Kennedy's letter to Salisbury dated February 26, 1880, reported on his meeting with Minister of Home Affairs Itō the previous day (25th). When Kennedy asked Itō about the letter by John Russell Young (who was accompanying Grant) published in *The Times* on December 19, 1879,[92] which Kennedy said provided more detailed information on the Ryūkyū question than previously published, Itō acknowledged that the letter was largely correct, and said, "Last summer General Grant was asked by the Chinese Government to arbitrate the Loochoo question. This office he declined, but promised his good offices with Japan. After hearing the Japanese case, ... [he] recommended the appointment of Commissioners on both sides."[93]

In this way, between September 1879 and the time when the Satow Memorandum was written in February 1880, the British Legation in Japan was aware that the Ryūkyū issue was being discussed within the framework of international dispute resolution procedures, partly due to information provided by the Japanese Government, and that the possibility of referral to arbitration had been mentioned in the process.

4.2 *Applicability of International Law*

4.2.1 Perception Concerning the Intent of Japan and Qing

Even if the Ryūkyū Attribution Issue is positioned within the framework of international dispute resolution procedures and the possibility of referral to arbitration is recognized, the parties to the dispute can designate an alternative standard by agreement, and international law may not necessarily be the

---

the inquiry dated May 10, 1879, review dated July 16, 1879, and the inquiry dated August 22, 1879.

91 FO881/4718/38 (FO46/248, no. 205).

92 It is believed to be December 17, 1879 (see John Russell Young, "The Ryūkyū Question, The Times, 1879," in Yamaguchi and Arakawa (eds.), *supra* note 23, 75–79).

93 FO881/4718/51 (FO46/256, no. 36; *BDFA* 2, *supra* note 14, 29).

standard used for making a decision. In this case, however, there is evidence to suggest that Satow believed that both Japan and Qing wanted international law to be applied or that he recognized that international law could be applied between the two States.

First, in an inquiry to Foreign Minister Terashima dated August 22, 1879, the Zongli Yamen stated, "In these days, as the nations of the world are like the members of a family, and fixed rules of law are imposed for their obedience, some great and wise men would necessarily appear before us to dictate what is equity and justice."[94] This letter to Terashima was translated by the Japanese Government and personally delivered to Kennedy by Itō on October 23 of the same year.[95]

Going slightly further back in time, a letter from Qing Minister to Japan He Ruzhang to Foreign Minister Terashima dated October 7, 1878, also condemned Japan's disposition of Ryūkyū "in light of public law."[96] A translation of this letter was also attached to a letter from Parkes to the Foreign Secretary, the 3rd Marquess of Salisbury dated August 1, 1879. It is clearly translated as "in the light … of international law."[97] Regardless of whether directly

94 "'Ryūkyū Shozoku ni Kanshi Nisshin Ryōkoku Fungi Ikken' 103 (1879 Nen) 8 Gatsu 22 Nichi Shinkoku Sōri Kakkoku Jimu Ō Daijin yori Shinkoku Chūtaisatsu Shishido Kōshi Ate (Ryūkyū Shozoku o Ronji Waga Haihan Chiken ni Kōgi Mōshide no Ken)" 「琉球所属に関し日清両国紛議一件」103（1879年）8月 22日清国総理各国事務王大臣より清国駐岱割宍戸公使宛（琉球所属を論じ我廃藩置県に抗議申出の件）[Dispute between Japan and Qing regarding the attribution of Ryūkyū 103, August 22 (1879) the Zongli Yamen addressed to Minister Shishido in China (Discussing Ryūkyū's attribution and protesting against the abolition of Ryūkyū's feudal domains)], Ministry of Foreign Affairs of Japan (ed.), *supra* note 84, 187. The original text was "方今四海一家、公法具在、必有明白事理之人、出而主持公道." For a translation, see FO881/4718/20, FO881/4718/20(iv) (FO46/248, no. 187, and no. 187(iv)).

95 FO881/4718/20, FO881/4718/20(iv) (FO46/248, no. 187, and no. 187(iv)).

96 "'Ryūkyū Shozoku ni Kanshi Nisshin Ryōkoku Fungi Ikken' 124 (1878 Nen) 10 Gatsu 7 Ka Shinkoku Kōshi yori Terashima Gaimukyō Ate (Ryūkyū wa Ganrai Shinkoku no Hanzoku Jichi no Kuni Naruni Naze Nihon wa Sono Shinkō o Sashitometaruka no Ken)" 「琉球所属に関し日清両国紛議一件」124（1878年）10月 7日清国公使より寺島外務卿宛（琉球は元来清国の藩属自治の国なるに何故日本は其進貢を差止めたるか質問の件）[Dispute between Japan and Qing regarding the affiliation of Ryūkyū 124, October 7 (1878) From the Qing Minister to Foreign Minister Terashima (Regarding why Japan stopped the tribute from Ryūkyū which was originally a self-governing tributary state of Qing)], Ministry of Foreign Affairs of Japan (ed.), *Nihon Gaikō Bunsho* 日本外交文書 [Documents on Japanese Foreign Policy], vol. 11 (Tokyo: UN Association of Japan, 1950), 271. See Okamoto Takashi 岡本隆司, *Chūgoku no Tanjō* 中国の誕生 [The Birth of China] (Nagoya: Nagoya University Press, 2017), 90.

97 FO881/4718/5 and FO881/4718/5(i), (FO46/247, no. 140 and no. 140(i)).

or indirectly, it is reasonable to assume that Satow also encountered these letters.[98]

Thus, given that he encountered the letter of He Ruzhang dated October 7, 1878 and the inquiry of the Zongli Yamen dated August 22, 1879 or the translation thereof, there is at least some evidence to suggest that when Satow positioned the Ryūkyū Attribution Issue within the framework of international dispute resolution procedures, he sought international law as a standard, rather than the traditional East Asian view of the world order.

4.2.2 Satow's Knowledge of International Law

Nevertheless, questions may arise as to whether Satow had the ability to make an assessment based on international law. If books on the subject had been referenced in the debate on newspapers between Japan and Qing, it is conceivable that his assessment would have been based on them, but they were not referenced in the debate. In addition, the Satow Memorandum did not refer to any books related to international law. The author intends to conduct a full-fledged examination of this point in future works but, for now, will provide below a sketch of the aspects of Satow's career that are of relevance to this point and explore the possibility that Satow used international law as a standard.

Satow graduated in 1861 with a degree from University College London, and although there is no record of him studying law or international law, he is believed to have begun studying law in 1875 during his administrative leave, attended lectures on Roman law at the University of Marburg in Germany in 1876, passed the British bar examination in 1883, and qualified as a barrister in 1887.[99]

---

98 In addition, regarding the debate within Qing on the use of international law in dealing with the Ryūkyū issue, see Hakoda, *supra* note 2, 4; Zhang Tian-en, *supra* note 10, 29–32; Nishizato, *supra* note 2, 301–305. In a meeting with Grant during his visit to China, Lee Hongzhang said that the disposition of Ryūkyū "would violate public law," and that he urged attention to international law regarding the Ryūkyū issue (*ibid.* (Nishizato), 325; Okamoto, *supra* note 96, 92). The record of this meeting written by Young, who accompanied Grant, was published in the *New York Herald* ("Around the World: General Grant's Mediation between China and Japan," in *New York Herald*, Aug. 16, 1879, 4), in which the words "international law" are used several times. It is conceivable that the British Legation in Japan was also aware of this information.

99 Ian C. Ruxton (ed.), *The Diaries and Letters of Sir Ernest Mason Satow (1843–1929): A Scholar-Diplomat in East Asia* (Lewiston, Queenston, Lampeter: The Edwin Mellen Press, 1998) 437 note 20, 109, 111, 153, 172. From the point of interest of this paper, it is worth noting that he started studying law in the late 1870s, but the significance of these matters will be left for future research.

In later years, Satow was also "appointed for … British member of the Court of Arbitration, … act[ed] as the second British Delegate to the Second Hague Peace Conference in 1907, … received the honorary degree of D.C.L. from the university of Oxford and that of L.L.D. from the university of Cambridge … and wrote various studies on international law and history."[100] Satow's catalogue of writings also lists more than 10 essays related to international law after 1910.[101]

Furthermore, Satow's *A Guide to Diplomatic Practice* published in 1917 dealt with many issues in international law, with a focus on diplomatic law and the law of treaties.[102] In addition to listing several manuals of international law in Appendix I (List of Works Referred to),[103] it also featured a detailed list of works, primarily manuals, by British, American, French, German, Italian, Spanish, Dutch, Russian, Portuguese, Brazilian, and Spanish-speaking South American essayists, together with annotations, in Appendix II (International Law Literature for Diplomatists).[104] In light of this, it can be assumed that Satow had a wealth of knowledge of international law at the time of its publication.

However, this does not necessarily indicate that Satow had a wealth of knowledge of international law in 1880. Moreover, the fact that Satow had begun studying law in the late 1870s suggests that he was in the process of acquiring a certain level of legal knowledge at the time of the memorandum, but the extent of this and the state of the intellectual environment[105] around Satow at that time must be examined in future works.

Here, the author would like to introduce a work that was very readily available to Satow and concerned a subject that was very close to him, as well as a manual of international law referenced therein.

The former work is *Is Aboriginal Formosa a part of the Chinese Empire?: An Unbiased Statement of the Question, with Eight Maps of Formosa*, which was

100 Harold W. V. Temperley, "Satow, Sir Earnest Mason (1843–1929)," in John R. H. Weaver (ed.), *The Dictionary of National Biography: 1929–1930* (Oxford: Oxford University Press, 1937), 748–749. See Ruxton, *supra* note 99, 349–351.

101 *Ibid.* See appendix (1) and 363 ("Published Works").

102 Ernest Satow, *A Guide to Diplomatic Practice* (London: Longman, Green & Co., 1917).

103 *Ibid.*, vol. 2, 363–369.

104 *Ibid.*, 370–374.

105 For example, it is noted that Vattel's work (Emer de Vattel, *Le droit des gens, ou principes de la loi naturelle, appliqués à la conduite & aux affaires des nations & des Souverains* (London: Apud Liberos Tutior, 1758)) was frequently referred to for diplomatic relations in the 19th century, particularly the first half of the century (Arthur Nussbaum, *A Concise History of the Law of Nations* (London: Macmillan, 1947), 161). Whether Satow referred to it or to other books related to international law should be the subject of future works.

authored by Charles Le Gendre and published in Yokohama in 1874.[106] Le Gendre was an American who constructed the logic that "aboriginal land is *kegai no chi* (land outside of enlightened rule) and is *terra nullius*" at the time of the Taiwan Expedition, providing the basis for the dispatch of Japan's military forces.[107] In the same book, Le Gendre pointed out that "sovereignty of the state exists only when it is *de facto* exercised"[108] while referring to Bluntschli, and from this he derived the logic that the aboriginal land where China's sovereignty was not exercised was *terra nullius*.

The latter work is one by Bluntschli referred to in the former. Le Gendre merely stated, "Mr. Bluntschli says [International Law, codified, page 165, §281,]" and gives no exact bibliographic information, but as far as the author knows, it is *Das moderne Völkerrecht der civilisirten Staten als Rechtsbuch dargestellt*,[109] published in 1868 by Johann Casper Bluntshli. In fact, page 166, §281 of the same book pointed out that "no state has any right to incorporate more territory, uninhabited or inhabited by other states, than she has the ability (Macht) to civilize or politically organize."[110] The book is also listed in Appendix II (International Law Literature for Diplomatists) of Satow's *A Guide to Diplomatic Practice*, with the edition unspecified.[111]

These findings are consistent with Satow's focus on sovereignty and authority, which he used as the basis for his assessment. It is not possible to clarify here whether Satow referred to these works, but the former was published also in Yokohama, and it can be said that such discussions occurred around Satow, who had been stationed in Japan since that time. Here, the author wishes to present this only as a hypothesis and to address this matter, including establishing Satow's background and the intellectual environment around him in 1880, in future works.

---

106 Anonymous (Charles Le Gendre), *Is Aboriginal Formosa a Part of the Chinese Empire?: An Unbiased Statement of the Question, with Eight Maps of Formosa* (Shanghai, Hongkong and Yokohama: Lane, Crawford & Co.; Foochow: Hedge & Co.; Amoy: Wilson, Nichols & Co., 1874). For author, see Robert Eskildsen, "Ajia no Naka no Amerikajin" アジアの中のアメリカ人 [Americans in Asia], in *Meiji Ishin to Gaikō* 明治維新と外交 [Meiji Restoration and Diplomacy], Meiji Ishin Shigakukai 明治維新史学会 (ed.) (Tokyo: Yūshisha, 2017), 113.

107 See the works cited in note 9 above regarding the fact that Japan incorporated Le Gendre's opinion in formulating this logic.

108 Anonymous (Le Gendre), *supra* note 106, 8.

109 Johann Casper Bluntschli, *Das moderne Völkerrecht der civilisirten Staten als Rechtsbuch dargestellt* (Munich: C. H. Beck, 1868), 166.

110 *Ibid.* Same as in the second edition published in 1872 (169), and the third edition published in 1878 (170).

111 Satow, *supra* note 102, vol. 2, 373.

5 Conclusion

The author has examined Ernest Satow's memorandum on the Ryūkyū Attribution Issue. As a result, it has become clear that Satow, having taken into consideration the de facto dispute between Japan and China, supported Japan's claims by focusing on the exercise of authority, without delving deeply into the significance of imperial tributes or the theory of dual affiliation within the historical debate. It can be said that this memorandum was based on the order under modern international law, rather than the traditional East Asian view of the world order such as imperial tributes and dual affiliation as seen in the prior views expressed by Parkes and Satow.

However, it cannot be said that the Satow Memorandum represented or reflected a shift in Britain's basis for assessing Sino-Japanese relations. Although the memorandum reflected Japan and Qing's position on the specific case of the Ryūkyū Attribution Issue, it concerned the debate on newspapers between Japan and Qing and was written by Satow in his position as a secretary of the British Legation in Japan, and no instructions from the British Government regarding a shift in the basis of assessment have been found to the best of the author's knowledge. Nor is it the case that the Satow Memorandum indicated that Qing recognized the application of international law in Sino-Japanese relations.[112]

On the other hand, it is thought that Satow, who had sufficient knowledge of the traditional East Asian view of the world order, wrote this memorandum against a backdrop of this issue coming to be positioned in the context of international dispute resolution procedures under the order based on modern international law, which was prompted by the involvement of former US President Grant, and the British Legation in Japan also being aware of this development. If that is indeed the case, it can be said that the fact that the assessment in the memorandum was made in accordance with the order based on modern international law, together with its background, offers a snapshot of the changing view of order in and related to East Asia.

As pointed out in Section 1 of this chapter, in the past, such changes in the view of order have been discussed in a way that connects several major points over time. While such macroscopic discussions are important, it is also

112 See the text corresponding to note 68 above. In addition, in the process of negotiating an agreement once reached between Japan and Qing regarding the resolution of this issue, the Qing side strongly desired that Ryūkyū remain its vassal state, and in that respect, it is thought that Qing maintained its traditional East Asian view of order (see the documents listed in note 2 above).

important to examine the process of change in greater details. The author hopes that this chapter represents one such attempt. In addition, the author intends to more concretely examine the flow of events from this issue to the Sino-Japanese War, as well as the changes after the Sino-Japanese War, in future works. Such an examination will surely contribute to a more complete study of the "acceptance of international law" in East Asia.[113]

Furthermore, the importance of examining the process of change more precisely seems to apply to historical examinations of international law in general. For certain concepts and institutions, there is room to look more closely at the process of change, at least from the standpoint of historical research. How such concepts and systems were understood at a particular time may also be important in relation to, for example, specific territorial disputes.[114]

Bibliography

Primary Sources

Japanese

"Bakugi Dai 1 Pen" 駁議第一編 [Rebuttal Part 1]. *Tokyo Nichi Nichi Shimbun* 東京日日新聞, January 28, 1880.

"Bakugi Dai 2 Hen" 駁議第二編 [Rebuttal Part 2]. *Tokyo Nichi Nichi Shimbun* 東京日日新聞, January 29, 1880.

"Bakugi Dai 3 Pen" 駁議第三編 [Rebuttal Part 3]. *Tokyo Nichi Nichi Shimbun* 東京日日新聞, January 31, 1880.

"Bakugi Dai 4 Pen" 駁議第四編 [Rebuttal Part 4]. *Tokyo Nichi Nichi Shimbun* 東京日日新聞, February 5, 1880.

113 In this respect, Hakoda Keiko's research (*supra* note 2, note 79, and "Shinmatsu Chūgoku no Shimbun, Zasshi ni Miru Chūsai Saibankan" 清末中国の新聞・雑誌にみる仲裁裁判観 [Chinese Understanding of Arbitration Extracted from the Analysis of the Periodicals in Late Qing China], in *Shisō* 史窓, no. 78 (2021), 47–71) and Yanagihara's works (*supra* note 2 as well as "Nihon ni okeru Kindai Yōroppa Kokusaihō no Juyō" 日本における近代ヨーロッパ国際法の受容 [Reception of Modern European International Law in Japan], in *Kokusai Hōgaku no Shosō* 国際法学の諸相 [Aspects of International Law Studies] Etō Junichi 江藤淳一 (ed.) (Tokyo: Shinzansha, 2015), 47–64) are very important.

114 See 3.2.2 of Chapter 1 (Yanagihara) in this book. Similar issues of relevance to this chapter include how the theory of territorial titles was understood in 1880, when Satow created the memorandum.

Inoue Kowashi Denki Hensan Iinkai 井上毅傳記編纂委員會, ed. *Inoue Kowashi den. Shiryō hen no. 5* 井上毅傳 史料編第5 [Life of Kowashi Inoue, Historical Materials, vol. 5]. Tokyo: Kokugakuin University Library, 1975.

Ministry of Foreign Affairs of Japan, ed. *Nihon Gaikō Bunsho* 日本外交文書 [Diplomatic Documents of Japan], vol. 11, 12. Tokyo: United Nations Association of Japan, 1950, 1949.

Yokoyama, Manabu 横山学, ed. *Ryūkyū Shozoku Mondai Kankei Shiryō* 琉球所属問題関係資料 [Ryūkyū Attribution Issue Related Documents], vol. 4. Tokyo: Honpō Shoseki, 1980.

Western Language

"Around the World: General Grant's Mediation between China and Japan." *New York Herald*, August 16, 1879.

Nish, Ian, ed. *British Documents on Foreign Affairs: Reports and Papers from the Foreign Office Confidential Print, Part 1, From the Mid-Nineteenth Century to the First World War, Series E, Asia, 1860–1914, vol. 2, Korea, the Ryūkyū Islands, and North-East Asia, 1875–1888*. Federick: University Publications of America, 1989.

Nish, Ian, ed. *British Documents on Foreign Affairs: Reports and Papers from the Foreign Office Confidential Print, Part 1, From the Mid-Nineteenth Century to the First World War, Series E, Asia, 1860–1914, vol. 21, Treaty Revision and Sino-Japanese Dispute over Taiwan, 1868–1876*. Federick: University Publications of America, 1989.

Simon, John Y., ed. *The Papers of Ulysses S. Grant, vol. 29: October 1, 1878–September 30, 1880*. Illinois: Southern Illinois University Press, 2008.

The National Archives of the UK. FO17/676; FO46/247; FO46/248; FO46/256; FO881/4718.

Secondary Sources

Japanese

Aoyama, Harutoshi 青山治世. "Taiwan Shuppei Jiken" 台湾出兵事件 [Taiwan Expedition Incident]. In *Handobukku Kindai Chūgoku Gaikōshi* ハンドブック近代中国外交史 [Handbook of Modern Chinese Diplomatic History], edited by Okamoto Takashi 岡本隆司 and Hakoda Keiko 箱田恵子. Tokyo: Minerva Shobō, 2019.

Arano, Yasunori 荒野泰典. *Kinsei Nihon to Higashi Ajia* 近世日本と東アジア [Modern Japan and East Asia]. Tokyo: University of Tokyo Press, 1988.

Dickens, Frederick Victor. *Pākusu Den – Nihon Chūzai no Hibi* パークス伝 – 日本駐在の日々 [The Life of Sir Harry Parkes: Minister Plenipotentiary to Japan]. Translated by Takanashi Kenkichi 高梨健吉. Tokyo: Heibonsha, 1984.

Eskildsen, Robert. "Meiji 7 Nen Taiwan Shuppei no Shokuminchiteki Sokumen" 明治7年台湾出兵の植民地的側面 [Colonial Aspects of the 1874 Taiwan Expedition]. In

Meiji Ishin to Ajia 明治維新とアジア [Meiji Restoration and Asia], edited by Meiji Ishin Shigakukai. Tokyo: Yoshikawa Kōbunkan, 2001.

Eskildsen, Robert. "Ajia no Naka no Amerikajin" アジアの中のアメリカ人 [Americans in Asia]. In *Meiji Ishin to Gaikō* 明治維新と外交 [Meiji Restoration and Diplomacy], edited by Meiji Ishin Shigakukai 明治維新史学会. Tokyo: Yūshisha, 2017.

Hakoda, Keiko 箱田恵子. "Ryūkyū Shobun o Meguru Nisshin Kōshō to Chūsai Saiban Seido" 琉球処分をめぐる日清交渉と仲裁裁判制度 [The Arbitration System and the Sino-Japanese Negotiation over the Annexation of Ryūkyū]. *Shisō* 史窓 77 (2020): 1–23.

Hakoda, Keiko 箱田恵子. "Shinmatu Chūgoku ni Okeru Chūsaisaibankan – 1860, 70 Nendai o Chūshin ni" 清末中国における仲裁裁判観 – 1860、70年代を中心に [The Understanding of Arbitration in Late Qing: Focusing on the Decades of the 1860s and 70s]. *Kyōto Joshi Daigaku Daigakuin Bungaku Kenkyūka Kenkyūkiyō Shigakuhen* 京都女子大学大学院文学研究科研究紀要史学編 17 (2018): 1–32.

Higashi Ajia Kindaishi 東アジア近代史 no. 2 (1999).

Higashi Ajia Kindaishi 東アジア近代史 no. 3 (2000).

Ichinose, Norie 一瀬啓恵. "Meiji Shoki ni okeru Taiwan Shuppei Seisaku to Kokusaihō no Tekiyō" 明治初期における台湾出兵政策と国際法の適用 [Taiwan Expedition Policy and Application of International Law in the Early Meiji Era]. *Hokudaishigaku* 北大史学 35 (1995): 23–49.

Kawashima, Shin 川島真. *Chūgoku Kindai Gaikō no Keisei* 中国近代外交の形成 [Formation of Modern Chinese Diplomacy]. Nagoya: Nagoya University Press, 2004.

Kobayashi, Takao 小林隆夫. "Taiwan Jiken to Ryūkyū Shobun – Rujandoru no Yakuwari Saikō – (2)" 台湾事件と琉球処分 – ルジャンドルの役割再考 –(2) [Taiwan Incident and Ryūkyū Disposition: Reconsidering the role of Le Gendre (2)]. *Seiji Keizai Shigaku* 政治経済史学 341 (1994): 13–32.

Kobayashi, Takao 小林隆夫. *19 Seiki Igirisu Gaikō to Higashi Ajia* 19世紀イギリス外交と東アジア [19th Century British Diplomacy and East Asia]. Tokyo: Sairyūsha, 2012.

Kurihara, Jun 栗原純. "Taiwan Jiken (1871–1874 Nen) – Ryūkyū Seisaku no Tenki to Shiteno Taiwan Shuppei" 台湾事件(1871–1874年) – 琉球政策の転機としての台湾出兵 [Taiwan Incident (1871–1874): Dispatch of troops to Taiwan as a turning point in Ryūkyū policy]. *Shigaku Zasshi* 史学雑誌 87, no. 9 (1978): 60–85.

Matsui, Yoshirō 松井芳郎. *Kokusaihō gakusha ga Yomu Senkaku Mondai* 国際法学者がよむ尖閣問題 [The Senkaku Issue as Read by International Law Scholars]. Tokyo: Nippon Hyōronsha, 2014.

Mitani, Hiroshi 三谷博. *Nihonshi no Naka no 'Fuhen'* 日本史のなかの「普遍」 [Searching for Generalities in Japanese History]. Tokyo: University of Tokyo Press, 2020.

Motegi, Toshio 茂木敏夫. "Chūkateikoku no 'Kindai' teki Saihen to Nihon" 中華帝国の『近代』的再編と日本 [The Modern Reorganization of the Chinese Empire and Japan]. In *Iwanami Kōza Kindai Nihon to Shokuminchi 1 Shokuminchi Teikoku Nihon*

岩波講座近代日本と植民地 1 植民地帝国日本 [Iwanami Lectures Modern Japan and Colonies vol. 1 Colonial Empire Japan], edited by Ōe Shinobu 大江志乃夫, et al. Tokyo: Iwanami Shoten, 1992.

Namihira, Tsuneo 波平恒男. *Kindai Higashi Ajiashi no Nakano Ryūkyū Heigō – Chūka Sekai Chitsujo kara Shokuminchi Teikoku Nihon e* 近代東アジア史のなかの琉球併合 – 中華世界秩序から植民地帝国日本へ [The Disposition of Ryūkyū in the History of Modern East Asia: From the Chinese World Order to the Colonial Empire of Japan]. Tokyo: Iwanami Shoten, 2014.

Nishizato, Kikō 西里喜行. *Shinmatsu Chū Ryū Nichi Kankeishi no Kenkyū* 清末中琉日関係史の研究 [A Study of Relations between China, Ryukyu and Japan in Late Qing Period]. Kyoto: Kyoto University Press, 2005.

Okamoto, Takashi 岡本隆司. *Chūgoku no Tanjō* 中国の誕生 [The Birth of China]. Nagoya: Nagoya University Press, 2017.

Ōkubo, Yasuo 大久保泰甫. *Bowasonādo to Kokusaihō – Taiwan Shuppeijiken no Tōshizu* ボワソナードと国際法 – 台湾出兵事件の透視図 [Boissonade and International Law: Perspective of the Taiwan Expedition]. Tokyo: Iwanami Shoten, 2016.

Toyota, Tetsuya 豊田哲也. "19 Seiki Higashi Ajia to Kindaikokusaihō no Kokkachūshinshugi no Keisei" 19世紀東アジアと近代国際法の国家中心主義の形成 [19th-century East Asia and the Formation of State-Centrism in Modern International Law]. *Kokusaihō Gaikō Zasshi* 国際法外交雑誌 116, no. 4 (2018): 1–19.

Ueda, Toshio 植田捷雄. "Ryūkyū no Kizoku o Meguru Nisshin Kōshō" 琉球の帰属を繞る日清交渉 [Sino-Japanese Negotiations Concerning the Ryūkyū Attribution]. *Tōyō Bunka Kenkyūsyo Kiyō* 東洋文化研究所紀要2 (1951): 151–201.

Yamamoto, Sōji 山本草二. *Kokusaihō* 国際法 [International Law]. Tokyo: Yūhikaku, 1994 (New Edition).

Yamashita, Shigekazu 山下重一. "'Japan Gazetto' Ronsetsu no Ryūkyū Shobun Hihan to Inoue Kowashi no Hanron" 『ジャパン・ガゼット』論説の琉球処分批判と井上毅の反論 [Criticism of the Ryūkyū Disposition in the Japan Gazette Article and Kowashi Inoue's Counterargument]. *Kokugakuin Hōgaku* 國學院法學 40, no. 1 (2002): 53–94.

Yamashita, Shigekazu 山下重一. *Zoku Ryūkyū Okinawashi Kenkyū Josetsu* 続 琉球・沖縄史研究序説 [Continued Introduction to Ryūkyū and Okinawan History Research]. Tokyo: Ochanomizu Shobō, 2004.

Yanagihara, Masaharu. "Nihon ni okeru Kindai Yōroppa Kokusaihō no Juyō" 日本における近代ヨーロッパ国際法の受容 [Reception of Modern European International Law in Japan]. In *Kokusai Hōgaku no Shosō* 国際法学の諸相 [Aspects of International Law Studies], edited by Etō Junichi 江藤淳一. Tokyo: Shinzansha, 2015.

Watanabe, Miki 渡辺美季. "'Ryūkyū Shobun' to Ryūkyū Bunkatsu Kōshō – Nisshin Kankei no Tenki" 『琉球処分』と琉球分割交渉 – 日清関係の転機 [Ryūkyū Disposition and Negotiation on Ryūkyū Partitioning: Turning Point of Japan–Qing Relations]. In *Handobukku Kindai Chūgoku Gaikōshi* ハンドブック近代中国外交史

[Handbook of Modern Chinese Diplomatic History], edited by Okamoto Takashi 岡本隆司 and Hakoda Keiko 箱田恵子. Tokyo: Minerva Shobō, 2019.

Zhang, Chixiong 張啓雄. "Nisshin Gokan Jyōyaku ni Oite Ryūkyū no Kizoku wa Kettei Saretaka?" 日清互換條約において琉球の帰屬は決定されたか [Did the Sino-Japanese Treaty Determine the Attribution of Ryūkyū?]. *Okinawa Bunka Kenkyū* 沖縄文化研究 19 (1992): 95–129.

Zhang, Tian-en 張天恩. "Ryūkyū Mondai o Meguru Nisshin Kōshō to Kokusaihō" 琉球問題をめぐる日清交渉と国際法 [Sino-Japanese Negotiations and International Law over the Ryūkyū Issue]. *Socio-science* ソシオサイエンス 26 (2020): 18–39.

Western Languages

Anonymous (Charles Le Gendre). *Is Aboriginal Formosa a Part of the Chinese Empire?: An Unbiased Statement of the Question, with Eight Maps of Formosa.* Shanghai, Hongkong and Yokohama: Lane, Crawford & Co.; Foochow: Hedge & Co.; Amoy: Wilson, Nichols & Co., 1874.

Beillevaire, Patrick, ed. *Ryūkyū Studies Since 1854*, vol. 2. London: Curzon Press and Tokyo: Edition Synapse, 2002.

Casper, Johann Bluntschli. *Das moderne Völkerrecht der civilisirten Staten als Rechtsbuch dargestellt.* Munich: C. H. Beck, 1868.

Hall, William Edward. *International Law.* Oxford: Clarendon Press, 1880.

Hamamoto, Shōtarō. "International Law, Regional Developments: East Asia." In *The Max Planck Encyclopedia of Public International Law*, vol. 5, edited by Rüdiger Wolfrum. Oxford: Oxford University Press, 2012.

Nussbaum, Arthur. *A Concise History of the Law of Nations*. London: Macmillan, 1947.

Ōnuma, Yasuaki. "When was the Law of International Society Born? – An Inquiry of the History of International Law from an Intercivilizational Perspective." *Journal of the History of International Law* 2 (2000): 1–66.

Ruxton, Ian C., ed. *The Diaries and Letters of Sir Ernest Mason Satow (1843–1929): A Scholar-Diplomat in East Asia*. Lewiston, Queenston, Lampeter: The Edwin Mellen Press, 1998.

Satow, Ernest. *A Guide to Diplomatic Practice*. London: Longman, Green & Co., 1917.

Suzuki, Shōgo. *Civilization and Empire: China and Japan's Encounter with European International Society*. London: Routledge, 2009.

Temperley, Harold W. V. "Satow, Sir Earnest Mason (1843–1929)." In *The Dictionary of National Biography: 1929–1930* edited by John R. H. Weaver. Oxford: Oxford University Press, 1937.

Yamaguchi, Eitetsu and Yūkō Arakawa, eds. *The Demise of the Ryūkyū Kingdom: Western Accounts and Controversy*. Ginowan: Yōjushorin, 2002.

Yanagihara, Masaharu. "Significance of the History of the Law of Nations in Europe and East Asia." *Recueil des Cours de l'Academie de droit international de la Haye* 371 (2015): 317–349.

Yanagihara, Masaharu. "Shioki, Fuyō, Zokkoku and Sovereignty." The Japan Institute of International Affairs, 2021. https://www.jiia-jic.jp/en/resourcelibrary/pdf/Shioki_Fuyo_Zokkoku_and_Sovereignty.pdf.

Yanagihara, Masaharu. "Some Thoughts on the Concept of Territory in the Late Edo and Early Meiji Periods." The Japan Institute of International Affairs, 2021. https://www.jiia-jic.jp/en/resourcelibrary/pdf/Shioki_Fuyo_Zokkoku_and_Sovereignty.pdf.

PART 2

Territorial Extensions in Modern Japan

CHAPTER 3

Acquisition of "Colonies" and Legal System of Japan

Tetsuya Yamada

1 Introduction

This chapter explores how Japan perceived the concept of "territory" when it acquired so-called *gaichi* (overseas territory of Japan or colony) and how that impacted legislation. The term *ryōiki* (domain; especially territory) is a translation of the English word "territory," is considered a Japanese-made Chinese word derived from *ryōchi* (appanage),[1] and is believed to differ from a traditional understanding of territory consisting of *hanto* (territory), *kyōdo* (territory within a boundary), and *kyōiki* (territory). As will be discussed below, the Constitution of the Empire of Japan (hereinafter, "Meiji Constitution") did not stipulate the limits of Japan's territory, nor did it mention anything about the gain or loss of territory after its promulgation. Therefore, whether it was the cession of Taiwan in 1895 or the annexation of Korea in 1910, the question of whether the Meiji Constitution would apply to Taiwan and Korea became a matter of debate both practically and academically. Furthermore, the decision of what type of legislation to be established in *gaichi* was the basis of controlling such *gaichi*. Japan's acquisition of *gaichi* is often described as (national) imperialization or imperial(istic) expansion, and one of its characteristics is that "the home country and the territory under control [colony] exist as a union of different jurisdictions based on the principle of disparity and integration."[2]

1 Okamoto Takashi 岡本隆司, "Chūgoku ni Okeru Ryōdo Gainen no Keisei" 中国における『領土』概念の形成 [Formation of the Concept of Sovereignty in China], Okamoto Takashi 岡本隆司 (ed.), *Sōshuken no Sekaishi – Tōzai Ajia no Kindai to Honyaku Gainen* 宗主権の世界史—東西アジアの近代と翻訳概念 (Nagoya: The Nagoya University Press, 2014), 294; and Matsui Yoshiro 松井芳郎, "Kokusaihō ni Okeru Ryōiki to Kokkyō – Sono Henyō no Kizashi" 国際法における『領域』と『国境』—その変容のきざし [Concepts of "Territory" and "Boundary" under International Law: Indications of Their Change], *Higashi Ajia Kindaishi* 東アジア近代史, no. 17 (2014), 6.

2 Yamamuro Shinichi 山室信一, "Kokumin Teikoku Nihon ni Okeru Ihōiki no Tōgō to Kakusa" 国民帝国日本における異法域の統合と格差 [Integration and discrimination in the Japanese nation-empire], *Jinbun Gakuhō* 人文學報, no. 101 (2011), 64.

 | DOI:10.1163/9789004706361_004

As Asano Toyomi points out, "Japan's 'imperialization' is not characterized by an expansion to *terra nullius*, but rather an expansion to the surrounding areas where the system of Western 'settlements' already existed."[3] Consequently, for Japan, the acquisition of *gaichi* was not only defined by relations with the State from which it was acquiring territory, but also required the political support and approval of the Western countries that had advanced into East Asia. In this context, Japan attempted to replace Japan–China–Korea relations based on traditional East Asian logic with those based on the logic of modern international law, thereby maintaining its own independence and ensuring its security.

An examination of this from the perspective of "sovereignty" can be summarized as follows. First, sovereignty is transferred through treaties. In chronological order, this is the Treaty of Shimonoseki in 1895, the Treaty of Portsmouth in 1905, and the Japan-Korea Annexation Treaty in 1910. In addition, the Mandate for the German Possessions in the Pacific Ocean Lying North of the Equator of 1922 can also be added here, but as will be described below, the question of sovereignty over the mandated territories was a great source of international debate at the time, and no conclusion was ever reached. In any case, through these, Japan acquired *gaichi* and exercised its sovereignty domestically. Although it is difficult to firmly define what constitutes sovereignty, if considered in terms of internal supremacy and external independence, sovereignty means the basis under international law on which a State exclusively exercises domestic governance.

The sovereign State under (modern) international law is premised on the exercise of effective control over territory and the exercise of jurisdiction based on the principle of territoriality. In addition, the different branches of the federal State may have different legal systems, and, as a whole, it may be a State with more than one system of law. In the rule of a colony, however, for several reasons, a legal system that is different from the suzerain State and intrinsically discriminatory may be promulgated, resulting in the creation of different laws (or jurisdictions) in one whole state. This condition was also described in German *Staatsrecht*[4] at the time as "domestic under international law but foreign under the constitution." Since the enactment of laws over colonies (the

3 Asano Toyomi 浅野豊美, *Teikoku Nihon no Shokuminchi Hōsei* 帝国日本の植民地法制 [Colonial Legislation of Imperial Japan] (Nagoya: The Nagoya University Press, 2008), 2.

4 *Staatsrecht* was a distinctive field of 19th century German jurisprudence that sought to analyze the nature of States from a legal standpoint. In the Anglosphere, it generally equated to constitutional law and administrative law, but to avoid confusion, the term *Staatsrecht* will be used in this chapter.

periphery) is carried out by the colonial power (the center), it is not accurate to describe them as "foreign." Rather, the word "foreign" should probably be regarded as something metaphorical, implying the unequal and discriminatory nature of center-periphery relations. In any case, after the cession of Taiwan, Japan was forced not only to carry out the simple spatial unification of Japan and its *gaichi*, but also to establish an order based on nationality that included relations with the foreign nationals living in its *gaichi*.

Prompted by Commodore Perry's arrival in 1853, Japan demarcated territories by drawing "borders" under the (modern) international legal sense and established a system of effective control based on sovereignty. For Japan, this involved a process of translating, understanding, interpreting, and applying (hereinafter collectively referred to as "accepting," etc.) international law, as well as the task of repositioning the traditional system of rule in East Asia within the framework of international law based on Japanese logic. Typical examples are Ryūkyū (Okinawa), Hokkaido, the Kuril Islands, and Sakhalin. After the "incorporation" of these regions, the space that made up Japan was demarcated both domestically and internationally.

This process involved Japan's participation and accession to the international order of Western origin, as well as the conflict, coordination, and reorganization of the East Asian regional order headed by China (Qing and the Republic of China). After the Opium Wars, Qing continued to adhere to the Chinese order and accepted international law based on its own understanding thereof. At the same time, Western States established settlements in East Asia and placed Southeast Asia under colonial rule except for Thailand. The question of how to position Taiwan and Korea, which were on the periphery of Japan geographically, had been major issues in Japan's domestic and diplomatic affairs since the early Meiji Era, taking the form of the *seitairon* and *seikanron* debates, respectively, and both of these issues related to relations with China. Japan and China showed different levels of acceptance towards international law, with Japan deemed to have been more proactive.[5] This manifested itself in the difference of views between Japan and China regarding the status of Korea, as will be discussed later.

Below, this chapter summarizes how Japan understood sovereignty at the time. Needless to say, sovereignty is a concept in international law as well as a concept in domestic law, particularly at the constitutional law level. Given

5 See, for instance, Ōhata Tokushirō 大畑篤四郎, "Higashi Ajia ni Okeru Kokusaihō (Bankokukōhō) no Juyō to Tekiyō" 東アジアにおける国際法（万国公法）の受容と適用 [Reception and Application of International Law in East Asia], *Higashi Ajia Kindaishi* 東アジア近代史, no. 2 (March 1999), 5–6.

that Japan was under Imperial rule at the time, it would be necessary to verify how Japan accepted sovereignty, and whether it understood sovereignty as "control" over "territory" in the international legal sense. Next, this chapter will examine how Japan acquired *gaichi* and what kind of legislation it established there, on a case-by-case basis. It will focus in particular on the cession of Taiwan in 1895, in light of the fact that, as will be described later, there was intense debate at the time on whether or not to apply the Meiji Constitution to "territorial expansion" that was not planned for under said Constitution, a typical example of which is the issue of "Act No. 63." This chapter will also outline how academic theory, particularly in the field of constitutional law, responded to the imperial expansion of Japan.

2 Constitution and International Law, and Sovereignty

2.1 *Introduction of the Concept of Sovereignty*

It is not necessarily clear when *shuken*, used as a translation of "sovereignty," became a widely accepted Japanese word. Supposing that the Chinese translation of Henry Wheaton's *Elements of International Law* (1836) was subsequently translated into Japanese, *shuken* would have been derived from the Chinese language.[6] In said work, *shuken* or "sovereignty" is defined as "the supreme power by which any State is governed"[7] and its contents correspond to today's internal sovereignty (supremacy) and external sovereignty (independence); i.e., "that which is inherent in the people of any State, or vested in its ruler, by its municipal Constitution" and "the independence of one political society, in respect to all other political societies,"[8] but there is no description of the territoriality of the State. *Shuken* also appears in *The Laws of Western Countries* by Tsuda Masamichi published in 1868.[9] Therefore, it is necessary to conduct

6 Okamoto Takashi 岡本隆司, "Sōshuken to Kokusaihō to Honyaku – 'Tōhō Mondai' kara 'Chōsen Mondai' e" 宗主権と国際法と翻訳—『東方問題』から『朝鮮問題』へ [Suzerainty, International Law, and Translation: From 'Eastern Issues' to 'Korean Issues'], Okamoto, *supra* note 1, 98–99.

7 Ministry of Justice Collection of *Elements of International Law by Henry Wheaton* (1883) (National Diet Library Digital Collections NDLBibID S00001116), 35 (last accessed on September 21, 2021).

8 *Ibid.*, 36.

9 Tsuda Masamichi (Shinichirō) 津田真道（真一郎）, *Taisei Kokuhōron* 泰西国法論 [*The Laws of Western Countries*] (Waseda University Library Classical Books Comprehensive Database https://archive.wul.waseda.ac.jp/kosho/wa07/wa07_00839/wa07_00839_0001/wa07_00839_0001.pdf). (Quoted passage from the 19th image; last accessed on September 21, 2021).

further study of the origin of the term *shuken* while expanding the scope to include literature other than the two aforementioned works. According to Tsuda, *shuken* is explained as "the authority to govern an entire country" and "it is the monarch who holds this *shuken*." The debate over where or with whom sovereignty resides in Japan, be it the "ruler" or the "monarch," would later be associated with Japan's own theory of national polity and would define the structure and interpretation of the Meiji Constitution. However, chronologically speaking, the theory of national polity appears first, and then the debate over the Meiji Constitution, including the concept of *shuken* or sovereignty, emerges; thus, the concept of sovereignty is interpreted based on the concept of national polity. It can therefore be understood that there was little awareness of territory (territorial land) in Japan, and that the rule by the Emperor based on the theory of national polity, with the Emperor as the "holder of the right of sovereignty," was pushed to the fore.

2.2 *Existence of the Theory of National Polity*

The question of how to define the national polity, i.e., the constitutional foundation of the country or the fundamental system of the State, was related to the question of how to position Japan after the Meiji Era and how to build a system of governance through the ensuing Meiji Constitution. What should be confirmed here is that the theory of national polity eventually converged on the "sovereign monarch," and furthermore, the basis for this was sought in the myths of the *Kiki* mythology (the *Kojiki* [*The Records of Ancient Matters*] and *Nihonshoki* [*Chronicles of Japan*]). As a clear illustration of this understanding, an editorial published in the *Tokyo Nichinichi Shimbun* on January 27, 1882, for example, which claimed that "it is clear that the sovereignty of Japan has always been held by the Imperial Family since the time of the first emperor,"[10] is deemed to have played an important role.[11]

The influence of this understanding on the provisions of the Meiji Constitution and its interpretation will be discussed below. It should be first established that the perception of the Emperor, belonging to an unbroken line of Imperial pedigree, as being eternal did not diminish thereafter, despite debate on the subject intensifying up to Japan's defeat in World War II. The

10 "The Fourth Sovereignty Deliberation," *Tokyo Nichi Nichi Shimbun*, January 27, 1882.

11 See Yonehara Ken 米原謙, *Kokutairon wa Naze Umaretaka – Meiji Kokka no Chi no Chikeizu* 国体論はなぜ生まれたか—明治国家の知の地形図 [*Why was the Idea of Polity Born?: Topography of the Knowledge of the Meiji State*] (Kyoto: Minerva Shobō, 2015), 208–213 for the role Tokyo Nichi Nichi Shimbun played in the formation of the idea of polity.

culmination of this perception can be seen in *Kokutai no Hongi* [*The Essence of Japan's Polity*][12] of 1937. At its outset, the work explains, regarding "Japan's polity, which has not changed since ancient times," that "the unbroken line of Emperors, receiving the divine edict of the founder of the nation, shall rule forever over the Empire of Japan." It is well known that this book was intended as a denunciation of Minobe Tatsukichi's theory of the Emperor as an organ of government. At the same time, there is no doubt that it curtailed the discourse of other legal scholars,[13] and it should be noted here that it had a considerable impact on "laws in *gaichi*" (theory/studies), which will be reviewed below.

2.3 *Sovereignty in International Law*

Under international law, States have sovereignty, which is the basis upon which they control their territories. The rights afforded by sovereignty over land is generally called territorial sovereignty[14] (or dominion). This is sometimes referred to as State possession or State dominion.[15] The legal nature of territorial sovereignty has been the subject of much historical debate. This debate can be broadly divided into those that perceive territory either as *dominium* that can be used and disposed of freely by the State, or *imperium* over people, property, and facts within the territory.[16] However, today, territorial sovereignty is commonly understood as having the properties of both *dominium* and *imperium*, and it is said that there are aspects of "ownership (possession), governance, and disposition."[17]

In addition, the term *ryōdoken* (territorial rights) is generally used in Japan, including the debate between Minobe Tatsukichi and Tachi Sakutarō triggered

---

12 Ministry of Education (ed.), *The Essence of Japan's Polity* (National Diet Library Digital Collections NDL BibID 000000713777) (last accessed on September 21, 2021).

13 *Ibid.*, 9.

14 Iwasawa Yūji 岩沢雄司, *Kokusaihō* 国際法 [*International Law*] (Tokyo: University of Tokyo Press, 2020), 220; and Yanagihara Masaharu 柳原正治, Morikawa Kōichi 森川幸一, and Kanehara Atsuko 兼原敦子 (eds.), *Purakutisu Kokusaihō Kōgi* [*Dai 2 Han*] プラクティス国際法講義[第 2 版] (Tokyo: Shinzansha, 2016), 186 (written by Fukamachi Tomoko), and so on.

15 Yanagihara Masaharu 柳原正治, *Kyōiki, Hanto, Hōdo, Soshite Ryōiki* ["The Concept of 'Territory' in Europe and East Asia"], *Kokusai Mondai* 国際問題, no. 624 (September 2013), 2.

16 Iwasawa, *supra* Note 14.

17 While it is not clear when this view took hold in the field of international law in Japan, this positioning can already be found in Yokota Kisaburō 横田喜三郎, *Kokusaihō II* (*Hōritsugaku Zenshū 56*) 国際法 II (法律学全集 56) [International Law II (Complete Works of Law 56)] (Tokyo: Yūhikaku, 1958), 1. (The same is also true of the new 1972 edition.)

by the annexation of Korea in 1910. Whether *ryōdoken* is the same as today's territorial sovereignty and dominion is debatable. Setting this debate aside, the Minobe-Tachi debate was over the nature of annexation under international law, as was also evidenced by the fact that it was triggered by Tachi's "The Annexation of Korea as Viewed under International Law."[18] From there, as the specific content of *ryōdoken* and its relationship with sovereignty were discussed, the debate expanded to include the relationship between international law and domestic law.[19] Without going into too much detail, it is necessary to take into account how *ryōdoken* and *tōchiken* (rights of sovereignty), as terms found in constitutional law and *Staatsrecht* at the time, relate to the *dominium* and *imperium* used when discussing sovereignty in international law today.

2.4 *Shuken* (Sovereignty) and *Tōchiken* (Rights of Sovereignty) in the Meiji Constitution

In the Meiji Constitution, *shuken* was understood to be synonymous with the *tōchiken* of the Emperor. The fact that Itō Hirobumi also used the two interchangeably can be seen in his *Commentaries on the Constitution of the Empire of Japan*.[20] First, Article 1 stipulated that "The Empire of Japan shall be reigned over and governed by a line of Emperors unbroken for ages eternal," and Article 4 provided that "The Emperor is the head of the Empire, combining in

---

18 Tachi Sakutarō 立作太郎, "Kankoku Heigō Kokusaihōkan" 韓国併合国際法観 [The Annexation of Korea as Viewed under International Law], *Hōgakukyōkai Zasshi* 法学協会雑誌, vol. 28, no. 11 (1910), 1–19.

19 Previous research examining the history and discussion points of the Minobe-Tachi controversy include Nakahara Seiichi 中原精一, "Minobe Tachi Ryōhakase Ronsō no Sobyō – Kokunaihō to Kokusaihō tono Kankeiron ni Tsuite" 美濃部・立両博士論争の素描—国内法と国際法との関係論について [A Sketch of the Controversy between Prof. Minobe and Prof. Tachi: On the Relationship between Domestic Law and International Law], *Meijidaigaku Shakaikagaku Kenkyūsyo Kiyō* 明治大学社会科学研究所紀要, No. 7 (1969), 37–54; Ebara Yoshiyasu 頴原善徳, "Kokusaihō to Kokunaihō no Kankei o Meguru Minobe Tachi Ronsō" 国際法と国内法の関係をめぐる美濃部・立論争—韓国併合と領土権・主権論争 [Minobe-Tachi Debate over the Relationship between International Law and Domestic Law: Annexation of Korea and Territorial Rights/Sovereignty Debate], *Hisutoria* ヒストリア, no. 181 (2002), 1–25; and Nishimura Yūichi 西村裕一, "Nihon ni Okeru Shukenron – Senzen Kara no Shikaku" 日本における主権論—戦前からの視角 [The Theory of Sovereignty in Prewar Japan: A Perspective from the Prewar Period], *Shuken wa Ima* (*Nenpō Seijigaku 2019–1*) 主権はいま(年報政治学2019–1) (2019), 113–136.

20 Itō Hirobumi 伊藤博文 (annotation by Miyazawa Toshiyoshi 宮沢俊義), *Kenpō Gikai* 憲法義解 [*Commentaries on the Constitution of the Empire of Japan*] (Tokyo: Iwanami Shoten, 2019).

Himself the rights of sovereignty." It is evident that these terms are directly connected to the theory of national polity discussed above. In addition, Itō stated that "the body of sovereignty is the control of the rights to sovereignty," and Miyazawa noted that in the English translation by Itō Miyoji, the term *tōchiken* was translated as "the rights of sovereignty."[21] On the other hand, the basis of the Emperor's rights of sovereignty is "the supreme power We inherit from Our Imperial Ancestors" as stated in the Imperial Speech on the Promulgation of the Constitution, and the proclamation of the Meiji Constitution was also based on this "supreme power" (authority). Based on this premise, Itō also wrote, with regard to Article 1, that "[the Emperor] shall wield the authority and govern the land and subjects."[22]

Furthermore, that which was to be reigned over and governed was the people, and it is not clear to what extent the possession and control of land and space in the international legal sense was envisaged, whether by the Meiji Constitution itself or by the "govern the land" in the *Commentaries on the Constitution of the Empire of Japan*. This point is evident in the Imperial Speech. In other words, what is emphasized as being reigned over and governed by the Emperor is "Our beloved subjects," "the very same that have been favoured with the benevolent care and affectionate vigilance of Our Ancestors."[23] The Imperial Speech further mentions that "The right of sovereignty of the State, We have inherited from Our Ancestors, and We shall bequeath them to Our descendants." These are the origins of the "one great family-like nation," mentioned in *Kokutai no Hongi* [*The Essence of Japan's Polity*].[24] This led to a reliance on the "fictional history"[25] that the Imperial ancestors created the land and space of Japan, and the Emperors of the unbroken Imperial pedigree expanded it and passed it down from generation to generation. This point had fundamentally different roots to the Christian and European beliefs that separate God from man and keep the creation of heaven and earth exclusively in the domain of God.

As mentioned above, the Meiji Constitution has no territorial provisions. Usually, the territory of a State has the possibility of expansion or contraction, and there are other countries with constitutions that include pre-determined

21 *Ibid.*, 27–28.

22 *Ibid.*, 21.

23 *Ibid.*, 223.

24 Ministry of Education (ed.), *supra* note 12, 9.

25 Okamoto Kōichi 岡本公一, "Ryōdomondai to Dainihonteikoku Kenpō" 領土問題と大日本帝国憲法 [Territory, Expansionism and the Meiji Constitution], *Waseda Global Forum*, no. 7 (2010), 237.

rules for such scenarios. The draft of the Meiji Constitution, which was prepared in accordance with the Meiji Emperor's decree to "consider the laws of foreign countries,"[26] included territorial provisions. However, just before the Privy Council held its deliberations, Itō deleted the provisions and submitted the new draft for consideration.[27] As for the reason for not establishing territorial provisions, Inoue Kowashi explained, "Japan has not changed its borders for 2,500 years, so we do not recognize any need to do so now."[28] Itō also collectively referred to Ōyashima, as well as Hokkaido, Okinawa (Ryūkyū) and the Ogasawara Islands, which were incorporated after the Meiji Restoration, as the territory or land of Japan, while making reference to the *Kojiki* [*Records of Ancient Matters*] and the *Nihonshoki* [*Chronicles of Japan*].[29] Furthermore, in Japan's case, the fact that there are naturally limits to its expansion due to the geographical condition of being surrounded by the sea on all sides, and the fact that it had not experienced a reduction in its territory may have played a role. Even today, it is an implicit domestic understanding that the space of Japan entails Hokkaido, Honshu, Shikoku, Kyushu, Okinawa, and its accompanying islands, and there is no territorial provision in the current constitution. There is no doubt, both from Japan's own understanding and that internationally, that Japan's territory falls within the scope defined in Paragraph 8 of the Potsdam Declaration. While the problems surrounding the interpretation of "various small islands" (Northern Territories, Senkaku Islands, Takeshima/Dokdo) remain even now, the territory of Japan is nevertheless rarely discussed in the context of constitutional law today.[30]

How does this spatial perception of Japan differ from the concept of "territory" in international law? Also, what is its relationship with the perception of land in the East Asia region, such as *hanto* (territory) and *kyōdo* (territory within a boundary)? Furthermore, despite both being located in East Asia, was the understanding of territory in China the same as in Japan? These issues are deeply related to those concerning East Asia's integration into the European

26 Kokken Kisō no Mikotonori 国憲起草の詔 [Imperial Edict for the Drafting of the Constitution] (National Archives of Japan Digital Archive https://www.digital.archives.go.jp/gallery/0000000004 [last accessed on September 21, 2021]).

27 Okamoto, *supra* note 6, 228–232.

28 "Records of the Privy Council Meeting, 1. Draft of the Constitution, 18th June to 13th July, 1888," Center for Asian Historical Records, National Archives of Japan (JACAR) Ref. A03033487900 (last accessed on September 21, 2021).

29 Itō, *supra* note 20, 21–22.

30 Ishimura Osamu 石村修, "Kenpō ni Okeru Ryōdo" 憲法における領土 [Territory in the Constitution], *Hōseiriron* 法政理論, vol. 39, No. 4 (2007), 158.

international order and its acceptance of international law, as well as the ensuing reorganization of the international order in East Asia.[31]

3 Formation of *Gaichi* (Overseas Territory of Japan) and Its Concept

3.1 Colonial Lands (*Gaichi*) and Legislation

While the Prussian Constitution, which served as the model of the Meiji Constitution, also did not contain territorial provisions, the cession of Alsace-Lorraine and the acquisition of colonies (protectorates) in non-European regions led to the implementation of a colonial system and control over local populations that were different from the domestic equivalents in Germany, and such a state of unconstitutional governance became difficult to explain.[32] As will be discussed below, Japan found itself in the same situation with the cession of Taiwan in 1905.

As mentioned above, colonies are explained as having different jurisdictions, or legal status, to their colonial rulers. Moreover, different jurisdictions may exist even within the same colonial power itself.[33] Generally, in Japan, the areas that have been under control before the promulgation of the Meiji Constitution are referred to as *naichi* (domestic territory), while areas acquired thereafter are referred to as *gaichi* (overseas territory). However, the "center and periphery" in Japan is not exactly the same as its "*naichi* and *gaichi*." This is because periphery areas such as Ryūkyū (Okinawa) and Hokkaido also existed

31 There is much previous research on these issues. See, for example, Yanagihara Masaharu 柳原正治, "Bakumatsuki Meijishoki no 'Ryōiki' Gainen ni Kansuru Ichi Kōsatsu" 幕末期・明治初期の『領域』概念に関する一考察 [A study on the concept of territories in the late Edo period and the early Meiji period], Matsuda Takeo 松田竹男, Tanaka Norio 田中則夫, Yakushiji Kimio 薬師寺公夫, and Sakamoto Shigeki 坂元茂樹 (eds.), *Gendaikokusaihō no Shisō to Kōzō I Rekishi, Kokka, Kikō, Jōyaku, Jinken* 現代国際法の思想と構造I 歴史、国家、機構、条約、人権 (Tokyo: Toshindo, 2012), 45–73; and Kawashima Shin 川島真, "Kingendai Chūgoku ni Okeru Kokkyō no Kioku – 'Honrai no Chūgoku no Ryōiki o Meguru" 近現代中国における国境の記憶—『本来の中国の領域』をめぐる [The Memory of the National Border in Modern and Contemporary China: China's Imagined Original Territory], *Kyōkaikenkyū* 境界研究, no. 1 (2010), 1–17.

32 Ishikawa Kenji 石川健治, "Kenpō no Naka no 'Gaikoku'" 憲法の中の『外国』 [Foreign Countries in the Constitution], Waseda University Comparative Law Research Institute (ed.), *Nihon no Naka no Gaikokuhō – Kihonhō no Hikakuhōteki Kōsatsu* 日本法の中の外国法—基本法の比較法的考察 (Tokyo: Seibundo, 2014), 15–16.

33 A typical example in Japan is that the conscription ordinance based on the proclamation of conscription (Dajōkan Proclamation no.379 of November 28, 1872) was not enforced in Okinawa and Ogasawara until January 1, 1898.

within Japan's *naichi*.[34] In addition, since the Meiji Constitution did not have territorial provisions, the boundary between *naichi* and *gaichi* was not necessarily clear. In terms of legislation, Article 1, Paragraph 1 of the Common Law of 1918 (Law No. 39) stipulates that "the term 'region' refers to *naichi* (domestic territories), Korea, Taiwan or Kwantung," so among the areas controlled by Japan, Korea, Taiwan and Kwantung were *gaichi*, and other areas were *naichi* (according to Paragraph 2, Article 2, Sakhalin belongs to *naichi*.) In any case, there is no legal definition of *gaichi* as a term or which areas it corresponds to. It is said that *gaichi* came into regular use after the establishment of the Ministry of Colonial Affairs in 1929 and that it became a legal term after the promulgation of the Foreign Territory Telephone Communication Regulations (Ministry of Communications Ordinance No. 51 of 1934) and the Personal Income Tax and Corporate Income Tax Internal and Foreign Territory Relations Law (Act No. 55 of 1940).[35]

In Kiyomiya Shirō's *Introduction to Foreign Territory Law*, published in 1944, the following five examples of the use of *gaichi* are as follows.[36] (1) Taiwan, South Sakhalin, Korea, Kwantung Leased Territory and the South Sea Islands, which became territories or quasi-territories after the enactment of the Meiji Constitution; are positioned as "the most common usage"; (2) In addition, territories occupied by Japan as a result of the Second Sino-Japanese War and the Greater East Asia War are included; (3) "Foreign countries that have special relations with Japan" such as Manchuria are included; (4) The territory of foreign countries and foreign States themselves are *gaichi*; and (5) Only Honshu is *naichi*, while all other land is *gaichi*. Yamazaki Tanshō shared the same understanding as (1) in Kiyomiya's classification, and defined "Korea, Taiwan, Sakhalin, the leased territory of Kwantung, and the mandated territory of the

34 On this point, see Okazaki Mayumi 岡崎まゆみ, "'Naikoku Shokuminchi' Toshite no Hokkaidō Kindaihō Shiron – 'Minji Hanketsu' Bunseki o Tsūjita Gaichi Hōshi tono Hikaku Kanōsei o Mezashite"『内国植民地』としての北海道近代法史論—「民事判決」分析を通じた外地法史との比較可能性を目指して [Considerations on the Modern Legal History of Hokkaido: Aiming for comparability with foreign legal history through the analysis of 'civil judgments'], *Horitsu Ronsō* 法律論叢, vol. 90, no. 2–3 (2017) 139–163. For example, even today, the terms *naichi* (domestic territory) and *hondo* (mainland) are used almost interchangeably in the local dialects in Hokkaido and Okinawa. (However, the geographical scope of these terms is not necessarily definitive.)

35 Legal Affairs Division, Treaty Bureau, Ministry of Foreign Affairs, *Gaichi Hōrei Seido no Gaiyō* (*Gaichi Hōseishi Dai 2 Bu*) 外地法令制度の概要(外地法制誌第2部) [Overview of Legal Systems in Foreign Territories (Journal of Legal Systems in Foreign Territories, Part 2)] (Tokyo: Bunsei Shoin, 1990 [reprint]), 1–3.

36 Kiyomiya Shirō 清宮四郎, *Gaichihōjosetsu* 外地法序説 [Introduction to Foreign Territory Law] (Tokyo: Yūhikaku, 1944), 3–5.

South Sea Islands" as *gaichi*.[37] Research conducted in relatively recent years on laws in *gaichi*, focusing particularly on the family register system, also follows the general terminology of the time and defines *gaichi* as "a territory of a different jurisdiction that was under Japanese rule."[38] In addition, among previous studies that comprehensively examined *gaichi*, there are also those that have considered Taiwan and Korea as "colonies" without using the word "*gaichi*."[39]

Nevertheless, Kiyomiya separated Japan's territory and its quasi-territory, while, as seen in Yamazaki's definition, Kwantung is sometimes explained as "leased territory" and the South Sea Islands as "a mandated territory." It is thus not clear how each author understood the difference in legal nature between cession, annexation, lease, and mandated territory. In any case, focusing on the degree to which sovereignty was transferred, it can be seen that it was implicitly recognized that there were three types of *gaichi*: Taiwan and Sakhalin (both ceded), as well as Korea (annexation), sovereignty over which can be understood to have been completely transferred; Kwantung, where the residual sovereignty of the lessor State was recognized; and the South Sea Islands (mandate), sovereignty over which was the subject of international debate.

3.2 *Cession of Taiwan*

3.2.1 Background

As an outcome of the Sino-Japanese War, Taiwan Island and the Pescadores Islands were ceded to Japan from Qing (Paragraphs 2 and 3, Article 2 of the Sino-Japanese Peace Treaty signed on April 17, 1895, entered into force May 8, 1895). The Liaodong Peninsula was also to be ceded according to Paragraph 1, but it was returned by a further treaty with Qing in November of the same year following the Triple Intervention. Sino-Japanese relations after the Meiji

37 Yamazaki Tanshō 山崎丹照, *Gaichi Tōchi Kikō no Kenkyū* 外地統治機構の研究 [Research on Foreign Territory Organizations] (Tokyo: Takayama Shoin, 1943), 1. In addition, Minami Karafuto was incorporated into the *naichi* in 1943, regarding which Yamazaki stated, "It goes without saying that we can no longer call this a *gaichi*" (*ibid.*).

38 Mukai Hidehiro 向英洋, *Shōkai Kyū Gaichihō* 詳解旧外地法 [Detailed Explanation of the Old Foreign Land Law] (Tokyo: Nihon Kajo Publishing, 2007), 9.

39 For example, see Endō Masataka 遠藤正敬, *Kindai Nihon no Shokuminchi Tōchi ni Okeru Kokuseki to Koseki -Manshū, Chōsen, Taiwan* 近代日本の植民地統治における国籍と戸籍—満洲・朝鮮・台湾 [Nationality and Family Register in Modern Japanese Colonial Rule: Manchuria, Korea, and Taiwan] (Tokyo: Akashi Shoten, 2011); and Yamanaka Einosuke 山中永之佑, *Teikoku Nihon no Tōchihō – Naichi to Shokuminchi Chōsen, Taiwan no Chihōseido o Shōten Tosuru* 帝国日本の統治法—内地と植民地朝鮮・台湾の地方制度を焦点とする [Governance Law of Imperial Japan: Local Systems of Domestic Territory and Colonial Korea and Taiwan] (Osaka: Osaka University Press, 2021).

Restoration meant the reorganization of the East Asian order through the Taiwan Expedition (1874) and the Ryūkyū Disposition (1879).[40] In particular, Article 1 of the Treaty of Shimonoseki denied that the tribute paid by Korea to Qing amounted to Korea being part of the Chinese tributary system, stating, "China recognizes definitively the full and complete independence and autonomy of Korea, and, in consequence, the payment of tribute and the performance of ceremonies and formalities by Korea to China in derogation of such independence and autonomy, shall wholly cease for the future."

On the other hand, despite the fact that "the question of how to govern modern Japan's first colony was, for the Meiji Government, an important issue in relation to the constitutional system,"[41] there was much confusion in the initial debate on the cession. One of the reasons for this was the situation on the ground in Taiwan, where Japan had no choice but to prioritize pacification "unconstrained by laws and regulations"[42] in response to the fierce resistance of the Taiwanese people. However, as an even more fundamental issue, there was a difference of opinion on how to position Taiwan and how to govern it, both in terms of colonial (rule) policy and the legal system to support it. As part of the discussion on this point, Hara Takashi, who was Vice Minister of Foreign Affairs and a member of the Taiwan Secretariat, wrote, in *Two Proposals on the Taiwan Issue*,[43] "A. Deem Taiwan to be a kind of 'colony.' B. Taiwan is somewhat different from the *naichi*, but it should not be regarded as a type of colony." (Punctuation added by the author.) Hara himself "advocated" the second proposal because Taiwan and its people "represented a completely different situation from the case of European countries controlling people of other races." Rather than being based on any legal position, this stance can be appropriately

40 Okamoto also positions the Sino-Japanese War as a watershed moment in world history. Okamoto Takashi 岡本隆司, "Nisshin Sensō to Higashi Ajia" 日清戦争と東アジア [The Sino-Japanese War and East Asia], Yamauchi Masayuki 山内昌之 and Hosoya Yūichi 細谷雄一 (eds.), *Nihon Kingendaishi Kōgi – Seikō to Shippai no Rekishi ni Manabu* 日本近現代史講義—成功と失敗の歴史に学ぶ (Tokyo: Chuokoron-Shinsha, 2019), 56.

41 Kurihara Jun 栗原純, "Meiji Kenpō Taisei to Shokuminchi – Taiwan Ryōyū to Rokusanhō o Meguru Shomondai" 明治憲法体制と植民地—台湾領有と六三法をめぐる諸問題 [Meiji Constitutional System and Colonies: Various Issues Concerning Sovereignty over Taiwan and Act no.63], *Tokyo Joshidaigaku Hikakubunka Kenkyūsyo Kiyō* 東京女子大学比較文化研究所紀要, No. 54 (1993), 56.

42 "Naikakusōridaijin no Kunrei" 内閣總理大臣ノ訓令 [Instruction of the Prime Minister of the Cabinet] (July 16, 1895), Itō Hirobumi 伊藤博文 (ed.), *Hisho Ruisan Dai 18 Kan Taiwan Shiryō* 秘書類纂第18巻臺灣資料 (hereinafter referred to as "Taiwan Materials") (1936), 444 (NDL Digital Collection bibID 000000855219). (Last accessed on September 21, 2021).

43 *Ibid.*, 32–34.

viewed as being based on Hara's position of so-called "*naichi* extensionism."[44] If one is to take this standpoint, however, the same laws as Japan's *naichi* should, in principle, be enforced in Taiwan as much as possible, and the power of the Governor-General of Taiwan should be weakened.

In reality, however, the "Act on Laws and Regulations to be Enforced in Taiwan" (Act No. 63 of March 30, 1896; hereinafter referred to as "Act No. 63") gave the Governor-General of Taiwan broad power to enact laws.

3.2.2 Establishment of Taiwan's Legislation: Confusion over Act No. 63

Issues arose regarding what type of legislation to create for Taiwan's territory, especially how to understand its relationship with the Meiji Constitution. *Taiwan Materials* includes documents by an unknown author entitled "Position of Taiwan in Japanese Law"[45] and "Authority to Govern Territory."[46] First, "Position of Taiwan in Japanese Law" can be summarized as follows.

Based on the premise that "Taiwan is a new territory acquired by the Empire in accordance with international law," it is understood as being "a newly acquired territory, with the fact of its incorporation into the Empire meaning that the borders of the Empire will change." However, since the Meiji Constitution does not provide any procedure for changing borders, Taiwan's status under Japanese law has to be determined through the "Ordinary Principles of the State" and the "Spirit of the Imperial Constitution." The State is free to decide whether or not to incorporate a new territory. The existence of foreign constitutions that provide for procedures for changing borders means that the method of expressing the intention to incorporate a new territory after acquiring it has been stipulated. Then, in the case of Japan, how can it express its intentions? One would be to amend the Meiji Constitution, and the other would be to understand it as part of the prerogative of the Emperor. Whichever position is adopted, the conclusion is the same: "Taiwan is not part of the Empire even though it is under the sovereignty of the Empire," and therefore, "the Empire's Constitution and its various laws and regulations cannot directly be promulgated in Taiwan."

---

44 For the relationship between policy on Taiwan before and after the possession of Taiwan and the Constitution, and Hara's theory of colonial policy in general, see Haruyama Meitetsu 春山明哲, "Kindai Nihon to Taiwan – Musha Jiken, Shokuminchi Tōchi Seisaku no Kenkyū" 近代日本と台湾—霧社事件・植民地統治政策の研究 [Modern Japan and Taiwan: A Study of the Wushe Incident and Colonial Policy] (Tokyo: Fujiwara Shoten, 2008), 155–221, especially 173–179.

45 *Taiwan Materials*, (note 42), 71–74. Page numbers are omitted when quoting. (The same applies hereinafter for this reference material.)

46 *Ibid.*, 75–77.

Based on this understanding, the following arguments are developed in the "Authority to Govern Territory." Although Japan has not promulgated its constitution or laws in Taiwan, it is also not the case that Japan is governing the independent State of Taiwan under a personal union; thus, the Emperor is exercising "the sovereignty of the Japanese Empire as the sovereign of the Japanese Empire" over Taiwan. "The Emperor is the head of the Empire, combining in Himself the rights of sovereignty," as stipulated in Article 4 of the Meiji Constitution, and this is those rights being exercised. Such an exercise is in accordance with the provisions of the Meiji Constitution. When legislating with regard to Taiwan, Article 55, Paragraph 2 of the Meiji Constitution required the countersignature of a Minister of State, but it did not require the consent of the Imperial Diet, and "the authority of the Emperor is unlimited in this respect." This is the same as for diplomatic authority, and "the authority over the territory can also be summed up and called the authority to govern territory under the Meiji Constitution, so long as it is invoked for the territory and does not relate to internal affairs."

The following can be pointed out about these two documents. First, while they recognize the border change as a fact, if, due to the absence of a procedure for changing borders, Taiwan is "not part of the Empire" and neither the Meiji Constitution nor the laws and regulations are promulgated, then no legal restrictions would be imposed on the Emperor's possession and control of Taiwan. This synonymous treatment of *shuken* and *tōchiken* is the same as in Itō's *Commentaries on the Constitution of the Empire of Japan*, but it is a contradiction or circular theory to derive the authority to govern territory under the Meiji Constitution as a positive law through analogical inference from diplomatic authority. The diplomatic authority under Article 13 of the Meiji Constitution to "declar[e] war, mak[e] peace, and conclud[e] treaties" is believed to "belong to the authority of the Emperor and does not require the consent of the Diet," and the reason for this was "the unity of the sovereignty of representing the State to foreign countries."[47] Although it is a trivial point, it is possible to infer the cession of territory (Taiwan and Sakhalin) and the acquisition of leased land through peace treaties in this diplomatic authority, but when this is "authority ... under the Meiji Constitution," then the argument for removing the need for the consent of the Imperial Diet would be extremely weak if the authority is regarded as being pre-constitutional in nature.

In response, William Montague Hammett Kirkwood, an adviser to the Ministry of Justice, summarized the arguments in his "Opinion on the Taiwan

47 Itō, *supra* note 20, 43.

System, the Emperor's Authority, and the Imperial Diet"[48] as follows, stating that both are valid interpretations of the Meiji Constitution.

a) Since the authority of the Emperor is not restricted by the Meiji Constitution in Taiwan, it is constitutional to formulate laws concerning Taiwan without the approval of the Diet.

b) As long as Taiwan is a Japanese territory, the Meiji Constitution applies, and laws concerning Taiwan require the support of the Diet.

Kirkwood then pointed out, as a legislative policy issue, that, "In the current Japanese public opinion, there is a strong democratic tendency, and if my interpretation is carried out, it is difficult to predict whether a Diet that is not close to the existing Government may give rise to more aggressive arguments against the government or not."[49] Thus, he advised making a decision from a political and practical perspective rather than a legal one, placing emphasis on parliamentary strategy rather than constitutional interpretation.

After that, the government began to formulate the "Act on Laws and Regulations to be Enforced in Taiwan." After many twists and turns, it was promulgated as Act No. 63 of 1896 (March 30), commonly known as "Act No. 63." The law was intended to settle the question of what powers should be given to the Governor-General's Office and how to harmonize it with Japan's own system of governance, in light of the ongoing but sporadic uprisings on the island of Taiwan, despite it having been pacified.

According to the original "Statement of Reasons for the Bill," the recognition at the time was as follows:

> Taiwan has only just been included in the Japanese Empire, and not only are all matters still in their infancy, but there are also concerns about uprisings by armed groups in the region. Despite this, this island is located far from the capital of Tokyo and transportation between the two lands is still completely undeveloped. The emotions and social customs of the people of this island are also completely different from those of Japan, so they should not be governed by the same laws and regulations as the home country. This is why we are submitting this proposal.[50]

---

48 "Mr. Kirkwood's Opinion on the Taiwan System, the Emperor's Authority, and the Imperial Diet" (July 24, 1895), *Taiwan Materials* (note 42), 78–107.

49 *Ibid.*, 105.

50 Establishing ordinance on laws and ordinances to be enforced in Taiwan (JACAR Ref. A01200843100).

What was the nature of the draft of the Act? The validity of Act No. 63 under the Meiji Constitution was questioned for a long time after that for the reason that Article 1 of the Act stipulated, "the Governor-General of Taiwan may issue ordinances having the power of law within his jurisdiction" and Article 5 stipulated "any existing law or a law to be promulgated in the future which is necessary to be enforced in whole or in part in Taiwan shall be determined by Imperial Ordinance."

This was "nothing more than a bill with provisions concerning the legislative power of the Governor-General, which were included in the draft bylaws of the Governor-General's Office,"[51] but, at the same time, it also contained an element of danger in that "granting legislative power to the Governor-General, who is the bearer of administrative authority, and recognizing administrative ordinances as having the same power as laws clearly runs counter to the principles of constitutional government."[52] Even in the Imperial Diet, which deliberated Act No. 63, there was debate about whether the Meiji Constitution would extend to Taiwan, and, if so, how it would be extended, but it is unlikely that either the Government or the Diet fully understood and digested the issues. Below, the author will cover the background to the law's enactment using historical reference materials.[53]

Attending the Diet as a Government committee member (since March 17, 1896) was Mizuno Jun, Director of the Civil Affairs Bureau of the Office of the Governor-General of Taiwan. First, Mizuno explained the reasons for the proposal to almost the same effect as above. In response, Nakamura Katsumasa asked,[54] "As stated in Articles 8 and 9 of the Meiji Constitution, in Japan, no one but the Emperor has the authority to issue laws and ordinances, but does this actually apply to all matters under civil administration?" Article 8 of the Meiji Constitution is a provision concerning "Imperial Ordinances in the place

---

51 Kurihara, *supra* note 41, 49.

52 Komagome Takeshi 駒込武, "Kokusai Seiji no Naka no Shokuminchi Shihai" 国際政治の中の植民地支配 [Colonial Rule in International Politics], Kawashima Shin 川島真 and Hattori Ryūji 服部龍二 (eds.), *Higashi Ajia Kokusai Seijishi* 東アジア国際政治史 (Aichi: Nagoya University Press, 2007), 184.

53 As will be explained below in the main text of this chapter, Act no.64 was enacted as a three-year time-limited law. It was extended to four years by Law no.31 in 1906, and further revised according to Law no.3 in 1921. The relevant minutes of the Imperial Diet are summarized in Legal Affairs Division, Treaty Bureau, Ministry of Foreign Affairs, *Minutes of the Laws Concerning Taiwan's Enforcement Laws (Acts no.63, no.31 and No.3) (Journal of Foreign Legislation Part 3, Annex)* (Tokyo: Bunsei Shoin, 1990 [reprint]). According to the preface of the same book, the original stenographic records of the proceedings were created and published by the Governor-General of Taiwan in 1921.

54 *Ibid.*, 4.

of law" (emergency ordinances) to maintain public safety when the Imperial Diet is not sitting, and Article 9 refers to "Ordinances" to enforce the laws. However, could the Governor-General of Taiwan be delegated the authority to issue "ordinances having the power of law" in the first place? In other words, if, according to Article 4, "The Emperor is the head of the Empire, combining in Himself the rights of sovereignty," and, having "exercise[d] the legislative power with the consent of the Imperial Diet," as stated in Article 5, "gives sanction to laws, and orders them to be promulgated and executed," as stated in Article 6, then it is unlikely to be coherent to have a "legislative" process that ignores the Emperor's procedure for promulgating laws (including the consent of the Diet), and allows the Governor-General to issue "ordinances having the power of law" and obtain Imperial sanction through the Minister of Colonial Affairs. Setting that point aside, Mizuno's response was also extremely unclear. Specifically, in response to Nakamura's question, he replied, "This has nothing to do with the Meiji Constitution, which is to say that the Meiji Constitution has no power in Taiwan."[55]

If it has nothing to do with the Meiji Constitution, the basis of the Emperor's rights of sovereignty under Article 4 is lost, and it means that Taiwan would be ruled based on a pre-constitutional authority. On this point, Sakurai Yoshiki once again asked, "You have said that the Meiji Constitution has not been enacted in Taiwan, but it is a matter of course that the Meiji Constitution would be enforced once a land comes into the possession of the Empire of Japan, no matter where it is, and I believe there is something mistaken in your assertion that the Meiji Constitution is not even partially enforced in Taiwan." In response, Mizuno replied, "The Meiji Constitution has, in its entirety, not been promulgated there. To put it another way, even within the Constitution, the 'Rights and Duties of Subjects' do not apply to Taiwanese subjects. However, it goes without saying that the authority of the Emperor under the Meiji Constitution is exercised over Taiwan." The relationship between authority and the Meiji Constitution was also extremely unclear.[56] However, if the "Emperor's authority" extended to Taiwan, then some form of the Emperor's rights of sovereignty extended there and Taiwan's status as a "territory" of Japan were confirmed.

The Government temporarily withdrew the bill (March 24), but resubmitted it (March 26) with a provision (Article 6) that the bill would be legislated for a period of three years, and it was passed by the House of Peers.

55 *Ibid.*

56 *Ibid.*, 6.

3.2.3 Evaluation of Act No. 63

It is not clear where the true intention of removing the need for the consent of the Imperial Diet through Act No. 63 lay. Ariga Nagao shared an episode about the budget related to Taiwan saying, "It is troublesome to have to get approval for each and every matter, so we decided that Taiwanese matters would be decided at the discretion of the Governor-General's Office, and that there is legal power in these decisions made at its discretion."[57] Based on the opportunistic idea that "Itō would take on Itagaki's Liberal Party" and "it would be convenient later if the delegated power were to be passed at that time,"[58] a precautionary front was set up in preparation for the emergence of a "Diet that is not close to the Government," as Kirkwood was concerned about.

Since then, the relationship between Act No. 63 and the Meiji Constitution has been a controversial topic among scholars of constitutional law and *Staatsrecht*.

Act No. 63 was subsequently prolonged by revisions in 1899, 1902, and 1905. In addition, Act No. 31 of 1906 required the Governor-General of Taiwan to obtain "Imperial sanction through the competent minister" (Article 2) when prescribing ordinances. On top of that, according to Act No. 3 of 1922, when all or part of the law was enforced in Taiwan, an Imperial Ordinance would be required in principle (Article 1). Furthermore, the authority of the Governor-General to issue ordinances was exceptional, and there was a shift to *naichi* extensionism (Article 2).

3.3 *Background of the Sakhalin Cession*

As a result of the Russo-Japanese War, in September 1905, Japan was ceded Sakhalin south of the 50th parallel (Article 9, Paragraph 1 of the Treaty of Portsmouth). The Treaty of Portsmouth also stipulated that, "The Imperial Russian Government, acknowledging that Japan possesses in Korea paramount political, military and economical interests engages neither to obstruct nor interfere with measures for guidance, protection and control which the Imperial Government of Japan may find necessary to take in Korea" (Article 2). The Russo-Japanese War was about the hegemony of both countries on the Korean Peninsula. More details will be covered in the next section, but first a brief description of Sakhalin will be provided here.

57 Ariga Nagao 有賀長雄, "Taiwan ni Kansuru Rippō no Sakugo (Takano Mondai ni Tsuite)" 臺灣ニ關スル立法ノ錯誤(附高野問題) [Taiwan's Legislative Error (附高野問題)], *Kokka Gakkai Zasshi* 国家学会雑誌, vol. 14, no. 172 (June 1901), 4.

58 *Ibid.*, 5.

At first, military administration was established for Sakhalin, but in 1907, the Sakhalin Agency was established and placed in charge of governance. The "Act on Laws and Regulations to Be Enforced in Sakhalin" (Act No. 25 of 1908) stipulated that "those laws that need to be enforced in whole or in part in Sakhalin shall be made by Imperial Ordinance, but special provisions may be made by Imperial Ordinance with respect to the matters listed above." Examples of such matters were those related to indigenous persons; the powers of administrative offices or public offices; legal periods; and counsel, litigation attorneys, or successors appointed or selected by the court or the presiding judge. Unlike Taiwan, the head of the Sakhalin Agency was not given the authority to issue ordinances. It has been pointed out that the background to this is that Sakhalin "was not recognized as being *gaichi* in nature."[59] This is thought to be due to the fact that, from the beginning, 90% of the inhabitants (10,000 people) were Japanese (from the *naichi*), while there were only a small number of Ainu and other local people, and Russians.[60]

Partly because of these circumstances, Sakhalin was completely incorporated into the *naichi* on April 1, 1943.

3.4 *Korea*

3.4.1 Background to the Korean Annexation[61]

One issue in Japanese diplomacy in the Meiji Era, or an issue of concern between Japan and Qing and between Japan and Russia, was the handling of

59 Legal Affairs Division, Treaty Bureau, Ministry of Foreign Affairs, *Nihon Tōchika no Karafuto* (*Gaichi Hōseishi Dai 13 Bu*) 日本統治下の樺太(外地法制誌第 13 部) [Sakhalin under Japanese Rule (Journal of Foreign Legislation Part 13)] (Tokyo: Bunsei Shoin, 1990 [reprint]), 53.

60 *Ibid.*, 5. According to the same book, by the end of 1941, the number of domestic Japanese and Koreans had increased to over 400,000, while the number of other residents was less than 1,000. In addition, the population density was about one-sixth that of the South Sea Islands (6–7).

61 With regard to the annexation of Korea, as symbolized by the stipulation of Article 2 in The Treaty on Basic Relations between Japan and the Republic of Korea, which declares that "It is confirmed that all treaties or agreements concluded between the Empire of Japan and the Empire of Korea on or before August 22, 1910 are already null and void," the debate over its legality and illegality under international law has not been resolved between Japan and the Republic of Korea, and between Japan and North Korea. In addition, controversy continues at the level of historical materials over the signature of Park Jae-sun, Minister of External Affairs (Foreign Affairs) of the Korean Empire, and the circumstances leading up to the signing of the Second Japan-Korea Agreement (Eulsa Treaty). However, regardless of the perceptions of the parties concerned, this chapter will not go into discussion on the legality or illegality of the annexation of Korea itself, based

Korea. Without going into the significance and background of this matter,[62] the author would like to briefly summarize Korea's status at the time under international law. Article 1 of the Sino-Japanese Treaty of Amity of July 29, 1871 stipulated non-aggression toward "land belonging to" Qing with Korea in mind. From this article, it can be inferred that Qing regarded Korea at that time as not a fully sovereign State, but Article 1 of the Japan-Korea Treaty of Amity of February 1876 stipulated that "[Korea], being a sovereign and independent State, enjoys the same equal rights as does Japan," with the premise that Japan recognized Korea as an independent sovereign State or, in other words, had the expectation of its independence from Qing.

However, Korea itself did not believe that this established a sovereign State relationship, at least in terms of its relations with Japan, but rather recognized it as a restoration of the old relations between the two. Thus, there was a gap in understanding between Japan and Korea.[63] Through the subsequent Treaty of Peace, Amity, Commerce and Navigation between the United States and Korea (1882), Western countries opened their legations in Hanseong (present-day Seoul). Based on these facts, it can be assumed that other countries regarded Korea as a State in the sense according to international law. However, for Qing, Korea continued to be a vassal State but retained a relationship as an "autonomous vassal State" whereby its autonomy in the handling of ordinary political affairs was recognized.[64]

Subsequently, with the Sino-Japanese Peace Treaty (1895) eliminating traditional Qing-Korean relations and the Treaty of Portsmouth (1905) establishing Japan's supremacy over Russia in Korea, Japan made Korea a protectorate. Article 1 of the Japan-Korea Protocol of February 1904 stipulated that

---

on the fact that the Potsdam Declaration and the San Francisco Peace Treaty were drafted on the premise that Japan actually ruled Korea.

62 As a matter of course, there are countless previous studies dealing with the annexation of Korea. Examples of research that analyzed the annexation in terms of the resonance between Qing-Korean relations with Korea as an "autonomous Vassal State" and international relations include Okamoto Takashi 岡本隆司, *Zokkoku to Jishu no Aida – Kindai Shinkan Kankei to Higashi Ajia no Meiun* 属国と自主のあいだ—近代清韓関係と東アジアの命運 [Between Vassal State and Independence: Modern Qing-Korean Relations and the Fate of East Asia] (Aichi: Nagoya University Press, 2004); and Okamoto Takashi 岡本隆司, *Sekai no Naka no Nisshinkan Kankeishi – Kōrin to Zokkoku, Jishu to Dokuritsu* 世界のなかの日清韓関係史—交隣と属国、自主と独立 [*History of Japan-China-Korea Relations in the World: Neighborhood and Vassal State, Autonomy and Independence*] (Tokyo: Kodansha, 2008).

63 Okamoto, *Sekai no Naka no Nisshinkan Kankeishi* 世界のなかの日清韓関係史 [History of Japan-China-Korea Relations in the World] (note 62), 67–68.

64 *Ibid.*

"the Imperial Government of Korea shall place full confidence in the Imperial Government of Japan, and adopt the advice of the latter in regard to improvements in administration." Furthermore, the first Japan-Korea Agreement of August of the same year allowed the acceptance of financial advisors and diplomatic advisers, and the second Japan-Korea Agreement of November 1905 stripped Korea of its diplomatic rights. Needless to say, behind this series of events was the support and approval of the United Kingdom and the United States through the Anglo-Japanese Alliance (1902) and the Katsura-Taft Agreement (1905). The third Japan-Korea Agreement of July 1907 further expanded the involvement of Japanese people in all aspects of Korea's domestic affairs, and the financial advisory and diplomatic advisory system based on the first Japan-Korea Agreement was abolished.

On August 22, 1910, the Japan-Korea Annexation Treaty was signed (promulgated on August 29). Article 1 stipulated that "His Majesty the Emperor of Korea makes the complete and permanent cession to His Majesty the Emperor of Japan of all rights of sovereignty over the whole of Korea," and Article 2 stipulated that "His Majesty the Emperor of Japan accepts the cession mentioned in the preceding article and consents to the complete annexation of Korea to the Empire of Japan."

3.4.2 Structure of the Korea Governance Act

The question of what kind of legislation should be used to govern Korea was also an issue. In the Cabinet decision of June 3, prior to the signing of the Japan-Korea Annexation Treaty, entitled "Administrative Policy for Korea after the Annexation," it was decided that "the Constitution shall not be enforced in Korea for the moment and Korea shall be ruled based on the Emperor's prerogative"; "The Governor-General shall be directly subordinate to the Emperor and have the power to preside over all political affairs in Korea" and "The Governor-General shall be empowered to issue orders on legal matters in accordance with the authority (omitted)."[65] In other words, the principle of governance over Korea was based on prerogative.[66] One month later, however,

65 Unno Fukuju 海野福寿, *Kankoku Heigōshi no Kenkyū* 韓国併合史の研究 [Research on the History of the Annexation of Korea] (Tokyo: Iwanami Shoten, 2000), 351–352. Legal Affairs Division, Treaty Bureau, Ministry of Foreign Affairs, *Korea in the Japanese Colonial Period* (*Journal of Foreign Legislation Part 9*) (Tokyo: Bunsei Shoin, 1990 [reprint]), 12.

66 Ogawara Hiroyuki 小川原宏幸, Kankoku Heigō to Chōsen eno Kenpō Sikō Mondai 韓国併合と朝鮮への憲法施行問題——朝鮮における植民地法制度の形成過程 [The issue of constitution enforcement to Korea on Korean annexation], *Nihon Shokuminchi Kenkyū* 日本植民地研究, no. 17 (2005), 19.

it was decided in an ambiguous way that the Meiji Constitution would be promulgated in Korea, but it would not be applied in practice. This is considered to stem from an effort to ensure consistency with the official view that the Meiji Constitution was interpreted as being applied to Taiwan.[67]

In response to this, Article 1 of the "Act on Laws and Regulations to be Enforced in Korea"[68] stipulated that "matters in Korea for which laws are required shall be prescribed by ordinance of the Governor-General of Korea," and such ordinances were collectively referred to as "Regulations" (Article 6). Article 1 is the same as the aforementioned Act No. 63. However, while Act No. 63 was revised by Act No. 3 of 1922 and shifted to *naichi* extensionism, Korea continued to be ruled by the Emperor's prerogative until the end. According to Unno, there was an ambiguous handling of the matter as, "According to the 'Interpretation,' the Meiji Constitution was enforced in Korea, but it was not enforced in reality, and the title of Korean rule is based on the prerogative of the Emperor, not the Meiji Constitution."[69]

3.5 *South Sea Islands*

The South Sea Islands (the Marianas, Caroline and Marshall Islands) became subject to the League of Nations mandate system as a result of World War I, and was placed under the administration of Japan by the "Class C Mandate Clause Imperial Mandate Clause for the South Sea Islands" (Ministry of Foreign Affairs Notification No. 16 of April 29, 1922) of 1921. Article 22 (6) of the Covenant of the League of Nations stated that it "can be best administered under the laws of the Mandatory as integral portions of its territory." Therefore, at first glance, it can be immediately determined that it is a territory to which the sovereignty of the mandatory extends. However, the Cabinet Decision entitled "Decision on Matters Concerning the Governance of the South Sea Islands"[70] stated with regard to the South Sea Islands, which were governed by the South Sea Islands Agency under the Cabinet, "It shall be interpreted that, as in the case of the Kwantung Leased Territory, the Meiji Constitution shall be exercised" (Paragraph 6). Even before addressing the issue of whether or not to apply the Meiji Constitution, there were conflicting theories regarding the sovereignty over the mandated territories. According to the summary in Taoka Ryōichi's *The Essence of the Mandate*, there were the "League of Nations

67 *Ibid.*, 22–23.

68 JACAR Ref. A01200064500 (last accessed on September 25, 2021).

69 Unno, *supra* note 65, 353.

70 "Decision on matters concerning the governance of the South Sea Islands" (JACAR Ref. A01200193500 [last accessed on September 25, 2021]).

sovereignty theory," "mandate sovereignty theory," "major power sovereignty theory," "German sovereignty theory," and "mandatory sovereignty theory."[71]

Although it is not possible to go into the details of each theory here, the author would like to summarize the understanding of the Japanese Government by focusing on the fact that Japan continued its mandate over the South Sea Islands even after its withdrawal from the League of Nations (notification of March 27, 1933, effective on the same day in 1935). Immediately before the notice of withdrawal, the Japanese Government compiled the "Cabinet Decision on the Policy Determination Method of the Imperial Government Concerning the Consequences of the South Sea Islands Mandate after the Empire's Withdrawal from the League of Nations."[72] The sovereignty of the mandated territories was determined by the Treaty of Versailles, as "Germany renounces in favour of the Principal Allied and Associated Powers all her rights and titles over her oversea possessions," (Article 119) expressing the understanding that the territories belonged to the Principal Allied and Associated Powers, including Japan. Therefore, withdrawal from the League of Nations would not affect Japan's sovereignty over the mandated territories in any way. Based on this premise, Minister for Foreign Affairs Uchida Kōsai (Yasuya) stated, "Since our mandate is a Class C Mandate, we can carry out all forms of administration as part of our territory. Therefore, there is absolutely no need to return it to the League, even after our withdrawal therefrom. Simply submitting an annual report shall suffice."[73] It was not always clear whether "territory" under the Covenant of the League of Nations and territory under domestic law (Meiji Constitution) were considered to be the same thing. This was because, "the view is taken that laws are not implemented in the South Sea Islands, but on the other hand, there is no delegation of law and even matters which should be stipulated by law are stipulated by ordinance," so the view that "contrary to the clear fact that the Imperial Constitution extends to Korea, Taiwan, and Sakhalin, the situation of the South Sea Islands is completely different; that is, the South Sea Islands is not recognized as territory under the application of the Meiji Constitution,[74] also exists."[75] In addition, Tōmatsu Haruo, after analyzing the discussions at

71 Taoka Ryōichi 田岡良一, *Inin Tōchi no Honshitsu* 委任統治の本質 [The Essence of the Mandate] (Tokyo: Yuhikaku, 1941), 155–259.

72 Legal Division, Treaty Bureau, Ministry of Foreign Affairs, *Mandatory Territory of the South Sea Islands, Part 1* (*Journal of Foreign Legislation Part 10*) (Bunsei Shoin, 1990 [reprint]), 62–64.

73 *Ibid.*, 65.

74 *Ibid.*, 58–59.

75 As an example of evaluating this treatment as "custom," see Sakai Kazuomi 酒井一臣, "'Bunmei no Shimei' to Shite no Nihon no Nanyō Guntō Inin Tōchi – Kajō Tōchi no Haikei"

the Permanent Mandate Committee (PMC), stated that "to whom sovereignty of the mandate belonged was ultimately inconclusive."[76]

Furthermore, the situation was unique in that the residents of the South Sea Islands (islanders) were not granted Japanese nationality. As a background to this, a resolution at the Council of the League of Nations was passed in April 1923 to the effect that native inhabitants of Class C Mandates could voluntarily naturalize, but that they would not necessarily acquire the nationality of the mandatory.[77] In the report presented by the chairman at the first session of the PMC in 1922, it was stated that "the mandate system was established because it was recognized that there was a strict distinction between higher civilizations and mandated territories, and if the nationalities of the two are equated, there would essentially be no distinction made between them."[78] Thus, the Japanese Government simply referred to the inhabitants of the South Sea Islands as "islanders" and distinguished them from "subjects."

In this regard, as in the case of the Kwantung Leased Territory, there were statements that cited, as evidence, the fact that the mandated territories were "not pure territories of Japan under international law"[79] or that they "were quasi-territories."[80] Certainly, views were divided on whether the sovereignty of a mandated territory had been completely transferred to the mandatory, but the debate at the League of Nations was only about whether or not to grant nationality based on the difference in the degree of civilization, not the difference in the legal status of the area in question. If one considers that the intention of this discussion was not to prohibit the granting of nationality, it is reasonable to assume that it was only a policy measure. In addition, in the Common Law of 1918 (Act No. 39 of 1918), Paragraph 1, Article 1 and others were revised by Act No. 25 of 1923 five years later to add the South Sea Islands.[81]

『文明の使命』としての日本の南洋群島委任統治—過剰統治の背景 [Japan's Mandatory Rule of the South Sea Islands as a 'Mission of Civilization': The Background of Overrule], Institute of Social Science, Chukyo University, Edited by Asano Toyomi 浅野豊美 (ed.), *Nanyō Guntō to Teikoku Kokusai Chitsujo* (*Shakaikagaku Kenkyūsho* Sōsho 21) 南洋群島と帝国・国際秩序（社会科学研究所叢書 21）(Aichi[Nagoya?]: Chukyō University Social Science Research Institute, 2007), 82.

76 Tōmatsu Haruo 等松春夫, *Nihon Teikoku to Inin Tōchi – Nanyō Shotō o Meguru Kokusai Seiji 1914–1947* 日本帝国と委任統治—南洋群島をめぐる国際政治 1914–1947 [The Japanese Empire and the Mandate: International Politics of the South Sea Islands 1914–1947] (Aichi: Nagoya University Press, 2011), 32.

77 Ministry of Foreign Affairs, *supra* note 72, 59.

78 *Supra* note 39, 53–54.

79 *Ibid.*, 52–53.

80 *Ibid.*, 132.

81 JACAR Ref. A03021426100 (last accessed on September 25, 2021).

From this, it is appropriate to assume that even with the islanders of the South Sea Islands who did not have nationality, conflict of law between the laws of *naichi* and the laws of *gaichi* could be expected, as will be described below.

4 Systematization of the Laws of *Gaichi* and Their Problems

4.1 *Questions Raised by Minobe Tatsukichi*

The first call for systematic study of the laws of *gaichi* or colonial law (hereinafter "colonial law") was probably Minobe Tatsukichi's report[82] at the Jurisprudence Research Seminar on May 18, 1911, and his essay[83] based on said report. Minobe points out, as evidence of the necessity of colonial law research, that "the laws applied to people in the *naichi* and to indigenous populations are often different ... that is to say, in a sense, the nationality principle is applied."[84] He points out that, as a result, "a relationship similar to private international law has formed between the laws of *naichi* and colonial law, as well as between indigenous laws and the laws of *naichi*, and there is a need to alleviate potential conflicts between them according to certain rules."[85] Minobe then defines "the legal concept of a colony" as "a part of the territory of the *naichi*, in principle, whose laws differ from those of other places in the *naichi*" or "land within the territory of a country to which, in principle, a jurisdiction other than that of the *naichi* applies." The term *hōiki*, a Japanese translation of the German *Rechtsgebiet* (jurisdiction), is said to have been established by Yamada Saburō, a scholar of private international law.[86] Minobe made the point that, while "*hōiki* (*Rechtsgebiet*; jurisdiction) and *ryōiki* (*Staatsgebiet*; domain) are usually compatible,"[87] further research of colonial law had become necessary due to

82 For an overview of the report given that day, see "Articles of the Law Research Society," *Hōgaku Kyōkai Zasshi*, vol. 29, no. 11 (November 1911), 162–168.

83 Minobe Tatsukichi 美濃部達吉, Nihon Shokuminchihō ni Tsuite (Meiji 44 Nen 5 Gatsu 18 Nichi Hōri Kenkyūkai ni Oite) 日本殖民地法に就て(明治44年5月 18日法理研究會に於て) [Japanese Colonial Law (at the Jurisprudence Research Seminar on May 18, 1911)], *Kokka Gakkai Zasshi* 国家学会雑誌, vol. 26, no. 1 (January 1912), 89–108.

84 *Ibid.*, 91.

85 *Ibid.*, 92.

86 Ishikawa Kenji 石川健治, 'Keijō' no Kiyomiya Shirō 『京城』の清宮四郎 [Kiyomiya Shirō of 'Keijō'], Sakai Tetsuya 酒井哲哉 and Matsuda Toshihiko 松田利彦 (eds.), *Teikoku Nihon to Shokuminchi Daigaku* 帝国日本と植民地大学 (Tokyo: Yumani Shobō, 2014), 322. The above work also notes that Minobe's understanding of the colonies was informed by Hermann Edler von Hoffmann's *Deutsches Kolonialrecht*.

87 Minobe, *supra* note 83, 99. As pointed out by Ishikawa in *supra* note 86, the *ryōiki* here refers to the *ryōiki* of Japan.

the acquisition of Korea, Taiwan, Sakhalin, and the Kwantung Leased Territory and the resulting creation of multiple *hōiki* or jurisdictions within Japan's *ryōiki* or domain.

The emergence of jurisdictions that differed from that of the *naichi*, i.e., a different jurisdiction, was semi-inevitable. This was because the *gaichi* of Japan were acquired as part of a State or as its whole via treaty, rather than by occupation of *terra nullius*. They were thus already territories, with inhabitants, under some form of domestic legal system. For this reason, it was necessary to respect the existing legal system and longstanding customs. In addition, in the cases of say Taiwan or Korea, since there were forces opposing their cession and annexation, it was necessary to have harsh laws for maintaining public order, such as the "Ordinance for the Punishment of Bandits"[88] in Taiwan (Ordinance No. 24 of 1898) and the "Ordinance for the Summary Judgment of Criminal Matters in Korea"[89] (Imperial Ordinance No. 240 of 1909), which existed before Japan's annexation of Korea. The application of these laws was geographically limited to Taiwan or Korea. In effect, however, it was inconceivable that they would be applied to the Japanese (from the *naichi*), and were effectively only applied to the Taiwanese and to Koreans. In this way, elements of the nationality principle accompanied Japan's colonial law (*gaichi* law), both formally and practically, until the end.

4.2 *Minobe's Theory on Constitutional Law and Gaichi*

At the beginning of the Minobe-Tachi debate, Tachi understood *ryōdoken* (territorial rights) to be "real rights under international law that consider a certain region as an object, and that include the function of a State exercising its own inherent sovereignty, in other words its *tōchiken* (rights of sovereignty), within the scope of the land, or allowing another State to exercise sovereignty on its behalf for a specific period of time (in the case certain types of leases, etc.)."[90] In response, Minobe argued that it was clear that "*ryōdoken* have a 'public' relevance while *dominium* has an exclusively 'private' relevance."[91] As background to this, Minobe had revered the intent in German *Staatsrecht* to break away from the medieval patrimonial State, which could not distinguish between public and private, in other words, the intent to form a nation-state.[92]

88 JACAR Ref. A01200876000.

89 JACAR Ref. A03020810800.

90 *Supra* note 18, 4 (note 2).

91 Minobe Tatsukichi 美濃部達吉, "Ryōdoken no Hōritsujō no Seishitsu o Ronzu" 領土権ノ法律上ノ性質ヲ論ス [Discussing the Legal Nature of Territorial Rights], *Hōgakukyōkai Zasshi* 法学協会雑誌, vol. 29, no. 2 (February 1911), 16.

92 For a detailed outline of the controversy, see Ishikawa, *supra* note 32, 20–25.

Subsequently, however, Minobe changed his position and began to regard *ryōdoken* as real rights as well.[93] The logical consequence of this, according to Ishikawa, was that,

> Under Minobe's formerly held theory, the annexation of Korea would have plunged the Japanese Empire into a crisis of identity, and depending on the circumstance, the previous Meiji State would have ended and a new 'Empire' would have to be established on August 29, 1910. However, under the theory newly advocated by Minobe, *ryōdoken* as real rights were simply transferred from the Korean Empire to the Japanese Empire, and the identity of the Meiji State would not be impaired. This amounts to no less than a theoretical shift towards Taisho 'Imperialism,' which envisioned the further acquisition of new territories in future.[94]

This is because, by defining territorial sovereignty as having both elements of possession and control, and positioning them as one aspect of *tōchiken*, the acquisition (possession) of any *gaichi* and the control (governance) of any acquired *gaichi* would be free from the Meiji Constitution. Whether or not to apply the Meiji Constitution to *gaichi* (i.e., to possess and govern them in accordance with the provisions of the Meiji Constitution) would be a matter of policy, not a matter of jurisprudence.

Minobe's description of colonies (colonial law) in the *Compendium of the Constitution* is largely in line with the views he presented in his report at the Jurisprudence Research Seminar. He again states that a colony is a different jurisdiction, and even within the text of the Meiji Constitution, except for "laws concerning the supreme body of government which by nature must be common throughout the country,"[95] the Constitution itself can differ. Minobe was of the opinion that, as a result, the incorporation of a colony into the *naichi* was no longer a constitutional issue. Rather it would be sufficient to amend the laws in force in the colony to have the same content as laws in the *naichi*.[96]

93 On the other hand, Tachi did not change his position on the "real rights theory" even after theories such as the "spatial theory" and the "authority theory" were introduced. Tachi Sakutarō, "The Concept of a State under International Law and the Territory of a State," *Journal of International Law and Diplomacy*, vol. 28, no. 3 (1929), 1–22.

94 Ishikawa, *supra* note 32, 25.

95 Minobe Tatsukichi 美濃部達吉, *Kenpō Satsuyō* (*Kaitei Dai 5 Han*) 憲法撮要（改訂第5版） [Constitutional Law (Revised 5th Edition)] (Tokyo: Yūhikaku, 1932). Discussion here is based on the reprint edition of the same book (Hiroshima: Kure PASS Publishing, 2019), 142.

96 *Ibid.*, 154.

5 Conclusion

The problems surrounding the laws of *gaichi* were subsequently taken up by scholars such as Kiyomiya Shirō of Keijo Imperial University and Nakamura Tetsu of Taipei Imperial University. However, with the loss of all *gaichi* on August 15, 1945, the subjects and significance of such studies had disappeared. As mentioned at the beginning of this chapter, the territory of Japan is rarely examined from the perspective of constitutional scholarship today. International legal scholarship also considers this issue within the context of the territorial issues that Japan is facing.

This chapter attempted to summarize how Japan as a colonial empire was formed by reviewing the formation of the laws of *gaichi* with a focus on the debate over the process of concluding treaties for acquiring *gaichi* and over the application of the constitution to *gaichi*. As Hatano Sumio points out, Japan's colonial rule, unlike that of European countries, targeted areas close to Japan, including Taiwan and the Korean Peninsula.[97] Since it opened itself up to the world, Japan had simultaneously undertaken modernization (acceptance of international law) and imperialization (the acquisition of colonies based on international law) in East Asia. Needless to say, the colonization of areas controlled by China (Qing), including not only Taiwan but also the Korean Peninsula, marked the beginning of various so-called "issues concerning the recognition of history" that continue to this day.

Setting that point aside, while the acquisition of colonies and what kind of legislation to promulgate there were theoretical issues, the issue of the application of the Meiji Constitution also involved political aspects, such as parliamentary strategy and factional strife within the Meiji Government. It is also important to note that under Japanese colonial rule, despite slogans such as "universal brotherhood" and "Japan and Korea as one," the colonies, with the exception of Sakhalin, were considered to be different jurisdictions until the end, and no progress was made in incorporating them into the *naichi*. On March 26, 1945, at the end of World War II, the House of Representatives adopted the "Petition for the Abolition of the Term *Gaichi*."[98] However, this

97 Hatano Sumio 波多野澄雄, *'Chōyōkō' Mondai towa Nanika – Chōsenjin Rōmu Dōin no Jittai to Nikkan Tairitsu*「徴用工」問題とは何か—朝鮮人労務動員の実態と日韓対立 [What is the 'Requisitioned Workers' Issue?: The Reality of Korean Labor Mobilization and the Japan-Korea Conflict] (Tokyo: Chūōkōron Shinsha, 2020), 3.

98 Mizuno Naoki 水野直樹, "Senjiki no Shokuminchi Shihai to 'Naigaichi Gyōsei Ichigenka'" 戦時期の植民地支配と『内外地行政一元化』 [Colonial Rule in Wartime and 'Unification of Domestic and Foreign Administrations'], *Journal of Humanistic Science*, vol. 79 (1997), 77–78.

was not done from the viewpoint of achieving equality between domestic and foreign people, but from the perspective of the war effort, and it was criticized for the fact that "this unification only served to strengthen colonial rule in that it led to stronger calls to reinforce and deepen the Imperial subjugation of the people of the *gaichi*."[99] Looking at this point from the perspective of *gaichi* legislation, Japan had to continue to rule and govern on the basis of the nationality principle based on disparity until the end, and it must be said that the laws of *gaichi* were potentially suppressing human rights (although the guarantee of human rights even in *naichi* during the prewar period was also generally restrictive).

There has been a certain amount of research on (the history of) *gaichi* legislation up to the present day, not only in terms of history but also in the context of research on the "Empire" (research on colonies) and constitutional law in relation to Japan. Much of this work has essentially been conducted from a domestic perspective, and there are relatively few systematic studies conducted with international relations in mind, like that of Asano Toyomi. In addition, in relation to the degree of acceptance of international law in Japan at that time, even fewer have examined *gaichi* legislation. As mentioned at the beginning of this chapter, there were already Western settlements in the *gaichi* of Japan, especially Taiwan and Korea, and it was necessary for Japan to negotiate treaties with the Western powers before engaging in its own colonization. Modern international law, which allowed colonial rule, supported the unequal (treaty) system of securing the economic interests of Western Powers and their nationals who maintained a presence there. How did Japan, having accepted such modern international law and worked to revise the unequal treaties it had concluded on the one hand, utilize the logic of modern international law in the development of its own interests, including the acquisition of "colonies," and engage in negotiations with the States concerned on the other? Due to the limited space available here, the author wishes to further consider this point in future research.

Acknowledgement

This chapter partly includes the outcomes of the 2021 Nanzan University Pache Research Grant I-A-2.

99 *Ibid.*, 98.

Bibliography

Primary Sources

Japanese

Center for Asian Historical Records, National Archives of Japan (JACAR) A01200064500; A01200193500; A01200843100; A01200876000; A03020810800; A03021426100; A03033487900.

Legal Affairs Division, Treaty Bureau, Ministry of Foreign Affairs of Japan 外務省条約局法規課. *Gaichi Hōrei Seido no Gaiyō* (*Gaichi Hōseishi Dai 2 Bu*) 外地法令制度の概要（外地法制誌第2部）[Overview of Legal Systems in Foreign Territories (Archives of Legal Systems in Overseas Territories, Part 2)]. Tokyo: Bunsei Shoin, 1990 [reprint].

Legal Affairs Division, Treaty Bureau, Ministry of Foreign Affairs of Japan 外務省条約局法規課. *Taiwan ni Shikō subeki Hōrei ni Kansuru Hōritsu* 台湾に施行スヘキ法令ニ関スル法律 [Minutes of the Laws Concerning Taiwan's Enforcement Laws (Acts No. 63, No. 31 and No. 3) (Archives of Legislation in Overseas Territories, Part 3, Annex)]. Tokyo: Bunsei Shoin, 1990 [reprint].

Legal Affairs Division, Treaty Bureau, Ministry of Foreign Affairs of Japan 外務省条約局法規課. *Nihon Tōchika no Karafuto* (*Gaichi Hōseishi Dai 13 Bu*) 日本統治下の樺太（外地法制誌第 13 部）[Sakhalin under Japanese Rule (Archives of Legislation in Overseas Territories, Part 13)]. Tokyo: Bunsei Shoin, 1990 [reprint].

Legal Affairs Division, Treaty Bureau, Ministry of Foreign Affairs of Japan 外務省条約局法規課. *Nihon Tochi Jidai no Chosen* (*Gaichi Hōseishi Dai 9 Bu*) 日本統治時代の朝鮮（外地法制誌第9部）[Korea in the Japanese Colonial Period (Archives of Legislation in Overseas Territories, Part 9)]. Tokyo: Bunsei Shoin, 1990 [reprint].

Legal Affairs Division, Treaty Bureau, Ministry of Foreign Affairs of Japan 外務省条約局法規課. *Inin Tōchi Ryō Nanyō Guntō* 委任統治領南洋群島 [Mandatory Territory of the South Sea Islands, Part 1 (Archives of Legislation in Overseas Territories, Part 10)]. Bunsei Shoin, 1990 [reprint].

“Shuken Benmō Dai 4” 主権弁妄第四 [The Fourth Sovereignty Deliberation]. *Tokyo Nichi Nichi Shimbun* 東京日日新聞, January 27, 1882.

Secondary Sources

Japanese

Ariga, Nagao 有賀長雄. “Taiwan ni Kansuru Rippō no Sakugo (Takano Mondai ni Tsuite)” 臺灣ニ關スル立法ノ錯誤（附高野問題）[Taiwan's Legislative Error (附高野問題)]. *Kokka Gakkai Zasshi* 国家学会雑誌 14, no. 172 (1901): 1–15.

Asano, Toyomi 浅野豊美. *Teikoku Nihon no Shokuminchi Hōsei* 帝国日本の植民地法制 [Colonial Legislation of Imperial Japan]. Nagoya: The Nagoya University Press, 2008.

Ebara, Yoshiyasu 頴原善徳. "Kokusaihō to Kokunaihō no Kankei o Meguru Minobe Tachi Ronsō" 国際法と国内法の関係をめぐる美濃部・立論争 – 韓国併合と領土権・主権論争 [Minobe-Tachi Debate over the Relationship between International Law and Domestic Law: Annexation of Korea and Territorial Rights/Sovereignty Debate]. *Hisutoria* ヒストリア 181 (2002): 1–25.

Endō, Masataka 遠藤正敬. *Kindai Nihon no Shokuminchi Tōchi ni Okeru Kokuseki to Koseki – Manshū, Chōsen, Taiwan* 近代日本の植民地統治における国籍と戸籍 – 満洲・朝鮮・台湾 [Nationality and Family Register in Modern Japanese Colonial Rule: Manchuria, Korea, and Taiwan]. Tokyo: Akashi Shoten, 2011.

Haruyama, Meitetsu 春山明哲. *Kindai Nihon to Taiwan – Musha Jiken, Shokuminchi Tōchi Seisaku no Kenkyū* 近代日本と台湾 – 霧社事件・植民地統治政策の研究 [Modern Japan and Taiwan: A Study of the Wushe Incident and Colonial Policy]. Tokyo: Fujiwara Shoten, 2008.

Hatano, Sumio 波多野澄雄. *'Chōyōkō' Mondai towa Nanika – Chōsenjin Rōmu Dōin no Jittai to Nikkan Tairitsu*「徴用工」問題とは何か – 朝鮮人労務動員の実態と日韓対立 [What is the 'Requisitioned Workers' Issue?: The Reality of Korean Labor Mobilization and the Japan-Korea Conflict]. Tokyo: Chūōkōron Shinsha, 2020.

Ishikawa, Kenji 石川健治. "Kenpō no Naka no 'Gaikoku'" 憲法の中の『外国』["Foreign Countries" in the Constitution]. In *Nihon no Naka no Gaikokuhō – Kihonhō no Hikakuhōteki Kōsatsu* 日本法の中の外国法 – 基本法の比較法的考察, edited by Waseda University Comparative Law Research Institute. Tokyo: Seibundō, 2014.

Ishikawa, Kenji 石川健治. "'Keijō' no Kiyomiya Shirō"『京城』の清宮四郎 [Kiyomiya Shirō in 'Keijō']. In *Teikoku Nihon to Shokuminchi Daigaku* 帝国日本と植民地大学, edited by Sakai Tetsuya 酒井哲哉 and Matsuda Toshihiko 松田利彦. Tokyo: Yumani Shobō, 2014.

Ishimura, Osamu 石村修. "Kenpō ni Okeru Ryōdo" 憲法における領土 [Territory in the Constitution]. *Hōseiriron* 法政理論 39, no. 4 (2007): 158–185.

Itō Hirobumi 伊藤博文 (ed.), *Hisho Ruisan Dai 18 Kan Taiwan Shiryō* 秘書類纂第 18 巻臺灣資料 (1936), 444.

Itō, Hirobumi 伊藤博文 (annotation by Miyazawa Toshiyoshi 宮沢俊義). *Kenpō Gikai* 憲法義解 [Commentaries on the Constitution of the Empire of Japan]. Tokyo: Iwanami Shoten, 2019.

Iwasawa, Yūji 岩沢雄司, *Kokusaihō* 国際法 [International Law]. Tokyo: University of Tokyo Press, 2020.

Kawashima, Shin 川島真. "Kingendai Chūgoku ni Okeru Kokkyō no Kioku – 'Honrai no Chūgoku no Ryōiki o Meguru" 近現代中国における国境の記憶 –『本来の中国の領域』をめぐる [The Memory of the National Border in Modern and Contemporary China: China's Imagined Original Territory]. *Kyōkaikenkyū* 境界研究 1 (2010): 1–17.

Kiyomiya, Shirō 清宮四郎. *Gaichihōjosetsu* 外地法序説 [Introduction to the Law concerning Overseas Territories]. Tokyo: Yūhikaku, 1944.

Komagome, Takeshi 駒込武. "Kokusai Seiji no Naka no Shokuminchi Shihai" 国際政治の中の植民地支配 [Colonial Rule in International Politics]. In *Higashi Ajia Kokusai Seijishi* 東アジア国際政治史, edited by Kawashima Shin 川島真 and Hattori Ryūji 服部龍二. Nagoya: The Nagoya University Press, 2007.

Kurihara, Jun 栗原純. "Meiji Kenpō Taisei to Shokuminchi – Taiwan Ryōyū to Rokusanhō o Meguru Shomondai" 明治憲法体制と植民地 – 台湾領有と六三法をめぐる諸問題 [Meiji Constitutional System and Colonies: Issues Concerning Taiwan and Act No. 63]. *Tokyo Joshidaigaku Hikakubunka Kenkyūsyo Kiyō* 東京女子大学比較文化研究所紀要 (1993): 37–62.

Matsui, Yoshiro 松井芳郎. "Kokusaihō ni Okeru Ryōiki to Kokkyō – Sono Henyō no Kizashi" 国際法における『領域』と『国境』 – その変容のきざし [Concepts of "Territory" and "Boundary" under International Law: Indications of Their Change]. *Higashi Ajia Kindaishi* 東アジア近代史 17 (2014): 56–71.

Ministry of Education (ed.), *The Essence of Japan's Polity*, (National Diet Library Digital Collections, NDL bibID 000000713777).

Ministry of Justice Collection of *Elements of International Law by Henry Wheaton* (1883) (National Diet Library Digital Collections, NDL bibID S00001116), 35.

Minobe, Tatsukichi 美濃部達吉. "Ryōdoken no Hōritsujō no Seishitsu o Ronzu" 領土權ノ法律上ノ性質ヲ論ス [Discussing the Legal Nature of Territorial Rights]. *Hōgakukyōkai Zasshi* 法学協会雑誌 29, no. 2 (1911): 182–212.

Minobe, Tatsukichi 美濃部達吉. "Hōri Kenkyūkai Kiji" 法理研究会記事 [Articles of the Jurisprudence Research Society]. *Hōgakukyōkai Zasshi* 法学協会雑誌 29, no. 11 (1911): 162–168.

Minobe, Tatsukichi 美濃部達吉. "Nihon Shokuminchihō ni Tsuite (Meiji 44 Nen 5 Gatsu 18 Nichi Hōri Kenkyūkai ni Oite)" 日本殖民地法に就て（明治 44年 5月 18日法理研究會に於て） [Japanese Colonial Law (at the Jurisprudence Research Society's Seminar on May 18, 1911)]. *Kokka Gakkai Zasshi* 国家学会雑誌 26, no. 1 (1912): 89–108.

Minobe, Tatsukichi 美濃部達吉. *Kenpō Satsuyō (Kaitei Dai 5 Han)* 憲法撮要（改訂第 5 版） [Constitutional Law (Revised 5th Edition)]. Tokyo: Yūhikaku, 1932.

Mizuno, Naoki 水野直樹. "Senjiki no Shokuminchi Shihai to 'Naigaichi Gyōsei Ichigenka'" 戦時期の植民地支配と『内外地行政一元化』 [Colonial Rule in Wartime and 'Unification of Administrations over Inland and Overseas Territory']. *Jinbun Gakuhō* 人文學報 79 (1997): 77–102.

Mukai, Hidehiro 向英洋. *Shōkai Kyū Gaichihō* 詳解旧外地法 [Detailed Explanation of the Former Laws of Overseas Territories]. Tokyo: Nihon Kajo Publishing, 2007.

Nakahara, Seiichi 中原精一. "Minobe Tachi Ryōhakase Ronsō no Sobyō – Kokunaihō to Kokusaihō tono Kankeiron ni Tsuite" 美濃部・立両博士論争の素描 – 国内法と国際法との関係論について [A Sketch of the Debates between Prof. Minobe and Prof. Tachi: On the Relationship between Domestic Law and International Law].

Meijidaigaku Shakaikagaku Kenkyūsyo Kiyō 明治大学社会科学研究所紀要 7 (1969): 37–54.

Nishimura, Yūichi 西村裕一. "Nihon ni Okeru Shukenron – Senzen Kara no Shikaku" 日本における主権論 – 戦前からの視角 [The Theory of Sovereignty in Japan: A Perspective from the Prewar Period]. *Shuken wa Ima (Nenpō Seijigaku 2019–1)* 主権はいま(年報政治学2019–1) (2019): 113–136.

Ogawara, Hiroyuki 小川原宏幸. "Kankoku Heigō to Chōsen eno Kenpō Sikō Mondai" 韓国併合と朝鮮への憲法施行問題 – 朝鮮における植民地法制度の形成過程 [The issue of constitution enforcement to Korea on Korean annexation]. *Nihon Shokuminchi Kenkyū* 日本植民地研究 17 (2005): 17–33.

Ōhata, Tokushirō 大畑篤四郎. "Higashi Ajia ni Okeru Kokusaihō (Bankokukōhō) no Juyō to Tekiyō" 東アジアにおける国際法(万国公法)の受容と適用 [Reception and Application of International Law in East Asia]. *Higashi Ajia Kindaishi* 東アジア近代史 2 (1999): 1–7.

Okamoto, Kōichi 岡本公一. "Ryōdomondai to Dainihonteikoku Kenpō" 領土問題と大日本帝国憲法 [Territory and the Meiji Constitution]. *Waseda Global Forum* 7 (2010): 217–241.

Okamoto, Takashi 岡本隆司. *Zokkoku to Jishu no Aida – Kindai Shinkan Kankei to Higashi Ajia no Meiun* 属国と自主のあいだ – 近代清韓関係と東アジアの命運 [Between Vassal State and Independence: Modern Qing-Korean Relations and the Fate of East Asia]. Nagoya: The Nagoya University Press, 2004.

Okamoto, Takashi 岡本隆司. *Sekai no Naka no Nisshinkan Kankeishi – Kōrin to Zokkoku, Jishu to Dokuritsu* 世界のなかの日清韓関係史 – 交隣と属国、自主と独立 [History of Japan-China-Korea Relations in the World: Neighborhood and Vassal State, Autonomy and Independence]. Tokyo: Kōdansha, 2008.

Okamoto, Takashi 岡本隆司. "Chūgoku ni Okeru Ryōdo Gainen no Keisei" 中国における『領土』概念の形成 [Formation of the Concept of Sovereignty in China]. In *Sōshuken no Sekaishi – Tōzai Ajia no Kindai to Honyaku Gainen* 宗主権の世界史 – 東西アジアの近代と翻訳概念, edited by Okamoto Takashi 岡本隆司. Nagoya: The Nagoya University Press, 2014.

Okamoto, Takashi 岡本隆司. "Sōshuken to Kokusaihō to Honyaku – 'Tōhō Mondai' kara 'Chōsen Mondai' e" 宗主権と国際法と翻訳 – 『東方問題』から『朝鮮問題』へ [Suzerainty, International Law, and Translation: From 'Eastern Issues' to 'Korean Issues']. In *Sōshuken no Sekaishi – Tōzai Ajia no Kindai to Honyaku Gainen* 宗主権の世界史 – 東西アジアの近代と翻訳概念, edited by Okamoto Takashi 岡本隆司. Nagoya: The Nagoya University Press, 2014.

Okamoto, Takashi 岡本隆司. "Nisshin Sensō to Higashi Ajia" 日清戦争と東アジア [The Sino-Japanese War and East Asia]. In *Nihon Kingendaishi Kōgi – Seikō to Shippai no Rekishi ni Manabu* 日本近現代史講義 – 成功と失敗の歴史に学ぶ, edited by Yamauchi Masayuki 山内昌之 and Hosoya Yūichi 細谷雄一. Tokyo: Chūōkōron Shinsha, 2019.

Okazaki, Mayumi 岡崎まゆみ. "'Naikoku Shokuminchi' Toshite no Hokkaidō Kindaihō Shiron – 'Minji Hanketsu' Bunseki o Tsūjita Gaichi Hōshi tono Hikaku Kanōsei o Mezashite"『内国植民地』としての北海道近代法史論 –「民事判決」分析を通じた外地法史との比較可能性を目指して [Considerations on the Modern Legal History of Hokkaido: Aiming for comparability with foreign legal history through the analysis of 'civil judgments']. *Hōritsu Ronsō* 法律論叢 90, no. 2–3 (2017): 139–163.

Sakai, Kazuomi 酒井一臣. "'Bunmei no Shimei' to Shite no Nihon no Nanyō Guntō Inin Tōchi – Kajō Tōchi no Haikei"『文明の使命』としての日本の南洋群島委任統治 – 過剰統治の背景 [Japan's Mandatory Rule of the South Sea Islands as a 'Mission of Civilization': The Background of Overrule]. In *Nanyō Guntō to Teikoku Kokusai Chitsujo* (*Shakaikagaku Kenkyūsho Sōsho 21*) 南洋群島と帝国・国際秩序（社会科学研究所叢書 21）, edited by Institute of Social Science, Chukyo University, Asano Toyomi 浅野豊美. Nagoya: Chūkyō University Social Science Research Institute, 2007.

Tachi, Sakutarō 立作太郎. "Kankoku Heigō Kokusaihōkan" 韓国併合国際法観 [The Annexation of Korea as Viewed under International Law]. *Hōgakukyōkai Zasshi* 法学協会雑誌 28, no. 11 (1910): 1–19.

Tachi, Sakutarō 立作太郎. "Kokusaihō jō no Kokka no Kannen to Kokka no Ryōdo" 國際法上の國家の觀念と國家の領土 [The Concept of a State under International Law and the Territory of a State]. *Kokusaihō Gaikō Zasshi* 国際法外交雑誌 28, no. 3 (1929): 1–22.

Taoka, Ryōichi 田岡良一. *Inin Tōchi no Honshitsu* 委任統治の本質 [The Essence of the Mandate]. Tokyo: Yūhikaku, 1941.

Tōmatsu, Haruo 等松春夫. *Nihon Teikoku to Inin Tōchi – Nanyō Shotō o Meguru Kokusai Seiji 1914–1947* 日本帝国と委任統治 – 南洋群島をめぐる国際政治 1914–1947 [The Japanese Empire and the Mandate: International Politics of the South Sea Islands 1914–1947]. Nagoya: Nagoya University Press, 2011.

Tsuda, Masamichi (Shinichirō) 津田真道（真一郎）, *Taisei Kokuhōron* 泰西国法論 [The Laws of Western Countries]. Waseda University Library Classical Books Comprehensive Database. https://archive.wul.waseda.ac.jp/kosho/wa07/wa07_00839/wa07_00839_0001/wa07_00839_0001.pdf.

Unno, Fukuju 海野福寿. *Kankoku Heigōshi no Kenkyū* 韓国併合史の研究 [Research on the History of the Annexation of Korea]. Tokyo: Iwanami Shoten, 2000.

Yamamuro, Shinichi 山室信一. "Kokumin Teikoku Nihon ni Okeru Ihōiki no Tōgō to Kakusa" 国民帝国日本における異法域の統合と格差 [Integration and discrimination in the Japanese nation-empire]. *Jinbun Gakuhō* 人文學報 101 (2011): 63–80.

Yamanaka, Einosuke 山中永之佑. *Teikoku Nihon no Tōchihō – Naichi to Shokuminchi Chōsen, Taiwan no Chihōseido o Shōten Tosuru* 帝国日本の統治法 – 内地と植民地朝鮮・台湾の地方制度を焦点とする [Governance Law of Imperial Japan: Local

Systems of Domestic Territory and Colonial Korea and Taiwan]. Osaka: Osaka University Press, 2021.

Yamazaki, Tanshō 山崎丹照. *Gaichi Tōchi Kikō no Kenkyū* 外地統治機構の研究 [Research on Overseas Territory's Administrative Organizations]. Tokyo: Takayama Shoin, 1943.

Yanagihara, Masaharu 柳原正治. "Bakumatsuki Meijishoki no 'Ryōiki' Gainen ni Kansuru Ichi Kōsatsu" 幕末期・明治初期の『領域』概念に関する一考察 [A study on the concept of territories in the late Edo period and the early Meiji period]. In *Gendaikokusaihō no Shisō to Kōzō I Rekishi, Kokka, Kikō, Jōyaku, Jinken* 現代国際法の思想と構造I 歴史、国家、機構、条約、人権, edited by Matsuda Takeo 松田竹男, Tanaka Norio 田中則夫, Yakushiji Kimio 薬師寺公夫, and Sakamoto Shigeki 坂元茂樹. Tokyo: Tōshindō, 2012.

Yanagihara, Masaharu 柳原正治. "Kyōiki, Hanto, Hōdo, Soshite Ryōiki" 彊域、版図、邦土、そして領域 ["East Asian and European Notions of Territory"]. *Kokusai Mondai* 国際問題 624 (2013): 1–4.

Yanagihara, Masaharu 柳原正治, Morikawa, Kōichi 森川幸一, and Kanehara, Atsuko 兼原敦子, eds. *Purakutisu Kokusaihō Kōgi* [Dai 2 Han] プラクティス国際法講義[第2版] [The Practice of International law (2nd edition)]. Tokyo: Shinzansha, 2016.

Yokota, Kisaburō 横田喜三郎. *Kokusaihō II* (*Hōritsugaku Zenshū 56*) 国際法 II（法律学全集 56）[International Law II (Complete Works of Law 56)]. Tokyo: Yūhikaku, 1958.

Yonehara, Ken 米原謙. *Kokutairon wa Naze Umaretaka – Meiji Kokka no Chi no Chikeizu* 国体論はなぜ生まれたか – 明治国家の知の地形図 [Why was the Idea of Polity Born?: Topography of the Knowledge of the Meiji State]. Kyoto: Minerva Shobō, 2015.

CHAPTER 4

The Concept of Leaseholds from the Perspective of Modern Japan

Yuichi Sasaki

1 Introduction

1.1 *The Subject of This Chapter*

The regional order in East Asia differed from the modern international order of the West until the 18th century. East Asian States did not form an international society tied together by diplomatic relations on an equal footing, nor did they have comprehensive and exclusive jurisdiction within their borders. State control did not extend homogeneously over domestic areas, and there was uncertainty about the scope and nature of territory. For example, the Ryūkyū Kingdom was effectively ruled by the Satsuma Domain of Japan yet had a tributary relationship with Chinese dynasties.

In the 19th century, the East Asian world was being incorporated into a modern Western-style international system. In this context, Japan and China defined the areas considered to be their territories and established State control within their borders. Through contact with the Western world, the multi-layered, ambiguous, and fluid nature of territory and control of the East Asian world disappeared.

However, another complex situation concerning territory and sovereignty arose in China as it faced the advances of the great powers through the Opium War, the Arrow War (the Second Opium War), and the Sino-Japanese War of 1894–95. Leasehold, the subject of this paper, is a good example of this.

What is a leasehold? According to Yokota Kisaburō, "A leasehold refers to a State leasing part of the territory of another State. Such territory is known as leased territory. The receiving State is the lessee State, while the owner State is the lessor State. The legal status is not the same across all leased territories. It needs to be confirmed based on the treaty applicable to that particular leased territory." Such territories are classified into political leased territory, military

 DOI:10.1163/9789004706361_005

leased territory, and commercial leased territory. Yokota gave the following explanation about political leased territory.[1]

> A lessee State's underlying purpose for leased territory is to obtain it in the hope of making the lessor State cede the leased territory. However, the lessee State takes the approach of leased territory to account for factors such as opposition from the lessor State, the antipathy of the lessor State's citizens, and the interference of third-party States. In this sense, leased territory is very political in nature. In addition, the lessee State holds all political power and conducts all politics in the leased territory. The lessee State carries out legislation, justice, and administration in the leased territory, stations its military forces and builds military bases there, and takes charge of the territory's defense. In these respects, the leased territory has virtually been ceded to the lessee State. … The most important political leased territories are those in China acquired by European countries and Japan from the end of the 19th century.

The complexity of the leasehold is apparent from this explanation. Today, the meaning of the leasehold as a concept under international law is well established, notwithstanding the complexity and diversity of the actual circumstances of the leaseholds. However, this was not the case in the past. Various discussions were held on the question of the nature of the leasehold.

Among those discussions, from the end of the 19th century, when the so-called partition of China took place, to around the time of World War I, the theory that leaseholds constituted disguised cession was widely advocated in the West. Later, instead, the understanding that a leasehold is not the equivalent of cession took root. Such a shift in theoretical trends has already been pointed out.[2]

However, in Japan, the view that a leasehold was not equivalent to cession came to be a dominant one at an earlier time than the rest of the world. To

---

1 Yokota Kisaburō 横田喜三郎, *Hōritsugaku Zenshū 56 Kokusaihō II (Shinban)* 法律学全集 56 国際法ii〔新版〕[Jurisprudence Complete Collection 56: International Law II (New Edition)] (Tokyo: Yūhikaku, 1972), 108–109.

2 C. Walter Young, *The International Legal Status of the Kwantung Leased Territory* (Baltimore: Johns Hopkins Press, 1931), 131–152; Ueda Toshio 植田捷雄, *Shina Soshakuchi Ron* 支那租借地論 [The Theory of Leased Territory of China] (Tokyo: Nikkō Shoin, 1943), 159–188; Yokota, *supra* note 1, 108; Yaël Ronen, "Territory, Lease," in *The Max Planck Encyclopedia of Public International Law, Volume IX*, Rüdiger Wolfrum (ed.) (Oxford: Oxford University Press, 2012), 905; Michael J. Strauss, *Territorial Leasing in Diplomacy and International Law* (Leiden: Brill Nijhoff, 2015), 89–91.

state it more precisely, the theory of not equating leaseholds with cession (hereinafter referred to as "non-cession theory") was not so dominant as to be overwhelming but was more predominant than the theory of disguised cession (hereinafter referred to as "disguised cession theory"). Focusing on this point, this chapter analyzes the historical development of the concept of leaseholds from the perspective of modern Japan.

1.2 *Prior Research*

As noted in Yokota's explanation above, the main impetus that brought attention to leaseholds was territorial leasing in China.[3] Therefore, many studies on leaseholds were published until the time of World War II with a focus on the leaseholds in China.[4] Since World War II, although leaseholds have not ceased to exist around the world, this subject has not been intensively studied, besides a few exceptions.[5]

---

3 In Japan, during the same period, the leasehold was often explained as a relatively recent phenomenon, with reference to precedents such as Cyprus and Bosnia-Herzegovina. Later, it was pointed out that the de facto leasehold relationship can be traced back to Portugal's lease of Macau from China.

Nakamura Shingo 中村進午, "Eikyū Senryō to Soshakuchi" 永久占領と租借地 [Perpetual Occupation and Leased Territory], *Hōsei Shinshi* 法政新誌, vol. 7, no. 12 (1903); Matsubara Kazuo 松原一雄, *Saikin Kokusai Kōhō Genron* 最近国際公法原論 [Recent Theory on Public International Law] (Tokyo: Tokyo Hōgakuin Daigaku, 1904), 123–124; Shinoda Jisaku 篠田治策, "Soshakuken no Seishitsu to Kantōshū no Soshakuchi" 租借権の性質と関東州の租借地 [The Nature of Leasehold Rights and the Kwantung Leased Territory], *Kokusaihō Zasshi* 国際法雑誌, vol. 5, no. 2 (1906): 12–24; Taoka Ryoichi 田岡良一, "Soshakuchi to Kokusai Chieki (3)" 租借地と国際地役(三) [Leased Territory and International Servitude (3)], *Kokusaihō Gaikō Zasshi* 国際法外交雑誌, vol. 32, no. 4 (1933): 54–61; Ueda, *supra* note 2, 140–158.

4 Louis Gérard, *Des cessions déguisées de territoires en droit international public* (Paris: Librairie de la Société du Recueil général des lois et des arrêts, 1904); Jean Perrinjaquet, *Des cessions temporaires de territoires* (Paris: V. Giard & F. Brière, 1904); Min-ch'ien T. Z. Tyau, *The Legal Obligations Arising out of Treaty Relations between China and Other States* (Shanghai: Commercial Press, 1917); Hersch Lauterpacht, *Private Law Sources and Analogies of International Law: With Special Reference to International Arbitration* (New York: Longmans, Green, 1927); Westel W. Willoughby, *Foreign Rights and Interests in China* [2nd ed.] vol. I (Baltimore: Johns Hopkins Press, 1927); Léon Yang (Yang Lieou-Fong), *Les Territoires à bail en Chine: Etude d'histoire diplomatique et de Droit International* (Paris: Presses universitaires de France, 1929); Young, *supra* note 2; Marc Alfonsi, *Les Cessions à Bail en Chine: Histoire diplomatique et de droit international public* (Paris: Domat-Montchrestien, 1940); Ueda, *supra* note 2. See also footnote 18. The discussion in Japan is as indicated in this chapter.

5 Michael J. Strauss, *The Leasing of Guantanamo Bay* (Santa Barbara: Praeger Security International, 2009); Strauss, *The Viability of Territorial Leases in Resolving International Sovereignty Disputes* (Paris: L'Harmattan, 2010); Strauss, *supra* note 2. Post-World War

Yet, that only applies in terms of general analyses from a legal and institutional point of view. Various specific case studies of leaseholds have been conducted, and they have raised some important points for understanding the concept of leaseholds in general. For example, with regard to the leasehold of Kiaochow Bay, Asada Shinji pointed out that the German side did not have a clear understanding of the concept of leaseholds before negotiating the treaty and devised a leasehold to be applied to China during the negotiations process. Also, he argued that Germany and the Qing Government concluded the treaty without a shared understanding of what a leasehold entailed.[6] The discussions in this chapter are premised upon this point on the fluidity of the concept of leaseholds at the end of the 19th century. However, rather than engaging in deeper analysis of the actual circumstances of leaseholds and specific diplomatic negotiations, this chapter aims to examine the concept of leaseholds with a focus on the logic and perceptions concerning leaseholds.

Furthermore, on a related note, although not covered in this chapter, there has been a vast amount of research on concessions, an issue adjacent to leaseholds. Also, recently, there has been widespread global research on how international law and related concepts were accepted, applied, formed, or transformed as the Western and East Asian worlds came into contact, including discussions on territorial sovereignty and perpetual lease rights, which are related to leaseholds.[7]

On the understanding of the concept of leaseholds in modern Japan, which is the main topic of this chapter, there is a pertinent article by Asada Shinji.[8] According to Asada's research, Japanese international law scholars argued that leaseholds were different from cession prior to the Russo-Japanese War, i.e.,

---

II research: Joseph Lazar, "The Status of the Leasehold in International Law" (Ph.D. diss., University of Minnesota, 1965).

6 Asada Shinji 浅田進史, *Doitsu Tōchika no Chintao Keizaiteki – Jiyū Shugi to Shokuminchi Shakai Chitsujo* ドイツ統治下の青島—経済的自由主義と植民地社会秩序 [Qingdao under German Rule: Economic Liberalism and the Colonial Social Order] (Tokyo: University of Tokyo Press, 2011), 42–62.

7 Douglas Howland, "The Japan House Tax Case, 1899–1905: Leases in Perpetuity and the Myth of International Equality," *Zeitschrift für ausländisches öffentliches Recht und Völkerrecht*, vol. 75, no. 2 (2015); Howland, *International Law and Japanese Sovereignty: The Emerging Global Order in the 19th Century* (Basingstoke: Palgrave Macmillan, 2016); Howland, "The Territorial Foundations of the Sovereign State in East Asia," *The Journal of Transcultural Studies*, vol. 9, no. 1–2 (2018).

8 Asada Shinji, "Colonizing Kiaochow Bay: From the Perspective of German-Japanese Relations," in *Japan and Germany: Two Latecomers to the World Stage, 1890–1945, Volume I, A Chance Encounter in East Asia*, Kudō Akira, Tajima Nobuo, and Erich Pauer (eds.) (Folkestone: Global Oriental, 2009).

from the time when Russia leased Lüshun [Ryojun in Japanese pronunciation, also known as Port Arthur] and Dalian [Dairen in Japanese pronunciation, may also be spelled Talien] and Japan did not have any leaseholds in China. However, after the Russo-Japanese War, when Japan came to hold the leasehold for Lüshun and Dalian, Japanese scholars began to argue that leaseholds were equivalent to cession using European theories. In other words, Japanese international law scholars interpreted the concept of leaseholds in a way that was advantageous to Japan's foreign expansion according to the situation at the time. Asada cited Ariga Nagao, Takahashi Sakue, Ninagawa Arata, and Egi Tasuku as specific examples of such scholars.

However, such explanations of Japanese theoretical trends on leaseholds seem to be at odds with contemporaneous accounts. Minobe Tatsukichi stated the following in 1912.

> As for the nature of leaseholds, many European scholars seem to consider them to be definite territory. In their interpretation, these may be leaseholds in name but the ceding of territory in reality. This was also reflected in official systems. For example, Germany's leasehold of Kiaochow Bay was treated as a so-called protectorate, exactly the same as other colonies, that is to say like a true territorial land. Contrary to this, in Japan, it has long been the prevailing theory to consider leased territories as being foreign land, and the official system also distinguishes the Kwantung leased territory from other colonies, treating it as foreign land.[9]

Kikuchi Komaji, who viewed leaseholds as being equivalent to cession, wrote in a 1923 article that the theory that "a leasehold treaty essentially promises the cession of territorial land, and is nothing more than a method of acquiring territorial rights" was the prevailing theory in European countries, but was only a minority one in Japan.[10] In a later paper, Kikuchi indicated a similar interpretation, naming about 30 scholars inside and outside Japan.[11]

---

9 Minobe Tatsukichi 美濃部達吉, "Nihon Shokuminchihō ni Tsuite" 日本殖民地法に就て [On Japanese colonial law], *Kokka Gakkai Zasshi* 国家学会雑誌, vol. 26, no. 1 (1912): 104.

10 Kikuchi Komaji 菊地駒次, "Soshakuchi no Hōritsu Kankei o Ronzu" 租借地の法律関係を論ず [Discussion of the Legal Relationship of Leased Territory], *Hōgaku Kyōkai Zasshi* 法学協会雑誌, vol. 41, no. 10 (1923): 3–4.

11 Kikuchi Komaji 菊地駒次, "Soshakuchi no Hōri o Ronzu" 租借地の法理を論ず [Discussion of the Legal Principles of Leased Territory], *Gaikō Jihō* 外交時報, no. 677 (1933): 59–62.

Yet, further examination suggests that it is not easy to conclude that non-cession was the predominant theory in Japan. This chapter reexamines the state of Japanese theory up to around the time of World War I.

Below is an overview of the basic facts concerning leaseholds in China and world trends in the theory on the nature of leaseholds, followed by an examination of modern Japan's understanding of the concept of leaseholds.

2 Leaseholds in China

After the Sino-Japanese War of 1894–95, European powers began to advance into China in earnest as a result of the decline of the international reputation of the Qing Dynasty, the Triple Intervention by Russia, France, and Germany, and the Qing Dynasty's need to raise funds to pay a large indemnity to Japan. Under such circumstances, in November 1897, Germany occupied Kiaochow Bay of Shandong Peninsula using the murder of German missionaries in China as a pretext and, after negotiations, concluded the Kiaochow Bay lease treaty with the Qing Government in March 1898. These moves prompted the European powers and Japan to advance into China in a variety of ways, including territorial leasing, acquiring various rights and interests, and demanding that China not cede its territory to other countries. This was the so-called partition of China.

As part of this, leaseholds for Chinese territory were concluded. Russia leased Lüshun and Dalian, Britain leased Weihaiwei and the Kowloon region, and France leased Guangzhou Bay. The leasehold terms were 99 years for Kiaochow Bay, the Kowloon region, and Guangzhou Bay, and 25 years for Lüshun and Dalian. The term for Weihaiwei was to be the duration for which Lüshun was leased to Russia. In terms of sovereignty, in principle, under the relevant treaties, China was considered to have sovereignty over the leased territories. However, Germany tried to treat the Kiaochow Bay leased territory in the same way as its other colonies. There were various differences in the provisions of each treaty.[12] Moreover, the meaning of the treaties was often not clear, and there were often discrepancies between the wording of a treaty and

12 For an overview of the systemic status of each leased territory, see Kawashima Shin 川島真, "Ryōiki to Kioku – Sokai, Soshakuchi, Seiryoku Han-i o Meguru Gensetsu to Seido" 領域と記憶—租界・租借地・勢力範囲をめぐる言説と制度 [Territory and Memory: Discourses and Institutions Concerning Concessions, Leased Territories, and Spheres of Influence], in *Mosakusuru Kindai Nicchū Kankei – Taiwa to Kyōzon no Jidai* 模索する近代日中関係—対話と競存の時代 [Dialogue and Competitive Cooperation in Modern Japan–China Relations], Kishi Toshihiko, Tanigaki Mariko, and Fukamachi

the reality.[13] As mentioned above, the actual circumstances of the leaseholds were complex and varied.

With regard to Lüshun and Dalian, a lease treaty was concluded between Russia and China in March 1898, and a subsequent agreement was concluded in April 1898. As an outcome of the Russo-Japanese War, Russia transferred the leasehold rights of Lüshun and Dalian to Japan under the peace treaty (Treaty of Portsmouth) of September 1905. Article V of the Treaty states, "The Imperial Russian Government transfer and assign to the Imperial Government of Japan, with the consent of the Government of China, the lease of Port Arthur, Talien and adjacent territory and territorial waters and all rights, privileges and concessions connected with or forming part of such lease ... The two High Contracting Parties mutually engage to obtain the consent of the Chinese Government mentioned in the foregoing stipulation."[14] In December of the same year, Japan and the Qing Government concluded a treaty concerning Manchuria, in which Qing agreed to the transfer of the leasehold and other rights from Russia to Japan.[15] The various issues surrounding the Japanese leased territory of Lüshun and Dalian (the Kwantung leased territory) and Japanese diplomacy will be discussed in Section 4.4.2.

3 World Theory on the Nature of Leaseholds

As mentioned above and as will be shown later, with regard to the theoretical situation in the world on leaseholds, the disguised cession theory was recognized in Japan as being the globally predominant one from the end of the 19th century to around the time of World War I. Examples of frequently cited

---

Hideo (eds.) (Tokyo: University of Tokyo Press, 2009), 168–169. For more details, see Ueda, *supra* note 2.

13 With regard to the leased territory of Lüshun and Dalian, which Japan came to hold after the Russo-Japanese War, an issue arose as to what they would be based on, the wording of the original treaties concluded between Russia and Qing China, or the actual situation during Russia's leasehold period, which was tacitly accepted by Qing China. See *Kantō Totoku no Meishō Sonota ni Kanshi Shinkoku Seifu Yori Kōgi Ikken* 関東都督の名称其他に関し清国政府より抗議一件 [A protest from the Qing Government regarding the name of the Governor-General of Kwantung and other matters] (JACAR: B15100712100).

14 Ministry of Foreign Affairs of Japan (ed.), *Nihon Gaikō Bunsho: Nichiro Sensō V*『日本外交文書』日露戦争V [Documents on Japanese Foreign Policy: Russo-Japan War V], (Tokyo: UN Association of Japan, 1960), 536.

15 Ministry of Foreign Affairs of Japan (ed.), *Nihon Gaikō Bunsho* 日本外交文書 [Documents on Japanese Foreign Policy], vol. 38, no. 1 (Tokyo: UN Association of Japan, 1958), 156.

proponents of the disguised cession theory were John Westlake and Thomas Joseph Lawrence.

Westlake referred to and endorsed Frantz Despagnet's view that the possibility of restoration of territory at the end of a lease was so small that leases in effect constituted cession. ("We must then agree with Despagnet who, after remarking that the restoration of the territory at the end of the specified term is very unlikely, says that these pretended leases are alienations disguised in order to spare the susceptibility of the state at whose cost they are made.")[16]

Lawrence also considered a lease to be a de facto cession and argued that the wording on reservation of sovereignty in a lease treaty disguised the reality of the territorial transfer. ("It amounts, in fact, to a cession of the leased territory for a limited time, and with a strong probability that the period mentioned in the lease will be prolonged indefinitely if the lessee-state finds it convenient to stay on. … The words which reserve the sovereignty of the lessor are fine phrases used for the purpose of disguising the reality of territorial transfer.")[17]

Kikuchi Komaji and Ueda Toshio cited many other famed scholars as proponents of this theory as well.[18] For a certain period of time from the end of the 19th century, the theory of disguised cession was certainly a popular one in the West.

In discussing such theory trends, Lassa Oppenheim is sometimes cited as evidence that the disguised cession theory was widely advocated.[19] Yet, his arguments on leaseholds differ depending on the time period.

In the first edition of *International Law: A Treatise, Vol. 1, Peace* (1905), Oppenheim referred to leaseholds as a form of cession and also stated that "Cession may also take place under the disguise of an agreement according to which territory comes under the 'administration' of a foreign State."[20] These

16 John Westlake, *International Law, Part 1, Peace* (Cambridge: Cambridge University Press, 1904), 136.

17 T. J. Lawrence, *War and Neutrality in the Far East* [2nd ed.] (New York: Macmillan, 1904), 272–273.

18 In addition to Westlake and Lawrence, Kikuchi and Ueda also cite the following as examples of proponents of the disguised cession theory, Kikuchi, *supra* note 11, 59–61 and Ueda, *supra* note 2, 164–167, 185–186: Lassa Oppenheim, Franz von Liszt, Karl Gareis, Karl Freiherr von Stengel, Alphonse Rivier, Paul Fauchille, Frantz Despagnet, Louis Gérard, Albert de Pouvourville, Jean Perrinjaquet, Coleman Phillipson, Pitt Cobbett, Earl of Birkenhead, James Leslie Brierly, Amos Shartle Hershey, Sterling Edwin Edmunds, Ellery Cory Stowell, Jan de Louter.

19 Teemu Ruskola, *Legal Orientalism: China, the United States, and Modern Law* (Cambridge: Harvard University Press, 2013), 288; Strauss, *supra* note 2, 90.

20 L. Oppenheim, *International Law: A Treatise, vol. 1, Peace* (New York: Longmans, Green, 1905), 271.

explanations remained basically unchanged in its second edition (1912) as well.[21] In the first edition, Oppenheim briefly argued that leaseholds were in effect a cession of territory. ("All these cases contain practically, although not theoretically, cession of pieces of territory, and the same statements are valid regarding them as regarding the forementioned cases of foreign administration.")[22] These arguments can be seen as the disguised cession theory.

However, an explanation of the nature of leaseholds was added in the second edition, stating that

> All such cases comprise, for all practical purposes, cessions of pieces of territory, but in strict law they remain the property of the leasing State. And such property is not a mere fiction, as some writers maintain, for it is possible that the lease comes to an end by expiration of time or by rescission. Thus the lease, granted in 1894 by Great Britain to the former Congo Free State, of the so-called Lado Enclave, was rescinded in 1906. However this may be, as long as the lease has not expired it is the lease-holder who exercises sovereignty over the territory concerned.[23]

This is an argument along the lines of the non-cession theory. The point that the lessee State exercises sovereignty over the territory concerned during the term of the lease is not denied even under the non-cession theory. There is a large difference in Oppenheim's explanation of the nature of leaseholds between the first and second editions.

A significant factor in this change in explanation was the example of the rescinding of the British-Congo lease. The impact of actual developments in international politics surrounding leaseholds on the theory is, as will be shown below, important when considering Japan's understanding of the concept of leaseholds.

---

21 L. Oppenheim, *International Law: A Treatise, vol. 1, Peace* [2nd ed.] (New York: Longmans, Green, 1912), 288.

22 Oppenheim, *supra* note 20, 221.

23 Oppenheim, *supra* note 21, 233–234.

4 Modern Japan's Understanding of the Concept of Leaseholds

4.1 *Disguised Cession Theory*

4.1.1 Takahashi Sakue

To begin, one Japanese proponent of the disguised cession theory was Takahashi Sakue (1867–1920). After graduating from Imperial University, Takahashi worked as a naval professor and served in the Sino-Japanese War of 1894–95. Later, he studied abroad and then became a professor of public international law at Tokyo Imperial University. From 1914 to 1916, he served as Director-General of the Cabinet Legislation Bureau in the second Ōkuma Shigenobu Cabinet.[24] He was the author of numerous books on international law. As seen in publications such as *Cases on International Law During the Chino-Japanese War* (Cambridge University Press, 1899), he took on the role of justifying Japan's positions and actions, and conveying to the world that Japan was a nation that abided by international law.

As is clear from his career as described above, Takahashi was one of Japan's leading international law scholars at the time and often served in government positions. He presented the disguised cession theory as the predominant global theory. After Japan's capture of Lüshun during the Russo-Japanese War, Takahashi wrote the following.

> The legal nature of the leased territories of Lüshun, Dalian, Kiaochow Bay, Weihaiwei, and Guangzhou Bay has been a novel question in international law, but there is now mostly agreement among European scholars.
>
> … The gist of the conclusion reached in the debate among prominent European scholars is extremely simple.

24 For biographical information on each person below, unless otherwise noted, see Hata Ikuhiko 秦郁彦 (ed.), *Nihon Kingendai Jinbutsu Rireki Jiten (Dai 2 Han)* 日本近現代人物履歴事典〔第2版〕 [Biographical Dictionary of Leaders of Modern Japan [2nd ed.]] (Tokyo: University of Tokyo Press, 2013). The following works discuss the field of international law and its scholars in Japan during the Meiji and Taisho periods and mention many of the figures discussed in this chapter. Ichimata Masao 一又正雄, Nihon no Kokusaihōgaku o Kizuita Hitobito 日本の国際法学を築いた人々 [The People Who Built the Study of International Law in Japan] (Japan Institute of International Affairs, 1973); and Yi Ping 易平, *Sensō to Heiwa no Aida – Hossokuki Nihon Kokusaihōgaku ni Okeru 'Tadashii Sensō' no Gainen to Sono Kiketsu* 戦争と平和の間—発足期日本国際法学における「正しい戦争」の観念とその帰結 [Between War and Peace: The 'Just War' Concept and its Consequences During the Early Period of International Law Research in Japan] (Beijing: Torkel Opsahl Academic EPublisher, 2013).

> Sovereignty over the leased territory is reserved by the lessor State, but this is only a diplomatic gesture. A leasehold is cession with a term, and that term is perpetual. Therefore, leased territory can be considered to be the territory of the lessee State. Accordingly, territories leased by Russia such as Lüshun and Dalian can be considered to be Russian land.[25]

At a later time, Takahashi also argued that "According to scholarly theories, leased territory is a form of cession. Of course, there are some contrary theories. However, the world's leading scholars of international law today, such as Westlake, Lawrence, Despagnet, Gérard, and de Pouvourville, are in agreement on the following points. … Under international law, leased territory is not truly leased land, but rather equivalent to territory."[26] Takahashi's argument was that leaseholds were in fact cessions, and that Lüshun and Dalian were ceded from China to Russia and then to Japan.[27]

Kikuchi Komaji stated that the abovementioned article, which Takahashi published during the Russo-Japanese War, only introduced European theories and that Takahashi's own position on the nature of the leaseholds was unclear.[28] However, that is not true. Takahashi advocated the disguised cession theory and was recognized as doing so at the time.[29]

25 Takahashi Sakue 高橋作衛, "Soshakuchi no Seishitsu o Ronjite Ryojun Kanraku no Kōka ni Oyobu" 租借地の性質を論して旅順陥落の効果に及ぶ [The Nature of the Leased Territory and the Effects of the Fall of Lüshun], *Kokka Gakkai Zasshi* 国家学会雑誌, vol. 19, no. 3 (1905): 32–33.

26 Takahashi Sakue 高橋作衛, "Shinkoku Dōran o Ronjite Manshū Soshakuchi wa Ryōdo Hozen no Kengai Naru Koto ni Ronkyūsu" 清国動乱を論じて満洲租借地は領土保全の圏外なることに論及す [Discussion on the Upheaval in China Referencing that the Manchurian Leased Territory was Outside the Sphere of Territorial Integrity], *Zaikai* 財界, vol. 16, no. 6 (1912): 9.

27 In addition to the abovementioned paper, see Takahashi Sakue 高橋作衛, "Shinkoku Ryōdo Hozen no Igi o Kenkyūshite Kantō-shū Soshakuchi no Kokusaihōjō no Seishitsu ni Ronkyūsu" 清国領土保全の意義を研究して関東州租借地の国際法上の性質に論及す [Study on the Significance of the Territorial Integrity of China and Discussion of the Nature of the Kwantung Leased Territory under International Law], *Kokusaihō Zasshi* 国際法雑誌, vol. 10, no. 7 (1912); and Takahashi Sakue 高橋作衛, "Chintao Fukanpu Ron" 青島不還附論 [Non-return of Qingdao], *Tokyo Nichinichi Shimbun* 東京日日新聞 (May 2, 1919).

28 Kikuchi, *supra* note 10, 4; Kikuchi, *supra* note 11, 62.

29 As an example of Takahashi's view on the nature of leaseholds being positioned as falling under the cession theory, see Imai Yoshiyuki 今井嘉幸, *Shina Kokusaihō Ron Dai 1 Kan – Gaikoku Saibanken to Gaikoku Gyōsei Chiiki* 支那国際法論 第一巻—外国裁判権と外国行政地域 [The International Law of China, vol. 1: Foreign Jurisdiction and Foreign Administrative Regions] (Tokyo: Maruzen, 1915), 153.

4.1.2 Ninagawa Arata

The strongest proponent of the disguised cession theory in Japan was Ninagawa Arata (1873–1959). Ninagawa studied at Tokyo Imperial University and its graduate school, and served in the Russo-Japanese War as an international law advisor. After working in some governmental positions in Korea, he served as a professor at Doshisha University and Komazawa University, and was involved in various diplomatic, social, and ideological activities.

Ninagawa declared, before the Russo-Japanese War, that leaseholds were not equivalent to cession as follows.

> An example would be if State A had promised to lease land to State B for a period of 99 years and State A clearly reserved the territorial sovereignty over the leased territory in the text of the treaty. If, despite this, State B were to say, 'State A's territorial sovereignty is in name only, and our real intention is cession of the territory,' there would clearly be an error in the elements of the legal act and the treaty would therefore inevitably be invalid from a legal standpoint. Thus, there is no reason why a leasehold would simply change in nature and become a cession. It is strange that some advocate such a theory. To interpret a leasehold as a cession of territory is either a politically-motivated or nonsensical theory.[30]

However, Ninagawa reversed his argument after the Russo-Japanese War and came to advocate the theory of treating leaseholds like cessions, with statements such as, "The teachings of public law scholars [in Europe and the United States with regard to leaseholds] are in the same way, that is, leasehold is a new system which has the same effect as ceding territory," and "If we study the texts of the treaties and the actual measures taken with regard to the Kwantung leased territory and interpret it from a legal standpoint, it is appropriate to assert that the leased territory was part of Russian territory, not Qing territory."[31] Ninagawa is a good example of the kind of scholar, like those pointed out in Asada Shinji's research, who interpreted the concept of leaseholds in a way that was advantageous to Japan's foreign expansion according to the circumstances of the time.

30 Ninagawa Arata 蜷川新, "Soshakuchijō no Kenri to Manshū Mondai" 租借 cession à bail 地上の権利と満州問題 [Rights on Leased Territory and the Manchurian Question], *Gaikō Jihō* 外交時報, no. 66 (1903): 78.

31 Ninagawa Arata 蜷川新, *Minami Manshū ni Okeru Teikoku no Kenri* 南満洲に於ける帝国の権利 [Imperial Rights in South Manchuria] (Tokyo: Shimizu Shoten, 1913), 24, 55–56.

However, it must be noted that Ninagawa's statements belonged to the extreme end of the spectrum in Japanese academia at the time. In 1923, Ninagawa debated the nature of leaseholds with Kyoto Imperial University professor Yamamoto Miono (1874–1941) in the journal *Gaikō Jihō*. The following is a passage from Ninagawa's article.

> Ryodai (Lüshun and Dalian) was Russian territory. … It is a land where Japanese power will be exercised in perpetuity. In other words, according to legal theory, it is Japan's territory. The Japanese people must not allow anyone to consider this territory as the territory of another State through foolish arguments. The Japanese people are not Chinese. It is a matter of course that no scholar with a Japanese conscience should explain a round object as being square. I, of course, express this opinion with a Japanese conscience.[32]

Ninagawa was declaring that Lüshun and Dalian were Japanese territory, and that he would advocate that point because he was Japanese. It was rare for a scholar to make such an argument so publicly, even if, in their heart, they intended to support or justify the Japanese position.

4.1.3 Other Proponents

Another person who requires consideration is Matsubara Kazuo (1877–1956). Matsubara studied international law at Tokyo Imperial University and its graduate school, and lectured at some universities. He then entered the Ministry of Foreign Affairs and worked there for a long time, before retiring and returning

---

32 Ninagawa Arata 蜷川新, "Soshakuchi to Yo no Byūken" 租借地と世の謬見 [Leased Territory and People's Mistaken Views], *Gaikō Jihō* 外交時報, no. 445 (1923): 150–151. Furthermore, the following are Ninagawa and Yamamoto's articles (all from 1923). Ninagawa Arata 蜷川新, "Ryodai Mondai to Naigai no Byūron" 旅大問題と内外の謬論 [The Lüshun and Dalian Issue and Domestic and Foreign Mistaken Opinions], *Gaikō Jihō* 外交時報, no. 438; Yamamoto Miono 山本美越乃, "Nisshi Kyōyaku Haiki Mondai" 日支協約廃棄問題 [Issue of the Rescinding of the Japan–China Pact], *Gaikō Jihō* 外交時報, no. 443; Ninagawa Arata 蜷川新, "Soshakuchi to Yo no Byūken" 租借地と世の謬見 [Leased Territory and People's Mistaken Views], *Gaikō Jihō* 外交時報, no. 445; Yamamoto Miono 山本美越乃, "'Soshakuchi to Yo no Byūken' o Yomite" 『租借地と世の謬見』を読みて [Reading "Soshakuchi to Yo no Byūken"], *Gaikō Jihō* 外交時報, no. 450; Ninagawa Arata 蜷川新, "Soshakuchi to Yo no Byūron" 租借地と世の謬論 [Leased Territory and People's Mistaken Opinions], *Gaikō Jihō* 外交時報, no. 454.

to a life of scholarship. He published many scholarly works from his student days.[33]

Matsubara is characterized by his assertion, in his papers from before the Russo-Japanese War, that leaseholds are de facto cessation. He stated that "In leasehold occupation, sovereignty lies with the great powers, not Qing China. … Although Qing may appear to have sovereignty in the treaties, that is not actually the case. It is sovereignty and territory in name only. Scholars often refer to this as *nudum jus*. Sovereignty as *nudum jus* is different from what we know sovereignty to be. … All issues must be decided on the basis that sovereignty is held by the great powers and the leased territories are the great powers' territories." He also stated, "Leaseholds are only a form of cession. The lessee State exercises legislative, executive, and judicial power in the area and therefore has sovereignty. The texts of treaties contain euphemistic and contradictory phrasing merely in order to soothe public sentiments."[34] In his later writings, too, Matsubara's stance was that which would fall under the disguised cession theory.[35] Kikuchi Komaji regarded Matsubara as the leading scholar among the few proponents of the disguised cession theory in Japan.[36]

Yet, Matsubara also explained that Qing China held sovereignty in treaties and in name, and that the leased territories were still Chinese territories.[37] In addition, during the Russo-Japanese War, Matsubara argued that Japan could not succeed to the leasehold rights without Qing China's consent in the peace treaty with Russia, and that it would not be beneficial to take over the leasehold with various restrictions.[38] It appears that his argument on leaseholds was not always consistent as a whole. Moreover, he did not present a full-fledged theory on leaseholds after the Russo-Japanese War.

---

33 For Matsubara's biography, see Yokota Kisaburō 横田喜三郎, "Matsubara Hakase no Fu" 松原博士の訃 [News of Dr. Matsubara's Death], *Kokusaihō Gaikō Zasshi* 国際法外交雑誌, vol. 55, no. 1 (1956).

34 Matsubara Kazuo 松原一雄, "Heiji Senryō Ron Tokuni Soshakuchi no Hōritsu Kankei (Shōzen)" 平時占領論特に租借地の法律関係（承前） [Theory of Occupation in Peacetime, Especially the Legal Relations of Leased Territory (Continued)], *Kokka Gakkai Zasshi* 国家学会雑誌, no. 182 (1902): 53. Matsubara Kazuo 松原一雄, "Ryojunkō Hōken Mondai" 旅順口法権問題 [Issue of Legal Rights of Lüshunkou], *Hōgaku Shinpō* 法学新報, vol. 13, no. 2 (1903): 25–26.

35 Matsubara Kazuo 松原一雄, *Genkō Kokusaihō Jōkan Dai 2 Bunsatsu* 現行国際法 上巻 第二分冊 [Current International Law, vol. 1, Part 2] (Tokyo: Chūō Daigaku, 1924), 348–349.

36 Kikuchi, *supra* note 10, 4, 19–22; Kikuchi, *supra* note 11, 60, 74–77.

37 Matsubara, *supra* note 3, 125.

38 Matsubara Kazuo 松原一雄, "Soshakuchi no Shobun Ikan" 租借地の処分如何 [How to Dispose of Leased Territory], *Hōgaku Shinpō* 法学新報, vol. 14, no. 7 (1904): 28–29.

Another proponent was Fukuoka Hidei (1871–1932), a professor of international law at the Tokyo School of Foreign Languages who studied in the West. One paper, albeit not his own, presented a dialogue in which Fukuoka gave an explanation of leaseholds that would fall under the disguised cession theory.[39] Tomizu Hirondo (1861–1935), a professor at Tokyo Imperial University known for his hardline views on foreign affairs, argued during the Russo-Japanese War that the 25-year term attached to the leasehold of Lüshun and Dalian by Russia was an empty statement, and that the leasehold was actually for an indefinite period. He claimed that Japan should not lease the territory from China, but rather should take over the leasehold from Russia.[40] The bureaucrat and politician Egi Tasuku (1873–1932) argued, "I believe that even though the Constitution of the Empire of Japan does not apply to the leased territory, it is Japanese territory where Japanese sovereignty is fully implemented."[41] Imai Yoshiyuki (1878–1951) studied at Tokyo Imperial University and its graduate school, became a judge, and was invited by Qing to teach at the Beiyang School of Law and Politics for several years. He wrote in his 1915 book that even if a leasehold initially meant a lease according to the wording of the treaty, the meaning of the treaty text was flexible according to subsequent practices and acquiescence. He argued, "It seems to be a reasonable view that the meaning of a leasehold has now changed from its original one to one meaning the abandonment of the territory of China."[42]

Furthermore, although it is not in the period up until World War I, which is the subject of this chapter's study, Kikuchi Komaji (1878–1935) was a proponent of the disguised cession theory in the 1920s and 1930s.[43] Kikuchi graduated from Tokyo Imperial University and worked at the Cabinet Legislation

---

39 Kei Nansei 景楠生, "Soshaku no Enkaku Oyobi Sono Kokusaihōjō no Seishitsu (Fukuoka Hidei-shi Kobanashi)" 租借(Lease)の沿革及其国際法上の性質《福岡秀猪氏小話》 [The Nature of Leasehold in International Law (A Small Talk of Fukuoka Hidei)], *Hōkō* 奉公, no. 13 (1904).

40 Tomizu Hirondo 戸水寛人, "Ryodai no Soshakuken" 旅大の租借権 [Lüshun and Dalian Leasehold Rights], *Gaikō Jihō* 外交時報, no. 93 (1905).

41 Egi Tasuku 江木翼, "Doitsu Teikoku Hogoryō Taru Kōshūwanryō Seido no Ichi Ni o Toki Waga Kantō-shū ni Oyobu" 独逸帝国保護領たる膠洲湾領制度の一二を説き我か関東州に及ふ [The System of Kiaochow Bay as a Protectorate of the German Empire and Japan's Kwantung], *Kokka Gakkai Zasshi* 国家学会雑誌, vol. 20, no. 12 (1906): 99; See also Egi Tasuku 江木翼, *Kōshūwan Ron* 膠州湾論 [Theory of Kiaochow Bay] (Yomiuri Shimbunsha, 1907), 40–44.

42 Imai, *supra* note 29, 152–153.

43 Kikuchi, *supra* note 10; Kikuchi Komaji 菊地駒次, "Soshakuchi no Hōri o Ronzu" 租借地の法理を論ず [Discussion of the Legal Principles of Leased Territory], *Kokusaihō Gaikō Zasshi* 国際法外交雑誌, vol. 29, no. 4 (1930); Kikuchi, *supra* note 11.

Bureau and the Ministry of Foreign Affairs. After leaving governmental posts, he worked as a lecturer at Tohoku Imperial University and Senshu University.[44] As mentioned above, Kikuchi developed his argument from the standpoint of the disguised cession theory, based on the premise that the Japanese majority theory was the non-cession theory. Ueda Toshio's *Shina Soshakuchi Ron* (The theory of leaseholds of China), the preeminent study on leaseholds in Japan, takes up Kikuchi's argument in detail as a major target of criticism.

4.2 *Non-cession Theory*

4.2.1 Shinoda Jisaku

The first scholar on the non-cession theory side is Shinoda Jisaku (1872–1946). After graduating from Tokyo Imperial University, Shinoda became a lawyer and served in the Russo-Japanese War as an international law advisor. After the Russo-Japanese War, he was involved in the administration of Korea during the period when it was a Protectorate and under Japanese rule. His works include *Nichiro Sen'eki Kokusai Kōhō* (Public international law in the Russo-Japanese War) (Hōsei Daigaku, 1911).

As can be seen from his career, Shinoda was basically a practitioner, but he was also a member of the Japanese international law academic community in a broad sense.[45] He was the first to propose a full-fledged non-cession theory with regard to leaseholds.[45] In 1906, he wrote, "In the previous issue of this journal [*Kokusaihō Zasshi*], an anonymous author asserted in 'The New Theory of Leased Territory' that it is the general theory of European public law scholars that leaseholds are a means of cession. However, in my view, this assertion is still not correct from the standpoint of legal theory." His analysis was as follows.

---

44 For a biography of Kikuchi, see the chronology included in Kikuchi Komaji 菊地駒次, *Kōhō Kenteki* 公法涓滴 [A Little Book on Public Law] (Tokyo: Nihon Gaikō Kyōkai, 1935).

45 In 1902, Shinoda joined the Japanese Society of International Law, which was founded in 1897. At that time, there were over 70 members in Tokyo. Incidentally, another member who joined at the same time as Shinoda was Ninagawa Arata ("Kaihō" 会報 [Bulletin], *Kokusaihō Zasshi* 国際法雑誌, vol. 1, no. 1 (1902): 79–80, 85–87).

Yi, *supra* note 24, 12, as "international law scholars in the broad sense of the term," refers to bureaucrats who gave lectures on international law while working for government agencies, military officers who became engaged in international law research through the Sino-Japanese and Russo-Japanese Wars, diplomats who wrote books on international law based on their experience participating in international conferences, and graduate students who published essays in international law journals. These include Shinoda, Ninagawa, Matsubara Kazuo, Akiyama Masanosuke, and Endō Genroku, all of whom have been mentioned in this chapter.

> These views [that treat leaseholds and cession the same way] are a kind of prejudice that has arisen from the following reasons: (1) The fact that the strong European nations have not been able to shed the unequal style of thinking that constantly ignores justice for other, weaker nations, similar to the old idea prior to the Sino-Japanese War that international law discussed among European scholars was applied only among Western civilized nations, or only among Christian nations; (2) The leasehold is a relatively new concept in international relations, and those leases that have a term of validity have yet to expire, so it is unclear what stances the States involved in the leasehold and third States will take when said term does expire; (3) Because strong European nations have their leased territories, many scholars are merely attempting to interpret leaseholds in a way that is convenient for their own States.[46]

This passage suggests that the way in which the concept of leaseholds was viewed changed and settled according to diplomatic and international political situations. Shinoda also stated, "As a political argument, it may, in a sense, be correct to assert that a leasehold is in fact a cession of territory, but in legal theory, such an argument would fundamentally be incorrect. With regard to our Kwantung leased territory, it is the territory of the Qing Dynasty and the sovereignty of that land still resides with the Qing Dynasty. It is certainly not Japanese territory."[47]

4.2.2 Other International Law Scholars and Practitioners

Other international law scholars and practitioners who took the view that leaseholds were not equivalent to cession included, for example, Akiyama Masanosuke (1866–1937). Akiyama graduated from Imperial University, joined the Ministry of Foreign Affairs, and gave lectures on international law at several schools.[48] On the nature of leased territory, he argued that this was a type of

---

46 Shinoda, *supra* note 3, 13–14.

47 Shinoda Jisaku 篠田治策, "Soshakuken no Seishitsu to Kantōshū no Soshakuchi (Shōzen)" 租借権の性質と関東州の租借地（承前） [The Nature of Leasehold Rights and the Kwantung Leased Territory (Continued)], *Kokusaihō Zasshi* 国際法雑誌, vol. 5, no. 3 (1906): 36–37.

48 There are many transcripts of his lectures, as well as books based thereon, including Akiyama Masanosuke 秋山雅之介, *Kokusai Kōhō* 国際公法 [Public International Law] (Tokyo: Tokyo Senmon Gakkō, 1893); Akiyama Masanosuke 秋山雅之介, *Kokusai Kōhō Kōgi Heiji* 国際公法講義平時 [Lectures on Public International Law in Peacetime] (Tokyo: Meiji Hōritsu Gakkō Shuppanbu Kōhokai, 1900); Akiyama Masanosuke 秋山雅之介, *Kokusai Kōhō Heiji* 国際公法 平時 [Public International Law in Peacetime] (Tokyo: Wafutsu Hōritsu Gakkō, 1902); Akiyama Masanosuke 秋山雅之介, *Kokusai Kōhō*

international servitude, and that "As long as there is no change in the content between the State parties, the land belongs to the territory of the lessor State, and the scope of sovereignty exercised by the lessee State must be interpreted in accordance with the legal theory of international servitude."[49]

The view of Endō Genroku (1872–1971) was similar to Akiyama's one. After graduating from Tokyo Imperial University, Endō went on to graduate school and joined the Ministry of the Navy, where he was in charge of tasks related to maritime capture during the Russo-Japanese War. After the Russo-Japanese War, he lectured on international law at Meiji University and published several works on international law.[50] He concluded that a leasehold was neither a cession nor a mandate, but a new system under international law as a kind of international servitude. He pointed out, "European scholars still argue today that it is nothing but a cession of territory. This is not a legal theory, but instead a political argument that is intended to lay the groundwork for the future protection of the rights of their own States."[51]

Among the few professional international law scholars of the time in Japan, Nakamura Shingo (1870–1939), a professor at Gakushuin and other schools, argued that a leasehold was not a cession of sovereignty. While referring to "leasing" as a form of acquiring territory or territorial sovereignty from before the Russo-Japanese War, Nakamura stated, "Occupation and leasing are not a cession of sovereignty, but merely permission for the exercise of sovereignty, and therefore should not be mentioned here. But as a matter of convenience, I will discuss them here." He also stated, "These are not a cession of sovereignty, but merely an act of permitting a foreign State to exercise sovereignty. However, because the result of the occupation and leasing is often equivalent to the cession of sovereignty, I mention them here, even though it is theoretically unjustified."[52] In addition, Nakamura condemned unlawful occupation and the monopolization of military interests under the guise of leasing.[53] In

---

Senji 国際公法 戦時 [Public International Law in Wartime] (Tokyo: Wafutsu Hōritsu Gakkō, 1903).

49 Akiyama Masanosuke 秋山雅之介, "Soshakuchi no Seishitsu" 租借地の性質 [The Nature of Leased Territory], Hōgaku Shirin 法学志林, vol. 10, no. 2 (1908): 30–31.

50 For Endō's biography, see *Sūmitsuin Kōtōkan Rirekisho* 枢密院高等官履歴書 (JACAR: A06051185700).

51 Endō Genroku 遠藤源六, *Kokusaihō Yōron* 国際法要論 [Elements of International Law] (Tokyo: Shimizu Shoten, 1908), 232–236.

52 Nakamura Shingo 中村進午, *Heiji Kokusaihō* 平時国際法 [International Law in Peacetime] (Tokyo: Tokyo Hōgakuin, 1902), 53; Nakamura Shingo 中村進午, *Heiji Kokusai Kōhō* 平時国際公法 [Public International Law in Peacetime] (Tokyo: Tokyo Senmon Gakkō Shuppanbu, 1902), 50.

53 Nakamura, *supra* note 3.

later years, he declared, "Scholars may say that a leasehold is in fact a cession of territory (Lawrence; Liszt, etc.), but it is quite clear from the texts of lease treaties that this theory is completely wrong."[54]

Senga Tsurutarō (1857–1929), a professor at Kyoto Imperial University, also rejected the view that leaseholds were the same as acquiring territory. He stated, for example, "Although Kiaochow Bay is almost the same as German territory, we should not confuse the leasehold with the acquisition of territory in legal theory. In addition, with regard to the reality, too, one cannot say that there is no distinction at all between the two."[55]

Yamada Saburō (1869–1965), a private international law scholar and professor at Tokyo Imperial University, also stated, "A leasehold differs from the cession of territory, in which the entire sovereignty is transferred. The lessor State retains territorial rights in its name. Thus, it cannot be said that the leased territory is purely the territory of the lessee State either under international law or national law." He wrote that European theories such as "leased territory is actually ceded territory" and "leaseholds are disguised cession" are "still premature dogma under current international law."[56]

As a proponent of the non-cession theory, Kikuchi Komaji also mentioned Tachi Sakutarō (1874–1943), a leading international law scholar in modern Japan.[57] Indeed, in Tachi's *Heiji Kokusaihō Ron* (International law theory in peacetime), which was published in 1930, for example, in the section on "International Servitude," he wrote, "State power exercised over leased territory … is that which allows the lessee State to use the leased territory in the exercise of its own inherent State power within the area of the leased territory, in accordance with the lease treaty." He also wrote, "If I set aside the theory advocated by some scholars that a leasehold is in effect a cession." However, in the following section on "leased territory," Tachi does not directly deny the disguised cession theory like other non-cession theory proponents.[58] In addition, before

54 Nakamura Shingo 中村進午, *Kokusai Kōhō Ron* 国際公法論 [Theory of Public International Law] (Tokyo: Shimizu Shoten, 1916), 101.

55 Senga Tsurutarō 千賀鶴太郎, *Kokusai Kōhō Yōgi* 国際公法要義 [Fundamentals of Public International Law] (Kyoto: Kyōto Hōsei Daigaku, 1909), 295–296; See also Senga Tsurutarō 千賀鶴太郎, *Kokusai Kōhō* 国際公法 [Public International Law] (Tokyo: Kōhōkai, Shimizu Shoten, 1917), 84.

56 Yamada Saburō 山田三良, "Shokuminchihō to Naichihō to no Kankei ni Tsuite" 殖民地法と内地法との関係に就て [On the Relationship between the Colonial Law and the Mainland Law], *Hōgaku Kyōkai Zasshi* 法学協会雑誌, vol. 30, no. 2 (1912): 108.

57 Kikuchi, *supra* note 10, 3; Kikuchi, *supra* note 11, 60–61.

58 Tachi Sakutarō 立作太郎, *Heiji Kokusaihō Ron* 平時国際法論 [Theory of International Law in Peacetime] (Tokyo: Nihon Hyōronsha, 1930), 321–328.

theoretical trends started to shift around the world, namely up to the time of World War I, there seems to be no explicit statement of Tachi's view regarding the nature of the leaseholds. We can only find a related passage in his lecture transcript, stating that "It can be said that Lüshun and Dalian are territories under Japan's domestic law, but they are not territories in the strict sense of international law."[59]

4.2.3 Scholars of Domestic Japanese Law

After the Russo-Japanese War, constitutional and administrative law scholars in Japan developed the argument that leaseholds were different from cessions partly due to the fact that in the case of Japan, leased territory and true territory were apparently distinguished in its legal system. At an early stage, Shimizu Tōru (1868–1947) argued as follows.

> It is incorrect to interpret the establishment of a leasehold via a treaty as a cession of territory. Therefore, I am convinced that it is not appropriate for the German Empire to have declared a leasehold as a protectorate.
>
> In addition, among international law scholars, Liszt and Lawrence recognize leasehold rights as territorial rights, but if the leased territory were indeed part of the territory of the State leasing it, treaties between the State permitting the leasehold and other States would no longer be valid with respect to the leased territory, and instead, treaties between the State leasing the territory and other States would be applied. Furthermore, this would mean that if the State leasing the land were to transfer it to another State, the consent of the State permitting the leasehold would not be required. However, this differs from actual precedent. Therefore, the interpretation that regards leased land as part of true territory cannot be recognized under international law.[60]

Minobe Tatsukichi (1873–1948), as already mentioned, stated that most European scholars regarded leased territory as the true territory of the lessee State, but in Japan, it was common practice to regard it as foreign land and the official system also treated it as such. He then argued that it was not appropriate to regard leased territory as either true territory or foreign land. His view

---

59 Tachi Sakutarō 立作太郎, *Heiji Kokusai Kōhō* 平時国際公法 [Public International Law in Peacetime] (Tokyo: Chūō Daigaku, 1914), 64.

60 Shimizu Tōru 清水澄, "Waga Kenpō wa Soshakuchi ni Okonawaruru Ya Ina" 我憲法は租借地に行はるるや否 [Whether Our Constitution Applies to Leased Territory], *Nihon Hōsei Shinshi* 日本法政新誌, vol. 10, no. 8 (1906): 7–8.

was that, "It is not completely territory, but it should correspond to territory, that is to say it is quasi-territory. In the sense that it is an area where only Japan's sovereignty is fully and exclusively exercised, it is not different in any way from true territory."[61] Minobe emphasized the equivalence of leased territory and true territory in some aspects in such a way, but he clearly rejected the disguised cession theory.[62]

Other scholars such as Hozumi Yatsuka (1860–1912), Soejima Gi-ichi (1866–1947), and Ichimura Mitsue (1875–1928) all stated that a leasehold was different from cession and that leased territory was not the territory of the lessee State, although they differed in how they made their arguments.[63]

4.3 *Examination of Theory in Japan*

As shown above, after the Russo-Japanese War, the non-cession theory was predominant in Japan with regard to the nature of leaseholds. Yet, that is not to say that the overwhelming majority advocated the non-cession theory while only a few advocated the disguised cession theory. Takahashi Sakue was a proponent of the disguised cession theory, and a considerable number of others also advocated that theory.[64] Among prominent international law scholars, Tachi Sakutarō's view is, as mentioned above, not certain, and the same is true for Ariga Nagao (1860–1921). Although Ariga published numerous papers related to leaseholds, he mainly discussed what kind of response would be possible or beneficial for Japan from the viewpoint of international law, and did not discuss the general concept of leaseholds.[65]

61 Minobe, *supra* note 9, 104.

62 Minobe Tatsukichi 美濃部達吉, "Soshakuchi no Hōritsujō no Seishitsu" 租借地の法律上の性質 [The Legal Nature of Leased Territory], *Hōgaku Shinpō* 法学新報, vol. 25, no. 1 (1915); Minobe Tatsukichi 美濃部達吉, *Kenpō Satsuyō* 憲法撮要 [Compendium of the Constitution] (Tokyo: Yūhikaku, 1923), 137–142.

63 Hozumi Yatsuka 穂積八束, *Kenpō Teiyō Jōkan* 憲法提要 上巻 [Compendium of Constitution, vol. 1] (Tokyo: Yūhikaku, 1910), 323–324, 331; Ichimura Mitsue 市村光恵, *Teikoku Kenpō Ron* 帝国憲法論 [Theory of Imperial Constitution] (Tokyo: Yūhikaku, 1915), 248–250; Soejima Giichi 副島義一, *Nihon Teikoku Kenpō Yōron* 日本帝国憲法要論 [Compendium of the Imperial Japanese Constitution] (Tokyo: Ganshōdō Shoten, 1917), 233–234.

64 In addition to those already mentioned, examples of the disguised cession theory can be found in Hirose Kyūjirō (or Hisajirō) 広瀬久次郎, "Soshakuchi no Seishitsu o Ronzu" 租借地の性質を論ず [Discussion on the Nature of Leased Territory], *Gunji Keisatsu Zasshi* 軍事警察雑誌, nos. 4–7 (1908); Hirose Kyūjirō (or Hisajirō) 広瀬久次郎, "Soshaku no Kōka o Ronzu" 租借の効果を論ず [Discussion on the Effects of Leaseholds], Gunji Keisatsu Zasshi 軍事警察雑誌, nos. 8–9 (1908).

65 Ariga Nagao 有賀長雄, "Shinkoku ni Okeru Rekkoku Soshakuchi no Senji Kankei" 清国に於ける列国租借地の戦時関係 [Wartime Relations of the Leased Territories of

However, among professional international law scholars, it was only Takahashi Sakue, who clearly proposed the disguised cession theory, while the non-cession theory was at least advocated by Nakamura Shingo, Senga Tsurutarō, and Yamada Saburo. In the wider international law academic community, which included practitioners who studied or lectured on international law, there were leading advocates of the non-cession theory such as Shinoda Jisaku, Akiyama Masanosuke, and Endō Genroku. It seems to be true that the non-cession theory was more influential than the disguised cession theory as a trend in the international law academic community in Japan. Besides, because domestic legal scholars were basically proponents of the non-cession theory, if they are included, non-cession becomes the clearly predominant theory in Japan after the Russo-Japanese War. As for the time before the Russo-Japanese War, few scholars seriously discussed the issue of leaseholds, and it is difficult to find anything that can be called a trend concerning that issue in Japanese academic circles.

In Japan, after the Russo-Japanese War, the non-cession theory prevailed, albeit with a shared understanding that globally, the disguised cession theory was advocated as the prevailing theory on leaseholds. What did this discrepancy stem from? Firstly, it should be noted that there is no significant difference in the points that are considered under the disguised cession theory and the non-cession theory, nor even under the current explanation of the nature of leaseholds. An example is the explanation that the lessor State has sovereignty over the leased territory and a lease term exists based on the articles of the lease treaty. Under the non-cession theory, therefore, the leased territory is not the true territory of the lessee State, and a leasehold is not the same as cession. Meanwhile, the disguised cession theory does not ignore such points, but argues that sovereignty in name only has no substantive meaning, or that a leasehold is the same as a cession because the leased territory will probably not actually be returned when the lease expires.

China], *Gaikō Jihō* 外交時報, no. 30 (1900); Ariga Nagao 有賀長雄, "Shinkoku ni Okeru Rekkoku Soshakuchi no Kokusaihōjō no Chii" 清国に於ける列国租借地の国際法上の地位 [Status under International Law of the Leased Territories of China], *Meiji Hōgaku* 明治法学, no. 52 (1903); Ariga Nagao 有賀長雄, *Manshū Inin Tōchi Ron* 満洲委任統治論 [The Theory of Manchuria Mandate] (Tokyo: Waseda Daigaku Shuppanbu, 1905); Ariga Nagao 有賀長雄, "Jikoku no Kaigan wa Fūsasuru Koto o Eru Ya – Tsuketari Fūsa Kuikinai ni Soshakuchi Naishi Kyoryūchi o Hōyū Shioru Ba-ai" 自国の海岸は封鎖することを得るや—附封鎖区域内に租借地乃至居留地を包有し居る場合 [Whether One State May Blockade Its Own Coasts: Cases Where There Are Leased Territory or Settlements within the Blockaded Area], *Kokusaihō Zasshi* 国際法雑誌, vol. 6, no. 3 (1907).

In other words, the difference between the disguised cession theory and the non-cession theory arose mainly from whether the emphasis was placed on the wording of treaties and form, or on the reality and actual situations. On this point, in the case of Japan, it is important to note that the factual situation surrounding leased territory was different from that of other countries such as Germany, which had acquired the Kiaochow Bay leased territory.

As already mentioned, the Treaty of Portsmouth between Japan and Russia stipulated that the transfer and assignment of leaseholds and other rights be subject to the consent of the Chinese Government, and a treaty between Japan and China was subsequently concluded. In this way, Japan came to possess leased territory.[66] In regard to this, Nakamura Shingo presented the texts of the treaties concluded between Japan and Russia, as well as between Japan and China, and argued that they "can be used as clear evidence that leased territory is not the lessee State's true territory."[67] Shinoda Jisaku also stated, "It is clear that the transfer of the leasehold rights needs the consent of the lessor State, just as the transfer of a claim needs the consent of the debtor under private law," and explained that Japan's leasehold rights for the Kwantung leased territory did not stem from a treaty between Japan and Russia, but by a treaty between Japan and China.[68] In response to such views that placed emphasis on China's consent, one could make the counterargument that if the Chinese Government did not provide its consent, the transfer of the leasehold rights from Russia to Japan would be invalid and the Russian leasehold would be continued or it would result in a reversion to the situation before Russia and Qing China concluded their lease treaty. Such scenarios would be inconceivable, and the Chinese Government's consent was therefore merely a formality.[69]

66 The transfer and assignment of leaseholds and other rights from Russia to Japan with the condition of China's consent is still raised as an example of the difference between a leasehold and a cession today. For example, Ronen, *supra* note 2, 905.

67 Nakamura, *supra* note 54, 102–103.

68 Shinoda, *supra* note 47, 34–36.

69 Kikuchi, *supra* note 10, 13–15. See also Iwai Takafumi 岩井尊文, "Kokusai Chieki o Ronjite Manshū Tetsudō no Fusetsuken Oyobi Kantō-shū no Soshakuchi no Hōritsujō no Seishitsu ni Oyobu (Shōzen)" 国際地役を論して満洲鉄道の布設権及関東洲の租借地の法律上の性質に及ふ(承前) [Discussion of International Servitude, Extending to the Right to Construct the Manchurian Railway and the Legal Nature of the Kwantung Leased Territory (Continued)], *Kyōto Hōgakkai Zasshi* 京都法学会雑誌, vol. 1, no. 11 (1906): 39–42. Iwai argued in this paper that "Even if Qing China refuses to give its consent, it will not affect the relationship between Japan and Russia in any way, and the leasehold rights of Russia will be transferred to Japan. Therefore, Qing China could not refuse Japan's exercise of its right as the lessee State on the grounds that Qing China did not give its consent," whereas he explained that the land subject to the leasehold rights

Nevertheless, in Japan's case, it was rather natural to draw the conclusion that leaseholds were not the same as cession by observing the actual phenomena, that is, the circumstances that led to Japan's possession of the leased territory and the fact that the Japanese government did not treat the leased territory of Kwantung Province as true territory.

4.4 *Views and Actions of the Japanese Government*

4.4.1 Statements in the Imperial Diet by Director-General of the Cabinet Legislation Bureau Okano Keijirō

That is not to say, however, that the Japanese Government recognized that a leasehold was not the same as cession and that leased territory was not true territory, and always acted in accordance with this principle. The situation was not that simple. This is well illustrated by the answers given in the Diet by Okano Keijirō (1865–1925), Director-General of the Cabinet Legislation Bureau under the first Saionji Kinmochi Cabinet. Okano was a commercial law scholar and professor at Tokyo Imperial University who also held various government positions.[70] The questions were asked by Hanai Takuzō (1868–1931), a lawyer and politician known for his defense of criminal and human rights cases.

First, on March 27, 1907, at a committee of the House of Representatives, Hanai sought to confirm whether the location of the Kwantung Governor-General Office court was foreign land.[71] Okano replied that, "One can only say that it is foreign land since it cannot be said to be domestic or Imperial territory." Hanai then stated that although Kiaochow Bay and other areas were leased territories, he had heard that Germany was handling legal matters there as if they were domestic land. He called for the Japanese Government to take a similar policy to Germany, in which "German interests on the leased territory have been developing as Germany first made people think that the leased land was a protected area, then there was an about-face on that protected area and it became like a true protectorate without a treaty, and finally, that protectorate

was China's territory, and both Japan and Russia respected the sovereignty of China and requested its consent to the transfer of the rights.

70 Okano was a law scholar and professor at Tokyo Imperial University, and also a member of the Japanese Society of International Law. Okano's expertise and views may have influenced the content of his answers in the Diet. However, Okano was not expressing a theory that differed from the Japanese Government's position. Okano's answers are considered to be the official statement of the Director-General of the Cabinet Legislation Bureau of the Japanese Government, not his opinion as an individual scholar, and can be analyzed as such.

71 Statements in the Diet are cited using the Database System for the Minutes of the Imperial Diet (https://teikokugikai-i.ndl.go.jp).

has given the impression to others that it has been a de facto territory of the German Empire."

On March 25 in 1908 the following year, the nature of leased territory again became the focus of discussion during deliberations on a draft bill concerning consular jurisdiction in Manchuria. At that time, Okano stated the following:

> There have been various discussions about the system of leased territory and the nature of leasehold rights. … There is a theory that interprets leaseholds as being disguised cession of territory. This may be a theory that has been developed because of the advantages to be gained by lessee States and is a convenient political argument for the lessee States. In all fairness, I think there are such tendencies behind that theory. I believe that such a theory has arisen because the leasehold system was established in recent years, but if we examine the treaties on leasehold directly and fairly, it is highly doubtful that a leasehold can be considered to be a cession of territory. While there are both long lease terms and short ones, there is no doubt, based on the treaties, that at least in the case of short term leases, the leased territory should be returned to the lessor State once the years stipulated by the treaties have expired.

In addition, as for Kwantung, referring to his own answer in the Diet in the previous year, Okano argued, "Although it is difficult to claim that it is a part of our territory under national law, the principle that we are governing this land by our State power remains unchanged today."

Hanai then sought to determine what Okano meant by asking him whether the Japanese Government's principle toward leased territory was a cession-based principle, in which the land was considered to be Japanese territory, or a contract-based principle, which regarded it as involving a lessee–lessor relationship. Okano avoided stating whether it was a cession-based or contract-based principle and responded, "At this point, I am not of the opinion that the land is ceded, but Japan shall govern the land to the maximum extent possible, as long as its State power extend and Japan can assert its interests, in the same way as ceded land. I can only answer so." When asked again whether Japan's principle was cession-based or contract-based, he responded as follows:

> My response is this: I think that the policy toward leased territory is relevant to our policy toward Kwantung, and, in turn, it becomes a factor in establishing the nature of leased territory in the future. Therefore, I cannot assert here that we have a contract-based principle. Nor can I assert that it is a cession of territory – that this land is part of our true territory.

> At any rate, on a treaty basis, it is difficult to position the land as ceded territory, but the leased territory is subject to Japan's State power as if it were part of our territory. It is appropriate to say so.

Okano was not in favor of the disguised cession theory and did not state that the Kwantung leased territory was Japanese territory. In general, his answer was based on a view in line with the non-cession theory. On the other hand, he also did not say that the Japanese Government's principle regarding leased territory was on a contract basis, which viewed leased territory as involving a lessee–lessor relationship. That was because, if that were the position of the Japanese Government, it would limit the possibility of pursuing national interests.

The way in which Okano answered the questions can be considered to be a reflection of the Japanese Government's position. The Japanese Government basically handled the Kwantung leased territory on the premise that a leasehold was not the same as cession and that the leased territory was not the territory of the lessee State, but at the same time, it strongly considered pursuing Japan's national interests and securing its rights. Therefore, as various problems over leased territory arose, what the Japanese Government specifically asserted and what diplomatic actions it would take were decided separately from how it viewed leaseholds in general. The following are some examples of this, albeit presented in a fragmentary manner.

4.4.2 Various Issues Concerning Leaseholds and Japanese Diplomacy

Soon after Japan acquired the Kwantung leased territory, a dispute arose between Japan and Qing China over the fisheries in the area surrounding Kwantung, which continued for some time. It was a dispute between Japan and Qing, and at the same time there were various positions and interests concerning the dispute within both countries. The wide-ranging points at issue included fishing rights, tax collection rights, territorial waters, sovereignty, specific tax amounts, and the scope of fishing.[72] In the process, the Qing side

---

72 Satō Ryōsei 佐藤良聖, "Higashi Ajia Kai-iki ni Okeru Ryōkai to Nitchūkan Gyogyō Funsō (1906–1912)" 東アジア海域における領海と日中韓漁業紛争（一九〇六—一九一二）[The Territorial Waters of East Asia: A Case Study of the 1906–1912 Fishing Dispute between Japan, China and Korea], Tōyō Gakuhō 東洋学報, vol. 103, no. 1 (2021); See also Tsunoda Jun 角田順, *Manshū Mondai to Kokubō Hōshin – Meiji Kōki ni Okeru Kokubō Kankyō no Hendō* 満州問題と国防方針—明治後期における国防環境の変動 [The Manchuria Issue and National Defense Policy: Changes in the National Defense Environment in the Late Meiji Era] (Tokyo: Harashobō, 1967), 332–339.

argued that the Bohai Sea was China's territorial sea and that even though Lüshun and Dalian was a leased territory, China had the right to protect fishermen in the area. Meanwhile, the Japanese side took the position that the claim that the entire Bohai Sea was China's territorial sea was unacceptable.[73] Yet, Ijūin Hikokichi, the Japanese Minister to China at the time, was concerned that if Japan tried to dispute this point, it would result in a dispute over China's assertion that the Bohai Sea was its territorial sea and over the sovereignty of the people of Kwantung, and that "The latter point in particular is a fundamental dispute concerning the lease treaty and a very difficult issue for us." He believed that it would be undesirable for Japan to have a full-fledged dispute over the nature of the leasehold due to issues concerning fisheries and tax collection.[74] Japanese Foreign Minister Komura Jutarō accepted Ijūin's opinion to avoid any complications in the situation, and the issues were later resolved in a practical manner that avoided the more fundamental issues, as Ijūin had urged. However, Komura reminded Ijūin that it was important to clearly state Japan's position regarding China's assertion that the Bohai Sea was its territorial sea.[75]

In terms of trade, the Kwantung leased territory was to be a purely free port except for restrictions necessary for military purposes. The free port principle was to be implemented to the maximum extent possible by, for example, not imposing import and export taxes on incoming and outgoing cargo. With regard to the collection of Chinese customs duties on cargo coming and going within China (outside the leased territory), Chinese customs were logically to be established at the border of the leased territory, but due to practical economic and logistics problems, it was decided to establish a customs office in Dalian. However, in establishing the Chinese (i.e. the lessor State's) customs office in the leased territory, Japan took into account some factors such as limiting China's involvement in its operations. At the same time, Japan considered the balance with establishing the Chinese customs office in North Manchuria, the Russian side.[76] There were legal positions and principles as well as actual

73 Minister to China Ijūin Hikokichi to Foreign Minister Komura Jutarō, March 5; Komura to Ijūin, March 24; Komura to Ijūin, tel., May 10; Komura to Ijūin, tel., May 12, 1910, in *Nihon Gaikō Bunsho* 日本外交文書 [Documents on Japanese Foreign Policy], vol. 43, no. 1, Ministry of Foreign Affairs of Japan (ed.) (Tokyo: UN Association of Japan, 1962), 356–357, 358, 360, 363.

74 Ijūin to Komura, tel., May 11 and 13, 1910 (ibid., 362–363, 365–366).

75 Komura to Ijūin, tel., May 12 and 16, 1910 (ibid., 363, 369).

76 Manchurian Management Investigation Committee Report, June 1906, in *Nihon Gaikō Bunsho* 日本外交文書 [Documents on Japanese Foreign Policy], vol. 39, no. 1, Ministry of Foreign Affairs of Japan (ed.) (Tokyo: UN Association of Japan, 1959), 253–254; Kitano Gō

interests and practical responses, and which took precedence depended on each issue and situation. The traffic of foreign vessels between Dalian and Japanese open ports was to remain as before and continued to be allowed even after Dalian became a Japanese leased territory. This was at the discretion of Japan. Later, the issue of the closure of the shipping routes arose. At that time, there were various debates both within and outside the Japanese Government as well as within Japan and abroad as to whether the Kwantung leased territory and Dalian were Japanese territory and ports, whether it was possible to prohibit foreign vessels from sailing between Japan's domestic territory and Dalian as part of coastal trade, and, if this was theoretically possible, whether it was beneficial for Japan to do so.[77]

The extension of the leasehold term was, as is well known, a serious issue. Russia had leased Lüshun and Dalian in 1898 for 25 years, and it was not long before the expiration of the lease. The disguised cession theory viewed it as unlikely that the leased territory would actually be returned upon the expiration of the lease, even though a lease term had been set. That view was, in a sense, correct. Japanese political and military leaders and diplomats had no intention of returning the Kwantung leased territory at the end of the lease period. However, how Japan should respond when the deadline actually approached was unclear.

In 1911, the Xinhai Revolution broke out in China. In Japan, the second Saionji Cabinet at the time generally took a restrained approach to the situation, even though it faced those who sought a policy of foreign expansion to take advantage of the upheaval. Although some called for an extension of the lease period, the Saionji Cabinet did not pursued it.[78] The document which

北野剛, *Meiji Taishōki no Nihon no Manmō Seisakushi Kenkyū* 明治・大正期の日本の満蒙政策史研究 [Historical Study of Japan's Manchuria-Mongolia Policy in the Meiji and Taisho Eras] (Tokyo: Fuyō Shobō Shuppan, 2012), 27–52; See also Laws and Regulations Division, Treaty Bureau, Ministry of Foreign Affairs of Japan, *Kantō-shū Soshakuchi to Minami Manshū Tetsudō Fuzokuchi Zenpen* 関東州租借地と南満洲鉄道付属地 前編 [Kwantung Leased Territory and the Annexed Land of the South Manchuria Railway, Part 1] (Tokyo: Laws and Regulations Division, Treaty Bureau, Ministry of Foreign Affairs of Japan, 1966), 132–133.

77 Yoshida Masumi 吉田ますみ, "Dai 1 Ji Sekai Taisengo no Nihon Gaimushō to 'Tsūshō Jiyū Shugi'" 第一次世界大戦後の日本外務省と『通商自由主義』 [The Ministry of Foreign Affairs of Japan and the "Principle of Free Trade" after the First World War], *Higashi Ajia Kindaishi* 東アジア近代史, no. 24 (2020).

78 Sasaki Yūichi 佐々木雄一, *Teikoku Nihon no Gaikō, 1894–1922 – Naze Hanto wa Kakudaishita Noka* 帝国日本の外交1894–1922—なぜ版図は拡大したのか [Japanese Diplomacy and the Dynamics of Imperial Expansion, 1894–1922] (Tokyo: University of Tokyo Press, 2017), 217–225.

set the Saionji Cabinet's policy for dealing with the situation in China at the outbreak of the Xinhai Revolution cited the provisions of the Russo-Qing lease treaty that stipulated that the lease term could be extended by agreement between the two countries, as well as the most-favored-nation treatment provisions of the Sino-Japanese treaty on Manchuria, and stated that "The issue of extending the lease term is a matter we have grounds in treaties."[79] In other words, at that point, the Saionji Cabinet believed that the issue of the lease expiration date could be managed without any reckless action. In the end, however, the lease term was not extended semi-automatically. In 1915, a new treaty was concluded between Japan and China after a great deal of controversy over the issue of the Twenty-One Demands, and the term of the lease was extended to 99 years.

Related to the extension of the lease term and Japan's Twenty-One Demands to China, there was also the issue of the Kiaochow Bay leased territory. In 1914, Japan entered World War I on the side of the Allied Powers, together with Great Britain, France, Russia, and others, and tried to capture Germany's Kiaochow Bay leased territory, return it to China, and, in return, have Japan's interests in Manchuria strengthened. Although there were twists and turns along the way, Japan basically intended to return the Kiaochow Bay leased territory to China, but at the Paris Peace Conference, Japan aimed to succeed to Germany's interests in Shandong, which included the Kiaochow Bay leased territory. Japan's plan was to hold renewed negotiations with China on the Shandong region afterwards and to obtain economic interests there. On the other hand, China was trying to prevent Japan from succeeding to its interests in Shandong. China had participated in World War I on the side of the Allies and was therefore one of the victors.[80]

In this connection, Makino Nobuaki, the Japanese representative at the summit meeting of the major powers during the Paris Peace Conference, refuted the claim that the Sino-German lease treaty had lapsed as a result of China's declaration of war against Germany. Makino's argument was that in view of the nature of the lease treaty, which allowed Germany to exercise sovereignty over the leased territory, the lease of Kiaochow Bay was a pure cession, except for its 99-year term limit, and the declaration of war did not annul

79 Cabinet Decision, October 24, 1911, in *Nihon Gaikō Bunsho – Shinkoku Jihen* (*Shingai Kakumei*) 日本外交文書—清国事変（辛亥革命） [Documents on Japanese Foreign Policy: Qing Incident (Xinhai Revolution)], Ministry of Foreign Affairs of Japan (ed.) (Tokyo: UN Association of Japan, 1961), 50.

80 Sasaki, *supra* note 78, 228–232, 237–241, 293–298.

the land cession treaty or other territorial agreements.[81] This point was already a source of interest in Japan at the time China declared war on Germany, and similar arguments were made that the leasehold was in effect a cession and that the lease treaty, which was equivalent to a land cession treaty, did not lapse with the declaration of war.[82] After World War I, the precedent of the transfer of the lease right of Kiaochow Bay from Germany to Japan under the Treaty of Versailles was sometimes positioned as evidence that lease treaties do not expire with the outbreak of war between the States party to them and that leaseholds and cession have the same nature.[83] However, this was not sufficiently influential to change the theoretical situation in Japan where the non-cession theory was predominant.

4.5 *Changes around World War I*

Lastly, this chapter looks at the discussion in Japan concerning the shift in global theoretical trends regarding the nature of leaseholds that occurred around the time of World War I.

In a 1933 article, Kikuchi Komaji pointed out that "In European academia, the recent repudiation of the disguised cession theory has been advocated by German and Austrian legal scholars." Kikuchi saw it as a result of the collapse of both the German and Russian empires through World War I, as well as the closure of the paths of German and Austrian overseas development, which led German and Austrian scholars to view "lease treaties as ultimately a relic of imperialism, and the disguised cession theory as a theory in defense of aggression policy." Kikuchi also stated, "I have the impression that the theory that was in the minority more than 20 years ago has become the prevailing theory in the last 10 years. The change of the times is significant."[84] A short while later, Ueda

81 Makino's statement at the summit meeting, April 22, 1919, in *Nihon Gaikō Bunsho Taishō 8 Nen Dai 3 Satsu Jōkan* 日本外交文書 大正 8年第 3冊上巻 [Documents on Japanese Foreign Policy: Taisho 8, vol. 3, Part 1], Ministry of Foreign Affairs of Japan (ed.) (Tokyo: Ministry of Foreign Affairs, 1971), 254, 257.

Asada, *supra* note 8 argues that Makino's statement was made against the backdrop of the Japanese theory that equated leaseholds and cession. However, as discussed in this chapter, the non-cession theory was predominant in Japan. In addition, at that time, Japan was insisting adamantly on the succession of the interests in Shandong, and used various logics practically to try to achieve this. Makino's statement did not reflect the Japanese Government's understanding of leaseholds in a general sense.

82 For example, Makino Yoshitomo 牧野義智, "Shina no Sensen no Soshaku Jōyaku ni Oyobosu Kōka" 支那の宣戦の租借条約に及ぼす効果 [Effects of China's Declaration of War on the Lease Treaty], *Kokka Oyobi Kokkagaku* 国家及国家学, vol. 5, no. 11 (1917).

83 Kikuchi, *supra* note 43 (1930), 27–31; Taoka, *supra* note 3, 64–65.

84 Kikuchi, *supra* note 11, 90.

Toshio summarized, "Before World War I, that is to say when imperialism was in its heyday, the theory of territorial cession was dominant. However, since the war, as anti-imperialist sentiment has become stronger, the non-cession theory has gradually been gaining influence."[85] Both authors' analysis was that imperialism faced difficulties in terms of ideology, norms, and actual foreign policy after World War I, and that this led to a change in the global theoretical trends regarding leaseholds.

Also, more interesting is that at a time when the world's theoretical trends had been changing, Japanese scholars wrote about the shift. International law and colonial policy scholar Izumi Akira (1873–1943) wrote in a 1919 paper, "Territory leaseholds, as the term suggests, means that the land is used for a certain period of time and then returned to the sovereign State. But at present, it is not believed that the return of territories will be realized. In addition, a large number of international legal scholars agree that this constitutes disguised cession of territory."[86] This was an explanation that the disguised cession theory was the world's prevailing theory.

However, in a paper in 1920 the following year, Izumi wrote, "To date, a large number of international law scholars have maintained that leased territory is a kind of method to acquire territory under disguised pretenses, but it seems that this theory is becoming a thing of the past. It is doubtful whether this theory will be clearly recognized under international law in the future, and instead, there is likely to be a shift to a theory such as the one advocated by Chinese people."[87]

In 1923, China scholar Aoyagi Atsutsune (1877–1951) wrote, "My suspicions about the theory that a leasehold is a cession gradually deepened," citing the transfer of leasehold rights between Japan and Russia after the Russo-Japanese War with Qing China's approval and the 1915 treaty between Japan and China that extended the lease term from 25 years to 99 years. He then referred to the statements made at the Washington Conference (1921–22) by Britain (Weihaiwei) and France (Guangzhou Bay) regarding the return of leased territory, and wrote, "I have been forced to reject with certainty and clarity the theory that a leasehold is a cession. … The return of the leased territories has already been announced. The new principle that a lease is not a cession has

85 Ueda, *supra* note 2, 159.

86 Izumi Akira 泉哲, "Inin Tōchi to Soshaku Tōchi" 委任統治と租借統治 [Mandate and Leasehold Administration], *Kokusaihō Gaikō Zasshi* 国際法外交雑誌, vol. 17, no. 10 (1919), 29.

87 Izumi Akira 泉哲, "Soshaku Tōchi Ron" 租借統治論 [The Theory of Leasehold Administration], *Kokka Oyobi Kokkagaku* 国家及国家学, vol. 8, no. 3 (1920): 8–9.

been established on the basis of fact. This will give rise to a new relationship and a new interpretation of the issue of the Kwantung leased territory."[88]

These are probably rare documents for anywhere in the world in that they described the impact of changes in international norms and the actual international political situation on the global theoretical trends concerning leaseholds, not as retrospective analyses in later years but as predictions and descriptions of the actual feeling from the same period.

5 Conclusion

From the end of the 19th century until around the time of World War I, the disguised session theory regarding the nature of leaseholds was widely advocated in the West, and in Japan, that theory was recognized as being the prevailing theory among international legal scholars around the world. However, after the Russo-Japanese War, the non-cession theory was predominant in Japan, although it could not be said that the overwhelming majority advocated that theory.

Forming the background to the emergence of this theoretical trend in Japan were the facts and circumstances surrounding Japan's leased territories. Firstly, Japan obtained the leasehold rights for Lüshun and Dalian from Russia on the condition of the consent of Qing China. Then, although there was room for debate as to how to interpret the nature of its consent, a treaty was actually concluded between Japan and Qing China, and the Qing Government gave its consent for the transfer of leasehold rights from Russia to Japan. Japan came to possess the leased territory, with the existence of the sovereignty of the lessor State over the leased territory and the difference between leaseholds and cession being impressed upon Japan. Also, the Japanese Government did not treat the Kwantung leased territory as true territory. The way of thinking of the disguised cession theory was that leaseholds were in fact or in effect a type of cession, regardless of the wording of the treaty. In Japan, however, the process of acquiring the leased territory and the subsequent measures taken by the Japanese Government led to the conclusion that leaseholds were different from cession, and that leased territories were not the true territory of the lessee State.

---

88 Aoyagi Atsutsune 青柳篤恒, "Kantō-shū Soshakuchi Kanpu Mondai o Kaiketsusuru Niwa" 関東州租借地還附問題を解決するには [To Resolve the Issue of the Return of the Kwantung Leased Territory], *Gaikō Jihō* 外交時報, no. 440 (1923): 12–13.

In terms of the theoretical trends in the world, after World War I, there was a shift away from the disguised cession theory, which had been supported by the norms and practices of the imperialist era, alongside the decline of imperialism. This situation was foreseen and observed in Japan.

As for the relationship between the Japanese Government's actions and the theory, the Japanese Government basically did not equate leaseholds and cessions, nor leased territory and true territory. It did not treat the Kwantung leased territory as Japanese territory. Such a perception and actions by the Japanese Government concerning leaseholds probably influenced the theoretical trend in Japan.

However, many issues arose concerning the Kwantung leased territory, and the Japanese Government was, of course, conscious of pursuing its national interests and securing its rights in dealing with these problems. The Japanese Government responded to those actual diplomatic problems in various ways by taking a middle ground between treating leased territory completely as the territory of the lessor State, and treating leased territory as its own (the lessee State's) territory.

Bibliography

Primary Sources

Japanese

Japan Center for Asian Historical Records. (1) National Archives of Japan, A06051185700. (2) Diplomatic Archives of the Ministry of Foreign Affairs, B15100712100.

Ministry of Foreign Affairs of Japan, ed. *Nihon Gaikō Bunsho* 日本外交文書 [Diplomatic Documents of Japan]. Supplement v of Meiji Era vol. 37–38, vol. 38 (no. 1), vol. 39 (no. 1), vol. 43 (no. 1), Supplement of vol. 44–45, and Taisho Era vol. 3 (Part 1). Tokyo: United Nations Association of Japan, 1958, 1959, 1960, 1961, 1962, 1971.

Secondary Sources

Japanese

Akiyama, Masanosuke 秋山雅之介. *Kokusai Kōhō* 国際公法 [Public International Law]. Tokyo: Tokyo Senmon Gakkō, 1893.

Akiyama, Masanosuke 秋山雅之介. *Kokusai Kōhō Kōgi Heiji* 国際公法講義 平時 [Lectures on Public International Law in Peacetime]. Tokyo: Meiji Hōritsu Gakkō Shuppanbu Kōhokai, 1900.

Akiyama, Masanosuke 秋山雅之介. *Kokusai Kōhō Heiji* 国際公法 平時 [Public International Law in Peacetime]. Tokyo: Wafutsu Hōritsu Gakkō, 1902.

Akiyama, Masanosuke 秋山雅之介. *Kokusai Kōhō Senji* 国際公法 戦時 [Public International Law in Wartime]. Tokyo: Wafutsu Hōritsu Gakkō, 1903.

Akiyama, Masanosuke 秋山雅之介. “Soshakuchi no Seishitsu” 租借地の性質 [The Nature of Leased Territory]. *Hōgaku Shirin* 法学志林 10, no. 2 (1908): 25–31.

Aoyagi, Atsutsune 青柳篤恒. “Kantō-shū Soshakuchi Kanpu Mondai o Kaiketsusuru Niwa” 関東州租借地還附問題を解決するには [To Resolve the Issue of the Return of the Kwantung Leased Territory]. *Gaikō Jihō* 外交時報, no. 440 (1923): 11–18.

Ariga, Nagao 有賀長雄. “Shinkoku ni Okeru Rekkoku Soshakuchi no Senji Kankei” 清国に於ける列国租借地の戦時関係 [Wartime Relations of the Leased Territories of China]. *Gaikō Jihō* 外交時報, no. 30 (1900): 187–196.

Ariga, Nagao 有賀長雄. “Shinkoku ni Okeru Rekkoku Soshakuchi no Kokusaihōjō no Chii” 清国に於ける列国租借地の国際法上の地位 [Status under International Law of the Leased Territories of China]. *Meiji Hōgaku* 明治法学, no. 52 (1903): 33–43.

Ariga, Nagao 有賀長雄. *Manshū Inin Tōchi Ron* 満洲委任統治論 [The Theory of Manchuria Mandate]. Tokyo: Waseda Daigaku Shuppanbu, 1905.

Ariga, Nagao 有賀長雄. “Jikoku no Kaigan wa Fūsasuru Koto o Eru Ya – Tsuketari Fūsa Kuikinai ni Soshakuchi Naishi Kyoryūchi o Hōyū Shioru Ba-ai” 自国の海岸は封鎖することを得るや – 附封鎖区域内に租借地乃至居留地を包有し居る場合 [Whether One State May Blockade Its Own Coasts: Cases Where There Are Leased Territory or Settlements within the Blockaded Area]. *Kokusaihō Zasshi* 国際法雑誌 6, no. 3 (1907): 36–39.

Asada, Shinji 浅田進史. *Doitsu Tōchika no Chintao Keizaiteki – Jiyū Shugi to Shokuminchi Shakai Chitsujo* ドイツ統治下の青島 – 経済的自由主義と植民地社会秩序 [Qingdao under German Rule: Economic Liberalism and the Colonial Social Order]. Tokyo: University of Tokyo Press, 2011.

Egi, Tasuku 江木翼. “Doitsu Teikoku Hogoryō Taru Kōshūwanryō Seido no Ichi Ni o Toki Waga Kantō-shū ni Oyobu” 独逸帝国保護領たる膠洲湾領制度の一二を説き我か関東州に及ふ [The System of Kiaochow Bay as a Protectorate of the German Empire and Japan’s Kwantung]. *Kokka Gakkai Zasshi* 国家学会雑誌 20, no. 12 (1906): 75–100.

Egi, Tasuku 江木翼. *Kōshūwan Ron* 膠州湾論 [Theory of Kiaochow Bay]. Tokyo: Yomiuri Shimbunsha, 1907.

Endō, Genroku 遠藤源六. *Kokusaihō Yōron* 国際法要論 [Elements of International Law]. Tokyo: Shimizu Shoten, 1908.

Hata, Ikuhiko 秦郁彦, ed. *Nihon Kingendai Jinbutsu Rireki Jiten* (Dai 2 Han) 日本近現代人物履歴事典〔第 2 版〕 [Biographical Dictionary of Leaders of Modern Japan [2nd ed.]]. Tokyo: University of Tokyo Press, 2013.

Hirose, Kyūjirō (or Hisajirō) 広瀬久次郎. “Soshakuchi no Seishitsu o Ronzu” 租借地の性質を論ず [Discussion on the Nature of Leased Territory]. *Gunji Keisatsu Zasshi* 軍事警察雑誌, nos. 4–7 (1908).

Hirose, Kyūjirō (or Hisajirō) 広瀬久次郎. "Soshaku no Kōka o Ronzu" 租借の効果を論ず [Discussion on the Effects of Leaseholds]. *Gunji Keisatsu Zasshi* 軍事警察雑誌, nos. 8–9 (1908).

Hozumi, Yatsuka 穂積八束. *Kenpō Teiyō Jōkan* 憲法提要 上巻 [Compendium of Constitution, vol. 1]. Tokyo: Yūhikaku, 1910.

Ichimata, Masao 一又正雄. *Nihon no Kokusaihōgaku o Kizuita Hitobito* 日本の国際法学を築いた人々 [The People Who Built the Study of International Law in Japan]. Tokyo: Japan Institute of International Affairs, 1973.

Ichimura, Mitsue 市村光恵. *Teikoku Kenpō Ron* 帝国憲法論 [Theory of Imperial Constitution]. Tokyo: Yūhikaku, 1915.

Imai, Yoshiyuki 今井嘉幸. *Shina Kokusaihō Ron Dai 1 Kan – Gaikoku Saibanken to Gaikoku Gyōsei Chiiki* 支那国際法論 第一巻 – 外国裁判権と外国行政地域 [The International Law of China, vol. 1: Foreign Jurisdiction and Foreign Administrative Regions]. Tokyo: Maruzen, 1915.

Iwai, Takafumi 岩井尊文. "Kokusai Chieki o Ronjite Manshū Tetsudō no Fusetsuken Oyobi Kantō-shū no Soshakuchi no Hōritsujō no Seishitsu ni Oyobu (Shōzen)" 国際地役を論して満洲鉄道の布設権及関東洲の租借地の法律上の性質に及ふ（承前）[Discussion of International Servitude, Extending to the Right to Construct the Manchurian Railway and the Legal Nature of the Kwantung Leased Territory (Continued)]. *Kyōto Hōgakkai Zasshi* 京都法学会雑誌 1, no. 11 (1906): 39–48.

Izumi, Akira 泉哲. "Inin Tōchi to Soshaku Tōchi" 委任統治と租借統治 [Mandate and Leasehold Administration]. *Kokusaihō Gaikō Zasshi* 国際法外交雑誌 17, no. 10 (1919): 22–30.

Izumi, Akira 泉哲. "Soshaku Tōchi Ron" 租借統治論 [The Theory of Leasehold Administration]. *Kokka Oyobi Kokkagaku* 国家及国家学 8, no. 3 (1920): 1–11.

"Kaihō" 会報 [Bulletin]. *Kokusaihō Zasshi* 国際法雑誌 1, no. 1 (1902): 79–80, 85–87.

Kawashima, Shin 川島真. "Ryōiki to Kioku – Sokai, Soshakuchi, Seiryoku Han-i o Meguru Gensetsu to Seido" 領域と記憶 – 租界・租借地・勢力範囲をめぐる言説と制度 [Territory and Memory: Discourses and Institutions Concerning Concessions, Leased Territories, and Spheres of Influence]. In *Mosakusuru Kindai Nicchū Kankei – Taiwa to Kyōzon no Jidai* 模索する近代日中関係 – 対話と競存の時代 [Dialogue and Competitive Cooperation in Modern Japan–China Relations], edited by Kishi Toshihiko, Tanigaki Mariko, and Fukamachi Hideo. Tokyo: University of Tokyo Press, 2009.

Kei, Nansei 景楠生. "Soshaku no Enkaku Oyobi Sono Kokusaihōjō no Seishitsu (Fukuoka Hidei-shi Kobanashi)" 租借（Lease）の沿革及其国際法上の性質《福岡秀猪氏小話》[The Nature of Leasehold in International Law (A Small Talk of Fukuoka Hidei)]. *Hōkō* 奉公, no. 13 (1904): 13–20.

Kikuchi, Komaji 菊地駒次. "Soshakuchi no Hōritsu Kankei o Ronzu" 租借地の法律関係を論ず [Discussion of the Legal Relationship of Leased Territory]. *Hōgaku Kyōkai Zasshi* 法学協会雑誌 41, no. 10 (1923): 1–28.

Kikuchi, Komaji 菊地駒次. "Soshakuchi no Hōri o Ronzu" 租借地の法理を論ず [Discussion of the Legal Principles of Leased Territory]. *Kokusaihō Gaikō Zasshi* 国際法外交雑誌 29, no. 4 (1930): 1–34.

Kikuchi, Komaji 菊地駒次. "Soshakuchi no Hōri o Ronzu" 租借地の法理を論ず [Discussion of the Legal Principles of Leased Territory]. *Gaikō Jihō* 外交時報, no. 677 (1933): 58–97.

Kikuchi, Komaji 菊地駒次. *Kōhō Kenteki* 公法涓滴 [A Little Book on Public Law]. Tokyo: Nihon Gaikō Kyōkai, 1935.

Kitano, Gō 北野剛. *Meiji Taishōki no Nihon no Manmō Seisakushi Kenkyū* 明治・大正期の日本の満蒙政策史研究 [Historical Study of Japan's Manchuria–Mongolia Policy in the Meiji and Taisho Eras]. Tokyo: Fuyō Shobō Shuppan, 2012.

Laws and Regulations Division, Treaty Bureau, Ministry of Foreign Affairs of Japan. *Kantō-shū Soshakuchi to Minami Manshū Tetsudō Fuzokuchi Zenpen* 関東州租借地と南満洲鉄道付属地 前編 [Kwantung Leased Territory and the Annexed Land of the South Manchuria Railway, Part 1]. Tokyo: Laws and Regulations Division, Treaty Bureau, Ministry of Foreign Affairs of Japan, 1966.

Makino, Yoshitomo 牧野義智. "Shina no Sensen no Soshaku Jōyaku ni Oyobosu Kōka" 支那の宣戦の租借条約に及ぼす効果 [Effects of China's Declaration of War on the Lease Treaty]. *Kokka Oyobi Kokkagaku* 国家及国家学 5, no. 11 (1917): 40–46.

Matsubara, Kazuo 松原一雄. "Heiji Senryō Ron Tokuni Soshakuchi no Hōritsu Kankei (Shōzen)" 平時占領論特に租借地の法律関係(承前) [Theory of Occupation in Peacetime, Especially the Legal Relations of Leased Territory (Continued)]. *Kokka Gakkai Zasshi* 国家学会雑誌, no. 182 (1902): 47–54.

Matsubara, Kazuo 松原一雄. "Ryojunkō Hōken Mondai" 旅順口法権問題 [Issue of Legal Rights of Lüshunkou]. *Hōgaku Shinpō* 法学新報 13, no. 2 (1903): 14–26.

Matsubara, Kazuo 松原一雄. *Saikin Kokusai Kōhō Genron* 最近国際公法原論 [Recent Theory on Public International Law]. Tokyo: Tokyo Hōgakuin Daigaku, 1904.

Matsubara, Kazuo 松原一雄. "Soshakuchi no Shobun Ikan" 租借地の処分如何 [How to Dispose of Leased Territory]. *Hōgaku Shinpō* 法学新報 14, no. 7 (1904): 26–30.

Matsubara, Kazuo 松原一雄. *Genkō Kokusaihō Jōkan Dai 2 Bunsatsu* 現行国際法 上巻 第二分冊 [Current International Law, vol. 1, Part 2]. Tokyo: Chūō Daigaku, 1924.

Minobe, Tatsukichi 美濃部達吉. "Nihon Shokuminchihō ni Tsuite" 日本殖民地法に就て [On Japanese colonial law]. *Kokka Gakkai Zasshi* 国家学会雑誌 26, no. 1 (1912): 89–108.

Minobe, Tatsukichi 美濃部達吉. "Soshakuchi no Hōritsujō no Seishitsu" 租借地の法律上の性質 [The Legal Nature of Leased Territory]. *Hōgaku Shinpō* 法学新報 25, no. 1 (1915): 33–41.

Minobe, Tatsukichi 美濃部達吉. *Kenpō Satsuyō* 憲法撮要 [Compendium of the Constitution]. Tokyo: Yūhikaku, 1923.

Nakamura, Shingo 中村進午. "Eikyū Senryō to Soshakuchi" 永久占領と租借地 [Perpetual Occupation and Leased Territory]. *Hōsei Shinshi* 法政新誌 7, no. 12 (1903): 1–6.

Nakamura, Shingo 中村進午. *Heiji Kokusaihō* 平時国際法 [International Law in Peacetime]. Tokyo: Tokyo Hōgakuin, 1902.

Nakamura, Shingo 中村進午. *Kokusai Kōhō Ron* 国際公法論 [Theory of Public International Law]. Tokyo: Shimizu Shoten, 1916.

Ninagawa, Arata 蜷川新. "Soshakuchijō no Kenri to Manshū Mondai" 租借 cession à bail 地上の権利と満州問題 [Rights on Leased Territory and the Manchurian Question]. *Gaikō Jihō* 外交時報, no. 66 (1903): 78–79.

Ninagawa, Arata 蜷川新. *Minami Manshū ni Okeru Teikoku no Kenri* 南満洲に於ける帝国の権利 [Imperial Rights in South Manchuria]. Tokyo: Shimizu Shoten, 1913.

Ninagawa, Arata 蜷川新. "Ryodai Mondai to Naigai no Byūron" 旅大問題と内外の謬論 [The Lüshun and Dalian Issue and Domestic and Foreign Mistaken Opinions]. *Gaikō Jihō* 外交時報, no. 438 (1923): 466–471.

Ninagawa, Arata 蜷川新. "Soshakuchi to Yo no Byūken" 租借地と世の謬見 [Leased Territory and People's Mistaken Views]. *Gaikō Jihō* 外交時報, no. 445 (1923): 147–151.

Ninagawa, Arata 蜷川新. "Soshakuchi to Yo no Byūken" 租借地と世の謬見 [Leased Territory and People's Mistaken Views]. *Gaikō Jihō* 外交時報, no. 454 (1923): 148–151.

Sasaki, Yūichi 佐々木雄一. *Teikoku Nihon no Gaikō, 1894–1922 – Naze Hanto wa Kakudaishita Noka* 帝国日本の外交1894–1922 – なぜ版図は拡大したのか [Japanese Diplomacy and the Dynamics of Imperial Expansion, 1894–1922]. Tokyo: University of Tokyo Press, 2017.

Satō, Ryōsei 佐藤良聖. "Higashi Ajia Kai-iki ni Okeru Ryōkai to Nitchūkan Gyogyō Funsō (1906–1912)" 東アジア海域における領海と日中韓漁業紛争（一九〇六 – 一九一二）[The Territorial Waters of East Asia: A Case Study of the 1906–1912 Fishing Dispute between Japan, China and Korea]. *Tōyō Gakuhō* 東洋学報 103, no. 1 (2021): 31–55.

Senga, Tsurutarō 千賀鶴太郎. *Kokusai Kōhō Yōgi* 国際公法要義 [Fundamentals of Public International Law]. Kyoto: Kyōto Hōsei Daigaku, 1909.

Senga, Tsurutarō 千賀鶴太郎. *Kokusai Kōhō* 国際公法 [Public International Law]. Tokyo: Kōhōkai, Shimizu Shoten, 1917.

Shimizu, Tōru 清水澄. "Waga Kenpō wa Soshakuchi ni Okonawaruru Ya Ina" 我憲法は租借地に行はるるや否 [Whether Our Constitution Applies to Leased Territory]. *Nihon Hōsei Shinshi* 日本法政新誌 10, no. 8 (1906): 6–11.

Shinoda, Jisaku 篠田治策. "Soshakuken no Seishitsu to Kantōshū no Soshakuchi" 租借権の性質と関東州の租借地 [The Nature of Leasehold Rights and the Kwantung Leased Territory]. *Kokusaihō Zasshi* 国際法雑誌 5, no. 2 (1906): 11–30.

Shinoda, Jisaku 篠田治策. "Soshakuken no Seishitsu to Kantōshū no Soshakuchi (Shōzen)" 租借権の性質と関東州の租借地（承前） [The Nature of Leasehold Rights and the Kwantung Leased Territory (Continued)]. *Kokusaihō Zasshi* 国際法雑誌 5, no. 3 (1906): 11–38.

Soejima, Giichi 副島義一. *Nihon Teikoku Kenpō Yōron* 日本帝国憲法要論 [Compendium of the Imperial Japanese Constitution]. Tokyo: Ganshōdō Shoten, 1917.

Tachi, Sakutarō 立作太郎. *Heiji Kokusai Kōhō* 平時国際公法 [Public International Law in Peacetime]. Tokyo: Chūō Daigaku, 1914.

Tachi, Sakutarō 立作太郎. *Heiji Kokusaihō Ron* 平時国際法論 [Theory of International Law in Peacetime]. Tokyo: Nihon Hyōronsha, 1930.

Takahashi, Sakue 高橋作衛. "Soshakuchi no Seishitsu o Ronjite Ryojun Kanraku no Kōka ni Oyobu" 租借地の性質を論して旅順陥落の効果に及ぶ [The Nature of the Leased Territory and the Effects of the Fall of Lüshun]. *Kokka Gakkai Zasshi* 国家学会雑誌 19, no. 3 (1905): 32–41.

Takahashi, Sakue 高橋作衛. "Shinkoku Dōran o Ronjite Manshū Soshakuchi wa Ryōdo Hozen no Kengai Naru Koto ni Ronkyūsu" 清国動乱を論じて満洲租借地は領土保全の圏外なることに論及す [Discussion on the Upheaval in China Referencing that the Manchurian Leased Territory was Outside the Sphere of Territorial Integrity]. *Zaikai* 財界 16, no. 6 (1912): 7–10.

Takahashi, Sakue 高橋作衛. "Shinkoku Ryōdo Hozen no Igi o Kenkyūshite Kantō-shū Soshakuchi no Kokusaihōjō no Seishitsu ni Ronkyūsu" 清国領土保全の意義を研究して関東州租借地の国際法上の性質に論及す [Study on the Significance of the Territorial Integrity of China and Discussion of the Nature of the Kwantung Leased Territory under International Law]. *Kokusaihō Zasshi* 国際法雑誌 10, no. 7 (1912): 1–27.

Takahashi, Sakue 高橋作衛. "Chintao Fukanpu Ron" 青島不還附論 [Non-return of Qingdao]. *Tokyo Nichinichi Shimbun* 東京日日新聞, May 2, 1919.

Taoka, Ryoichi 田岡良一. "Soshakuchi to Kokusai Chieki (3)" 租借地と国際地役（三） [Leased Territory and International Servitude (3)]. *Kokusaihō Gaikō Zasshi* 国際法外交雑誌 32, no. 4 (1933): 403–427.

Tomizu, Hirondo 戸水寛人. "Ryodai no Soshakuken" 旅大の租借権 [Lüshun and Dalian Leasehold Rights]. *Gaikō Jihō* 外交時報, no. 93 (1905): 193–196.

Tsunoda, Jun 角田順. *Manshū Mondai to Kokubō Hōshin – Meiji Kōki ni Okeru Kokubō Kankyō no Hendō* 満州問題と国防方針 – 明治後期における国防環境の変動 [The Manchuria Issue and National Defense Policy: Changes in the National Defense Environment in the Late Meiji Era]. Tokyo: Harashobō, 1967.

Yamada, Saburō 山田三良. "Shokuminchihō to Naichihō to no Kankei ni Tsuite" 殖民地法と内地法との関係に就て [On the Relationship between the Colonial Law and the Mainland Law]. *Hōgaku Kyōkai Zasshi* 法学協会雑誌 30, no. 2 (1912): 96–110.

Yamamoto, Miono 山本美越乃. "Nisshi Kyōyaku Haiki Mondai" 日支協約廃棄問題 [Issue of the Rescinding of the Japan–China Pact]. *Gaikō Jihō* 外交時報, no. 443 (1923): 1323–1333.

Yamamoto, Miono 山本美越乃. "'Soshakuchi to Yo no Byūken' o Yomite" 『租借地と世の謬見』を読みて [Reading "Soshakuchi to Yo no Byūken"]. *Gaikō Jihō* 外交時報, no. 450 (1923): 348–354.

Yi, Ping 易平, *Sensō to Heiwa no Aida – Hossokuki Nihon Kokusaihōgaku ni Okeru 'Tadashii Sensō' no Gainen to Sono Kiketsu* 戦争と平和の間 – 発足期日本国際法学における「正しい戦争」の観念とその帰結 [Between War and Peace: The 'Just War' Concept and its Consequences During the Early Period of International Law Research in Japan]. Beijing: Torkel Opsahl Academic EPublisher, 2013.

Yokota, Kisaburō 横田喜三郎. "Matsubara Hakase no Fu" 松原博士の訃 [News of Dr. Matsubara's Death]. *Kokusaihō Gaikō Zasshi* 国際法外交雑誌 55, no. 1 (1956): 77–78.

Yokota, Kisaburō 横田喜三郎. *Hōritsugaku Zenshū 56 Kokusaihō II (Shinban)* 法律学全集 56 国際法ii〔新版〕[Jurisprudence Complete Collection 56: International Law II (New Edition)]. Tokyo: Yūhikaku, 1972.

Yoshida, Masumi 吉田ますみ. "Dai 1 Ji Sekai Taisengo no Nihon Gaimushō to 'Tsūshō Jiyū Shugi'" 第一次世界大戦後の日本外務省と『通商自由主義』[The Ministry of Foreign Affairs of Japan and the "Principle of Free Trade" after the First World War]. *Higashi Ajia Kindaishi* 東アジア近代史, no. 24 (2020): 146–164.

Western Languages

Alfonsi, Marc. *Les Cessions à Bail en Chine: Histoire diplomatique et de droit international public*. Paris: Domat-Montchrestien, 1940.

Asada, Shinji. "Colonizing Kiaochow Bay: From the Perspective of German-Japanese Relations." In *Japan and Germany: Two Latecomers to the World Stage, 1890–1945, Volume I, A Chance Encounter in East Asia*, edited by Kudō Akira, Tajima Nobuo, and Erich Pauer. Folkestone: Global Oriental, 2009.

Gérard, Louis. *Des cessions déguisées de territoires en droit international public*. Paris: Librairie de la Société du Recueil général des lois et des arrêts, 1904.

Howland, Douglas. "The Japan House Tax Case, 1899–1905: Leases in Perpetuity and the Myth of International Equality." *Zeitschrift für ausländisches öffentliches Recht und Völkerrecht* 75, no. 2 (2015): 413–434.

Howland, Douglas. *International Law and Japanese Sovereignty: The Emerging Global Order in the 19th Century*. Basingstoke: Palgrave Macmillan, 2016.

Howland, Douglas. "The Territorial Foundations of the Sovereign State in East Asia." *The Journal of Transcultural Studies* 9, no. 1–2 (2018): 10–32.

Lauterpacht, Hersch. *Private Law Sources and Analogies of International Law: With Special Reference to International Arbitration*. New York: Longmans, Green, 1927.

Lawrence, Thomas J. *War and Neutrality in the Far East*. 2nd ed. New York: Macmillan, 1904.
Lazar, Joseph. "The Status of the Leasehold in International Law." Ph.D. diss., University of Minnesota, 1965.
Oppenheim, Lassa. *International Law: A Treatise, vol. 1, Peace*. New York: Longmans, Green, 1905.
Oppenheim, Lassa. *International Law: A Treatise, vol. 1, Peace*. 2nd ed. New York: Longmans, Green, 1912.
Perrinjaquet, Jean. *Des cessions temporaires de territoires*. Paris: V. Giard & F. Brière, 1904.
Ronen, Yaël. "Territory, Lease." In *The Max Planck Encyclopedia of Public International Law vol. 9*, edited by Rüdiger Wolfrum. Oxford: Oxford University Press, 2012.
Ruskola, Teemu. *Legal Orientalism: China, the United States, and Modern Law*. Cambridge: Harvard University Press, 2013.
Strauss, Michael J. *The Leasing of Guantanamo Bay*. Santa Barbara: Praeger Security International, 2009.
Strauss, Michael J. *The Viability of Territorial Leases in Resolving International Sovereignty Disputes*. Paris: L'Harmattan, 2010.
Strauss, Michael J. *Territorial Leasing in Diplomacy and International Law*. Leiden: Brill Nijhoff, 2015.
Tyau, Min-ch'ien T. Z. *The Legal Obligations Arising out of Treaty Relations between China and Other States*. Shanghai: Commercial Press, 1917.
Yang, Léon (Yang Lieou-Fong). *Les Territoires à bail en Chine: Etude d'histoire diplomatique et de Droit International*. Paris: Presses universitaires de France, 1929.
Young, C. Walter. *The International Legal Status of the Kwantung Leased Territory*. Baltimore: Johns Hopkins Press, 1931.
Westlake, John. *International Law, Part 1, Peace*. Cambridge: Cambridge University Press, 1904.
Willoughby, Westel W. *Foreign Rights and Interests in China*. 2nd ed., vol. 1. Baltimore: Johns Hopkins Press, 1927.

PART 3

Intent and Time in Territorial Disputes

CHAPTER 5

The Arguments Based on "Law" in Territorial Disputes

Atsuko Kanehara

1 Main Subject Matter of This Chapter*

1.1 *Discussions on the Relation to the Law*

The main subject matter of this chapter is how international law can ensure its own validity, specifically in the context of territorial issues.[1] Territorial disputes involve both legal[2] and non-legal arguments. However, even in the case of non-legal arguments, international law has the flexibility to include such arguments, perhaps thereby attempting to ensure its own validity. This chapter will consider what the dynamism of international law is, in the sense of how the regulation of international law is achieved in its application to people, objects, facts, and acts, or figuratively speaking, exactly how formidable the world of international law is.

The following specific example comes to mind. Japan adheres to the so-called "inherent territory" argument, which has been described as "not a legal concept" and "having no clear legal meaning."[3] In that regard, the following question arises from the perspective of international law. Can the unilateral

* All of the URLs were last accessed on September 27, 2021.

1 The territorial issues referred to here are the actual circumstances between Japan and its neighboring States in relation to the Northern Territories, Takeshima, and the Senkaku Islands. The official position of Japan on the Senkaku Islands is there is no "dispute" with China. The official position of Japan on the Four Northern Islands and Takeshima is there are "disputes" with Russia and Korea, respectively. The term territorial "issues" collectively refers to these individual disputes. The author will use either "dispute(s)" or "issue(s)" as is required and appropriate according to the context.

2 The term "law" in this chapter refers to international law, with a focus on "international law in relation to territorial disputes."

3 With the reservation that this likely also contains personal views, refer to Yamagami Shingo 山上信吾, Counsellor (as of writing this chapter) for the International Legal Affairs Bureau, Ministry of Foreign Affairs, Koyū no Ryōdo o Kangaeru "固有の領土"を考える [Considering inherent territory], *Nihon Gaikō Kyōkai Hō* 日本外交協会報 [The Society for Promotion of Japanese Diplomacy Magazine] November 20, 2012 edition (Tokyo: The Society for Promotion of Japanese Diplomacy, 2012), 1.

 | DOI:10.1163/9789004706361_006

argument of one State cause the severance of its relation from the legal world? If Japan's "inherent territory" argument implies a blurring and denial of a relation to the legal world, then historic rights[4] are conversely asserted as rights under international law despite the existence of some doubt as to whether they are indeed such rights. China asserts that it has historic rights in the vast sea area that is the South China Sea. This assertion is not founded on the United Nations Convention on the Law of the Sea (UNCLOS), but rather based on customary international law.[5] Ever since the Fisheries Case[6] of 1951, there has been debate about the relationship between historic rights and international law. This is an unavoidable theme when constructing Japan's objection to China's assertion of historic rights regarding the Senkaku Islands.

1.2 *Structure of This Chapter*

The "inherent territory" argument will be dealt with elsewhere. This chapter focuses on the extent to which assertions and claims of a relation to the law will be incorporated into the legal world. It will consider this in the following order: 1) Elaboration of the subject matter; 2) Claims of a relation to the law – "historic rights"; 3) Main elements of determining a relation to the law – intent and time; 4) Reconsideration of the elements of the "effect of intent" in territorial disputes; and 5) Proposal for the building of Japan's integrated position as a sovereign State on the Senkaku Islands issue. This position is constructed with references to the territorial title argument, the law of the sea, and the concept of disputes, and contributes to the realization of the common interests of the international community as well.

The author believes it would be beneficial to also frankly express her own perceptions, and has therefore described the subject matter of this chapter to be the "blurring and denial of a relation to the law" and "claims of a relation to the law." Prior to considering these themes in Section 2 and onwards, the author will here clarify her perceptions by using the term "validity" of the law.

4 "Historic rights," "historic title," and other such terms will be dealt with later.

5 The arbitral award (merits) on the South China Sea dispute carefully confirms, in several official documents, the arguments of China that did not appear in the tribunal. Kanehara Atsuko, "Validity of International Law over Historic Rights: The Arbitral Award (Merits) on the South China Sea Dispute," *Japan Review*, vol. 2, no. 3 (2018, Winter), 9–11. The South China Sea Arbitration (The Republic of Philippines v. The Republic of China), Award of 12 July 2016, at https://pcacases.com/web/sendAttach/2086.

6 *Fisheries Case* (*United Kingdom v. Norway*), Judgment of December 18th, 1951, *ICJ Reports* 1951.

1.3 *"Validity" of the Law*

In this chapter, the existence of a relation to the law is described as the validity of the law being extended. This means the law applies those standards of legal assessment to people, objects, facts, and acts. This is described as the law extending regulation over people, objects, facts, and acts, and can also be called "prescriptive jurisdiction." The term "validity extends" is how the author expresses her perception of "people, objects, facts, and acts being included in the world of law." The law extends regulation and subsequently the people, objects, facts, and acts are legally assessed (legal or illegal) by the law.[7]

The usage of "validity" in precedents and so forth is not necessarily unambiguous. The usage of "validity" in this chapter, as the author has explained it to mean, also includes the following meanings depending on the context: "effectiveness," "relevancy," "usefulness," and "applicability."

2 Claims of a Relation to the Law – "Historic Rights"

2.1 *"Historic Rights"*

The following is a clarification of the main terms used in this section. Historic "rights" can also refer to "historic title," "historic rights," "(rights to) historic bays," "(rights to) historic waters," and so forth; however, these concepts will be collectively referred to as "historic rights."[8] These concepts will be applied according to the context, including the use of "historic rights" in a particularly narrow sense.

This section will consider the legal and non-legal aspects of arguments in territorial disputes, in regard to historic rights. The term "non-legal" that is used here includes all aspects (justice, historic, political, cultural, etc.) other than the legal elements. "Non-legal" is not used only in the sense of justice as "justice" in contraposition to law.

There are two types of "law" in relation to historic rights, as follows. The first type is international law that governs the relationship between historic rights and the matters of international law (for example, international law on territorial title, maritime delimitation, and border delimitation). For this type

---

7 Later in this chapter, a legal assessment of the "existence or absence of opposability" will also be introduced.

8 The substantive reason for this is that the considerations in this chapter generally apply to "historic" rights and "historic" title, etc. Furthermore, in the same sense, the arbitration award (merits) in the South China Sea disputes also use "historic rights" as "a generic term." Kanehara, *supra* note 5, 13.

of law, "general international law" is assumed that can take the form of customary international law and treaties. The term "special (not excluding bilateral) international law"[9] will be used as required. The second type is international law that concerns historic rights per se. (This brings to mind customary international law, but also does not exclude treaties.) Typical international law is that which governs the definition of historic rights and their requirements for establishment.[10] A clear distinction cannot always be made between the first and second types of international law. For example, in the first type of international law governing maritime delimitation, when some kind of legal effect is given to historic rights, it is possible to also stipulate (second type of international law) the requirements for qualifying as historic rights.[11] Therefore, the author will clarify, as much as possible and according to the individual context, whether an issue of international law pertains to the first or second type.

2.2 *Relationship between International Law and Arguments That Do Not Conform with International Law*

The relationship between international law and historic rights has been debated since 1951, prompted by the International Court of Justice (ICJ) judgment in the Fisheries Case.[12] The ICJ ruled that Norway's straight baseline method is "the application of general international law."[13] The "general international law" referred to here is that in relation to the straight baseline. In the terminology used in this chapter, it is the international law that governs the relationship between historic rights and the matters of international law. The United Kingdom argued that there was a 10 nautical mile rule for closing lines across the mouths of bays, and that the assertion of any exceptions to that rule would need to be based on historic grounds. The United Kingdom asserted that Norway's straight baseline method was what it deemed an exception to general international law, and that Norway had the burden of proving that the method was founded on historic grounds. The ICJ dismissed this assertion.[14]

9 "Special (bilateral) international law" and "opposability" will be considered later in Section 2.

10 Although prudent evaluation is required, China bases its assertions of historic rights in the South China Sea on general international law and customary international law.

11 In contrast, Article 15 of UNCLOS recognizes the special consideration of historic title in the maritime delimitation of territorial waters, but it does not stipulate the requirements for the establishment of historic title.

12 *Supra* note, 6.

13 *Ibid.*, 131.

14 *Ibid.*, 130–131.

Following the Fisheries Case judgment, the International Law Commission (ILC) examined matters in relation to historic waters and historic bays,[15] including the logic of the ICJ in the Fisheries Case judgment and the logic of the United Kingdom's assertion. This was an examination of the rights applying to historic waters; therefore, based on the terminology of this chapter, and provided that doing so is not particularly inappropriate, the term "historic rights" is used when referring to these considerations of the ILC.

It is difficult to substantially differentiate between the view that historic rights are an exception to general international law, and the view that historic rights are an application of general international law, when considered in the following manner, namely, when general international law provides for an abstract provision, which allows a certain amount of room to consider individual and specific circumstances. In this type of general international law, it is difficult to substantially differentiate between cases where the "application" of the law recognizes and gives certain consideration to historic rights as individual and specific circumstances, and cases where historic rights are recognized as deviating from general international law only as an "exception." In the former case, the legality (or illegality) of historic rights (and their corresponding assertions, etc.) is determined by the application of international law with reference to individual and specific circumstances. In the latter case, the legality (or illegality) of historic rights (and their corresponding assertions, etc.) is determined by whether or not they are an "exception." Put simply, whether or not historic rights are themselves an "exception" is primarily determined by the content of general international law.

From the perspective of this chapter's subject matter of the validity of general international law, a number of points can be made as outlined further below. First, however, it should be noted that the terms "general international law" and "exception" will be used in the following manner. The subject matter of this chapter is the validity of "international law" and the issue of ensuring and maintaining the world of "international law," in which case there is no particular need to limit this to "general international law." The term "general international law" refers to the type of international law that applies to and is in effect on all States, as opposed to "special international law," which applies, for instance, only between the party States to the dispute. Then, it can also

15 *Juridical Regime of Historic Waters, Including Historic Bays*, Study Prepared by the Secretariat, 19 March 1962, Document A/CN.4/143. Hereinafter written as the "ILC report." The ILC report takes heed of the terminology of "historic waters" and "historic bays," while not seeking further differentiation between the two, as historic bays are regarded as being included in historic waters. *Ibid.*, para. 34.

be argued that an "exception" of "general international law" is "special international law." However, in such a case, it is clear that this "exception" does not mean "outside of the law." In contrast, this chapter uses the term "general international law" in relation to, needless to say, discussions on the two logical structures presented by the ICJ in the Fisheries Case, and also when its use would not cause confusion in discussions on the validity of international law.

With these terms thus having been clarified, an examination of the two aforementioned views, from the perspective of this chapter, indicates that, if historic rights are positioned as an "application" of general international law, it is possible to ensure the validity of general international law in regard to historic rights. In other words, this may imply that "historic rights can be included in the world of international law." In comparison, when historic rights are perceived to be an "exception" to general international law, it can perhaps be posited that historic rights are dismissed from the world of international law. However, even when historic rights are positioned as an "exception" to general international law, it is, albeit by formal logic, general international law that positions them as an "exception." In that sense, it can also be suggested that general international law governs historic rights, and "historic rights are included in the world of international law" as an "exception."

The establishment of customary international law in regard to historic rights per se, as well as the adoption of provisions on historic rights by way of treaties, are also not excluded. The "international law" (both customary law and treaty) described here is, in accordance with the terminology of this chapter, that which stipulates the definition and requirements of historic rights. Then, if general international law in regard to historic rights per se is established, it is not necessary to position historic rights as an "exception" to general international law. For example, if historic rights are established upon fulfilling the requirements stipulated in general international law in regard to historic rights per se, the extent to which those historic rights have an impact in the maritime delimitation is determined by the relationship between the application of general international law in relation to the maritime delimitation and general international law in regard to historic rights per se.

Historic rights are referred to in the following manner in judicial and arbitral practice. In the Eritrea-Yemen Arbitration[16] of 2006, the Permanent Court of Arbitration stated, "if there is indeed an established [historic] title ... then it is

16 The Eritrea-Yemen Arbitration, Phase I: Territorial Sovereignty and Scope of Dispute, *Reports of International Arbitral Awards*, vol. XXII (1998), 211–234. Hereinafter referred to as the "Eritrea-Yemen Case."

by definition a prior right."[17] In the Qatar and Bahrain Case[18] of 2001, the joint dissenting opinion of Judges Bedjaoui, Ranjeva, and Koroma criticized the ICJ for not ruling on the validity of the parties' arguments on *the legal ground* of their rights, including "*the competing historical titles*."[19]

When asserting historic rights as an "exception" to general international law, the relationship between historic rights and general international law follows the course stated below, from the perspectives of the lapse of time and development of the law.

When general international law is in the process of being created and formed, those rights that are asserted and exercised as ones prior to general international law, and that do not conform with it in terms of content, are to be upheld as legal historic rights even if they are an "exception" under the international law that is being created and formed. Or, in the case of rights that conform with general international law, even when those rights come to no longer conform due to changes in general international law, in order to uphold such rights as legal rights, historic rights are asserted as an "exception." If general international law that allows for historic rights is established, then historic rights are no longer an "exception" to such international law.

If that is the case, in the relationship between historic rights and international law, it raises the issue of whether historic rights will be definitely overridden by the agreements (i.e., treaties) of the relevant States or the States of the international community in general.[20] This point will be considered later when examining the "attitude of foreign States," which is a requirement for establishing historic rights, while also considering the issue of the range of States expressing consent.

The above subsection has explained the relationship between historic rights and the "international law that governs the relationship between historic rights and the matters of international law." The next subsection will examine international law in regard to historic rights per se.

---

17 *Ibid.*, para. 107.

18 *Maritime Delimitation and Territorial Questions between Qatar and Bahrain* (Merits), Judgment of 16 March 2001, *ICJ Reports, 2001*, 40. Hereinafter referred to as the "Qatar and Bahrain Case."

19 Joint Dissenting Opinion of Judges Bedjaoui, Ranjeva, and Koroma, *ibid.*, para. 52.

20 There may also be a relationship between historic rights and customary international law. There is also debate as to whether customary international law treats "tacit agreement" as true agreement. Accordingly, in discussions of historic rights and the relation to the agreement of the specific States concerned or the States of the international community in general, this mainly pertains to agreement and the treaties that shape said consent.

2.3 *International Law on Historic Rights*[21]

2.3.1

As an underlying consideration, Subsection 2.3 will address the issue as to whether there are any differences in the logical constructs that are the basis for rights in the land and sea. The reasons for the argument that there are differences are as follows: 1) On land, physical effective occupation is an important element of territorial acquisition, whereas in the sea, legal logic is an important element. 2) On land, there is occupation of *terra nullius* or acquisition of land from the prior owner, whereas in the sea, rights are allocated on the basis of *res communis*. 3) On land, weight is placed on physical occupation and effective rule, with facts being more significant than norms, whereas in the sea (particularly in the current law of the sea), the focus is on the use of resources. In order to be able to derive profits from the development of resources, global markets need to function, and in order for those markets to function and to be utilized, it is necessary to follow norms rather than facts.[22]

Each argument is likely to apply to a certain degree, but what is important is that they cannot definitively be said to lead to differences in the logical constructs that are the basis for rights in the land and sea. Rather, it suffices simply to be aware that there may be such differences when determining elements such as effective occupation, the long-term use of authority, and acquiescence[23] from foreign States. Consequently, as will be explained below, it is primarily areas of the sea that are considered in regard to historic rights, and such considerations can also be applicable to the land, "*mutatis mutandis*."

2.3.2

The classification criteria and classifications of historic rights are presented in theory.[24] When forming the logical construct of historic rights as being legal rights, there is the possible issue of the extent of the applicability of this logic – namely, when following these classifications, do the logical constructs

21 For a comprehensive consideration of historic rights, refer to Clive Symmons, *Historic Waters in the Law of the Sea: A Modern Re-Appraisal* (Leiden: Brill, 2007).

22 For a comparative discussion of territorial sovereignty in the land and sea, refer to Lea Brilmayer, Natalie Klein, "Land and Sea: Two Sovereignty Regimes in Search of a Common Denominator," *New York University Journal of International Law and Politics*, vol. 33 (2001), 704; and also Irina Buga, "Territorial Sovereignty Issues in Maritime Disputes: A Jurisdictional Dilemma for Law of the Sea Tribunals," *International Journal of Marine and Coastal Law*, vol. 27 (2012), 59 *et seq.*

23 Terminology for expressing intent will be explained later.

24 See, for example, the articles listed in *supra* note 22 and the theories to which they refer, etc.

themselves need to be distinguished; in other words, does following these classifications require the application of different logical constructs? Nevertheless, it is difficult to conceive of classifications that would require the distinguishing of the logical constructs themselves. Rather, in considering the requirements for acquiring historic rights, the factors taken into (particular) account are indicated in the following classification criteria.

The classification criteria are: 1) Target of rights: Land or sea;[25] 2) Sovereignty or (complete and comprehensive) rights / partial rights; 3) Exclusive rights; and 4) Rights *erga omnes* or rights in relation to specific States.

2.4 *Requirements for the Establishment of Historic Rights*

2.4.1

The ILC report sets out three factors for the establishment of historic rights,[26] following the ICJ judgment in the 1951 Fisheries Case. These are: 1) The exercise of authority; 2) The attitude of foreign States; 3) Continuity. Generally, even in theory, and in judicial and arbitral precedents, historic rights are considered to converge on these three factors,[27] which will be examined in 2.4.2 to 2.4.4, respectively.

2.4.2

The first factor is "the exercise of authority."

2.3.2 stated that irrespective of the discussions on classifications surrounding historic rights, such classifications do not require the distinguishing of the logical constructs for asserting historic rights; however, they may be factors

25 The following points should be kept in mind in regard to islands. An island is a land, and so historic rights to such land can be assumed. On the other hand, the definition by international law of marine features such as islands or rocks and the types of marine area and seabed that are generated therefrom are in accordance with the law of the sea. An island requires "human habitation" as set out in Article 121 of UNCLOS, so as to have an exclusive economic zone (EEZ) and continental shelf status. In the territorial acquisition of land, in order to establish and continue effective rule, it is important to have either the habitation of people who are rulers of the land or a process of dealing with native inhabitants of the land, etc. However, it is difficult to understand the relationship between that and the "human habitation" requirement of Article 121 of UNCLOS. In the meaning shown here, the "human habitation" requirement from the perspective of the law of the sea, and the emphasis on the habitation of people who are rulers of the land or a process of dealing with native inhabitants of the land, etc., from the perspective of territorial acquisition may perhaps each be due to separate reasons.

26 ILC Report, para. 80.

27 Refer to the theories, etc., considered in the ILC Report.

to be accounted for when considering whether the requirements for acquiring historic rights have been fulfilled. This point is noticeably evident in the factor "the exercise of authority." It will be confirmed across several different elements below.

Firstly, in regard to the "subject of an act," this must be a part of the domestic (legal) system and the act must emanate from the State. The ILC report reached this conclusion by aggregating several theories.[28] The same is true of the view of the arbitral tribunal in the 1968 Indo-Pakistan Western Boundary (Rann of Kutch) Case[29] between India and Pakistan and the view regarding the Pulau Islands in the 2002 Pulau Ligitan and Pulau Sipadan (Indonesia/Malaysia) Case judgment.[30]

Secondly, as for the requisite content and extent of the exercise of authority, this is regarded as differing from case to case.[31] Upon closer examination, from the perspective of the land and sea being different, it has been pointed out that while it is physically easy to effectively occupy land, it is not necessarily the same in the sea (particularly the deep sea).[32]

Thirdly, concerning the assertion of sovereignty or complete and comprehensive rights, or that of partial rights, there is perhaps also the line of thinking that the degree of proof required differs depending on the content of the rights being asserted (sovereignty or rights that do not reach the level of sovereignty). Sovereignty naturally includes exclusivity. It can perhaps be said that in rights for a "specific purpose and function," exclusivity will become an even more important factor of consideration.[33]

For example, in the Gulf of Maine Case,[34] in regard to the traditional fisheries industry of the United States, the ICJ stated that any mere factual

28 ILC Report, para. 95.

29 The Indo-Pakistan Western Boundary (Rann of Kutch) between India and Pakistan, *Reports of International Arbitral Awards*, vol. XVII (1968), 416.

30 *Case Concerning Sovereignty over Pulau Ligitan and Pulau Sipadan (Indonesia/Malaysia)*, Judgment of 17 December 2002, *ICJ Reports, 2002*, 625.

31 In the same vein, refer to the Island of Palmas Case (Netherland/U.S.A.), Award of April 4, 1928, *Reports of International Arbitration Awards*, vol. II (1949), 867.

32 For works that consider topics on territorial sovereignty in comparison between the land and sea, see *supra* note 22.

33 It has also been pointed out that in the ocean, it is not easy to extend effective and physical rule in vast areas of the sea; rather, it becomes a case of States making assertions based on the exclusivity of legal rights to marine resources. Brilmayer and Klein, *supra* note 22, 735.

34 Affaire de la Délimitation de la Frontière Maritime dans la Région du Golfe du Maine (Canada/États-Unis D'Amérique), Arrêt du 12 Octobre 1984 Rendu par la Chambre Constitué par Ordonnance de la Cour du 20 Janvier 1982.

predominance could not support legal validity in relation to an (established) exclusive fishery zone.[35] In the Qatar and Bahrain Case[36] of 2001 as well, Bahrain's right in regard to its pearling industry was not deemed a special circumstance in the delimitation of boundaries, the reason being that Bahrain's right was not established as being "an exclusive and quasi-territorial (territorial) right."

Fourthly, as for rights *erga omnes* or rights in relation to specific States, assertions of rights *erga omnes* are perhaps considered to need to meet higher standards to fulfil "the exercise of authority" requirement, compared to the assertions of rights in relation to specific States; or these classification standards may only relate to the "attitude of foreign States," which will be examined next.

Similarly, the acts and public announcements (they cannot be secret acts) recognized by foreign States can also be considered in relation to the following factor of "the attitude of foreign States."

2.4.3

Under 2.4.3, the second factor, "attitude of foreign States," will be taken up.

1) Not only in practice and the ILC report but in theory as well, the unilateral assertion of rights to secure historic rights is considered to be insufficient on its own; the attitude of foreign States has also become a requirement.

As stated above, there are two possible logical constructs: asserting historic rights as an "exception" to general international law, or asserting historic rights as part of the application of general international law.[37] Whether or not the attitude of foreign States becomes a requirement depends on which of these logical constructs is applied. If historic rights are included in the scope of general international law as an application of such law, then the attitude of foreign States is not a requirement.

In this regard, similar to the Fisheries Case judgement, the ILC report has taken the position of historic rights being included in the application of general international law. (It frequently indicates criticisms of and questions about theories that use logical constructs that explain historic rights as an "exception" to general international law.) However, it states that "the attitude of foreign States" is a requirement to secure historic rights.[38] Logically, while positioning historic rights as a part of considering individual and specific circumstances

35 *Ibid.*, para. 235.

36 *Supra* note 18, para. 236.

37 2.2.

38 ILC Report, para. 80.

within the scope of the application of general international law, it can call for certain requirements to be fulfilled in order to secure historic rights.[39]

The conclusion of the ILC report is that, in confirming the ICJ judgment on the Fisheries Case, "the general toleration of the international community" is a requirement.[40] That this does not refer to "interested States" but rather to "*the general attitude of the international community and requires toleration*" will be elaborated on later. Logically, either of the other factors of an "exercise of authority," and also "(long term) continuity," which will be elaborated on in some sense later, can be connected to discussions on whether assertions of historic rights are an exception to or an application of general international law. That being said, this issue is actually most prominent in relation to the "attitude of foreign States" factor.

In the Fisheries Case judgment, the straight baseline method of Norway satisfied the three factors set by the ICJ. However, it is notable that, beyond recognizing that point, the ICJ also confirmed: (a) the attitude of the United Kingdom, an interested State, and also (b) the lack of opposition from the general international community.[41] This can be understood to a certain extent when taking into account that on the one hand, particularly in regard to (a), the ICJ played a role in resolving disputes between the United Kingdom and Norway; and on the other hand, particularly in regard to (b), the ICJ also made a legal declaration in general to the international community that Norway's straight baseline method conformed with international law.

While the ICJ adopted the logic that the straight baseline method is an application of general international law and not an exception, it nonetheless considered the toleration of the United Kingdom and also of the international community, and the absence of opposition. In other words, "foreign States," whose attitude is to be taken into consideration, were extended beyond the United Kingdom to the general international community. Although the ILC report has taken the stance of positioning historic rights as being an application of general international law, it, too, states that "the general toleration of the international community" is required to secure historic rights. This can perhaps be described as adhering to the Fisheries Case judgment.

Based on this underlying consideration, several elements of the "attitude of foreign States" will now be addressed.

---

39 In that case, using the terminology of this chapter, it can be said that the international law of historic rights per se is included in the general international law that governs the relationship between historic rights and the matters of international law rules and order.

40 ILC Report, paras. 120, 132.

41 *Supra* note 6, 136–139. Kanehara, *supra* note 5, 24–25.

2) What is required in terms of the attitude of foreign States?

It is easy to explain the need to consider the attitude of foreign States if historic rights are taken to be an "exception" to general international law. However, if acquiescence and recognition are required as the attitude of foreign States, and if these can be termed the "tacit *agreement*" of foreign States, this would render assertions of historic rights superfluous to begin with.[42] The reason is that the legal effect of such assertions of historic rights can be acquired by the "agreement" of foreign States. This is a consequence of the "*pacta sunt servanda*" principle.

Those scholars who adopt the "exception" theory explain that the attitude of foreign States need only to be "weak and negative (i.e., not reaching an agreement)" in the sense of toleration or inaction, which is different from a response of positive approval, in other words agreement. The point has also been made that if that is the extent to which the attitude of foreign States is required, it diminishes the substantive difference between the explanation of historic rights being within the scope of the application of general international law and the explanation of them being an "exception" to general international law.[43]

In the elements that comprise this attitude of foreign States, the issue of the scope of "foreign States," namely whether this entails specific States or the international community in general, may also be pertinent. The meaning of "opposability" in regard to foreign States will be elaborated on below, but first, it is necessary to explain how the scope of foreign States and the effect of historic rights are connected.

In order for historic rights to have "opposability" against interested States, the response (either a positive agreement or negative inaction) of those States is necessary in order to secure historic rights. This can also be perceived as similar to the so-called logic of distinguishing "special law" from "general law." Alternatively, if legality and opposability are distinguished as the concept of "opposability" having a different legal effect to "legality (or illegality)," the following logical construct can also be posited. On the one hand, in order to establish the "opposability" of historic rights between interested States and the State asserting historic rights, the attitude of the interested States is required. On the other hand, if a binding effect *erga omnes* – "legality" – is not asserted in regard to historic rights, the attitude of *States other than* interested States

42 ILC Report, para. 107.

43 ILC Report, para. 109.

is not required. Although logically this can be considered to be "opposability" *erga omnes*, it is difficult to find meaning in distinguishing that from "legality."

It could be argued that the degree to which relations with specific foreign States becomes an issue varies between cases of the delimitation of maritime boundaries and cases of territorial sovereignty in regard to land. Regarding the former, it is worth considering whether or not the attitude of specific foreign States can be described as necessary. As confirmed above, the ILC report states that the "general toleration of the international community" is required to secure historic rights. In the Gulf of Maine Case, in regard to the United States' similar argument regarding historic rights on the fishing activities of its fishermen, the Special Chamber said "no reliance could any longer be placed on that predominance," as "a valid ground for its now claiming the incorporation into its own exclusive fishery zone of any area which, in law, has become part of Canada's."[44]

In the Fisheries Case, the ICJ adopted the logic that Norway's straight baseline method is "the application of general international law and not an exception to it" and declared three criteria that can be interpreted as the content of general international law. In spite of acknowledging that the straight baseline method of Norway satisfied the three factors, the ICJ also confirmed the attitude of the United Kingdom – the (interested) State in dispute with Norway – as well as the absence of protests by the general international community. In regard to the effect of Norway's straight baseline method in relation to the United Kingdom, the French version of the judgment uses the term "*opposer*"[45] although the English version does not use the expression "opposable." Furthermore, in the Tunisia-Libya Case, both Libya and the ICJ argue "opposability."[46]

3), the meaning of "opposability" will be clarified in terms of its use in this chapter. "Opposability" can be used as a concept indicating *a legal effect that differs from* "legality/illegality." Accordingly, it can explain the following situations.

Firstly, if the foreign State is a specific one, as to the establishment of historic rights being determined by the negative attitude of the specific foreign State, even though the establishment of historic rights would not be recognized by the "unilateral assertion" of the State asserting its historic rights, the

44 *Supra* note 34, paras. 235–236.
45 *Supra* note 6, 138, in French.
46 *Continental Shelf* (*Tunisia v. Libyan Arab Jamahiriya*), Judgment of 24 February 1982, *ICJ Report, 1982*, for instance, paras. 15, 90, 92, 97, 101, 105.

attitude of the "specific" foreign State alone would negate the establishment of historic rights (as being legal). There is thus an imbalance. The "opposability" concept is useful in upholding the point that the establishment of historic rights cannot be determined by "only" a specific foreign State, while still somewhat acknowledging the effect of the foreign State's opposition.

The underlying logic is as follows. If a specific foreign State has expressed its opposition, this negates the "opposability" against said foreign State; namely, one cannot go so far as to say that historic rights are "illegal." In this case, "opposability" becomes a concept indicating *a legal effect that differs from* that of "legality/illegality." It follows, then, that this leaves the possibility for the historic rights to acquire legality, regardless of whether the "opposability" is affirmed or negated in relation to the specific foreign State. In such a situation, historic rights will not be established (will not become legal rights) merely by "the unilateral assertion of the one State" that is asserting its historic rights. At the same time, it is also not possible to determine the establishment (legality or illegality) of those historic rights "only" by the specific foreign State's intent to oppose. In this way, balance between the two can be achieved.

Secondly, if the "foreign State" entails "States covering the general scope of the international community," it can be interpreted that the "legality" of historic rights will be negated by the protest and negative attitude of the foreign State.

Taking this approach, on the one hand, even though the first element for establishing historic rights, namely, the exercise of authority, is not fulfilled (for example, the exercise of insufficiently effective authority, only sporadic acts of the State and individuals, etc.), and if the foreign State has an affirmative attitude, the possibility of the historic rights having "opposability" in relation to the foreign State is not negated. On the other hand, historic rights that have "legality" cannot be established in relation to States covering the general scope of the international community by the affirmative attitude of (only) the relevant foreign State.

Considering only the logical possibilities, this may give rise to "opposability" in relation to States covering the general scope of the international community and also the legal effect of "legality" in relation to an interested State. However, it is difficult to find any significance in this beyond logical possibilities.

That is to say, "opposability" is a concept indicating a legal effect that differs from "legality/illegality." In contrast, generally, the legal effect against States covering the general scope of the international community is "legality (or illegality)." It may also be possible to deal with this by distinguishing between bilateral (regional/special) customary international law and general customary international law, as in 2.4.3 point 4) and 5) below.[47]

4) Another meaning of "opposability" is a concept describing the effect of special international law as opposed to the effect of general international law.

As explained above, there are theories that divide historic rights into "rights *erga omnes*" and "rights in relation to specific States." When discussing the two in terms of the "legality" of historic rights, "rights *erga omnes*" would be "historic rights in general international law" and "rights in relation to specific States" would be "historic rights in special international law." Based on this view, in the case of "rights in relation to specific States," historic rights are established by the "tacit agreement" of specific States; in the case of "rights *erga omnes*," historic rights are acquired by "custom(ary law)." This distinction is perhaps due to the fact that, in the first place, general practice is not established by the assertion and exercise of historic rights of "only one State," and so it cannot be considered to be customary law.[48]

From the perspective of treating both "rights in relation to specific States" and "rights *erga omnes*" as being the same as the concept describing the legal effect of "legality/illegality," the concepts of "opposability" and "legality" can be contrasted as follows. Essentially, opposability is a concept describing the "legality (or illegality)" of historic rights in relation to specific States, and "legality" is a concept describing the "legality (or illegality)" of historic rights in relation to States covering the general international community.

In regard to "tacit agreement and customary law," "bilateral/special/regional customary law (special law) and general customary law (general law)," "opposability and legality" and so forth, the theories are not unambiguous. However, in any case, the common issue is that one of their purposes is to distinguish between the legal effect that historic rights can have in relation to specific States, and the legal effect that historic rights can have in relation to the general international community.

With respect to this, the ILC report describes the logically inconsistent approach of affording greater weight to the attitude of "specific interested States" in the case of logical constructs that take historic rights to be an "exception" to general international law.[49] The "general international law" here is that which is binding on all States in the international community, and the "exception" in this context can be interpreted as meaning that *all States* in the

47 In regard to the effect of historic rights, in treaties, i.e., express agreement, the attitude of foreign States does not readily become an issue.

48 For similar considerations, refer to the ILC Report, paras. 102, 116–117.

49 ILC Report, para. 118.

international community *are equal*, each with the opportunity to react and have their own interests.

This logic does not allow for the explanation that historic rights acquire opposability against specific interested States by the attitude of said States. However, unlike the ILC report, when taking historic rights to be rights of general international law, and even when acknowledging that States in the general international community have the opportunity to react and have their own interests in regard to the assertion of historic rights, in actual fact, this does not necessarily exclude the affording of greater weight to the attitude of specific interested States.[50]

5) Academics of legal positivism view tacit agreement and customary international law as being the same. However, provided such a view is not adopted, a distinction is made between both of these concepts.

If the attitudes of foreign States in regard to the assertion of historic rights can be ones of toleration, inaction, acquiescence, and recognition, even if *opinio juris*, one of the requirements in the establishment of customary international law, is satisfied, it is not possible to acknowledge the establishment of customary international law in relation to such historic rights. This is because general practice, which is another requirement of customary international law, is not established only by one State's (a single) assertion and exercise of historic rights. If a certain number of States assert and exercise historic rights, and if a maximum number of common factors can be identified in the content of said historic rights, and also if it is supported by the *opinio juris* of the international community, said historic rights will become customary international law. In that case, may the historic rights become “territorial title?” That it is possible to discuss *customary international law in regard to specific historic rights* here does not, however, mean that it is generally possible to discuss, as a matter of course, the topics of historic rights becoming territorial title and, in such a case, the customary international law that stipulates the definition, requirements and other elements of historic rights.[51]

The ILC report states that national usage can develop into international usage based on the international reaction thereto.[52] From the perspective of the ILC report's use of the logical construct of historic rights being “an application of general international law,” does this mean historic rights become international usage, which in turn becomes customary international law? If that is

50 ILC Report, paras. 117–118.

51 The discussion on whether historic rights become territorial title will be considered in Section 4 of this chapter.

52 ILC Report, paras. 102–105.

the case, then international usage can be used to describe one State's assertion of international rights spurring similar acts in foreign States. However, even if (only) one State's assertion of international rights is met with an attitude of toleration by States covering the scope of the general international community, this does not imply that general practice, which is a requirement of customary international law, is established, nor can this be considered international usage in terms of customary international law.

6) If the acquiescence of foreign States is required to establish historic rights, and if this acquiescence is understood to be the same as "tacit agreement," would this render the other requirements unnecessary to begin with? Similarly, if there is opposition (similar to protests or a clear expression of opposition) from foreign States toward the assertion of historic rights, could this be deemed a *reversal of the "pacta sunt servanda principle"* and negation of said historic rights for the reason of a "lack of consent"?

If there is the (tacit) agreement of foreign States, then on the grounds of consent, the historic rights will have a legal effect. Taking that approach renders meaningless the other requirements that historic rights should satisfy.[53]

In the resolution of territorial disputes, the consent of foreign States (treaties, tacit agreement) is "decisive." With it, could it perhaps be said that territorial sovereignty is established *regardless of* other elements? Or, in international law, which sets the standard for the resolution of territorial disputes, is it also possible to modify, relax, or make relative the fundamental principle of "*pacta sunt servanda*?" These questions will be considered in Section 4.

2.4.4

2.4.4 will briefly outline the third factor, "continuity." "Continuity" here refers to recurring acts by a specific State.

The terms "ancient title" and "original title" are similar concepts to custom. In the 2008 Pedra Branca Case, although the party State made an assertion of historic title, the ICJ used the term "ancient original title."[54] Supposedly influenced by the Fisheries Case judgment, in the 2001 Cameroon-Nigeria Case, Nigeria contended the notion of historical consolidation, but the ICJ deemed

---

53 ILC Report, para. 107. For a point of view that refutes the notion of acquisitive prescription and recognizes tacit agreement as a requirement for historic rights, refer to Zhang Zuxing, "A Deconstruction of the Notion of Acquisitive Prescription and Its Implications for the Diaoyu Islands Dispute," *Asian Journal of International Law*, vol. 2 (2012), 328.

54 *Case Concerning Sovereignty over Pedra Branca / Pulau Batu Puteh, Middle Rocks and South Ledge (Malaysia/Singapore)*, Judgement of 23 May 2008, *ICJ Reports, 2008*, paras. 42, 75, 290. Hereinafter referred to as the "Pedra Branca Case."

this to be highly controversial.[55] Furthermore, in the Eritrea-Yemen Case, the Permanent Court of Arbitration used the terms "original," "traditional," and "original historic title" in regard to Yemen's historic assertions. It stated, "a historic title ... that has been created, or consolidated, by a process of prescription, or acquiescence, or by possession so long continued as to have become accepted by the law as a title."[56] The ILC report deems the term "ancient title" to be appropriate when assertions of historic rights are used to strengthen the legal effect of long-term occupation.[57]

Section 2 examined historic rights as typical examples of assertions of rights whereby these rights have grounds in international law or whereby they are rights under international law, while also being assertions that are different in contents to international law. It considered how international law can ensure its validity against such assertions, and how to incorporate historic rights into the world of international law under any requirements. Section 3 will consider in detail the relevant elements for international law to ensure its validity, with a particular focus on the elements of the intent of a State and temporal elements, and in the specific context of the Senkaku Islands.

3 Intent and Time – The Main Elements in Determining the Relationship with the Law

3.1 *"International Law"*

This chapter takes up subjects concerning the validity of international law. With regard to the Senkaku Islands issue, there are, in the first place, a variety of issues about applicable "international law." They are: 1) The intertemporal law and critical date[58] for determining the applicable law; 2) "The East Asian

55 Affaire de la Frontiére Terrestre et Maritime entre le Cameroun et Nigéria (Cameroun c. Nigéria; Guinée Équatriale (intervenant)), Arrêt du 10 Octobre 2002, *CIJ Recueil, 2002*, para. 65. Hereinafter referred to as the "Cameroon-Nigeria Case."

56 *Supra* note 16, para. 106.

57 ILC Report, para. 71.

58 In regard to critical dates, refer, for example, to Sakai Hironobu 酒井啓亘, "Ryōiki Funsō ni Okeru 'Ketteiteki Kijitsu' no Igi – Kokusai Shihō Saibansho no Saibanrei o Chūshin ni –" 領域紛争における『決定的期日』の意義—国際司法裁判所の裁判例を中心に— [The Significance of 'Critical Dates' in Territorial Disputes: Centering on Precedents of the International Court of Justice] in *Kokusai Kankei to Hō no Shihai (Owada Kokusai Shihō Saibansho Saibankan Taikan Kinen)* 国際関係と法の支配(小和田恆国際司法裁判所裁判官退官記念) [International Relations and the Rule of Law: Festschrift for Judge Owada Hisashi in Commemoration of His Retirement from

World Order" that was established by China in the 14th to 19th centuries, which forms the basis of "historic title"; 3) The stance of courts concerning the application of "the East Asian World Order"; and other such issues. This chapter will only indicate where these issues exist.

Hereinafter, the Senkaku Islands will be referred to as "the Islands."

3.2 *Relationship between Protests and the Temporal Element of "Critical Dates"*

3.2.1

Japan asserts its occupation of the Islands as *terra nullius*. However, when said assertion is not recognized, Japan may, alternatively, assert acquisitive prescription, although this is not its official position. The (absence) of protests of the foreign State becomes a key requirement to establish acquisitive prescription. Thus, for Japan to build its position, it must, in relation to the point in time when China is required to have started protests, consider the critical date and (the absence of) China's protests in a manner that will be advantageous to Japan. This chapter will stop short of considering the critical date but will briefly examine points that concern the protest element, as well as the "impetus" and "crystallization" of the dispute.

3.2.2

In territorial disputes surrounding occupation of *terra nullius*, the critical date[59] is deemed to be the point in time when disputes occur over "whether or not the land is *terra nullius*." There are cases of both clear and unclear critical dates; in (precedents involving) the latter case, a critical date is determined by the crystallization[60] of a dispute. In terms of the Japan-China situation, 1895 can perhaps be said to be the point in time when there was the crystallization of a dispute between the two States.

Certainly, the initial (impetus) point in time when "the question of whether or not the land is *terra nullius*" may have become an issue is likely to be the time of a related Cabinet decision by Japan in 1895. However, this was only an "impetus" that would not even "trigger" a dispute. The "crystallization" of a

---

the International Court of Justice], Iwasawa Yūji 岩澤雄司, Okano Masataka 岡野正敬 (eds.) (Tokyo: Shinzansha, 2021), 147–180.

59 Gerald Fitzmaurice, "The Law and Procedure of the International Court of Justice, 1951–4," *British Year Book of International Law*, vol. 32 (1955–1956), 30.

60 In regard to the "crystallization" of disputes, refer to *The Minquiers and Ecrehos Case (France / United Kingdom)*, Judgment of November 17th, 1953, *ICJ Reports, 1953*, 59–60, and *supra* note 58 by Sakai, 159–161.

dispute likely occurred subsequently, after the results (indicating the existence of prospective offshore oil fields) of the United Nations Economic Commission for Asia and the Far East (ECAFE) study around 1970.

3.2.3

The period of ongoing protests can be considered as the time from the crystallization of a dispute up to the critical date. It can be described as such when acts taken after the critical date are not deemed to be acts that serve a party's self-interest in the territorial dispute. Although the party State to the dispute is likely to continue its protests even after the critical date, such acts are not taken into consideration in court and do not "strengthen" the claims of the protesting State. The latter can also be said to be a negative effect of critical dates.

However, if the effect of the critical date is relative, there is no clear meaning in deeming the period of protest to be that up to the critical date.[61]

3.3 *Intent of Occupation and/or the Relationship between Effective Control and Protests*

3.3.1

There are various reasons as to why China did not make any protest for many years after 1895.[62] Japan likely asserted the acquisition of territorial sovereignty even by prescription in case 2), since 1) China did not protest against Japan's "occupation of *terra nullius*" and, 2) as an alternative assertion, even if the Islands were not *terra nullius* and were the territory of China, China did not protest after the Japanese Cabinet's decision in 1895.

---

61 Not protesting and "abandoning" are different. The relationship between not protesting and acquiescence will be explored later.

62 For an explanation of why China was unable to protest, including Taiwanese authorities, refer to Hungdah Chiu, "An Analysis of the Sino-Japanese Dispute over the T'iaoyutai Islets (Senkaku Gunto)," *Chinese (Taiwan) Yearbook of International Law and Affairs*, vol. 15, 21, 25; Carlos Tal Cheng, "The Sino-Japanese Dispute over the Tiao-yu-tai (Senkaku) Islands and the Law of Territorial Acquisition," *Virginia Journal of International Law*, vol. 14, N. 2 (1974), 259–260; Carlos Ramos-Mrosovsky, "International Law's Unhelpful Role in the Senkaku Islands," *University of Pennsylvania Journal of International Law*, vol. 29, N. 4 (2008), 930; Han-yi Shaw, "Revisiting the Diaoyutai/Senkaku Islands Dispute: Examining Legal Claims and New Historical Evidence under International Law and the Traditional East Asian World Order," *Chinese (Taiwan) Yearbook of International Law and Affairs*, vol. 26, 114.

3.3.2

Then, assuming that protest is required, are, firstly, an official declaration / public announcement / notification likely to be elements of effective control in occupation? A negative stance can be deduced from precedents, such as in the arbitral award in the Island of Palmas Case[63] and the award in the Clipperton Island Case.[64] First of all, whether a "notification" pertains to both the intent of occupation and effective control or to either of the two cannot be specified. Moreover, the intended recipient of the "notification" could either be "other powers" or, more broadly, various States in general.

Secondly, what is the "assertion of rights"? For example, in the Libya/Malta Continental Shelf Case,[65] the ICJ did not permit the intervention of a third State (Italy),[66] and the area that Italy was "claiming" (rights to) was excluded from the geographic range covered by the judgment. In regard to this, Judge Schwebel criticized the judgment for not distinguishing between the "claims" and "rights," which, consequently, endorsed the limitation of the ICJ's competence (in the maritime delimitation) by the (mere) "claims" of a third State.[67] Similarly, the Georgia-Russian Federation Case concerning the application of the International Convention on the Elimination of All Forms of Racial Discrimination,[68] and even the Ukraine-Russian Federation Case Concerning Coastal State Rights,[69] hint at facts and situations that do not reach the level of a dispute.[70]

The distinction between "assertion of rights" or "claims" is not merely an issue of terminology, but has the following significance. The practice relating to the "*difference* between protests and an assertion of rights (assertion of opposition)" and the "*distinction* between an assertion of rights and claims (that can be described as one-sided arguments and false accusations that do not reach the level of an assertion of rights)," can provide a starting point for explaining

63 *Supra* note 31, 868.

64 *Affaire de l'île de Clipperton* (*Mexique c. France*), sentence de 28 janvier 1931, *Recueil de sentences arbitrales, Vol. II*.

65 *Libya/Malta Continental Shelf Case*, Judgment of 3 June 1985, *ICJ Reports 1985*, 13.

66 *Libya/Malta Continental Shelf Case*, Application by Italy for Permission to Intervene, Judgment of 21 March 1984, *ICJ Reports, 1984*, para. 47.

67 Dissenting Opinion of Judge Schwebel, *ibid.*, paras. 6, 12.

68 *Case Concerning Application of the International Convention on the Elimination of All Forms of Racial Discrimination* (*Georgia v. Russian Federation*), Preliminary Objections, Judgment of 1 April 2011, *ICJ Reports, 2011*, para. 129 *et seq.*

69 *Dispute Concerning Coastal State Rights in the Black Sea, Sea of Azov, and Kerch Strait* (*Ukraine and Russian Federation*), Award, Concerning the Preliminary Objections of the Russian Federation, 21 February 2020, at https://pcacases.com/web/sendAttach/9272.

70 *Ibid.*, paras. 183 *et seq.*

Japan's position of deeming China's "complaints" about the Islands as "one-sided arguments and false accusations" and not acknowledging a dispute. The proposal of this chapter, from the perspective of the structure of Japan's integrated response, will be presented in the Conclusion.

Moreover, even if the absence of protest can be viewed as the "absence of an assertion of rights," it is difficult to extend this line of thinking further to the point of concluding that there was acquiescence on the part of China. The elements of intent are not easy to assess. If the absence of protests is the absence of an assertion of rights, and if the element of the lapse of time is added to that, do these, combined, constitute acquiescence?

3.4 *Absence of Protests from China Regarding Occupation and Acquisitive Prescription*

3.4.1

It is possible for Japan to argue, as an alternative assertion, for acquisitive prescription of the Islands due to the absence of protests from China. There have, however, been doubts raised, including in theory, as to whether acquisitive prescription is a type of territorial title.[71]

3.4.2

The first requirement of acquisitive prescription is the existence of a holder (A) of prior territorial sovereignty. Accordingly, the subject (B) that acquires territorial title by prescription will be illegally establishing sovereignty. This "illegality" is recognized as being "an infringement/encroachment on the rights of foreign States," "illegal," and "invalid."[72] Second is the lapse of time, during which there needs to be a continuous exercise of sovereignty by B. Third is the acquiescence by A. Fourth, albeit not, strictly speaking, a requirement, is the eventual abandonment of sovereignty by A.

If one is to focus on the third requirement of whether there was acquiescence by China, one needs to consider 1) the range of the subject(s) expressing

71 For the point of view that the acquisitive prescription of territory is an effect of acquiescence rather than temporal elements, even though there is a system of prescription in international law, refer to Yanagihara Masaharu 柳原正治, "Dai 9 Shō 'Kokka Ryōiki'" 第 9 章「国家領域」[Chapter 9 'Territory'], in *Kōgi Kokusaihō* 講義国際法 [Lectures on International Law], Kotera Akira 小寺彰 et al. (eds.) (Tokyo: Yūhikaku, 2010), 246. For questions on acquisitive prescription, refer to Robert Jennings, "The Acquisition of Territory in International Law," in Robert Jennings, *Collected Writings of Sir Robert Jennings* (The Hague: Kluwer Law International, 1998), 953; Ian Brownlie, *The Rule of Law in International Affairs* (The Hague: Martinus Nijhoff, 1998), 153–155; Zhang, *supra* note 53.

72 Fitzmaurice, *supra* note 59, 31–34; Ramos-Mrosovsky, *supra* note 62, 915–916.

acquiescence (the party State to the dispute, other States in the international community, etc.) and, 2) the substance of the acquiescence – the "effect of intent" but more specifically which type, namely toleration, acquiescence or tacit agreement. Moreover, if acquiescence can be taken to mean tacit agreement, then it is possible to provide grounds for the transfer of territorial sovereignty by consent, and the question arises as to whether the element of "(the lapse of) time" is rendered unnecessary to begin with. This will be elaborated on later.

Furthermore, Japan does not need to prove China's "abandonment," provided that "abandonment" is not a requirement of acquisitive prescription. The logic for Japan's position can be constructed in the following order: a. the land was *terra nullius*, b. occupation of *terra nullius* was enforced, and c. as an alternative assertion, even supposing that the land was not *terra nullius*, China's inaction from 1895 until around 1970 formed the basis for Japan's acquisitive prescription of the Islands.

3.5 *Relationship between Prescription and Historic Title*

3.5.1

Can, therefore, historic title be considered a type of territorial title, one that is separate from acquisitive prescription?

Regardless of the terminology, the following is an example of discussions when "historic title" is viewed as a type of territorial title. Firstly, there is a point of view that acknowledges this as being the case for an assertion of rights over a long period of time, even if the requirements of acquisitive prescription are not satisfied. According to said view, acknowledgement of the requirements of acquisitive prescription is not required for an assertion of rights "since the dawn of time."[73] Secondly, there is also a point of view[74] that, for an assertion of ancient rights from time immemorial, determining the attribution of those rights depends on the relative weight among the respective claims of the States concerned (although it is possible to debate whether this can be limited to the party States to disputes).[75]

A certain theory of China does not recognize acquisitive prescription as a type of territorial title; rather, acquisitive prescription comprises the two separate requirements of a. historic title, b. tacit agreement. Furthermore, this

---

73 Fitzmaurice, *supra* note 59, 31.

74 *Ibid.*, 34.

75 From this perspective, the terms "ancient title" and "original title," etc., likely need to be referenced and considered in terms of their usage and effect in judicial and arbitral practice.

must be "tacit agreement,"[76] not "acquiescence." Such a view proposes a new type of territorial title of "historic title & tacit agreement" as an alternative to acquisitive prescription, and can be said to strictly require "acquiescence or tacit agreement," which are deemed to be requirements of acquisitive prescription.[77] This is probably an assertion that, if Japan makes an alternative assertion of acquisitive prescription in regard to the Islands, it must satisfy the "historic title & tacit agreement" requirement.

If there is consent (albeit tacit), then the "lapse of time" element will no longer be required. This is in accordance with the *pacta sunt servanda* principle of international law. If that is the case, it raises questions as to where the features of "historic title" are. Furthermore, if territorial title is established by consent, this brings one back to the original question of "is historic title a type of territorial title?" with the conclusion being there is no need for it.

The ILC report requires the element of intent of the conflicting party State to the dispute (setting aside the issue of the range of the State) for establishing historic rights. However, the ILC states that territorial title is established by consent if there is a tacit "agreement," which renders meaningless the temporal element. Accordingly, the element of intent is toleration that is "not at the level of" consent.[78]

Lastly, this chapter will summarize the key issues relating to the effect of intent in territorial disputes, while referring to the foundation that is the *pacta sunt servanda* principle.

4 Reconsideration of the Element of the "Effect of Intent" in Territorial Disputes

4.1 *Aspects Involving the "Effect of Intent"*

Focusing on the considerations in this chapter, the effect of intent in territorial disputes appears in the following aspects: 1) the possibility of differences and distinctions among the "absence of protests," the "absence of an assertion of (opposing) rights" and "tolerance, acquiescence and tacit agreement"; 2) requirements of acquisitive prescription;[79] and 3) requirements for the establishment of historic rights.

---

76 Zhang, *supra* note 53, 328.

77 *Ibid.*, 328–331.

78 2.4.3, point 2).

79 If that effect of intent is a "(tacit) agreement," then, to begin with, the acquisition of territory is the result of a consent, which renders meaningless temporal elements. In that case,

With regard to the Fisheries Case, this chapter focused on whether Norway's straight baseline method could be opposable to the United Kingdom or if there was general toleration by the international community. Adhering to the terminology of this chapter, it also considered the legal effect that arises from the effect of intent as either an issue of "opposability" or of "legality (or illegality)," or an effect of general international law or special (regional) international law.

4.2 *"Consent" in the Effect of Intent*

4.2.1

It is possible for there to be "degrees" of the effect of intent, and this chapter thus far has considered toleration, acquiescence, and a tacit agreement. Indeed, the difference between acquiescence and a tacit agreement is not always clear. Moreover, even when distinguishing between toleration and acquiescence,[80] there remain questions as to whether such a distinction can be actually determined by the courts.

As for the "degrees" of the effect of intent, the following points must be kept in mind when considering Japan's response regarding the Islands. Although Japan asserts occupation of *terra nullius*, as an alternative assertion, it is possible to argue acquisitive prescription by Japan. In that case, 1) Can the absence of protests be called acquiescence?; and 2) If acquiescence includes consent, this renders meaningless the temporal element of acquisitive prescription from the start, and it is thus possible to assert the establishment of Japan's territorial sovereignty by a tacit agreement, rather than by acquisitive prescription.[81] In doing so, it is also important to invoke the following legal principles.

4.2.2

For a more detailed consideration of the effect of intent, (judicial) doctrines and principles that corroborate the formation of consent can be found in theories and judicial and arbitral practices. For example, there are silence and estoppel, and, as slightly more general principles, good faith and stability. It is not always easy to logically organize these (judicial) doctrines and other principles in terms of which phase to position them at. Perhaps there is an original means of organizing them in the setting of territorial disputes, and it may also

the question also arises as to whether acquisitive prescription can be perceived as a type of territorial title.

80 ILC Report, paras. 107, 109.

81 Even in such a case, it is still possible to maintain an assertion of acquisitive prescription as a concurrent assertion.

be possible and appropriate to propose a logical construct that is applicable in general in international law.[82]

4.3 *"Consent" in Territorial Disputes*

The "*pacta sunt servanda* principle" is a fundamental principle in international law. In the transfer of territorial sovereignty by "consent" there is "successive acquisition." This notion is based on the idea of there being a holder of territorial sovereignty (A), and another subject (B) that receives the transfer of territorial sovereignty by consent.

On the one hand, in the case of the assertion of historic title, if this is recognized by the "consent" of various States, the idea is not that territorial sovereignty is transferred from the holder (A) of territorial sovereignty to the subject (B) that is asserting historic title, but one that is clearly different from the notion of successive acquisition. On the other hand, in the case of acquisitive prescription, if this is recognized by a "tacit agreement," it is not impossible to understand, as a type of successive acquisition, the transfer of territorial sovereignty, by the tacit agreement of the prior holder of territorial sovereignty (A), to the subject (B) that is asserting acquisitive prescription, despite the temporal elements being rendered meaningless. When arranged in the traditional theory of territorial title, if acquisitive prescription could be taken to be an original acquisition and not a successive acquisition, then it would be necessary to restructure the theory of territorial title.

The *pacta sunt servanda* principle is a fundamental principle in international law. However, does it make sense for temporal elements to be rendered meaningless by the involvement of "consent?" In the unique context that is the theory of territorial title, is it not conceivable that "consent" is given a unique effect and that effect is diminished? Furthermore, is it also possible that there are differences in the notions of "State" and "consent" in different legal orders, such as (modern) Western international law and the East Asia world order? In that regard as well, there is perhaps still room for further consideration of "consent." At the very least, in the territorial issues of Japan, which belongs to East Asia, there can be said to be room to reconsider the significance of consent in territorial disputes from such perspectives.

82 See, Chapter 6 (Kitamura) of this book.

5 Conclusion

This chapter focused on the Senkaku Islands ("the Islands") and examined the validity of international law. It mainly dealt with historic rights, prescription, and the effect of intent as issues of the principles of territorial acquisition. Indeed, with regard to the Islands, Japan's response to the activities of Chinese vessels (government vessels, warships, and fishing boats) in the surrounding waters of the Islands is primarily based on the law of the sea. Lastly, in this Conclusion, in regard to the Islands issue, this chapter proposes that Japan, as a sovereign State, maintains an "integrated position" built on assertions that are based, in particular, on the theory of territorial title, the law of the sea, and the concept of disputes, respectively.[83] The reason for this is that the considerations in this chapter, which focused mainly on the theory of territorial title, should serve their intended functions, precisely as part of Japan's integrated position.

Japan's official position is that there is "no dispute" concerning territorial sovereignty of the Islands. To maintain this position, Japan appears to adopt, in principle, an approach of being *passive* in its response to China's assertions and acts, basically "not letting itself be provoked, *remaining silent, and shrinking away*."[84] This, consequently, also invites further provocations and other unbridled acts by China.

It is possible to conceive of a *proactive* response to prevent this from occurring, namely, a response grounded in the "rule of law,"[85] which is the central pillar of Japan's foreign policy, and criticizes China's attempts to unilaterally change the status quo by force, while at the same time maintaining Japan's position that there is no dispute over the Islands. Similarly, in another central pillar of Japan's foreign policy as well, that of a "Free and Open

83 The details are provided in a separate paper. Kanehara Atsuko, "Refining Japan's Integrative Position on the Territorial Sovereignty of the Senkaku Islands," *International Law Studies* (2021), vol. 97.

84 Not all of Japan's response to China's government vessels can necessarily be called "passive." See, for example, *ibid.*, III.1.(2). This is also closely related to the discussions on improving China–Japan relations held on November 7, 2014 (https://www.mofa.go.jp/a_o/c_m1/cn/page4e_000150.html), which mentions "the emergence of tense situations in recent years in the waters."

85 In the keynote speech by (then) Prime Minister Abe Shinzo in the Shangri-La Dialogue on May 30, 2014, he emphasized the "rule of law" at sea, which refers to the three principles of 1) Claims based on international law, 2) Not using "force or coercion," and 3) Peaceful settlement. https://www.mofa.go.jp/fp/nsp/page4e_000086.html.

Indo-Pacific,"[86] the "rule of law" is the first of the three central pillars. These pillars are also becoming established as common interests of the international community.

If that is the case, Japan should perhaps respond proactively to China's attempts to unilaterally change the status quo by force in the following manner:[87] 1) rather than a passive approach of avoiding the establishment of a dispute, 2) state clearly that China's assertions are nothing more than "false accusations" and do not constitute oppositional assertions that establish a dispute, and 3) proactively criticize and prevent China's attempts to unilaterally change the status quo by force. Specifically, based on the theory of territorial title, such an approach entails proving that there are no rational grounds whatsoever to China's assertions, and thoroughly refuting those assertions. Furthermore, in accordance with the notion of a dispute, Japan should deny the establishment of a dispute on the basis of China's assertions being nothing more than "false accusations." China and Japan are not in an equal position as mutual "party States to a dispute." Moreover, in response to China's unilateral attempts to change the status quo by force in the waters around the Senkaku Islands, besides of course taking steps based on the law of the sea, Japan should also implement effective measures[88] by invoking the fundamental principle of international law of the "respect of sovereignty" with the evidence of an infringement of Japan's sovereignty.

This would constitute and realize the sovereign State of Japan's "integrated" position, which leverages multiple perspectives based on the fundamental principles of international law of the theory of territorial title, the law of the sea, the notion of disputes, and the respect of sovereignty. Moreover, in the realization of this "integrated" position, Japan would not only be protecting its own rights but also simultaneously contributing to the realization of the common interests of the international community. This would be no less than an expression of Japan's wisdom as a sovereign State meriting the label of being a subject of international law.

---

86 https://www.mofa.go.jp/files/000407643.pdf.

87 The Coast Guard Law of China, which was enacted in February 2021, is perhaps precisely what promotes such attempts to change the status quo by force.

88 Kanehara, *supra* note 83, 4.(3).

Bibliography

Secondary Sources

Japanese

Sakai, Hironobu 酒井啓亘. "Ryōiki Funsō ni Okeru 'Ketteiteki Kijitsu' no Igi – Kokusai Shihō Saibansho no Saibanrei o Chūshin ni –" 領域紛争における『決定的期日』の意義 – 国際司法裁判所の裁判例を中心に – [The Significance of 'Critical Dates' in Territorial Disputes: Centering on Precedents of the International Court of Justice]. In *Kokusai Kankei to Hō no Shihai (Owada Kokusai Shihō Saibansho Saibankan Taikan Kinen)* 国際関係と法の支配（小和田恆国際司法裁判所裁判官退官記念）[International Relations and the Rule of Law: Festschrift for Judge Owada Hisashi in Commemoration of His Retirement from the International Court of Justice], edited by Iwanaga Yūji 岩澤雄司 and Okano Masataka 岡野正敬, 147–180. Tokyo: Shinzansha, 2021.

Yamagami, Shingo 山上信吾. "'Koyū no Ryōdo' o Kangaeru" "固有の領土"を考える [Considering inherent territory]. In *Nihon Gaikō Kyōkai Hō* 日本外交協会報 [The Society for Promotion of Japanese Diplomacy Magazine], 1. Tokyo: The Society for Promotion of Japanese Diplomacy, 2012.

Yanagihara, Masaharu 柳原正治. "Dai 9 Shō 'Kokka Ryōiki'" 第 9 章「国家領域」[Chapter 9 'Territory']. In *Kōgi Kokusaihō* 講義国際法 [Lectures on International Law], edited by Kotera Akira 小寺彰 et al., 246. Tokyo: Yūhikaku, 2010.

Western Language

Brilmayer, Lea and Natalie Klein. "Land and Sea: Two Sovereignty Regimes in Search of a Common Denominator." *New York University Journal of International Law and Politics* 33 (2001): 703–768.

Brownlie, Ian. *The Rule of Law in International Affairs*. The Hague: Martinus Nijhoff, 1998.

Buga, Irina. "Territorial Sovereignty Issues in Maritime Disputes: A Jurisdictional Dilemma for Law of the Sea Tribunals." *International Journal of Marine and Coastal Law* 27 (2012): 59–95.

Cheng, Carlos Tal. "The Sino-Japanese Dispute over the Tiao-yu-tai (Senkaku) Islands and the Law of Territorial Acquisition." *Virginia Journal of International Law* 14, no. 2 (1974): 221–266.

Chiu, Hungdah. "An Analysis of the Sino-Japanese Dispute over the T'iaoyutai Islets (Senkaku Gunto)." *Chinese (Taiwan) Yearbook of International Law and Affairs* 15 (1996–1997): 1–27.

Fitzmaurice, Gerald. "The Law and Procedure of the International Court of Justice, 1951–4." *British Year Book of International Law* 32 (1955–1956): 20–96.

Jennings, Robert. "The Acquisition of Territory in International Law." In Robert Jennings, *Collected Writings of Sir Robert Jennings*. The Hague: Kluwer Law International, 1998.

"*Judicial Regime of Historic Waters, Including Historic Bays: Study Prepared by the Secretariat.*" UN Doc. A/CN.4/143, March 9, 1962.

Kanehara, Atsuko. "Validity of International Law over Historic Rights: The Arbitral Award (Merits) on the South China Sea Dispute." *Japan Review* 2, no. 3 (2018): 8–35.

Kanehara, Atsuko. "Refining Japan's Integrative Position on the Territorial Sovereignty of the Senkaku Islands." *International Law Studies* 97 (2021): 1588–1632.

Ramos-Mrosovsky, Carlos. "International Law's Unhelpful Role in the Senkaku Islands." *University of Pennsylvania Journal of International Law* 29, no. 4 (2008): 903–946.

Shaw, Han-yi. "Revisiting the Diaoyutai/Senkaku Islands Dispute: Examining Legal Claims and New Historical Evidence under International Law and the Traditional East Asian World Order." *Chinese (Taiwan) Yearbook of International Law and Affairs* 26 (2008): 95–168.

Symmons, Clive. *Historic Waters in the Law of the Sea: A Modern Re-Appraisal.* Leiden: Brill, 2007.

Zhang, Zuxing. "A Deconstruction of the Notion of Acquisitive Prescription and Its Implications for the Diaoyu Islands Dispute." *Asian Journal of International Law* 2 (2012): 323–338.

CHAPTER 6

Significance of Silence in Territorial Disputes

Toward Legal Construction on "75 Years of Silence" regarding the Senkaku Islands (Pinnacle Islands)

Tomofumi Kitamura

1 Introduction

Silence, or the fact of failure to act via an absence of protest, reservation, or other reaction, is often given decisive importance in territorial disputes. This applies to the territorial issues facing Japan, and particularly to the Senkaku Islands issue. In fact, some theories in Japan regarding territorial sovereignty to the Senkaku Islands emphasize that neither China nor others made any protests from Japan's incorporation of the islands in 1895 until 1971. Japan asserts that it acquired territorial sovereignty over the Senkaku Islands through occupation of *terra nullius*. Even if the Senkaku Islands were not *terra nullius*, it has been pointed out that as a result of the absence of protests by China and others in the subsequent 75 years, Japan acquired territorial sovereignty. However, the reasons given for why the absence of protests would result in Japan's acquisition of the territorial sovereignty differ depending on the proponent. For example, while Taijudō suggests that the absence of China's protest signifies "acquiescence" of Japan's territorial sovereignty and thus justifies the transfer of territorial sovereignty,[1] Matsui treats the absence of protest as establishing a title via a "continuous and peaceful display of territorial sovereignty."[2] Miyoshi, on the other hand, states that China's absence of protest indicates "acquiescence" of Japan's territorial sovereignty and thereby creates an "estoppel" effect,[3] although he also acknowledges the role of the absence of

1 Taijudō Kanae 太壽堂鼎, *Ryōdo Kizoku no Kokusaihō* 領土帰属の国際法 [International Law of Territory Possession] (Tokyo: Tōshindō, 1998), 204.

2 Matsui Yoshirō 松井芳郎, *Kokusaihō Gakusha ga Yomu Senkaku Mondai* 国際法学者が読む尖閣問題 [International Law Theorists' View of the Senkaku Islands Issue] (Tokyo: Nippon Hyōronsha, 2014), 141–142.

3 Miyoshi Masahiro 三好正弘, "Ryōdo Shutoku ni Okeru Kōgi to Mokunin" 領土取得における抗議と黙認 [Protest and Acquiescence in Territorial Acquisition], *Tōsho Kenkyu Jyānaru* 島嶼研究ジャーナル, vol. 4, no. 2 (2015), 44.

 DOI:10.1163/9789004706361_007

protest in providing grounds for "prescriptive title or historic title."[4] There is as yet no agreement among theories regarding how to legally define the "75 years of silence" regarding the Senkaku Islands, or, in other words, what type of legal effect to determine from this silence and via what concept.

The background to the abovementioned lack of agreement regarding the Senkaku Islands issue is disagreement or confusion about the concepts themselves of acquiescence, estoppel, prescription, etc. For example, Marques Antunes, under the item "acquiescence" in the Encyclopedia of Public International Law, refers to the legal maxim that "he who keeps silent is held to consent if he must and can speak" (*Qui tacit consentire videtur si loqui debuisset ac potuisset*) and defines the concept as "a consent tacitly conveyed by a State, unilaterally, through silence or inaction, in circumstances such that a response expressing disagreement or objection in relation to the conduct of another State would be called for" with a recommendation to refer also to the entry for "Unilateral Acts of States in International Law."[5] Therefore, acquiescence in this case seems to be understood as an "instantaneous act" of tacit consent (expression of intent) through silence as a juridical act with the effect of "changes in substantive rights." However, the author also explains that acquiescence requires a "lengthy lapse of time"[6] and may produce the effect of "estoppel,"[7] and it is hence unclear how the author understands this concept. Furthermore, even though the author states that acquiescence differs from prescription because it involves consent along with the requirement for a "lengthy lapse of time,"[8] there are also scholars who argue that "acquiescence" is important in establishing prescription.[9] In this way, the concepts of acquiescence, estoppel, and prescription are discussed in a closely intertwined manner, and there are disagreement and confusion broadly across the spectrum from the conditions and effects of these concepts, as well as whether or not they exist.

The interconnectedness of the concepts of acquiescence, estoppel, and prescription, etc., has distant roots. This chapter, in consideration of the abovementioned issues and with the ultimate aim of finding insights for addressing

4 *Ibid.*, 26.

5 N. S. Marques Antunes, "Acquiescence," in *Max Planck Encyclopedia of Public International Law* (online edition, last updated in September 2006), para. 2.

6 *Ibid.*, para. 25.

7 *Ibid.*, para. 24.

8 *Ibid.*, para. 25.

9 For example, James Crawford, *Brownlie's Principles of Public International Law*, 9th ed. (Oxford: Oxford University Press, 2019), 219–220.

the Senkaku Islands issue, attempts to untangle the relationship among these concepts and ascertain whether or not they exist, as well as their content. For this purpose, the chapter reviews judicial practices from before World War II and theories regarding acquiescence, estoppel, and prescription (Section 2) and early judicial practices of the International Court of Justice (ICJ) and related theories (Section 3). In terms of the latter, i.e., judicial practices of the ICJ, this chapter conducts in-depth reviews of the Fisheries Case judgement and the Preah Vihear Temple Case judgement. Both judgements stand, respectively as major precedents on historic title (prescription) and acquiescence, and acquiescence and estoppel. At the same time, there are fundamental disagreements in how these judgements are understood, including differing opinions on which concepts and what understanding of them were used in determining the judgements, making them highly useful judicial practices for comprehending these concepts. Nevertheless, it is obviously not possible to obtain definitive answers for understanding these concepts and finding insights for addressing the Senkaku Islands issue just by reviewing the ICJ's early judicial practices. The final section therefore sketches out a provisional understanding of the various concepts gleaned from the abovementioned review and presents suggestions and key points in looking at subsequent judicial practices (Section 4).

This chapter provisionally defines acquiescence as a tacit consent (expression of intent) through silence without prejudice to its effect. Prescription in this chapter refers to acquisitive prescription. In the review covered by this chapter, prescription and title of "continuous and peaceful display of territorial sovereignty," as well as historic title, are understood as coming under the same legal framework with the same purpose and content. In any discussion that does not delineate these items, the term "prescription, etc." is used.

2 Judicial Practices and Theories before World War II

2.1 *Prescription and Correlation between Prescription and Acquiescence*

2.1.1 Theories

The modes of territorial acquisition in international law have been discussed in an analogy from Roman law that regulated acquisition of land by individuals. Prescription is one such mode of acquisition. Grotius was the precursor of this discussion and heavily influenced subsequent theories. Grotius pointed out that, because usucaption was introduced from Roman law to municipal law (time in fact, in its own nature has no effective force), it had no place in the relations between States. At the same time, however, he wondered if that would therefore mean that contests about kingdoms and the boundaries of kingdoms never come to an end with lapse of time.[10] Grotius' answer to this question is the theory of immemorial possession and assumed abandonment of rights through silence. According to Grotius, human expression of intent occurs not just with words but also through acts and failure to act. A person who knows that their property is in the possession of another but is silent of their own free will is assumed to have abandoned their right thereto. The lapse of time offers many opportunities for cognizance of one's property in the possession of another and taking counsel against fear, in other words, to overcome constraints on one's free will. Therefore, silence over a long period of time implies the abandonment of a right, and specifically if a length of time exceeding the memory of man has passed, it will always seem sufficient to imply such an abandonment.[11]

Therefore, for Grotius, it is the tacit expression of intent, in other words acquiescence, that results in the abandonment of a right by the right holder and the acquisition of a right by the possessor,[12] and this acquiescence is presumed based on possession exceeding the memory of man and silence regarding such possession. However, Grotius also mentions roughly 100 years as possession exceeding the memory of man,[13] and seems to wish to set a limit on the period of time required to infer acquiescence. Moreover, while Grotius explains, as the reason for presuming acquiescence from silence over a long period of time, that the lapse of time suggests that the right holder knows of the possession but is silent of their own free will, he also states that it is to the interest of human society that governments be established on a sure basis and beyond the hazard of dispute and all implications which point in that direction ought to be looked upon with favor.[14] This leaves a question about whether he truly aimed to identify the intent of the right holder. Grotius rejects

10 Hugo Grotius, *De jure belli ac pacis*, book ii, chap. iv, s. 1.

11 *Ibid.*, ss. 3–7.

12 Grotius explains the effect of acquiescence as abandonment rather than transfer of rights. Although possession of another party's property actually occurs prior to abandoning the right, he positions acquisition of territory in this manner as "assumed abandonment of ownership and occupation consequent thereon" (*ibid.* (chapter title)) and keeps it within the scope of original acquisition. For more on these points, as well as Grotius' discussion of *ius voluntarium*, refer in particular to Yanagihara Masaharu 柳原正治, "Shoyūken, Shihaiken" 所有権・支配権 [Ownership Rights and Control Rights], in Sensō to Heiwa no Hō [Hoseiban] 戦争と平和の法［補正版］ [*Laws of War and Peace* (*Revised Edition*)], Ōnuma Yasuaki 大沼保昭 (ed.) (Tokyo: Tōshindo, 1995), 237–238.

13 Grotius, *supra* note 10, s. 7.

14 *Ibid.*, s. 8.

the existence of prescription in natural law on the ground that time in its own nature has no effective force. However, his intention could be understood to be to "introduce" prescription into natural law and thus in relations between States for the interest of peace and stability by using the "technique" of the presumption of acquiescence.

Scholars of natural law subsequently understood that the Grotius theory explained above recognized the existence of prescription in natural law, and, based on this theory, they discussed whether or not prescription did in fact exist, as well as its content. For example, Pufendorf introduces the Grotius theory and criticizes the basis as not always being valid. He points out that a long continued silence does not necessarily give sufficient ground to suppose a tacit derelict for it may happen that a man might either have been ignorant of his right, or hindered from asserting it through apprehension or want of power.[15] Having raised that point, Pufendorf then argues that, as the propriety of things was introduced out of a regard to the common peace, based on the same principle, they who have been let into the possession of anything upon a fair and honest presumption should be freed from perpetual suits and quarrels about their title. Furthermore, he states that, while the space of time is not determined by natural reason or the universal consent of nations, this can be decided by each particular case considering the various circumstances affecting the ancient owner and the new possessor.[16] Pufendorf understood that Grotius's intention was to establish the existence of prescription under natural law and thus in relations between States as being a framework for the purpose of a stable order and therefore considered that long continued silence on possession should always result in the acquisition of rights. Recognizing, however, that this is not guaranteed by assumed acquiescence, Pufendorf based prescription under natural law directly on the interest of peace and stability, drawing on his theory of the propriety of things being introduced for the same interest.

In contrast, Wolff retains and consistently upholds the logic of assumed acquiescence. He states that prescription refers to the acquisition of ownership from presumed abandonment of a thing and argues that abandonment is presumed from long continued silence for the reason that it is not credible that in so great a space of time the other party should not have obtained knowledge of his right, or that no opportunity of questioning it had arisen. Wolff further explains that, if reasons for long-continued silence are alleged,

15 Samuel von Pufendorf, *De jure naturae et gentium libri octo*, book iv, chap. xii, s. 8.

16 *Ibid.*, s. 9.

the reason for the presumption fails, and consequently also the prescription.[17] While Pufendorf positions prescription as a title that produces a right based on possession and long continued silence, for Wolff, they are merely facts which allow the presumption that the right holder was, at some point, placed in a situation where he "could and ought to speak"[18] but, by failing to do so, acquiesced in the right of the possessor. Here, it is the acquiescence, that is to say the consent, of the right holder, not public interests such as peace and a stable order, that creates the right of the possessor.[19] Prescription in this context therefore, rather than being a title, refers to acquisition of a right produced by acquiescence derived through a specific method of presumption based on possession and long continued silence. Wolff consistently upholds this logic of assumed acquiescence and positions it as a literal presumption (*juris tantum*) that allows for rebuttal based on lack of knowledge, constraints on free will, and other defenses.

Vattel, meanwhile, defines prescription as a framework that creates acquisition of a title only on the basis of the fact of long-term possession uninterrupted and undisputed, while also referring to Wolff's view of prescription and stating that the two stances are easily harmonized and not in conflict.[20] He argues that natural law demands respect for ownership rights for the purpose of protecting peace, safety, and welfare in human society, and, therefore, according to natural law, it can be assumed that an owner who ignores their own rights over a long period of time without a legitimate reason has abandoned said rights.[21] In this way, Vattel also mentions the logic of assumed acquiescence, but bases his reasons for the presumption on the interests of human society, such as peace, instead of probability in the form of the unlikeliness that lack of knowledge and constraints on free will would continue over a long period of time. The main issue then becomes the nature of such a presumption. In this regard, Vattel states that, considering the need for peace among States, even those States that remain silent due to reasons such as fear must endure the loss of rights,[22] and therefore seems to consider that at least in the case

17 Christian Wolff, *Jus gentium methodo scientifica pertractatum*, book iv, chap. vii, ss. 358 and 363.

18 *Ibid.*, s. 359.

19 Wolff also describes the abandonment of a right as being an effect of acquiescence, while stating that a right cannot be "transferred" without the consent of the owner (*ibid.*, s. 363). In contrast to Grotius (refer to previous footnote 12), he does not use the construction of "assumed abandonment of ownership and 'occupation consequent thereon.'"

20 Emer de Vattel, *Le droit de gens*, book ii, chap. xi, s. 140.

21 *Ibid.*, s. 141.

22 *Ibid.*, s. 149.

of prescription in relations among States, the nature of the presumption is one without room for rebuttal (*juris et de jure*). Even though he speaks of presumed acquiescence, if the presumption does not actually allow rebuttal and the acquiescence is fictious in the interest of peace, this is tantamount to arguing for the existence of a title that results in the acquisition of a right based only on long-term possession uninterrupted and undisputed for the purpose of maintaining peace and stability.

As explained above, there exists, among scholars of natural law, the understanding of prescription as a title that produces a right premised on possession and long continued silence for the purpose of maintaining peace and stability, and also as an acquisition of a right produced by acquiescence derived through a specific method of presumption based on possession and long continued silence. (Hereinafter, the former shall be referred to as prescription for the purpose of peace and stability and the latter as prescription premised on acquiescence.) Theories at the end of the 19th century and early 20th century more frequently understood prescription in international law in the former sense.[23] The following opinion from Hall is a representative example.

> Title by prescription arises out of a long-continued possession, where no original source of proprietary right can be shown to exist, or where possession in the first instance being wrongful, the legitimate proprietor has neglected to assert his right, or is unable to do so. … [T]he object of prescription as between states is mainly to assist in creating a stability of international order which is of more practical advantage than the bare possibility of an ultimate victory of right.[24]

Hall explains prescription in international law as title with the purpose of maintaining peace and stability and accepts the establishment of prescription in not only cases of negligence in asserting the right by the right holder but also when it could not be done, that is to say when the right holder did not consent. Hall also argues that prescription can be established regardless of whether there is an actual right holder. If the basis for prescription is the consent of the right holder, a true right holder must exist and be identified because it is not possible to give something that you do not possess (*nemo dat quod non habet*). However, this does not apply in a case of prescription for the

---

23 For example, refer to documents listed in D. H. N. Johnson, "Acquisitive Prescription in International Law," 27 *British Year Book of International Law* (1950), 333, n. 1; Y. Z. Blum, *Historic Titles in International Law* (The Hague: M. Nijhoff, 1965), 12–13.

24 W. E. Hall, *A Treatise on International Law*, 4th ed. (Oxford: Clarendon Press, 1895), 123.

purpose of peace and stability. If things are settled through possession without interruption over a long period of time, this should provide the basis for rights enforceable against all parties.

It is unclear why in this period the prevalent view became that of prescription for the purpose of peace and stability. However, the transition from thinking based on natural law to legal positivism may have provided liberation from the difficult issue of how to establish a basis, under natural law, for the existence of a framework that allows the acquisition of rights through the lapse of time and reduced the necessity of relying on the "technique" of assuming acquiescence. That being said, there are no statutes under international law that establish the prescription period, and some theorists used this as the basis for rejecting the existence of prescription.[25] Furthermore, the transition from thinking based on natural law to legal positivism instead raised the need to ground the existence of prescription in international practice. While judicial practices invoking prescription started to appear, particularly from the 20th century, how is prescription utilized as a concept and what are the judgements regarding it in these judicial practices?

2.1.2 Judicial Practices

The Grisbådarna Case (1909) in which Norway and Sweden filed suits with the Permanent Court of Arbitration (PCA) to delimit their maritime boundary is an early practice that could be deemed a precedent regarding prescription in international law. The PCA decided that according to the international law of the 17th-century, in which parities asserted that a boundary line in the disputed sea areas was automatically drawn as a result of cession of the adjoining land territory, the line should be made according to the general direction of the land territory. However, the PCA attributed all of the Grisbådarna banks, which based on the aforementioned boundary line would have been partly owned by both parties, to Sweden[26] and explained its reasoning in the following manner.

> [I]t is a well established principle of the law of nations that the state of things that actually exists and has existed for a long time should be changed as little as possible; this principle is especially applicable in the

25 For example, A. W. Heffter, *Le Droit international de l'Europe*, 4th ed. (Paris: A. Cotillon, 1883), 39–40. Fauchille criticizes this theory because it rejects the existence of the principle itself based on a lack of rules regarding the application of the principle. (Paul Fauchille, *Traité de droit international public*, 8th ed. (Paris: Rousseau, 1925), vol. 1, pt. 2, 755.)

26 Affaire des Grisbadarna (Norvège, Suède), 23 October 1909, XI *RIAA*, 160.

> case of private interests which, once disregarded, cannot be effectively preserved by any manner of sacrifice on the part of the Government of which the interested parties are subjects; … from these various circumstances it appears so probable as to be almost certain that the Swedes exploited the banks in question much earlier and much more effectively than the Norwegians.[27]

In this case, both parties invoked prescription, but the PCA did not mention this term. Furthermore, looking at subsequent judicial practices, questions linger as to whether effective exploitation by a private entity could be rightly called effective control by a State. Nevertheless, the aforementioned decision attributed to Sweden a sea area that would have been attributed to Norway based precisely on the principle to not move settled things (*quieta non movere*), and therefore this case can be understood as a practice that granted rights to one of the parties premised on prescription for the purpose of peace and stability.

The Chamizal Case (1911) is a precedent involving a detailed decision on the conditions for prescription in international law. In this case, while the United States and Mexico concluded a treaty in 1848 that stipulated the Rio Grande River as the boundary line, there was a dispute regarding the possession of a tract of land that shifted from the southern side to the northern side due to changes in the river's channel. While the United States contended that it acquired the title of the tract in question by prescription alleged to result from "the undisturbed, uninterrupted, and unchallenged possession of the territory since 1848,"[28] the International Boundary Commission reached the following decision on this assertion.

> Without thinking it necessary to discuss the very controversial question as to whether the right of prescription invoked by the United States is an accepted principle of the law of nations, in the absence of any convention establishing a term of prescription, the commissioners are unanimous in coming to the conclusion that the possession of the United States in the present case was not of such a character as to found a prescriptive title. … On the contrary, it may be said that the physical possession taken by citizens of the United States and the political control exercised by the local and Federal Governments, have been constantly challenged and

27 *Ibid.*, 161.

28 The Chamizal Case (Mexico, United States), 15 June 1911, XI *RIAA*, 317.

> questioned by the Republic of Mexico, through its accredited diplomatic agents.[29]

The Commission refrains from discussing the existence of prescription in international law but cites prescription in domestic law and addresses the conditions for its application. The point explained in the award that "(i)n private law, the interruption of prescription is effected by a suit, but in dealings between nations this is of course impossible, unless and until an international tribunal is established for such purpose"[30] deserves attention. While this could be interpreted as stating that it is necessary to file a suit in the case of the existence of an international tribunal,[31] if the basis of prescription in international law is acquiescence of the right holder, it is unclear why protest is not enough.

Furthermore, the Island of Palmas Case (1928) is an important precedent as a case in which the PCA mentioned prescription and acknowledged the right of one of the parties based on it. In this case, the United States argued that Spain discovered and acquired sovereignty over the Island of Palmas before 1648 and subsequently ceded it to the United States, while the Netherlands asserted that it held sovereignty over the island and exercised it from 1677 or a date prior to 1648.[32] The PCA acknowledged the Netherlands' title based on the following decision.

> practice, as well as doctrine, recognizes – though under different legal formulae and with certain differences as to the conditions required – that the continuous and peaceful display of territorial sovereignty (peaceful in relation to other States) is as good as a title.[33]
>
> Since the moment when the Spaniards, in withdrawing from the Moluccas in 1666, made express reservations as to the maintenance of their sovereign rights, up to the contestation made by the United States in 1906, no contestation or other action whatever or protest against the exercise of territorial sovereignty by the Netherlands over the Talautse (Sangi) Isles and their dependencies (Miangas included) has been recorded. The peaceful character of the display of Netherland's sovereignty for the entire period to which the evidence concerning acts of display relates (1700–1906) must be admitted.[34]

---

29 *Ibid.*, 328.

30 *Ibid.*, 329.

31 Johnson, *supra* note 23, 340–342.

32 Island of Palmas Case (Netherlands, USA), 4 April 1928, II *RIAA*, 837–838.

33 *Ibid.*, 839.

34 *Ibid.*, 868.

The award introduces new language of "continuous and peaceful display of territorial sovereignty" to explain the title of the Netherlands to the Island of Palmas. Furthermore, while it does not recognize the Island of Palmas as being *terra nullius* at the time of the start of the acts of display, it also does not recognize it as Spanish territory. Due to these points, opinions are split on how to understand the award, with some viewing it as approving occupation,[35] others viewing it as not distinguishing between occupation and prescription and applying conditions shared by both,[36] and yet others viewing it as presenting "new territorial law" distinct from the existing theories on the modes of territorial acquisition.[37]

However, the award rephrases "continuous and peaceful display of territorial sovereignty" as "so-called prescription,"[38] asserts that doctrine has approved this title, explains that federal States applying international law to interstate relations have also recognized it, and cites a US Supreme Court decision that included quotations from "Vattel and Wheaton, who both admit prescription founded on length of time as a valid and incontestable title."[39]

The split in opinions on how to understand the title of "continuous and peaceful display of territorial sovereignty" despite these points seems to stem from a view that prescription requires the existence of a true right holder.[40] As already noted above, however, prescription for the purpose of peace and stability can be established even if the origin of the right is not certain. In other words, it is not necessary to confirm that the Island of Palmas was Spanish territory. Meanwhile, in order to ascertain that things are settled through long-term possession and establish a right enforceable against all others, it is necessary to show that the possession was not generally contested. This is why the award uses the term "peaceful" to mean "peaceful in relation to other States," and confirmed the absence of protests from not only Spain but all States.

Considering these points and that "continuous and peaceful display of territorial sovereignty" fit the conditions of "possession and long continued silence" or "long-term possession uninterrupted and undisputed," it is reasonable to understand that the award acknowledged the existence of prescription

35 Taijudō, *supra* note 1, 66.

36 Robert Jennings and Arthur Watts, *Oppenheim's International Law*, 9th ed. (London: Longman, 1996), vol. 1, pts. 2–4, 709–710.

37 Huh Sookyeon 許淑娟, *Ryōiki Kengen Ron* 領域権原論 [The Acquisition of Territory in International Law] (Tokyo: University of Tokyo Publishing, 2012), 137–138.

38 Island of Palmas Case, *supra* note 32, 868.

39 *Ibid.*, 840.

40 Taijudō, *supra* note 1, 11; Jennings and Watts, *supra* note 36, 710; Huh, *supra* note 37, 100–101.

for the purpose of peace and stability, clarified some detailed standards, such as the public (not clandestine) nature of display of sovereignty,[41] and approved the sovereignty of the Netherlands based on prescription thus understood.

However, after acknowledging the title for the Netherlands in this manner, the award addresses the question of "whether the United States as successors of Spain are in a position to bring forward an equivalent or stronger title." The explanation it gives, in answering in the negative,[42] deserves attention.

> [T]he acquiescence of Spain in the situation created after 1677 would deprive her and her successors of the possibility of still invoking conventional rights (rights based on the Treaty of Munster from 1648 that the United States claimed as recognition of Spain's rights) at the present time.[43]

The award, as explained above, acknowledged the Netherlands' title based on "continuous and peaceful display of State authority (so-called prescription)" and also noted that this title "may prevail even over a prior, definitive title."[44] While it mentioned Spain's acquiescence and possible loss of rights due to the acquiescence, the award did not conduct any examination of whether Spain had knowledge of the display of sovereignty by the Netherlands. Therefore, it is questionable whether the award genuinely intended to identify Spain's intent and reject the Netherlands' sovereignty if it was confirmed that Spain did not consent. This type of nominal mention of acquiescence is reminiscent of the theory described by Vattel and others that refers to the presumption of acquiescence but rejects the possibility of rebuttal. In this sense, it can be said that traces of the correlation between prescription and acquiescence can be found in international practice as well.

As shown above, while courts and tribunals rarely made overt references to prescription because of the historical division of views on prescription in international law, they acknowledged the existence of prescription in international law as a title which creates the right of a possessor for the purpose of maintaining peace and stability and on the conditions of "continuous and peaceful display of territorial sovereignty," regardless of whether a true right holder existed. However, following World War II, the understanding of prescription in international law became the subject of much debate in the ICJ

41 *Island of Palmas Case, supra* note 32, 868.

42 *Ibid.*

43 *Ibid.*, 869. Author's note added in parentheses.

44 *Ibid.*, 846.

under the concept of historic title. The next section looks at what judgements were reached by the Court and how these judgements were understood.

2.2 *Estoppel and Correlation between Estoppel and Acquiescence*

2.2.1 Judicial Practices

While prescription in international law was initially debated in theories and later accepted in international practice, estoppel is a concept that emerged in international law through international judicial practices from the latter half of the 19th century. Estoppel has long existed in a wide range of forms in common law, many of which did not themselves result in a change of rights under substantive law and instead had the effect of dismissing assertions of facts and rights in court cases.[45] It makes sense, therefore, that its application to international law would need to wait until the emergence and development of an international court and tribunal. While there are many cases that involve estoppel,[46] because the purpose in this chapter is to clarify the concept of estoppel, as well as the origin and nature of the correlation between this concept and acquiescence, the review looks at three cases: the Serbian Loans Case, the Eastern Greenland Case, and the Costa Rica-Nicaragua Treaty of Limits Case.

The Serbian Loans Case (1929) involved French holders of Serbian bonds requesting payment of interest and principal in gold francs as stipulated in the bond contract. Since Serbia asserted that it would pay in paper francs, the French side protested, and this case was brought before the Permanent Court of International Justice (PCIJ). In this case, Serbia invoked estoppel, asserting that, because the bondholders had accepted payment in paper francs over a lengthy period of time, they could not enlist the right to payment in gold francs.[47] The PCIJ reached the following decision regarding Serbia's assertion.

45 Estoppel in common law includes estoppel by record, estoppel by deed, estoppel by convention, estoppel by representation, proprietary estoppel, and promissory estoppel. Excluding the first two types, the other types are jointly referred to as "estoppel by conduct," among other terms. Among them, proprietary estoppel itself creates rights and obligations in substantive law and can serve as the cause of claims. The others previously only had a role as a principle in procedural law of preventing the assertion of facts or rights by a claimant before a court, thereby acting as a "shield" against the establishment of a claim. At present, they are understood to be a principle in substantive law that creates rights and obligations in substantive law and can also function as a "sword," in the sense of preventing rebuttal against facts and rights that serve as causes of claims and thereby enabling relief that would not have been given otherwise. Piers Feltham et al., *Spencer Bower: Reliance-Based Estoppel*, 5th ed. (London: Bloomsbury Professional, 2017), 31–43.

46 For details regarding international judicial practices on estoppel, refer to Antoine Martin, *L'Estoppel en droit international public* (Paris: A. Pedone, 1979), 93–172.

47 *Serbian Loans, Speeches Made in Court, PCIJ, Series C, No. 16/3-II*, 155–157.

> when the requirements of the principle of estoppel to establish a loss of right are considered, it is quite clear that no sufficient basis has been shown for applying the principle in this case. There has been no clear and unequivocal representation by the bondholders upon which the debtor State was entitled to rely and has relied. There has been no change in position on the part of the debtor State.[48]

In this case, the two parties described estoppel as "forbidden to speak against his own act or deed" and "cannot blow hot and cold"[49] and presented it as a principle that prevents assertions that contradict clear past conduct. However, the judgement cited factors such as clear representation, reliance upon the representation by the other party, and whether there was a disadvantageous change in position, and treated them as conditions for estoppel. This understanding shares points in common with the forms of estoppel referred to as "estoppel by conduct," among other terms, in common law, and the judgement can be said to have confirmed the applicability of this type of estoppel in international law.

Meanwhile, the Eastern Greenland Case (1933) is an example in which the parties asserted a rigorous understanding of estoppel similar to the above-mentioned Serbian Loans Case judgement, but the PCIJ seemed to have interpreted it as a principle that prevents assertions that contradict clear past conduct and approved the estoppel. In this case, Denmark asserted that Norway's past recognition of Denmark's sovereignty over the whole of Greenland and acceptance of compensation in exchange prevented Norway from contesting the sovereignty via estoppel,[50] and the PCIJ reached the following decision regarding the assertion.

> It has already been said that when the Treaty of 1826 speaks of 'Greenland', this can only denote ... the whole of Greenland. ... In accepting these bilateral and multilateral agreements as binding upon herself, Norway reaffirmed that she recognized the whole of Greenland as Danish; and thereby she has debarred herself from contesting Danish sovereignty over the whole of Greenland, and, in consequence, from proceeding to occupy any part of it.[51]

48 *Serbian Loans, Judgement of 12 July 1929, PCIJ, Series A, Nos. 20/21*, 39.

49 *Serbian Loans (Speeches), supra* note 47, 157, 255.

50 *Legal Status of Eastern Greenland, Documents of the Written Proceedings, PCIJ, Series C, No. 63/2*, 841–842.

51 *Legal Status of Eastern Greenland, Judgement of 5 April 1933, PCIJ, Series A/B, No. 53*, 68–69.

The judgement does not mention the term "estoppel." It explains that Norway recognized the whole of Greenland as Denmark's territory, and, with that being the case, the PCIJ needed perhaps only to state that this thereby debarred Norway from occupation. However, the PCIJ instead explains that as the effect of Norway's recognition, Norway "debarred herself from contesting Danish sovereignty," and, in consequence, from proceeding to occupy any part of Greenland. Although Denmark asserted that Norway received compensation (in other words, showing that Denmark disadvantageously changed positions), the PCIJ did not review this point and dismissed Norway's assertion. Based on these points, the judgement can be deemed to have shown an understanding of permissive estoppel, expressed as "cannot blow hot and cold," and recognized the establishment of estoppel.

The Eastern Greenland Case discussed above is a precedent in which a counterpart's rights are recognized through an action such as the conclusion of a treaty, resulting in the dismissal of assertions that run contrary thereto. Meanwhile, the Costa Rica-Nicaragua Treaty of Limits Case (1888) is a precedent in which the acquiescence of the validity of a treaty through the inaction of silence was recognized as having the effect of a dismissal of an assertion. In this case, the two parties concluded the "Treaty of Limits" in 1858, but Nicaragua subsequently asserted the invalidity of the treaty and the case was brought before an arbitrator. Nicaragua asserted the invalidity of the treaty due to the absence of ratification by the San Salvador Government despite Article 10 of the treaty guaranteeing observance by said government,[52] but the arbitrator dismissed the assertion, stating the following.

> The arguments now advanced by Nicaragua, as establishing the invalidity of the Treaty, might perhaps have been urged as reasons for refusing to exchange the ratifications until San Salvador was ready to unite in the act. But the Government of Nicaragua was silent when it ought to have spoken, and so waived the objection now made. It saw fit to proceed to the exchange of ratifications without waiting for San Salvador. The Treaty was complete without Article X. … neither may now be heard to allege, as reasons for rescinding this completed Treaty, any facts which existed and were known at the time of its consummation.[53]

52 *Award of the President of the United States in Regard to the Validity of the Treaty of Limits between Costa Rica and Nicaragua of 15 July 1858, 22 March 1888*, XXVIII RIAA, 201–202.

53 *Ibid.*, 206.

While the award does not discuss acquiescence, its statement that Nicaragua "was silent when it ought to have spoken" indicates that it acknowledged Nicaragua's acquiescence in accordance with the legal maxim that "he who keeps silent is held to consent if he must and can speak." The award also does not mention estoppel, though the result of the assertion "neither may … be heard" is the same effect as estoppel. The award recognized Nicaragua's acquiescence and, with that being the case, needed perhaps only to state that, as a result, the treaty was valid, but it instead proceeded to identify an effect of estoppel from acquiescence and acquiescence alone.

As explained above, this period has many judicial practices that were examples of the application of estoppel as a principle with the effect of dismissing an assertion. Regarding the conditions, while there were some decisions involving a strict understanding that requires clear representation, reliance upon the representation, and a disadvantageous change in position, there were also those that seemed to approve estoppel without examining, for example, whether or not there had been a disadvantageous change in position. However, it is important to note that the latter type of decisions involved cases with recognition or acquiescence and did not overtly mention estoppel. The next section addresses academic discussion of the conditions for estoppel in international law and the relationship between estoppel and recognition or acquiescence.

2.2.2 Theories

Prior to World War II, theories did not discuss the topic of estoppel in international law much. Even in the few cases in which it is addressed, tension is evident between strict and permissive views of estoppel. For example, McNair argues regarding "estoppel by conduct" in domestic law that it must be proven that the party setting up the estoppel acted or abstained from action upon it to his detriment and that this opinion is also evident in estoppel under international law.[54] At the same time, however, he also mentions that although it is not literally estoppel, the principle of "cannot blow hot and cold" and "*allegans contraria non audiendus est*" (a person adducing to the contrary is not to be heard) is to some extent accepted in international courts,[55] and thus leaves unclear what serves as the basis for establishing estoppel in international law.

Additionally, Lauterpacht introduces "estoppel by conduct" in English law, which has the effect of dismissing assertions under strict conditions such as a

54 A. D. McNair, "The Legality of the Occupation of the Ruhr," 5 *British Year Book of International Law* (1924), 34–35.

55 *Ibid.*, 35.

disadvantageous change in position, and argues that the principle underlying estoppel is recognized by all systems of private law and that this principle is also applicable in relationships among States.[56] He then lists seven examples of judicial practice in which parties invoked the principles of estoppel and preclusion and international courts used them as the basis for the judgements.[57] However, many of these are not literal cases of estoppel as defined by McNair and instead are invocations or applications of permissive estoppel expressed as "cannot blow hot and cold."[58] It is unclear how Lauterpacht understood the principle of estoppel which, he alleges, is a general principle of law.

Anzilotti, Rousseau, and other scholars from the same period discuss treaties and unilateral acts of States as juridical acts and address recognition and tacit expressions of intent through silence, i.e., acquiescence.[59] According to these views, it is incomprehensible to interpret recognition or acquiescence as having the effect of dismissing assertions, because they result in changes in rights under substantive law themselves. However, arguments by McNair, etc., do not express this concern. Hidden in the background of this state of theories, as well as in the abovementioned judicial practices, which do not refer to estoppel itself but recognize the effect of recognition or acquiescence in dismissing assertions, seems to be the divergence between civil law scholars, who know the concept of a juridical act, and common law scholars, who do not accept the effect of raw intent that lacks consideration and who seek equity among parties using the estoppel principle. How did the relationship between these concepts come to be understood in the postwar period?

3 Early Judicial Practices of the International Court of Justice

3.1 *Fisheries Case (1951) – Prescription, Etc., and Acquiescence*

3.1.1 Overview of the Judgement

The Fisheries Case was an example of the ICJ's recognition of the right of one of the parties based on historic title, which strongly influenced theories related to historic title, prescription, and acquiescence. The case involved a dispute

56 Hersch Lauterpacht, *Private Law Sources and Analogies of International Law* (London: Longman, 1927), 203–204.

57 *Ibid.*, 205–206.

58 Martin, *supra* note 46, 175–180.

59 Dionisio Anzilotti, *Cours de droit international*, vol. 1 (Paris: R. Sirey, 1929), 344; Charles Rousseau, *Principes généraux du droit international public*, vol. 1 (Paris: A. Pedone, 1944), 126–127.

between Norway and the United Kingdom about the validity of Norway's straight base-lines method. The United Kingdom asserted that Norway's straight base-lines method violated international law because this method can only be applied to bays and no base-line can extend beyond 10 nautical miles. Norway, meanwhile, counterargued that the straight base-lines method did not violate international law, its rights were confirmed by historical aspects of long-term usage and absence of protests by the international community, and the straight base-lines method was justified by historic title even if the method deviated from international law.[60]

The ICJ rejected the existence of the rules argued for by the United Kingdom and then presented standards such as "certain economic benefits peculiar to a region, the reality and importance of which are clearly evidenced by a long usage" as the principle for determining the validity of the system applied by Norway to delimit its territorial waters.[61] The ICJ made its judgment on Norway's assertion of historic title in the context of discussing the above-mentioned "long usage." While the Court found that "the Norwegian authorities applied their system of delimitation consistently and uninterruptedly from 1869 until the time when the dispute arose,"[62] it proceeded to state that "[f]rom the standpoint of international law, it is now necessary to consider whether the application of the Norwegian system encountered any opposition from foreign States,"[63] and reached the following judgement.

> Norway has been in a position to argue without any contradiction that neither the promulgation of her delimitation Decrees in 1869 and in 1889, nor their application, gave rise to any opposition on the part of foreign States. Since, moreover, these Decrees constitute, as has been shown above, the application of a well-defined and uniform system, it is indeed this system itself which would reap the benefit of general toleration, the basis of a historical consolidation which would make it enforceable as against all States.
>
> The general toleration of foreign States with regard to the Norwegian practice is an unchallenged fact. For a period of more than sixty years the United Kingdom Government itself in no way contested it.
>
> The United Kingdom Government has argued that the Norwegian system of delimitation was not known to it and that the system therefore

60 Fisheries Case, Pleadings, Oral Arguments, Documents, vol. IV, 307–308.
61 Fisheries Case, Judgment of December 18th, 1951, *I.C.J. Reports* 1951, 133.
62 *Ibid.*, 138.
63 *Ibid.*

> lacked the notoriety essential to provide the basis of an historic title enforceable against it. The Court is unable to accept this view. ... the United Kingdom could not have been ignorant of the Decree of 1869. Nor, knowing of it, could it have been under any misapprehension as to the significance of its terms, which clearly described it as constituting the application of a system.
>
> The notoriety of the facts, the general toleration of the international community, Great Britain's position in the North Sea, her own interest in the question, and her prolonged abstention would in any case warrant Norway's enforcement of her system against the United Kingdom.[64]

3.1.2 Review of the Judgement

In this case, both parties engaged in a detailed discussion of the basis and conditions for historic title. The United Kingdom considered that the demonstration of acquiescence is necessary for establishing historic title, and historic usage is relevant precisely to the extent that it shows acquiescence by inference.[65] It also explained that the acquiescence of States can only be deduced from their attitude towards acts of another State of such a kind as they can be expected to notice and to which they should react.[66] In this case, however, the United Kingdom claimed that it did not have knowledge of the Norwegian system, nor could it have reasonably been expected to have knowledge of it.[67] It hence rejected the existence of acquiescence and establishment of historic title.

On the other hand, Norway argued that the concept of historical consolidation reflects the need for stability.[68] According to Norway, history obviously has a role in historic title, and the lapse of time is an important condition. While historic title requires the peaceful exercise of sovereignty and therefore the absence of opposition from the international community, this differs from acquiescence. The argument can be made that, if historic title requires acquiescence, a State that did not protest against the usage of other States due to reasons such as lack of knowledge of the usage should not be bound by that usage, because in such a situation, silence does not necessarily mean acquiescence. However, from the perspective of Norway's view of historic title, such an argument cannot be made, because according to this view, once the situation is consolidated with the lapse of time, any opposition should be set aside.

64 *Ibid.*, 138–139.
65 Fisheries Case (Pleadings), *supra* note 60, 122.
66 *Ibid.*, 136–137.
67 *Ibid.*, 140–141.
68 *Ibid.*, 308–309.

Both parties rely on theories related to prescription in their discussion on historic title, and the United Kingdom utilizes these concepts interchangeably. However, while the United Kingdom highlights acquiescence as the cause and derives the necessity of having knowledge of the system from that premise, Norway argues that the purpose of historic title is the stability of order and title comes solely from continuous and peaceful exercise of sovereignty. These arguments correspond to the two different understandings of prescription reviewed in the previous section and it was demanded that the ICJ respond to this historical difference of opinions.

Many academic works present the view that the judgement agreed with the United Kingdom's understanding. For example, Fitzmaurice explained that Norway presented a "legal principle of historical right" as confirmation of an existing right rather than creation of a right that did not originally exist, and noted that "[o]n that basis, … the consent or acquiescence of other States would not so much be unnecessary as irrelevant – and so Norway argued."[69] Then, he cited statements in the judgement such as "it is … necessary to consider whether the application of the Norwegian system encountered any opposition from foreign States" and "the general toleration of foreign States … is an unchallenged fact" to support an interpretation that the ICJ did not adopt Norway's legal principle and "considered the acquiescence, the consent in some form, or at least the toleration of the other State, to be necessary."[70]

Fitzmaurice claims that the judgement favored the United Kingdom's understanding and acknowledged that the ICJ reviewed whether there was acquiescence in confirming the historic title. However, he harshly criticizes the judgement as a departure from traditional law in concluding that the United Kingdom had knowledge of the system and consequently confirming acquiescence. This is because traditional law dictates that "neither knowledge nor acquiescence would be presumed except from circumstances in which it could unmistakably … be inferred," while the judgement ruled that the United Kingdom had knowledge and acquiesced despite factors including its extreme difficulties in acquiring information about the system.[71]

---

69 Gerald Fitzmaurice, "The Law and Procedures of the International Court of Justice," 30 *British Year Book of International Law* (1953), 28.

70 *Ibid.*, 32–33. See also, I. C. MacGibbon, "The Scope of Acquiescence in International Law," 31 *British Year Book of International Law* (1954), 164–165; and Yamamoto Soji 山本草二, "Gyogyō Jiken" 漁業事件 [Fisheries Case], in *Hanrei Kenkyu Kokusai Shihō Saibansho* 判例研究国際司法裁判所 [Research on International Court of Justice Practices], Takano Yuichi (ed.) (Tokyo: University of Tokyo Publishing, 1965), 49.

71 Fitzmaurice, *supra* note 69, 35–39. See also, MacGibbon, *supra* note 70, 169; and Yamamoto, *supra* note 70, 49–50.

However, this understanding leaves some doubts for the following reasons. The first is that Norway did not propose the historic title as confirmation of existing rights and instead focused on the pursuit of the stability of order as the purpose and hence asserted that acquiescence was not required. Norway rejected the view that acquiescence was required to establish the historic title but did state that the absence of opposition from the international community was necessary, and just because the judgement considered whether or not there was opposition from foreign States does not imply a rejection of such an understanding. The second is that the judgement confirmed general toleration based on the absence of opposition from foreign States against Norway's long-term use and thus concluded that the system was enforceable against all States. If general toleration here means acquiescence, since silence does not necessarily imply acquiescence, it could not be said that general toleration existed even if there was no opposition from foreign States, nor that the system was enforceable against all States. Thus, the judgement's logic aligns conversely with Norway's understanding that historic title is established based on long-term use and absence of opposition from the international community.

Meanwhile, the judgement examined the legitimacy of the United Kingdom's assertion that it lacked knowledge of the system and thus the system was not enforceable against it. If the system was enforceable against all States based on general toleration, it should obviously also be enforceable against the United Kingdom. Therefore, while it is unclear for what purpose the ICJ examined the abovementioned assertion of the United Kingdom, comments such as "would in any case warrant … enforcement … against the United Kingdom" suggest that the examination was a precautionary *obiter dictum*. The conclusion that the United Kingdom could not have lacked knowledge, despite the extreme difficulty in acquiring information about the system and other factors, particularly considering that knowledge should not be presumed except in situations in which it can be presumed unmistakably, is indeed highly questionable. However, if knowledge was presumed in a situation in which it could not be presumed, this means that the ICJ approved rights enforceable against all States based only on long-term use and absence of opposition from the international community, or, in other words, continuous and peaceful display of sovereignty.

This judgement has the same structure as the Award in the Island of Palmas Case reviewed in the previous section in that it first recognizes the existence of title based on continuous and peaceful display of sovereignty alone and then mentions the presence of acquiescence or knowledge without clarifying the reason for it. However, this mention being only nominal, this case should also be viewed as a precedent where the right of one of the parties was recognized based on prescription for the purpose of peace and stability.

3.1.3 Prescription, Etc., and Acquiescence in Theories – Deepening Confusion

In the Fisheries Case, the United Kingdom emphasized acquiescence as the cause of prescription, etc., and argued for the necessity of knowledge. This argument is seen in UK and US theories in the same period and combines with theories that the judgement favored the United Kingdom's understanding to become the mainstream and steadily evolve further. For example, Johnson makes the following observations.

> Publicity is essential because acquiescence is essential. For acquisitive prescription depends upon acquiescence, express or implied. Acquiescence is often implied, in the interests of international order, in cases where it does not genuinely exist; but without knowledge there can be no acquiescence at all.[72]

MacGibbon, having explained that "[t]he most helpful definition of prescription is one which substitutes for the stipulation of a fixed term of years a conception which takes account of the consensual basis of the rules of international law,"[73] provided the following comments on the conditions.

> Although it is generally conceded that rights can be lost by inaction in the course of time, this is not to assert that failure to protest invariably entails this consequence. There may be circumstances which militate against the inference of acquiescence from failure to protest. Pleas of substance are available, by way of explanation, which, if well-founded, serve to rebut the presumption of consent which might otherwise be raised by a long, unexplained silence.[74]

Furthermore, Blum comments that acquiescence "removes the besetting difficulty which confronts the exponents of international prescription, namely, that it can dispense with the exacting requirements for the efflux of a fixed period of time"[75] and argues the following regarding conditions for historic title.

72 Johnson, *supra* note 23, 347.
73 MacGibbon, *supra* note 70, 166.
74 *Ibid.*, 172.
75 Blum, *supra* note 23, 59.

> [D]octrine and practice alike require for the establishment of an historic title an exercise by the claimant State of authority which is both continuous and peaceful. … [T]he [latter] – the requirement of peacefulness – is the invocation of acquiescence in disguise, for it indicates the lack of opposition to … an effective possession. … From the legal point of view it is of course not the fact of effective possession, but rather the presumption of acquiescence, that sets the seal of legal validity on the historic claim.[76]

While Johnson explains that prescription relies on acquiescence and requires knowledge, he also acknowledges that acquiescence is "implied, in the interests of international order" and seems to admit its fictious nature. However, MacGibbon consistently seeks the cause of prescription in acquiescence, with the intention to replace the definition of prescription with the concept of acquiescence. Blum argues that the source of historic title is acquiescence and not prescription, abandoning the latter concept.

This understanding clearly has roots in the prescription theory of natural law scholars, but it also seems to be influenced by the doctrine of "the presumption of a grant" related to prescription as the reason for the occurrence of easement in common law.[77] The presumption is thought to have been adopted by courts for the sake of accommodating the acquisition of rights in a shorter period of time, without changing the law itself, as a way of addressing the issue whereby proof of usage since the coronation of Richard the First (1189) had been required in British law but had become virtually impossible as time passed.[78] This doctrine is similar to the doctrine of presumed acquiescence advocated by natural law theories on prescription in that they both rely on the intent of the right holder to justify the acquisition of a right through usage or possession in the face of the obsolescence or inexistence of laws that provide effect to the lapse of time. What is even more notable is that the following points have also been made about the characteristics of this so-called presumption.

76 *Ibid.*, 99.

77 In particular, Blum conducted a comparative review of prescription, in the form of prescription in domestic law, in Roman law and British law and explained that lapse of time has decisive importance as a component factor in the former case, while it only has meaning as evidence that contributes to strengthening the presumption in the latter case (*ibid.*, 8–12). This indicates an association with his theory of historic title.

78 W. B. Stoebuck, "The Fiction of Presumed Grant," *University of Kansas Law Review*, vol. 15, no. 1 (1966), 19–22.

> Most courts that have considered the question have said the presumption cannot be rebutted by proof no grant was actually made. Otherwise stated, though the facts giving rise to the presumptive inference may be rebutted, the inference itself may not be. This really is only a way of saying that, as a rule of law, prescriptive use gives title to the incorporeal interest used, and presumed grant becomes a fictionalized rationale for the result of the rule. Such a rule and result accord with the generally accepted function of prescription. The minority of decisions holding that the presumptive inference is rebuttable thereby introduce an unwarranted restriction upon the doctrine of prescription.[79]
>
> [The minority of decisions], unfortunately, take the word 'acquiescence' literally. One result of this can be to defeat the presumption and to prevent prescription unless the owner has actual notice.[80]

Blum and others argue that the source of prescription, etc., is acquiescence as seen in the reliance on acquiescence and toleration in the Island of Palmas Case and the Fisheries Case[81] and therefore it is possible to hinder its establishment with a defense of lack of knowledge, etc. However, as indicated in this review, these decisions recognize title based on the continuous and peaceful display of sovereignty. Regarding acquiescence and other sometimes-mentioned terms, they do not appear to provide meaning beyond a fictitious reason for the title recognized in this way. Nevertheless, many theories seem to rely on these terms and have introduced an unwarranted restriction on prescription, etc.

3.2 *Temple of Preah Vihear Case (Merits) (1962) – Acquiescence and Estoppel*

3.2.1 Overview of the Judgement

The Temple of Preah Vihear Case is considered an important judicial practice for the concepts of acquiescence and estoppel, but has also generated a significant divergence of views about their interpretation. This case involves the dispute about the attribution of the Temple of Preah Vihear area located on the border between Cambodia and Thailand. France and Siam (Thailand) concluded a treaty in 1904 stipulating that the frontier in this area should adhere to the watershed line and a Mixed Commission should handle the actual delimitation work. However, the Commission did not complete its work, and French

---

79 *Ibid.*, 24.

80 *Ibid.*, 25–26. Author's note added in parentheses.

81 MacGibbon, *supra* note 70, 156–162; Blum, *supra* note 23, 67–78.

authorities, at the request of the Siam Government, handled map preparation and issuance. While the map was ready in 1907 and subsequently provided to the Siam Government, the frontier line placed the entire Temple area on the Cambodian side. In the case in question, Cambodia relied on this map for its claim of sovereignty, whereas Thailand asserted that it did not accept the map as having a binding character, among other arguments.[82]

The ICJ rendered the following judgment pointing out the circumstance that the map was allocated to the Siam Government as purporting to represent the outcome of the work of delimitation.[83]

> it is clear that the circumstances were such as called for some reaction, within a reasonable period, on the part of the Siamese authorities, if they wished to disagree with the map or had any serious question to raise in regard to it. They did not do so, either then or for many years, and thereby must be held to have acquiesced. *Qui tacet consentire videtur si loqui debuisset ac potuisset.*[84]

Furthermore, noting that Thailand did not contest the map thereafter (from 1909), that it created its own maps showing the temple as located in Cambodia, and that a member of the Thai royal family was officially received with the French flag flying on his visit to the temple,[85] the Court provided the following judgment.

> Even if there were any doubt as to Siam's acceptance of the map in 1908, and hence of the frontier indicated thereon, the Court would consider, in the light of the subsequent course of events, that Thailand is now precluded by her conduct from asserting that she did not accept it. She has, for fifty years, enjoyed such benefits as the Treaty of 1904 conferred on her, if only the benefit of a stable frontier. France, and through her Cambodia, relied on Thailand's acceptance of the map.[86]

---

82 *Case concerning the Temple of Preah Vihear (Cambodia v. Thailand), Merits, Judgement of 15 June 1962, ICJ Reports 1962*, 21.

83 *Ibid.*, 22–23.

84 *Ibid.*, 23.

85 *Ibid.*, 27–32.

86 *Ibid.*, 32.

3.2.2 Review of the Judgement

This judgement elicited a wide range of interpretations among theories. For example, Cot commented that Thailand accepted the map in Annex I and finalized the contract immediately in 1908–1909, and that its acts from 1909 were not elements of acquiescence,[87] whereas, he argued, the judgement regarding Thailand's attitude after 1909 applied the principle of estoppel.[88] In Cot's understanding, the rulings in the judgement were separated into those based on facts from 1909 and earlier and those based on facts thereafter, with the former recognizing Thailand's acquiescence and the binding character of the map, and the latter as *obiter dictum* explaining that Thailand, in any case, could not reject the binding character of the map due to estoppel.

Meanwhile, Marques Antunes explained that Thailand did not contest the map for over fifty years, and the ICJ used that fact to conclude that Thailand had "accepted the frontier ... as it was drawn on the map" and that Thailand was "precluded ... from asserting that she [had] not accept[ed] it."[89] Considering that Marques Antunes mentions that "elapsed time is ... of extreme importance" for establishing acquiescence and acquiescence is "used ... to impede an acquiescing State from contesting its previous conduct,"[90] he seems to interpret the judgement as recognizing Thailand's acquiescence based on silence of over fifty years and recognizing an estoppel effect from this.

Kolb, on the other hand, criticized the judgement for precluding Thailand's assertion, pointing out that the absence of change in the relative positions between the parties meant the conditions for estoppel were not met, and noted that "it is manifest that the decision ... was heavily coloured by the principle of acquiescence, which does not require a detrimental reliance" and "[this] principle did seem relevant in view of the prolonged silence."[91] This view asserts that while the judgement appears to have applied estoppel, it actually confirmed Thailand's acquiescence based on over fifty years of silence and thereby recognized the binding character of the map.

As indicated above, while theories disputed what period and facts were the basis for the judgement's confirmation of acquiescence or estoppel and

87 Jean-Pierre Cot, "L'arrêt de la Cour internationale de Justice dans l'affaire du *temple de Préah Vihéar* (Cambodge c. Thaïlande – Fond)," 8 *Annuaire français de droit international* (1962), 237.

88 *Ibid.*, 243–244.

89 N. S. Marques Antunes, "Estoppel, Acquiescence and Recognition in Territorial and Boundary Dispute Settlement," *Boundary & Territory Briefing*, vol. 2, no. 8 (2000), 13–14.

90 *Ibid.*, 31.

91 Robert Kolb, *Good Faith in International Law* (Oxford: Hart Publishing, 2017), 114.

what the effect of acquiescence was, a straightforward reading of the actual language of the judgement seems to obviously support the interpretation presented by Cot.

First, considering that, after explaining that it precluded Thailand's assertion on the basis of events after 1909, the judgement clearly states "the Court however considers that Thailand in 1908–1909 did accept the … map as representing the outcome of the work of delimitation, … the effect of which is to situate Preah Vihear in Cambodian territory,"[92] it is evident that the ICJ recognized Thailand's acquiescence based on the silence during the period and thereby acknowledged Cambodia's rights. The judgement immediately recognizes acquiescence based on a lack of a reaction over a reasonable period of time after Thailand was placed in a position in which it "must and can speak" and acknowledged the effect of a change in rights under substantive law.

Nevertheless, Marques Antunes and Kolb interpret the judgement as if it acknowledged Thailand's acquiescence based on a silence of over fifty years. The background to this understanding seems to involve a line of thinking whereby the decisions in the Fisheries Case and others are read as recognizing prescription, etc., premised on acquiescence, this leads to an understanding that "the backbone of acquiescence lies in the prolonged silence or passivity opposed to the claims of another subject,"[93] and this view is reflected in the judgement in the Temple of Preah Vihear Case.[94] However, as has already been noted, it is difficult to conclude that the Fisheries Case judgement recognized prescription, etc., premised on acquiescence.

Furthermore, the opinion that acquiescence requires the lapse of a lengthy period of time is problematic in that it misunderstands the reasoning involved in the doctrine of presumed acquiescence as the basis of prescription, etc. The doctrine implies that long-term possession puts the right holder in a position in which it "must and can speak" at some point and presumes acquiescence from the silence, on the ground that it is unlikely that lack of knowledge of the possession and constraints on free will would continue over a long period of time. The doctrine does not state that the acquiescence itself, that is to say a right holder remaining silent despite being in a position in which it "must and can speak," requires the lapse of a lengthy period of time. As noted by Cot, while explaining that the judgement in the Temple of Preah Vihear Case

92 Preah Vihear, *supra* note 82, 32.

93 Kolb, *supra* note 91, 92.

94 Marques Antunes and Kolb both quote the judgement in the Fisheries Case in explaining the importance of the lapse of time (Marques Antunes, *supra* note 89, 32; Kolb, *supra* note 91, 93).

accurately demonstrates the nature of acquiescence, acquiescence is "simply a method by which a State expresses its intent" and is "an instantaneous act and not something that emerges gradually over a period of time."[95]

Second, since the judgement recognizes Thailand's acquiescence based on silence prior to 1909 and does not include subsequent acts as part of the acquiescence, the portion of the judgement that dismisses Thailand's assertions based on these acts cannot be interpreted as granting an estoppel effect to the acquiescence. That portion of the judgement should be interpreted as *obiter dictum* that recognized the effect of precluding Thailand's assertions based on a strict understanding of estoppel consisting of clear representation, reliance upon the representation, and a disadvantageous change in position.

Judge Fitzmaurice offers a clear explanation in his separate opinion regarding this relationship between acquiescence and estoppel and the understanding of conditions for estoppel.

> A, having accepted a certain obligation, or having become bound by a certain instrument, cannot now be heard to deny the fact, to 'blow hot and cold'. True enough, A cannot be heard to deny it; but what this really means is simply that A is bound, and, being bound, cannot escape from the obligation merely by denying its existence. In other words, if the denial can be shown to be false, there is no room or need for any plea of preclusion or estoppel. Such a plea ... prevents the assertion of what might in fact be true. Its use must in consequence be subject to certain limitation.[96]

If Thailand's silence constituted acquiescence, the acquiescence binds Thailand, and it is unnecessary to mention the preclusion of the assertion by Thailand that it did not accept the map. The significance of estoppel is that, even if Thailand's silence did not actually constitute acquiescence, as the result of this representation, i.e., silence, Thailand is precluded from asserting that it did not accept the map, and this is why the use of estoppel is subject to the strict condition that the other party relied on the representation and changed its position to its detriment.[97]

While the judgement only explained that Thailand's assertion of not having accepted the map should be precluded, even if questions existed about

95 Cot, *supra* note 87, 237.

96 Preah Vihear, Separate Opinion of Sir Gerald Fitzmaurice, *ICJ Reports 1962*, 63.

97 However, as seen in Kolb's comment, there is criticism regarding whether France did in fact rely on Thailand's actions and changed its position to its detriment.

Thailand's acquiescence, this can be interpreted as meaning that, as a result of precluding this assertion, Preah Vihear is in any case positioned in Cambodian territory. In the past, "estoppel by conduct" in common law was understood as a principle in procedural law that served only to shield against the establishment of a claim by preventing assertions of facts and rights by a claimant.[98] Since this case recognizes estoppel in the context of affirming rights, if the estoppel precludes an assertion regarding the existence of a right, it essentially constitutes a change in rights under substantive law as the effect of precluding the assertion.

3.2.3 Acquiescence and Estoppel in Theories – New Confusion

The recognition of acquiescence in the Preah Vihear Temple Case judgement does not require the lapse of a lengthy period of time and fits with the prewar practice of recognizing acquiescence based on silence by a party in a situation in which it "must and can speak." On the other hand, in this case, the distinction between acquiescence and estoppel, as well as the understanding of strict estoppel, deviated from the prewar practice that could be interpreted as approving an effect of estoppel in acquiescence and allowing the effect without consideration of points such as a disadvantageous change in position. Behind this difference was a change in international legal theory, particularly the gradual acceptance of the concept of unilateral acts or juridical acts by common law theorists.

The following Schwarzenberger opinion is an example of this development.

> If a subject of international law chooses to take up a position in relation to a matter which is legally relevant and communicates this intent to others it is bound within such limits to accept the legal implications of such a unilateral act ... No doubt, in the formative stage of this rule, the obnoxiousness of self-contradictory behaviour and *venire contra factum proprium* assisted in creating the *opinio juris sive necessitatis* which marks the border-line between international comity and international customary law. Once, however, the rule on the binding character of unilateral declarations had come into existence, the necessity for reliance on good faith to justify this proposition had passed.[99]

98 Refer to footnote 45.

99 George Schwarzenberger, "The Fundamental Principles of International Law," 87 *Recueil des cours de l'académie de droit international de La Haye* (1955), 312.

This explains that there was recognition of a substantially binding character in cases of unilateral expression of intent for acquiescence and recognition, etc., based on the good faith principle, which disdains self-contradictory words and deeds, or, in other words, permissive estoppel, and that the stance has developed into recognition of these acts as juridical acts creating their own binding force.[100]

Meanwhile, based on a standpoint that assumes that acquiescence and recognition constitute juridical acts, the type of permissive estoppel seen in previous international practice is simply one form of expressing the effect that originates from juridical acts, etc., and estoppel as its own legal framework only existed as the strict estoppel that requires a disadvantageous change in position. For example, Dominicé discusses it in the following manner.

> Il résulte en définitive de l'analyse de la jurisprudence que tous les cas dans lesquels le préjudice n'est pas nécessaire pour que se produise une déchéance ont ceci de commun que cette déchéance est l'effet d'un acte juridique, ou de l'application d'une règle concrète. La forclusion, voire l'estoppel si l'on utilise ici ce terme, ne se présentent pas comme une institution juridique autonome, ce n'est qu'une manière de décrire la déchéance.
>
> En revanche, lorsque les comportements ne sont pas constitutifs d'un acte juridique, ou n'attestent pas le défaut d'action lorsque celle-ci était exigée de celui qui voulait sauvegarder son droit, ils ne sont susceptibles de lier définitivement leur auteur que si la position respective des parties a été modifiée.[101]

Prewar judicial practices confirming an effect of precluding assertions in recognition and acquiescence without mentioning estoppel are the product of doubts regarding the binding character of unilateral expressions of intent, and as the doubts faded after World War II, the understanding of recognition and acquiescence as juridical acts and a strict interpretation of estoppel become

100 Additionally, along with the abovementioned separate opinion, as literature that demonstrates the development of Fitzmaurice's understanding of the effect of unilateral expression of intent without *quid pro quo*, refer to Gerald Fitzmaurice, "The Law and Procedure of the International Court of Justice 1951–4," 33 *British Year Book of International Law* (1957), 229.

101 Christian Dominicé, "A propos du principe de l'estoppel en droit des gens," in M. Battelli et al. (eds.), *Recueil d'études de droit international en hommage à Paul Guggenheim* (Genève: Imprimerie de la Tribune de Genève, 1968), 364–365.

the main approach. The Preah Vihear Temple Case is a good example of this development in judicial practices. However, the opinions of theorists are split on the judgement because of the view that "acquiescence requires the lapse of a lengthy period of time," derived from an erroneous understanding of the reasoning involved in the doctrine of presumed acquiescence as the basis of prescription, etc., and this left confusion regarding the relationship between acquiescence and estoppel and the conditions for estoppel.

4 Conclusion

This chapter is a preliminary work for considering the significance of silence in territorial disputes, and particularly how to legally structure the "75 years of silence" regarding the Senkaku Islands. For this purpose, this chapter examined prewar judicial practices and theories, as well as early ICJ judicial practices and theories in relation to prescription, etc., acquiescence, and estoppel, and attempted to untangle the relationship among these concepts and ascertain whether or not they exist, as well as their content. The following points offer provisional conclusions from the analysis.

First, understandings of prescription, etc., include title that creates rights based on the continuous and peaceful display of sovereignty for the purpose of maintaining peace and stability, as well as the acquisition of a right from acquiescence derived via a specific method of presumption premised on display of sovereignty and long continued silence over this. Judicial decisions seem to have been in accordance with the former understanding. These titles create a right enforceable against all States without requiring the existence or identification of a true right holder and regardless of factors such as lack of knowledge of displays of sovereignty.

Acquiescence, meanwhile, refers to intent tacitly conveyed by silence by a party in a situation in which it "must and can speak." Whereas in prewar practice, some cases expressed the effect of this as estoppel, in postwar practice, acquiescence is interpreted as a juridical act that itself creates a change in substantive rights. Silence in this context is not limited to one related to displays of sovereignty and while it does not need to be something longstanding, if there is a lack of knowledge or the existence of a factor that invalidates consent, then acquiescence is not established.

Regarding estoppel, prewar practice included some judicial practices that could be seen as applying a permissive understanding expressed as "cannot blow hot and cold" and recognizing the establishment of this type of estoppel. In postwar judicial practices, courts have adopted a strict understanding that requires clear representation, reliance upon the representation, and a disadvantageous change in position. The clear representation mentioned here includes not only silence, i.e., inactions, but also actions. While estoppel is deemed to have the effect of precluding assertions, the result is a change in rights under substantive law in the sense of potentially recognizing a right that did not originally exist.

As for the "75 years of silence" regarding the Senkaku Islands, there is no doubt that China and other States were silent throughout the entire 75 years. Therefore, Japan would need to carefully assess in which period of silence (1) it can be said that there was a continuous display of sovereignty by Japan (prescription, etc.: in this case, whether there was a lack of knowledge or invalidating factor for consent on the part of China is irrelevant); (2) it can be said that there was not a lack of knowledge nor invalidating factor for consent on the part of China (acquiescence: China's silence in this case could be regarding the exercise of US administrative power or Japan's residual sovereignty and not the display of sovereignty by Japan); and (3) it can be said that Japan relied on China's silence and changed its position to its detriment (estoppel); etc. Japan should then select and invoke the appropriate concept.

That being said, the conceptual understandings explained above are simply conclusions based on some prewar and early ICJ judicial practices, and in order to obtain a conclusive conceptual understanding, a more in-depth review of international practices from the same period and a review of subsequent developments in international practices are required. Regarding this point, attention should be given to some subsequent ICJ practices that exhibit conflation of the acquiescence and prescription, etc., seen in theories. Specifically, it appears that the interpretation that "acquiescence requires the lapse of a lengthy period of time" and the resulting residual conflation of acquiescence and estoppel concepts have manifested themselves in a combined form, and acquiescence is being used as a concept that implies an approach of comprehensively determining a change in rights based on various actions or inactions (representation) that have occurred over a certain period of time (lengthy period of time) and that do not on their own constitute an expression of intent.[102]

---

102 For the beginning of this development, refer to Delimitation of the Maritime Boundary in the Gulf of Maine Area, Judgment, *ICJ Reports 1984*, paras. 126–154. As examples in which the rights of a State have been recognized using this new concept of "acquiescence," refer to Land, Island and Maritime Frontier Dispute, Judgment of 11 September 1992, *ICJ Reports 1992*, paras. 72–80 and Sovereignty over Pedra Branca/Pulau batu Puteh, Middle Rock and South Ledge, Judgment, *ICJ Reports 2008*, paras. 118–277. The latter judgement

The opinion presented in this chapter is that, even if it can be said that this approach of reaching a comprehensive assessment based on the new concept of "acquiescence" is established in international practice, it does not abolish the existing concepts which generate certain legal effects in rights under certain conditions as explained above, but may become a new option alongside these concepts as a legal construct concerning silence, etc. However, a review of the existence and significance of this type of new "acquiescence" concept obviously requires a separate serious consideration. The author intends to conduct such an assessment, as well as to present a review of the legal structure of the "75 years of silence" regarding the Senkaku Islands in light of a conclusive understanding of these concepts, as part of future work.

Bibliography

Secondary Sources

Japanese

Huh, Sookyeon 許淑娟. *Ryōiki Kengen Ron* 領域権原論 [The Acquisition of Territory in International Law]. Tokyo: University of Tokyo Publishing, 2012.

Miyoshi, Masahiro 三好正弘. "Ryōdo Shutoku ni Okeru Kōgi to Mokunin" 領土取得における抗議と黙認 [Protest and Acquiescence in Territorial Acquisition]. *Tōsho Kenkyu Jyānaru* 島嶼研究ジャーナル 4, no. 2 (2015): 25–46.

Matsui, Yoshirō 松井芳郎. *Kokusaihō Gakusha ga Yomu Senkaku Mondai* 国際法学者が読む尖閣問題 [International Law Theorists' View of the Senkaku Islands Issue]. Tokyo: Nippon Hyōronsha, 2014.

Taijudō, Kanae 太壽堂鼎. *Ryōdo Kizoku no Kokusaihō* 領土帰属の国際法 [International Law of Territory Possession]. Tokyo: Tōshindō, 1998.

Yamamoto, Soji 山本草二. "Gyogyō Jiken" 漁業事件 [Fisheries Case]. In *Hanrei Kenkyu Kokusai Shihō Saibansho* 判例研究国際司法裁判所 [Research on International Court of Justice Practices], edited by Takano Yuichi. Tokyo: University of Tokyo Publishing, 1965.

Yanagihara, Masaharu 柳原正治. "Shoyūken, Shihaiken" 所有権・支配権 [Ownership Rights and Control Rights]. In Sensō to Heiwa no Hō [Hoseiban] 戦争と平和の法[補正版] [*Laws of War and Peace* (*Revised Edition*)], edited by Ōnuma Yasuaki 大沼保昭. Tokyo: Tōshindo, 1995.

---

describes this new concept of "acquiescence" as "a convergent evolution of the positions of the Parties" (*ibid.*, para. 276).

Western Languages

Maruques Antunes, N. S. "Estoppel, Acquiescence and Recognition in Territorial and Boundary Dispute Settlement." *Boundary & Territory Briefing* 2, no. 8 (2000): 1–42.

Maruques Antunes, N. S. "Acquiescence." In *Max Planck Encyclopedia of Public International Law*, online edition, last updated in September 2006.

Anzilotti, Dionisio. *Cours de droit international*, vol. 1. Translated by Gilbert Gibel. Paris: Recueil Sirey, 1929.

Blum, Yehuda Zvi. *Historic Titles in International Law.* The Hague: M. Nijhoff, 1965.

Cot, Jean-Pierre. "L'arrêt de la Cour internationale de Justice dans l'affaire du *temple de Préah Vihéar* (Cambodge c. Thaïlande – Fond)." *Annuaire français de droit international* 8 (1962): 217–247.

Crawford, James. *Brownlie's Principles of Public International Law*, 9th ed. Oxford: Oxford University Press, 2019.

Dominicé, Christian. "A propos du principe de l'estoppel en droit des gens." In *Recueil d'études de droit international en hommage à Paul Guggenheim,* edited by M. Battelli et al., 327–365. Genève: Imprimerie de la Tribune de Genève, 1968.

Fauchille, Paul. *Traité de droit international public*, 8th ed., vol. 1. Paris: Rousseau, 1925.

Feltham, Piers, et al. *Spencer Bower: Reliance-Based Estoppel*, 5th ed. London: Bloomsbury Professional, 2017.

Fitzmaurice, Gerald. "The Law and Procedures of the International Court of Justice." *British Year Book of International Law* 30 (1953): 1–70.

Fitzmaurice, Gerald. "The Law and Procedure of the International Court of Justice 1951–4." *British Year Book of International Law* 33 (1957): 203–293.

Grotius, Hugo. *De jure belli ac pacis*, book ii.

Hall, William Edward. *A Treatise on International Law*, 4th ed. Oxford: Clarendon Press, 1895.

Heffter, August Wilhelm. *Le Droit international de l'Europe*, 4th ed. Paris: A. Cotillon, 1883.

Jennings, Robert and Arthur Watts. *Oppenheim's International Law*, 9th ed. vol. 1. London: Longman, 1996.

Johnson, David H. N. "Acquisitive Prescription in International Law." *British Year Book of International Law* 27 (1950): 332–354.

Kolb, Robert. *Good Faith in International Law*. Oxford: Hart Publishing, 2017.

Lauterpacht, Hersch. *Private Law Sources and Analogies of International Law.* London: Longman, 1927.

MacGibbon, Iain C. "The Scope of Acquiescence in International Law." *British Year Book of International Law* 31 (1954): 143–186.

Martin, Antoine. *L'Estoppel en droit international public.* Paris: A. Pedone, 1979.

McNair, Arnold D. "The Legality of the Occupation of the Ruhr." *British Year Book of International Law* 5 (1924): 17–37.

Rousseau, Charles. *Principes généraux du droit international public*, vol. 1. Paris: A. Pedone, 1944.
Schwarzenberger, George. "The Fundamental Principles of International Law." *Recueil des cours de l'académie de droit international de La Haye* 87 (1955): 191–385.
Stoebuck, William B. "The Fiction of Presumed Grant." *University of Kansas Law Review* 15, no. 1 (1966): 17–34.
Vattel, Emer de. *Le droit de gens*, book ii.
Von Pufendorf, Samuel. *De jure naturae et gentium libri octo*, book iv.
Wolff, Christian. *Jus gentium methodo scientifica pertractatum*, book iv.

CHAPTER 7

Temporal Elements and Their Regulation in Determining Territorial Disputes

Practical Application to Territorial Disputes of Japan

Hironobu Sakai

1 Introduction

"Time" can have a significant impact in determining the winner and loser in games.[1] This same effect applies to the resolution of territorial and border disputes under international law. Time rules events (*tempus regit factum*)[2] because of its role in defining facts and events related to territorial title and legal assessment. That being the case, the question of what kind of impact the concept of "time" has in such territorial disputes, and how that in turn influences the assertions of the parties involved in the dispute, as well as the decision of the dispute-resolving body and the reasoning for reaching said decision, are key points to consider in territorial disputes, not only for stakeholders asserting their own positions, but also for those in a position to propose measures for resolving a dispute.

Particularly in the field of the acquisition of territorial sovereignty, observers have cited critical date and intertemporal law as rules that regulate facts and acts from such a "time" perspective.[3] However, some are also of the view that the judgments and awards of courts and tribunals related to territorial disputes following the Second World War have not been successful in clarifying these two rules.[4] Furthermore, there are still considerable points of uncertainty about what kind of relation these two rules, which are applied to territorial disputes and have temporal elements, have with the actual judicial process.

---

1 M. Bennouna, *Le droit international entre la lettre et l'esprit* (Leiden: Brill, 2017), 264.

2 A. X. Fellmeth and M. Horwitz, *Guide to Latin in International Law, Second Edition* (Oxford: Oxford University Press, 2021), 287.

3 M. G. Kohen and M. Hébié, "Territory, Acquisition," in *The Max Planck Encyclopedia of Public International Law, Volume IX*, R. Wolfrum (ed.) (Oxford: Oxford University Press, 2012), 896–897.

4 Y. Onuma, *International Law in a Transcivilizational World* (Cambridge: Cambridge University Press, 2017), 310.

 | DOI:10.1163/9789004706361_008

This chapter will therefore first present a basic review of the respective roles of critical date and intertemporal law in territorial disputes, and examine how they have functioned in judicial practice. Then, based on the practical roles of the two rules that have been thus identified, it will home in on Japan's territorial issues and examine their application thereto.

2 Effect of Critical Date and Intertemporal Law in Judicial Practice

Critical date and intertemporal law are typically presented as rules that include temporal elements in relation to territorial disputes as explained above. Since these two rules have been formed and further clarified within international judicial practice, this section will look next at both the content and purpose of these rules in past judicial precedents.[5]

Critical date refers to "the date after which the actions or inaction of the parties cannot affect the legal situation."[6] Its main function, according to the Judgment by the International Court of Justice (ICJ) in the Territorial and Maritime Dispute between Nicaragua and Honduras in the Caribbean Sea case, is

> distinguishing between those acts performed *à titre de souverain* which are in principle relevant for the purpose of assessing and validating *effectivités*, and those acts occurring after such critical date, which are in general meaningless for that purpose, having been carried out by a State

5 The following explanation overlaps with some of the content in Sakai Hironobu 酒井啓亘, "Ryōiki Funsō ni Okeru 'Ketteiteki Kijitsu' no Igi –Kokusai Shihō Saibansho no Saibanrei o Chūshin ni–" 領域紛争における「決定的期日」の意義—国際司法裁判所の裁判例を中心に— [Significance of "Critical Date" in Territorial Disputes: Mainly from International Court of Justice Precedents]. In *Kokusai Kankei to Hō no Shihai* (*Owada Hisashi Kokusai Shihō Saibansyo Saibankan Taikan Kinen*) 国際関係と法の支配(小和田恆国際司法裁判所裁判官退官記念) [International Relations and the Rule of Law: Festschrift for Judge Owada Hisashi in commemoration of his retirement from the International Court of Justice], edited by Iwasawa Yuji 岩澤雄司 and Okano Masataka 岡野正敬 (Tokyo: Shinzansha, 2021), 147–179, and Sakai Hironobu 酒井啓亘, "Ryōiki Funsō ni Okeru Jisaihō Gensoku no Yakuwari ni tsuite – Kokusai Hanrei no Dōkō o Chushin ni" 領域紛争における時際法原則の役割について—国際判例の動向を中心に [The Roles of Intertemporal Law in the International Judicial and Arbitral Settlement of the Territorial Disputes], *Hōgaku Ronsō* 法学論叢, vol. 188 (2021), no. 4, 5, and 6, 87–126.

6 D. H. N. Johnson, "The Minquiers and Ecrehos Case," *International and Comparative Law Quarterly*, vol. 3 (1954), 208; L. F. E. Goldie, "The Critical Date," *International and Comparative Law Quarterly*, vol. 12 (1963), 1251.

> which, already having claims to assert in a legal dispute, could have taken those actions strictly with the aim of buttressing those claims. Thus a critical date will be the dividing line after which the parties' acts become irrelevant for the purposes of assessing the value of *effectivités*.[7]

As the ICJ explained in the Sovereignty over Pulau Ligitan and Pulau Sipadan Indonesia / Malaysia case, acts taken after the critical date do not have evidentiary value that contributes to assessing the existence of *effectivités* prior to the critical date, and from the ICJ's position, it "cannot take into consideration acts having taken place after the date on which the dispute between the Parties crystallized."[8]

In this way, the significance of the critical date lies in distinguishing between those acts *à titre de souverain* occurring prior to the date of crystallization of the dispute and those acts occurring after that date,[9] so that the critical date has the effect of instructing courts to consider only the former for the purpose of establishing and confirming sovereignty. Nevertheless, the function of the critical date is not necessarily applied strictly in actual territorial disputes. Even if the acts or facts come after the critical date, courts might consider them as long as they do not alter the legal relation at the time of the critical date and they do not improve the claims and territorial titles asserted by the parties to the dispute. In other words, the critical date has the value of confirming the situation at the time of the critical date in relation to subsequent facts and acts, while at the same time functioning to prevent any change to the situation that existed at that time.[10]

However, courts' leeway to use acts following the critical date to conditionally confirm a territorial title has relativized the designation of the time of the critical date and its effect, and this has given courts some flexibility in making decisions on substantive matters related to the creation and elimination of a territorial title.[11] In other words, since the designation of the critical date

---

7 *Territorial and Maritime Dispute between Nicaragua and Honduras in the Caribbean Sea (Nicaragua v. Honduras)*, *ICJ Reports 2007*, 697–698, para. 117.

8 *Sovereignty over Pulau Ligitan and Pulau Sipadan (Indonesia / Malaysia)*, *ICJ Reports 2002*, 682, para. 135.

9 *Territorial and Maritime Dispute (Nicaragua v. Colombia)*, *Merits*, *ICJ Reports 2012*, 652, paras. 67–68.

10 Kohen and Hébié, *supra* note 3, 897. See also, *The Minquiers and Ecrehos case*, *ICJ Reports 1953*, 59–60; *Case concerning the Location of Boundary Markers in Taba between Egypt and Israel. (Egypt / Israel)*, *Reports of International Arbitral Awards*, vol. XX, 45, para. 175.

11 D. Bardonnet, "Les faits postérieurs à la date critique dans les différends territoriaux et frontaliers," in *Le droit international au service de la paix, de la justice et du développement. Mélanges Michel Virally* (Paris: Pedone, 1991), 78.

relies on the unique circumstances of each case, it is difficult to generalize the method by which it is done, and the decision must depend on a discretionary ruling by a court, factoring in the uniqueness of each case.

Intertemporal law, the other rule that contains temporal elements, meanwhile, was defined in the Arbitral Award in the Island of Palmas case. According to the first principle, "a juridical fact must be appreciated in light of the law contemporary with it, and not of the law in force at the time when a dispute in regard to it arises or falls to be settled." This means an act should be assessed by laws in force at the time of the act. The second principle, based on the premise that "a distinction must be made between the creation of rights and the [continued] existence of rights," states that the continued existence of the right shall follow the conditions required by the evolution of law, and rights should adhere to the law in force at the respective times.[12] It can be said that intertemporal law is aimed at ensuring both the stability of the system of legal norms and the dynamism of law. However, the inclusion of the first principle as well as the second principle of intertemporal law resulted in the treatment of the modern international legal order, with established legal principles for territorial title, and the preceding pre-modern normative order as a single integrated normative system from the perspective of the abovementioned purpose. In particular, in response to the dynamism of law within this system, it acknowledged "continuous and peaceful display of territorial sovereignty" as a type of effective possession, and aimed to legally connect the stages of the creation of the right with the continued existence of the same right.

In this way, rational analysis of rules that contain temporal elements shows that, on the one hand, the critical date defines some delineation, albeit incomplete, within the timeframe of applicable laws, and, on the other hand, intertemporal law stipulates the content of the applicable law in the timeframe leading up to the critical date.[13]

However, while both rules deal with temporal elements, how they relate to each other in their practical application cannot be said to be unambiguous.

---

12 *The Island of Palmas Case* (*Netherlands / the United States of America*), *Reports of International Arbitral Awards*, vol. 11, 845.

13 Therefore, critical date "plays a preliminary role for the purposes of application of the principle of intertemporal law" (G. Distefano, "Time Factor and Territorial Disputes," in M. G. Kohen and M. Hébié (eds.), *Research Handbook on Territorial Disputes in International Law* (Cheltenham: Edward Elgar, 2018), 398) and "en précisant dans le temps le moment constitutif du différend, l'organe juridictionnel fixera de même, en termes de droit intertemporel, les principes et les normes juridiques applicables pour le règlement du litige" (L. I. Sánchez Rodríguez, "L'*uti possidetis* et les effectivités dans les contentieux territoriaux et frontaliers," *Recueil des cours*, Tome 263 (1997), 280–281).

From the judicial and arbitral decisions to date, as shown below, it is clear that the designation of the critical date, including whether or not it is defined as a specific time, is a matter falling under the discretion of the courts. Furthermore, the easing of the critical date function allows consideration of subsequent acts and facts, and, moreover, intertemporal law dictates the consideration of the evolution of law in its second principle, thereby creating leeway for a discretionary ruling by the courts and tribunals on the critical date and the content of the specific applicable laws. Since territorial disputes are related to State sovereignty and courts need to determine solutions whose content is acceptable to both States regarding the delimitation of stable territories and boundary lines, the fact that temporal elements have become important factors to be considered influences the formation of these substantive judgments.[14]

3 Application of the Doctrine of Critical Date and Intertemporal Law Principle in Judicial Practices regarding Territorial Disputes and Its Features

3.1 *Strict Application of the Critical Date and Court Perspective*

3.1.1 Application of Intertemporal Law from a "Current" Perspective

If the critical date function explained above takes strict effect, and if there has been evolution of international law and a shift in the legal order up until that date, the application of intertemporal law specifically becomes an issue. In other words, facts and acts that occurred prior to the critical date are subject to the law from their particular era. Regarding the acquisition of territorial title in territorial disputes, courts apply the law at the time to determine the legality of the acquisition and use the evolution of law to determine the legality of the subsequent retention of the title. When doing this, courts apply facts and acts from each period and the laws that regulate them. Therefore, they end up considering the evolution of law, applying, in particular, the second principle of intertemporal law. On the other hand, one of the purposes of the intemporal law principle is ensuring legal stability within the legal order, so it can be considered to be premised on the diachronic and sustained continuation of said

14 Sakai Hironobu 酒井啓亘, "Kokusai Saiban ni yoru Ryōiki Funsō no Kaiketsu – Saikin no Kokusai Shihō Saibansho no Hanrei no Dōkō" 国際裁判による領域紛争の解決－最近の国際司法裁判所の判例の動向 [Territorial Dispute Solutions by the International Courts and Tribunals: Trends in Recent ICJ Jurisprudence], *Kokusai Mondai* 国際問題, no. 624 (2013), 15–17.

legal order as a single legal system from the acquisition of the right by a party through to the retention of that right.

A typical example is the Permanent Court of International Justice's (PCIJ) Judgment in the Legal Status of Eastern Greenland case. In this Judgment, the PCIJ set the critical date as July 10, 1931, the time of Norway's attempted occupation,[15] and then reviewed the events in the period leading up to the critical date, particularly from the perspective of whether Denmark displayed authority to a degree sufficient to confer a valid title to the sovereignty. The PCIJ noted that from 1814 to 1915, Denmark exercised authority in the relevant area sufficiently to give it a valid claim to sovereignty therein[16] and cited applications which the Danish Government addressed to foreign governments between 1915 and 1921 seeking the recognition of Denmark's position in Greenland.[17] Ultimately, the PCIJ assessed Denmark's acts during the period from 1921 to the critical date of July 10, 1931 and concluded that "during this time Denmark regarded herself as possessing sovereignty over all Greenland and displayed and exercised her sovereign rights to an extent sufficient to constitute a valid title to sovereignty."[18]

However, it is important to note that, in judicial practice, critical date and intertemporal law are typically used by a court from the "current" time at which the laws and facts related to the subject of the claim are handled by the court. In fact, many judicial precedents in which the court has clarified the critical date rely on the perspective of evolution of law and transition in normative order from the "current" time at which the decision is being made. In cases where a party asserts territorial rights based on a historic title, the court does not rely simply on titles based on the laws and norms of the relevant time, but also replaces them with titles under subsequent modern international law or titles considered to be valid at the time of the critical date, to make a decision on whether territorial rights exist.

For example, in the Minquiers and Ecrehos case, the ICJ clarified the critical dates as being when France asserted sovereignty over Ecrehos and Minquiers in 1886 and 1888, respectively. At the same time, however, the ICJ determined

---

15 *Legal Status of Eastern Greenland (Denmark v. Norway), PCIJ Series A/B, no. 53, April 5th, 1933*, 45. The Court decided that the critical date must be the point at which Denmark lodged its protest against occupation by Norway, and selected the modern legal system as the applicable legal system. G. Cohn, "Statut juridique du Groënland oriental," *Revue de Droit international et de Législation comparée, 1933*, 566–567.

16 *PCIJ Series A/B, no.53*, 54.

17 *Ibid.*, 62.

18 *Ibid.*, 63.

that it did not need to resolve the historical controversies arising from the opposing assertions by the United Kingdom and France regarding conditions from 1066 to 1202, prior to the establishment of the system of modern sovereign States, and commented, "Such an alleged original feudal title of the Kings of France in respect of the Channel Islands could to-day produce no legal effect, unless it had been replaced by another title valid according to the law of the time of replacement,"[19] indicating the importance of providing evidence of the replacement of the original title under the pre-modern normative order by effective possession as demanded under the modern order based on international law. The ICJ observed the exercise of jurisdiction over Ecrehos by the King of England from the early 14th century, reconstructing his dominion from a modern perspective, and connected this to the exercise of State functions by the British authorities from the 19th century,[20] thereby presenting a position that emphasized effective control under modern international law.

A similar mechanism that has the function of connecting premodern and modern title is also found in agreements between the European powers and local rulers. In the Land and Maritime Boundary between Cameroon and Nigeria case, the ICJ recognized, regarding territorial rights to the Bakassi Peninsula, that the title originally lay with the Kings and Chiefs of Old Calabar, that sovereignty was transferred to Great Britain under the Treaty of Protection concluded between Great Britain and the Kings and Chiefs of Old Calabar in 1884, and that the Bakassi Peninsula passed from Great Britain to Germany under the Anglo-German Agreement of 1913 and subsequently became part of Cameroon.[21] Furthermore, in the Sovereignty over Pulau Ligitan and Pulau Sipadan case, the ICJ, pointing out that the dispute crystallized in 1969, interpreted that the island possessions of the Sultan under the 1878 contract concluded between the Netherlands and the Sultan of Bulungan did not include Pulau Ligitan and Pulau Sipadan, and rejected Indonesia's assertion that it inherited title to the islands from the Netherlands through these contracts

19 *ICJ Reports 1953*, 56.

20 According to the ICJ, Ecrehos was seen and treated as part of the Fief of the Channel Islands held by the King of England at the start of the 13th century and positioned under the premodern legal system at that time. The King of England exercised jurisdiction at the start of the 14th century, and British authorities exercised State functions in these islands in the 19–20th centuries. These acts placed Ecrehos under the modern legal system. *Ibid.*, 67. Similar logic was applied to the Minquiers. *Ibid.*, 70.

21 *Land and Maritime Boundary between Cameroon and Nigeria (Cameroon v. Nigeria: Equatorial Guinea intervening)*, *ICJ Reports 2002*, 404–405, para. 205.

with the Sultanate of Bulungan.[22] This can be considered another decision premised on the necessity of reconnecting a historic title to a title based on modern international law.

In almost all precedents, the courts reviewed laws that should apply within the framework of the modern international legal order from the perspective of the timing of the proceedings or the "current" perspective. In cases in which there was a split from the premodern normative order, courts consider a method for the replacement of the premodern normative concept related to territory with a concept under modern international law. Furthermore, utilizing "agreement" between the parties, a concept in modern international law, they seek to link the normative logic that existed previously and the legal principles used by courts, and assume the existence, albeit an artificial one, of a diachronic legal order that ensures legal stability, which is the purpose of applying intertemporal law. Strict application of the critical date sets the timing of the existence as close as possible to the modern era for the laws that are to be applied to the territorial dispute in question, while intertemporal law takes changes in law in the preceding period also into account when designating the laws that should be applied.

3.1.2 Respect for Contemporaneous Title and Supplementation with Modern Concepts

However, in certain exceptional cases, there are also times when courts place emphasis on the law prior to its evolution and the title based on such law, particularly assertions of rights under the premodern normative order, and reach decisions based on such grounds. In such cases, courts highlight and apply the first principle of intertemporal law. This approach respects the respective laws and normative orders of different eras.

For example, the Arbitral Tribunal in a case between Eritrea and Yemen concerning a matter of sovereignty ruled against the assertion by Yemen of ancient title and historic title to Red Sea islands that were part of Yemeni territory under the sovereignty of the Imam of Yemen over many centuries, pointing out that there is some question whether the Imam had sway over the islands, that it is not possible to assert territorial sovereignty by attributing to such a tribal, mountain and Muslim medieval society the modern Western concept of

22 *Sovereignty over Pulau Ligitan and Pulau Sipadan (Indonesia / Malaysia)*, *ibid.*, 669, para. 96.

a sovereignty title, and that Yemen did not prove its assertion that historic title actually existed.[23]

From an intertemporal law perspective, this Award demonstrates that even if a historical right exists under a premodern normative order at the stage of right creation, the Arbitral Tribunal cannot acknowledge a legitimate title to the disputed territory unless the right is exercised as territorial sovereignty such that it is maintained under the modern international order that subsequently emerged in the region. Furthermore, in cases of an assertion of historic title as the basis of territorial title, courts and tribunals can be seen to apply the law at the time of the act based on the first principle of intertemporal law, while also supplementing the historic title based on the premodern normative order with effective control by a modern sovereign State.[24]

The case concerning sovereignty over Pedra Branca / Batu Puteh between Malaysia and Singapore acknowledged a new development in the content of original title.[25] In this case, the ICJ set the critical dates at February 14, 1980, when Singapore protested against Malaysia's publication of a map with Pedra Branca[26] and February 6, 1993, when Singapore submitted its claim regarding Middle Rocks and South Ledge,[27] on the one hand, and acknowledged the possession of the original title to the islands by the Sultanate of Johor dating back to the 17th century.[28] On the other hand, it also reviewed whether Malaysia retained sovereignty over Pedra Branca following 1844 or whether sovereignty

23 *The Eritrea-Yemen Arbitration, First Stage: Territorial Sovereignty and Scope of the Dispute (Eritrea / Yemen), Reports of International Arbitral Awards*, vol. XXII, 310–311, paras. 441–447. According to the Arbitral Tribunal, classical Islamic law concepts practically ignored the principle of "territorial sovereignty," a basic feature of international law in 19th Western Europe. *Ibid.*, 245, para. 130.

24 In the above-mentioned Qatar-Bahrain case, Bahrain claimed possession of Zubarah based on historic title with a basis in the non-European normative order. However, the ICJ rejected Bahrain's assertion because Great Britain, of which Qatar and Bahrain were former protectorates, did not recognize Bahrain's sovereignty over the whole peninsula, including Zubarah, in the Anglo-Ottoman Convention of 1913. *Maritime Delimitation and Territorial Questions between Qatar and Bahrain (Qater v. Bahrain), Merits, ICJ Reports 2001*, 66–69, paras. 82–97.

25 M. Kohen, "Original Title in the Light of the ICJ Judgment on Sovereignty over Pedra Branca / Batu Puteh, Middle Rocks and South Ledge," *Journal of the History of International Law*, vol. 15 (2013), 151–171.

26 *Sovereignty over Pedra Branca / Pulau Batu Puteh, Middle Rocks and South Ledge (Malaysia / Singapore), ICJ Reports 2008*, 28, para. 33.

27 *Ibid.*, 28, para. 36.

28 *Ibid.*, 35, para. 59.

passed from Malaysia to Singapore and decided the matter in accordance with the relevant rules of international law.[29]

It should be noted that the ICJ's confirmation of the possession of the original right by the Sultanate of Johor included the condition of "continuous and peaceful display of territorial sovereignty" on the basis that it was never challenged by other Powers in this controlled territory. The expression used by the ICJ is obviously the same as the concept adopted in the Arbitral Award in the Island of Palmas case,[30] and the ICJ explained that the Sultanate of Johor, which had a confirmed existence from 1512, was a sovereign State in terms of the modern European concept,[31] noted that the title that passed to Malaysia and Singapore in later years was the original title, and considered that possession of the islands based thereon satisfied the condition of "continuous and peaceful display of territorial sovereignty."[32] In invoking original title, the ICJ applied the first principle of intertemporal law and thereby applied law from the time of the act to conduct an assessment from a premodern perspective, while at the same time supplementing this with modern terminology by deeming that the original title premised on the premodern normative order satisfies the condition of "continuous and peaceful display of territorial sovereignty" by a "sovereign State" in order to create the legal fiction of the continuous evolution of the normative order that underlies the application of intertemporal law.

While the ICJ decision in this case does indeed mention the standard of "continuous and peaceful display of territorial sovereignty," it does not actually review the sufficiency of effective control and simply has the "appearance of the recognition of original title and recognition of the conventional acquisition of title being fundamentally the same." It is therefore open to the criticism that the original title in this case differs from the "continuous and peaceful display of territorial sovereignty" that seeks grounds for territorial rights in the actual exercise of state authority.[33] In such a case, from a contemporaneous

---

29 *Ibid.*, 50, para. 119.

30 *Reports of International Arbitral Awards*, vol. 11, 839–840, 846, 855, 857, 867–870.

31 However, the ICJ emphasized that both parties were not contesting such a characterization of the Sultanate of Johor. *ICJ Reports 2008*, 33, para. 52.

32 *Ibid.*, 37, paras. 68–69.

33 Fukamachi Tomoko 深町朋子, "Ryōiki ni Kansuru Genshi Kengen – Ryōki Kengenron wa Nani o Dokomade Atsukaunoka" 領域に関する原始権原－領域権原論は何をどこまで扱うのか [Original Title to Territory: To What and To What Extent Is the Legal Framework of Title to Territory Applied?], *Hōgaku Seminā* 法学セミナー, no. 765 (2018), 28–29. and Huh Sookyeon 許淑娟, *Ryōiki Kengen Ron – Ryōiki Shihai no Jikkōsei to Seitōsei* 領域権原論－領域支配の実効性と正当性 [The Acquisition of Territory in International Law: The Effectiveness and Legitimacy of Territorial Control] (Tokyo: University of Tokyo Publishing, 2012), 329.

perspective, there is, through the application of the first principle of intertemporal law, an assertion of territorial rights based on the original title grounded in a premodern normative order,[34] and the possibility cannot be ruled out of an assertion being made under the modern order based on international law but relying primarily on original title, without replacement by a modern concept. However, even in the case of territorial disputes that deal with original title grounded in a premodern normative order, the logical structure of the decision in the Pedra Branca and other cases could be seen as indicating the need for supplementation with a modern concept, regardless of how much it appears that "continuous and peaceful display of territorial sovereignty" is being used as a fiction in relation to the assertion of rights grounded in normative orders that differ from the modern order based on international law.[35]

3.2 *Easing of the Critical Date Function and Intertemporal Law Principle*

3.2.1 Consideration of Facts and Acts That Occur after Critical Date and Applicability of Intertemporal Law Principle

The critical date function explained above is not always applied rigorously. Albeit on an exceptional basis, courts have taken into consideration acts that took place after the critical date in some cases as described above.[36] According to the ICJ's Judgment in the Minquiers and Ecrehos case, such an act could be used as a factor in deciding the attribution of a disputed territory, unless the act in question was taken with a view to improving the legal position of the party concerned.[37]

34 However, in the case of issues of territorial attribution after decolonization, even if intemporal law is applied, today's ICJ cannot adopt the logic of the Arbitral Award in the Island of Palmas case, which was made in a colonial context. See S. Huh, "Title to Territory in the Post-Colonial Era: Original Title and *Terra Nullius* in the ICJ Judgments on Cases Concerning *Ligitan / Sipadan* (2002) and *Pedra Branca* (2008)," *European Journal of International Law*, vol. 26 (2015), 724.

35 There is also a view that this is done in response to the unique characteristics of title grounded in the premodern normative order. K. Y. L. Tan, "The Role of History in International Territorial Dispute Settlement: The *Pedra Branca Case* (Singapore v Malaysia)," in J.-H. Paik, S.-W. Lee and K. Y. L. Tan (eds.), *Asian Approaches to International Law and the Legacy of Colonialism. The Law of the Sea, Territorial Disputes and International Dispute Settlement* (New York: Routledge, 2013), 76.

36 Kohen and Hébié, *supra* note 3, 897.

37 *ICJ Reports 1953*, 59–60. In the Judgment in the Pulau Ligitan and Pulau Sipadan case, even if the critical date is defined as the date of the crystallization of the dispute and subsequent acts are excluded, "such acts [that] are a normal continuation of prior acts and are not undertaken for the purpose of improving the legal position of the Party which relies on them" are deemed to not be excluded. *ICJ Reports 2002*, 682, para. 135.

The following are likely to be conditions under which facts and acts that occur after the critical date are nevertheless considered in the context of a territorial dispute. The first is absence of a fundamental difference in the relation between the parties to the dispute and the circumstances of the disputed territory before and after the critical date.[38] The second is the emergence of activities after the critical date that are the continuous evolution of the activities prior to the same critical date and the existence of the roots of said activities in some manner in the past.[39] Third is if the activities after the critical date were not conducted simply for the purpose of improving and strengthening the legal position of a party to the dispute compared to prior to the critical date, and that they are not seen as a paper claim or other tactical assertion, particularly from the perspective of the good faith principle.[40] The purpose of setting these conditions is the exclusion of clearly unreasonable grounds based on political strategy or other facts from after the critical date, conducted by a party with the aim of improving its position after the critical date.[41]

Furthermore, even if these conditions are met, facts and acts after the critical date should only be considered in order to confirm the legal relation at the critical date timing. Moreover, even if legal rules evolve with the lapse of time after the critical date, they are only invoked for interpreting the legal rules at the time of the critical date in order to confirm the legal relation at that time.

However, it must be noted that there is actually only a fine line between the task of confirming said legal relation by using facts and acts after the critical date for the sake of interpreting the legal relation at the time of the critical date, and the task of factoring in the legal evolution after the critical date and applying the evolved law in assessing the legal relation at the time of the critical date, as part of the application of the second principle of intertemporal law. In some cases, it is difficult to clearly distinguish between the consideration of subsequent facts and acts for the purpose of confirming an assessment of the legal relation at the time of the critical date and the assessment of the legal relation at the time of the critical date based on the legal evolution after the critical date. Under the critical date function, courts cannot directly acknowledge the application of evolved law after the critical date along the lines of the

38 *Reports of International Arbitral Awards*, vol. II, 866.

39 *ICJ Reports 1953*, 59–60.

40 *Ibid.*, 59.

41 R. Y. Jennings, *The Acquisition of Territory in International Law* (Manchester: Manchester University Press, 1963), 34.

latter case. However, the possibility cannot be ruled out of courts effectively considering the subsequent evolution of law for the stated purpose of confirming the legal relation at the time of the critical date, in order to find the most effective resolution of the dispute in a discretionary ruling.

3.2.2 Avoiding Designation of a Critical Date and Application of Intertemporal Law Principle

In territorial disputes, even if a party to the dispute asserts a specific critical date, a court may, in some cases, not accept it and avoid designation of a critical date. In the Arbitral Award in the Rann of Kutch case involving a dispute over the attribution of the Kutch region between India and Pakistan, the Tribunal did not accept any singular critical date based on the respective assertions of the two parties, but instead considered both to be relevant.[42] Additionally, the Arbitral Award in the Dubai-Sharjah Border Arbitration stated that if a critical date existed, it could only be that of the date of the signature of the Arbitration Agreement of November 30, 1976, while also pointing out that the critical date concept, although sometimes invoked in State practice, has not played a major role in territorial disputes.[43]

Courts' reluctance to adopt critical dates asserted by parties reflects a tendency to exclude assertions of a critical date that interfere with their discretion in reviewing all related evidence up to the reaching of a decision related to territorial attributions, including setting its own critical date that differs from the critical dates asserted by the parties.[44] Furthermore, the determination that

---

42 Both parties agreed to 1947, the year of India's independence, as one of the "relevant dates" (*Case concerning the Indo-Pakistan Western Boundary (Rann of Kutch), (India / Pakistan), Reports of International Arbitral Awards*, vol. XVII, 18–19). However, Pakistan also argued that 1819, when Kutch became a vassal of the British, was a critical date (*ibid.*, 64–65). According to the final Award of the Tribunal, the acts of the British Government during its rule was deemed by both parties to be of significance. In that sense, India's independence is of decisive importance. However, agreement on a precise critical date could not be reached (*ibid.*, 528). See also, A. L. W. Munkman, "Adjudication and Adjustment – International Judicial Decision and the Settlement of Territorial and Boundary Disputes," *British Year Book of International Law*, vol. XLVI (1972–1973), 74–75.

43 According to the same Arbitral Award, the concept of the critical date has only played a significant role in cases where it was necessary to establish exactly and precisely when in the past sovereignty was exercised by a State over a given territory, as in the Island of Palmas and Eastern Greenland cases, which was not the case in this dispute. *Dubai-Sharjah Border Arbitration (Dubai / Sharjah), International Law Reports*, vol. 91, 594.

44 Sir Robert Jennings and Sir Arthur Watts (eds.), *Oppenheim's International Law. Ninth Edition. vol. 1. Peace. Parts 2 to 4.* (London: Longman, 1992), 711.

the critical date is not important stems from concern about the potential insufficient review of related evidence due to the designation of a critical date that prevents a court from reaching a suitable ruling.[45] This can be seen as making clear that the designation of a critical date has been left up to the assessment of the court (particularly assessment of substantive issues) and prioritizing the opportunity to review more evidence in order to reach a suitable solution over designating a critical date.[46]

If a court does not designate a critical date, it can consider all facts and party activities that occurred until the submission of the claims to the court. In fact, although the court's review covers matters leading up to a designated fact or act that makes clear that the disputed territory is attributed to one of the parties to the dispute,[47] the application of intertemporal law could be conducted in parallel to said review. In that case, the closer the threshold of the timeframe of the court's review is to the present, the higher the probability of emphasis being placed on the effect of the second principle of intertemporal law and a decision being made that factors in legal evolution.

45 In the Arbitral Award in the Argentine-Chile Frontier case, since the parties agreed that the notion of the critical date is not a rigid one and that a good deal is left to the appreciation of the Court of Arbitration, and moreover that the critical date is not necessarily the same for all purposes, the Court deemed "the notion of the critical date to be of little value in the present litigation," and decided to "examin[e] all the evidence submitted to it, irrespective of the date of the acts to which such evidence relate." *Argentine-Chile Frontier Case (Argentine / Chile), Reports of International Arbitral Awards*, vol. XVI, 167.

46 Fukamachi Tomoko 深町朋子, "Ryōdo Kizoku Handan ni okeru Kanren Yōso no Kōryo" 領土帰属判断における関連要素の考慮 [Consideration of Related Elements in Territory Attribution Decisions], *Kokusai Mondai* 国際問題, no. 624 (2013), 37–38.

47 Therefore, this timing is the effective critical date designated by the court, and subsequent review aims to confirm the legal relationship at the time of the critical date. In the Cameroon-Nigeria case regarding a territorial issue related to the Bakassi Peninsula, while Cameroon asserted the date of the completion of the decolonization process (October 1, 1961) as the critical date (*Memoire de la Republique du Cameroun*, par. 3.384) and Nigeria, which had effective possession, called for January 1994, when Cameroon protested and the dispute emerged, to be the critical date (*Counter-Memorial of the Federal Republic of Nigeria*, para. 10.19), the ICJ did not specify a critical date. However, the ICJ decided that under the Anglo-German Agreement of 1913, the Bakassi Peninsula passed from Britain to Germany and subsequently became part of Cameroon, confirmed that the transfer of sovereignty based on the 1913 Agreement had a decisive influence on the attribution of the territory, and hence reviewed subsequent facts and State acts. *ICJ Reports 2002*, 407, para. 209, 409–412, paras. 212–217.

4 Application of Critical Date and Intertemporal Law in Territorial Issues Involving Japan

4.1 *Significance of Critical Date and Intertemporal Law in Territorial Disputes*

As explained above, a territorial title held by a party is grounded in facts and acts prior to the critical date, and while facts and acts after the critical date cannot create title to the disputed territory, these facts and acts occurring after the critical date are within the scope of legal assessment under certain conditions. If an act by a party to a dispute continues from before the critical date to after it and does not improve the party's own legal position, this act has evidentiary value in terms of consistently supporting a position that existed from prior to the critical date.[48]

Therefore, when parties to a dispute present the critical date, it is important that they assert a critical date that secures evidence that is advantageous to assertions premised on their current position. The critical date is a tool that a court can utilize at its discretion to reach an effective resolution to a dispute. At the same time, because of its flexibility as a standard, it is also something that the parties to the dispute can adapt to their assertions in a way that is favorable to their position. This means it could play roles that are suited to the characteristics of specific case and parties to a dispute. This also applies to territorial disputes in East Asia.[49]

Intertemporal law, which delineates the application timeframe based on the critical date, consists of its first principle of assessing an act in terms of law at the time of the act's occurrence and its second principle of the continued existence of a right needing to adhere to conditions regulated by the evolution of law. Due to its inclusion of these principles, intertemporal law enables the legal connection of territorial title across the stages of the creation of a right to the continued existence of said right, in response to the dynamism of law, in the form of effective possession via "continuous and peaceful display of territorial sovereignty." From a chronological perspective of order, it also facilitates the treatment of the modern order based on international law, with established legal principles for territorial title and the preceding premodern normative order as a single integrated normative system that retains legal stability.[50] This

48 Kohen and Hébié, *supra* note 3, 897.

49 S. Lee, "Intertemporal Law, Recent Judgments and Territorial Disputes in Asia," in S.-Y. Hong and J. M. Van Dyke (eds.), *Maritime Boundary Disputes, Settlement Processes, and the Law of the Sea* (Leiden: Brill, 2009), 124–126.

50 See Sakai, *supra* note 5, 125.

implies that the side that more convincingly asserts the established legal principles of territorial title under the modern order based on international law has the advantage in territorial disputes.

The following section will review territorial issues involving Japan from this perspective, particularly the Takeshima (Dokdo) issue and the Senkaku Islands (Diaoyu Islands) issue.[51] (The term "issues" is used because the question of whether disputes actually even exist is contested.)

4.2 *Takeshima Issue*

4.2.1 Critical Date

As candidate critical dates in the Takeshima (or, by its Korean name, Dokdo) issue, some observers assert January 28, 1952, when Japan voiced opposition to the establishment of a maritime boundary based on the Maritime Sovereignty Proclamation issued by the President of the Republic of Korea (ROK) Rhee Syngman (referred to as the Syngman Rhee Line).[52] Meanwhile, others assert

---

51 Japan also has the Northern Territories issue with Russia. The Northern Territories issue involves a complex interweaving of issues related to the effectiveness and interpretation of a number of related documents, including confirmation of territorial rights via the application of general rules of international law seen in many other territorial disputes, the effectiveness of the Yalta Agreement toward Japan, and interpretation of the scope of the Kuril Islands for which Japan abandoned its claims in accordance with Article 2 (c) of the San Francisco Peace Treaty (see Sugihara Takane 杉原高嶺, "Kokusaihō kara mita Hoppō Ryōdo" 国際法から見た北方領土 [Northern Territories from the Standpoint of International Law] in *Hoppō Ryōdo o Kangaeru* 北方領土を考える [Thinking of the Northern Territories], ed. Kimura Hiroshi (Hokkaido: Hokkaido Shimbunsha, 1981), 87–88). While critical date and application of intertemporal law might be issues in this matter (A. B. Quillen, "The "Kuril Islands" or the "Northern Territories": Who Owns Them Island Territorial Dispute Continues to Hinder Relations Between Russia and Japan," *North Carolina Journal of International & Comparative Regulation*, vol. 18 (1993), 645–646; regarding the critical date, see S. Lee, "Towards a Framework for the Resolution of the Territorial Dispute over the Kurile Islands," *Boundary & Territory Briefing*, vol. 3, no. 6 (2001), 11), the questions on the interpretation of these documents will not be taken up here and will be left to a separate review. Putting emphasis on current *effectivités*, let it only be said that the possibility of the non-designation of a critical date and the application of post-Second World War international law based on intertemporal law producing a favorable result for the occupying State applies to the Northern Territories issue too. E. V. Neverova, "The Southern Kuril Deadlock: Effectiveness v. Protest," *Moscow Journal of International Law*, vol. 3 (2019), 50–51.

52 Minagawa Takeshi 皆川洸, "Takeshima Funsō to Kokusai Hanrei" 竹島紛争と国際判例 [Takeshima Dispute and International Precedents], in *Maehara Mitsuo Kyōju Kanreki Kinen Kokusaihōgaku no Shomondai* 前原光雄教授還暦記念 国際法学の諸問題 [Festschrift for Professor Maehara Mitsuo in Commemoration of His 60th Birthday: Problems in International Law] (Tokyo: Keiō Tsushin, 1963), 354.

February 22, 1905, when the Japanese Government asserted the inclusion of Takeshima;[53] the date of the conclusion of the San Francisco Peace Treaty (September 8, 1951); the date when Japan proposed the referral of the issue to the ICJ (September 25, 1954);[54] and the date when both sides would agree to refer the matter to the ICJ and the procedure starts.[55]

Key issues related to the critical date in a territorial dispute are when the dispute emerged between the parties due to a clear act, such as the act of claiming sovereignty over the disputed territory by one of the parties and when the dispute crystalized.

Both Japan and the ROK have long asserted a historical basis for their assertions that Takeshima is their own territory.[56] Japan bases its assertion in its measure to incorporate Takeshima as a territory from 1905 and its subsequent effective control, while the ROK bases its assertions in measures taken by the Allied Powers starting from the Cairo Declaration and its own subsequent effective control. Opposition between the two sides regarding Takeshima's attribution first emerged with the establishment of a maritime boundary based on the Syngman Rhee Line on January 18, 1952 and Japan's response thereto. The ROK established a large maritime space around the Korean Peninsula with the Syngman Rhee Line. Since the space included Takeshima, the Japanese Government lodged a protest on January 28, 1952 that it did not recognize the ROK's territorial rights to Takeshima. The ROK counterargued that Takeshima was ROK territory. The opinions of the two sides were in direct opposition. The ROK subsequently stationed coast guard forces on Takeshima from 1954 and took other measures such as building a lighthouse there. Japan proposed the

53 Serita Kentarō, "Some Legal Aspects of Territorial Disputes over Islands," in Hong and Van Dyke (eds.), *supra* note 49, 142.

54 There is the view that the Japanese Government has indicated that, because it proposed to the ROK that the matter should be referred to the ICJ, it believes the timing of the proposal should be the critical date. H. K. Lee, "Korea's Territorial Rights to Tokdo in History and International Law," *Korea Observer*, vol. 29 (1998), 89.

55 Ha Yonsu 河錬洙, "'Takeshima Funsō' Saikō – Ryōiki Kengen o Meguru Kokusaihō no Kanten Kara" 「竹島紛争」再考－領域権原をめぐる国際法の観点から [Rethinking the Takeshima Dispute: From the Standpoint of International Law on Territorial Title], *Ryūkoku Hōgaku* 龍谷法学, vol. 32, no. 2 (1999), 36.

56 Regarding the ROK Government's assertion, see Ministry of Foreign Affairs, ROK, "The Korean Government's Basic Position on Dokdo," https://dokdo.mofa.go.kr/m/eng/dokdo/government_position.jsp. All websites quoted in this chapter were last accessed on November 9, 2021. For Japan's perception of the handling of Takeshima in the 17–18th centuries, refer to Nakano Tetsuya 中野徹也, *Takeshima Mondai to Kokusaihō* 竹島問題と国際法 [Takeshima Issue and International Law] (Shimane: Harvest Publishing, 2019) 55–58.

referral of the issue to the ICJ for resolution in the same year, but the ROK rejected this proposal and has continued to occupy the islets by force.[57]

Although the ROK has, since the 1965 Treaty on Basic Relations Between Japan and the Republic of Korea, consistently asserted that there is no dispute between the two States regarding Takeshima, it is not difficult to prove, based on the definition of the "dispute" concept adopted by the ICJ, that a dispute does exist between Japan and the ROK even while respecting the subjective perceptions of each party.[58]

When is the critical date in this dispute? The prevailing view in the Takeshima case is that the ROK's establishment of the Syngman Rhee Line and Japan's protest initiated the dispute between the two sides.[59] From the standpoint of the crystallization of the dispute, the critical date could also be set in 1954 when Japan first called for referral of the issue to the ICJ, as this indicated the possibility of a legal resolution of the dispute. Regardless of which timing is designated as the critical date, if the issue of *effectivités* is involved,[60] a key point in determining whether the acts by the ROK, which currently has effective control of Takeshima, have any legal significance is whether the acts possess temporal continuity from before the critical date to after it. Hence, determining which of the parties (the ROK or Japan) had "continuous and peaceful display of territorial sovereignty" prior to 1952 or 1954 and which acts should be deemed to be continuous acts extending from before to after the critical date are of decisive importance. If it is proven that the establishment

57 See Taijudo Kanae 太壽堂鼎, *Ryōdo Kizoku no Kokusaihō* 領土帰属の国際法 [Title to Territory in International Law] (Tokyo: Tōshindō, 1998) 125–156.

58 While a mere assertion of a dispute is not sufficient to prove its existence (*South West Africa Cases* (*Ethiopia v. South Africa; Liberia v. South Africa*), *Preliminary Objections, ICJ Reports 1962*, 328), if the validity or strength of the assertion need not be put to a plausibility or other test (*Dispute Concerning Coastal State Rights in the Black Sea, Sea of Azov, and Kerch Strait* (*Ukraine v. The Russian Federation*), *Preliminary Objections*, PCA Case no. 2017–06, para. 188.), then it should not be too difficult to prove the existence of a dispute based on the Japanese side's legal assertions, including its territorial title to Takeshima.

59 Nakano Tetsuya 中野徹也, "Takeshima no Kizoku ni Kansuru Ichi Kōsatsu" 竹島の帰属に関する一考察 [Thoughts on Takeshima's Attribution], *Kansai Daigaku Hōgakuronshu* 関西大学法学論集, vol. 60, no. 5 (2011), 120–121. See also N. J. Schrijver and V. Prislan, "Case Concerning Sovereignty over Islands before the International Court of Justice and the Dokdo / Takeshima Issue," *Ocean Development & International Law*, vol. 46 (2015), 296.

60 There is the view that, from the position of the ROK side, its *effectivités*, comprising its subsequent acts following discovery, would not only cure inchoate title but also confirm the validity of the original title (L. Mayali and J. Yoo, "Resolution of Territorial Disputes in East Asia: The Case of Dokdo," *Berkeley Journal of International Law*, vol. 36 (2018), 536), but such a view does not include a critical date perspective.

of the Syngman Rhee Line challenged Japan's prior sovereignty, it could be argued that any acts after that point are outside the scope of legal assessment based on the strict exercise of the critical date function.[61] In this case, Japan needs to have engaged in concrete acts to ensure that its acts after the critical date are not interpreted as acquiescence of the ROK's acts.[62]

However, the timing of the emergence of a dispute and its crystallization might not necessarily constitute the critical date. Other important events related to territorial rights to Takeshima include the conclusion of the San Francisco Peace Treaty and the Treaty on Basic Relations Between Japan and the Republic of Korea. It might also be argued, based on the relativity of the critical date, that all evidence should be acknowledged without deciding a clear timing.[63]

4.2.2 Application of Intertemporal Law

Both Japan and the ROK cite original title as a basis for territorial rights to Takeshima.[64] This means that the parties asserted their rights to this territory in the process of joining the modern international order, based on the premise that the territory at issue was positioned within the normative order of the East Asian region, prior to the region's acceptance of modern international law originating in Europe.[65] It is necessary to consider separately the characteristics of

61 The situation in this case is comparable to the Legal Status of Eastern Greenland case and the Minquiers and Ecrehos case. Miyoshi Masahiro 三好正弘, "Takeshima Mondai to Kuritikaru Dēto" 竹島問題とクリティカル・デート [Takeshima Issue and Critical Date], *Tōsho Kenkyu Jyānaru* 島嶼研究ジャーナル, vol. 3, no. 2 (2014), 45–46.

62 Serita Kentarō 芹田健太郎, *Nihon no Ryōdo* 日本の領土 [The Territory of Japan] (Tokyo: Chuo Koron Shinsha, 2010), 187–188. Conversely, the ROK side is likely to assert that its effective control after the critical date should be taken into consideration. As noted in the ICJ's Judgment in the Pulau Ligitan and Pulau Sipadan case, the inclusion of acts after the critical date occurs when "such acts are a normal continuation of prior acts and are not undertaken for the purpose of improving the legal position of the Party which relies on them." *ICJ Reports 2002*, 682, para. 135.

63 In particular, from the standpoint of the ROK side, which emphasizes its current effective control, the assertion would be made that all historical facts related to Takeshima (Dokdo) should be considered without setting a critical date. J. M. van Dyke, "Legal Issues Related to Sovereignty over Dokdo and Its Maritime Boundary," *Ocean Development & International Law*, vol. 38 (2007), 164.

64 Ha, *supra* note 55, 228.

65 Pae Keun Park 朴培根, "Nihon ni yoru Tosho Sensen no Sho-Senrei –Takeshima / Dokuto ni taisuru Tyoiki Kengen wo Chushin to shite–" 日本による島嶼先占の諸先例—竹島/独島に対する領域権原を中心として— [Some Observations on the Territorial Incorporation of Islands by Japan with Special Reference to the Territorial Title over Liancourt Rocks (Takeshima / Dokdo)], *Kokusaihō Gaikō Zasshi* 国際法外交雑誌, vol. 105, no. 2 (2006), 177.

the premodern regional normative order.[66] Furthermore, if this unique East Asian normative order still remains, even if only partially, effort must be made to clarify its content and its relation with modern international law.[67]

However, if the applicable legal rules change in the transition from a premodern normative order to the modern order based on international law and there is an assertion of territorial sovereignty under modern international law, which has been accepted at least in East Asia, according to the application of intertemporal law, the conditions required by modern international law must be fulfilled. Based on judicial precedents to date, effective possession of the islands being disputed replaces or supplements the original title asserted by the parties.[68] The reason is that "[t]he modern international law of the acquisition (or attribution) of territory generally requires that there be: intentional display of power and authority over the territory, by the exercise of jurisdiction and state functions, on a continuous and peaceful basis,"[69] according to the Arbitral Award in the case between Eritrea and Yemen concerning a matter of sovereignty.[70]

Whether Japan and the ROK are capable of arguing convincingly to satisfy the abovementioned conditions in the Takeshima issue hence depends on the intertemporal law function. The Japanese Government argues that its measure to incorporate Takeshima as a territory in 1905 reaffirmed its historic title, and that the incorporation measure and subsequent continuous display of state

66 As an example of research that examined the premodern normative order in East Asia and the acceptance of modern European international law, see Yanagihara Masaharu, "Significance of the History of the Law of Nations in Europe and East Asia," *Recueil des cours*, vol. 371 (2015), 317–349.

67 It has been mentioned above that there may be views that consider the possibility of the existence of normative orders separate from modern international law, in light of the content of the Pedra Branca and other cases. At the same time, the Separate Opinion of Judge Fortier accompanying the Judgment in the Qatar-Bahrain case indicates, while quoting from the Advisory Opinion in the Western Sahara case, that there exist different regional concepts of sovereignty as basis for territorial sovereignty. *Separate Opinion of Judge Fortier, ICJ Reports 2001*, 456–457, para. 28.

68 *ICJ Reports 1953*, 56–57.

69 *Reports International Arbitral Awards*, vol. XXII, 268, para. 239.

70 However, Nakano Tetsuya argues that "modern international law generally did not demand reaffirmation of territorial intent by States that, like Japan, became members of the 'international community' regulated by modern international law originating in Europe at a particular point in history." Nakano Tetsuya 中野徹也, "1905 Nen Nihon ni yoru Takeshima Ryōdo Hen'nyū Sochi no Hōteki Seishitsu" 1905年日本による竹島領土編入措置の法的性質 [Legal Nature of Japan's Measure to Incorporate Takeshima as Territory in 1905], *Kansai Daigaku Hōgaku Ronshū* 関西大学法学論集, vol. 61, no. 5 (2012), 126.

authority was sufficient to replace the title, which was validly established in the 17th century in accordance with international law at the time, in response to modern requirements.[71] Therefore, while this is just one example, the Japanese side needs to carefully argue that it has always satisfied the conditions dictated by the laws of the period, in accordance with intertemporal law, and to base its assertions on its practices fulfilling these requirements.

4.3 *Senkaku Islands (Diaoyu Islands) Issue*

4.3.1 Critical Date

According to Japan's assertion, it incorporated the Senkaku Islands as Japanese territory based on the Cabinet Decision of January 14, 1895. It asserts territorial rights to the Senkaku Islands premised on the legal principle of occupation of *terra nullius*.[72] China, on the other hand, argues that the Diaoyu Islands are its inherent territory from ancient times.[73] China explains that it held historic title to these islands in 1895 and hence that Diaoyu Islands were not *terra nullius* when Japan incorporated them as Japanese territory through occupation.[74] In fact, the Ministry of Foreign Affairs of the People's Republic of China officially asserted China's sovereignty to Diaoyu Dao on December 30, 1971. Taiwan conveyed its own stance to the Japanese side on February 24, 1971.[75]

The Japanese Government has consistently asserted that no dispute exists regarding the Senkaku Islands. Based on the ICJ's Judgment regarding the Preliminary Objections in the South West Africa cases that a mere assertion by one party is not sufficient to prove the existence of a dispute and that it must be shown that the claim of one party is positively opposed by the other,[76] some observers agree with the Japanese Government's stance that there is no dispute because exaggerated and unilateral claims that lack even the slightest bit

---

71 Taijudō, *supra* note 57, 143.

72 Ministry of Foreign Affairs of Japan, "Senkaku Islands Q & A," https://www.mofa.go.jp/region/asia-paci/senkaku/qa_1010.html#q1.

73 State Council Information Office, The People's Republic of China, "Diaoyu Dao, an inherent Territory of China (26 September 2012)," https://www.fmprc.gov.cn/mfa_eng/topics_665678/diaodao_665718/t973774.shtml.

74 Ministry of Foreign Affairs of the People's Republic of China, "Statement of the Ministry of Foreign Affairs of the People's Republic of China (10 September 2012)," https://www.fmprc.gov.cn/mfa_eng/topics_665678/diaodao_665718/t968188.shtml.

75 Tomabechi Masato 苫米地真理, *Senkaku Mondai – Seifu Kenkai wa Dō Hensenshita Noka* 尖閣問題－政府見解はどう変遷したのか [Senkaku Islands Issue: How Has the Government Opinion Changed] (Tokyo: Kashiwa Shobo, 2020), 30.

76 *ICJ Reports 1962*, 328.

of evidence should be treated as invalid.[77] While it might seem unreasonable to acknowledge a dispute based on an assertion that is "merely a false accusation,"[78] since the question of whether there exists an international dispute is a matter for objective determination by a court,[79] the possibility of a court recognizing the existence of a dispute cannot be ruled out in such a case.[80]

If a dispute over the Senkaku Islands exists between Japan and China or between Japan and Taiwan, there then arises the issue of when the critical date is. In a case in which one of the parties asserts acquisition by occupation, the point of contention is then whether the disputed area is *terra nullius*, and the critical date should therefore generally be the timing of the asserted acquisition by occupation.[81]

However, there did not exist a dispute when Japan asserted acquisition by occupation because there is no evidence of China lodging a protest against

77 Nakatani Kazuhiro 中谷和弘, "Nihon no Ryōdo Kanren Mondai to Kokusai Saiban Taiō" 日本の領土関連問題と国際裁判対応 [Japan's Territorial Issues and International Court Responses], *Tōsho Kenkyu Jyānaru* 島嶼研究ジャーナル, vol. 7, no. 1 (2017), 21. Tsukamoto Takashi 塚本孝, "Takeshima to Senkaku Shotō" 竹島と尖閣諸島 [Takeshima and Senkaku Islands] *Tōsho Kenkyū Jyānaru* 島嶼研究ジャーナル, vol. 5, no. 1 (2015), 29–33.

78 "Zadankai – Tanaage ni yoru Kaiketsu wa Kanouka" 座談会－棚上げによる解決は可能か [Panel Discussion: Is Shelving a Possible Solution?], in *Kenshō – Senkakumondai* 検証－尖閣問題 [Verification: Senkaku Islands Problems], ed. Magosaki Ukeru 孫崎享 (Tokyo: Iwanami Publishing, 2021), 140 (Kotera Akira's comment).

79 *Interpretation of Peace Treaties, ICJ Reports 1950*, 74.

80 This point is likely to be important in determining whether it can be convincingly shown that there does not exist a dispute in the case in question based on the definition of "dispute" in recent international judicial precedents. Regarding ICJ precedents on deciding the existence of a "dispute," refer to Etō Junichi 江藤淳一, "Funsō no Sonzai no Kettei o Meguru Kokusai Shihō Saibansho no Hanrei no Tenkai" 紛争の存在の決定をめぐる国際司法裁判所の判例の展開 [Development of International Court of Justice Precedents on Deciding the Existence of Disputes], in Iwasawa and Okano (eds.), *supra* note, note 5, 97–120.

81 Sir Gerald Fitzmaurice, *The Law and Procedure of the International Court of Justice, vol. I* (Cambridge: Cambridge University Press, 1993), 270. Therefore, the question of whether the Senkaku Islands were *terra nullius* when the Japanese Government implemented its measure to incorporate them as part of its territory is an important one. If the islands were *terra nullius*, China loses the legal basis it asserts. Conversely, there is a view that if China can prove that the islands were Chinese territory up to that time, Japan can no longer argue territorial possession based on effective possession (T. Cheng, "The Sino-Japanese Dispute Over the Tio-yu-tai (Senkaku) Islands and the Law of Territorial Acquisition," *Virginia Journal of International Law*, vol. 14 (1974), 262). In that case, the critical date would be January 14, 1895.

Japan at that time.[82] Even if the Senkaku Islands were Chinese territory based on historic title at that time as asserted by China, since China did not lodge protests thereafter, Japan could successfully assert that it acquired the Senkaku Islands through prescription[83] or through China's subsequent acquiescence.[84] In either case, some observers argue that the critical date cannot then be when Japan asserted its acquisition by occupation and instead should be the timing of the initial protests in February 24, 1971 (Taiwan) and December 30, 1971 (China) against Japan's assertion.[85]

4.3.2 Application of Intertemporal Law Principle

Looking at the Senkaku Islands issue from the standpoint of the critical date, Japan is clearly in an advantageous position vis-à-vis China and Taiwan considering its current effective control. This view reflects the fact that if the acts by China and Taiwan prior to the critical date explained above[86] do not have continuity/cohesion with their acts after it, the current assertions of territorial

---

82 R. M. Scoville, "A Defense of Japanese Sovereignty over the Senkaku / Diaoyu Islands," *The George Washington International Law Review*, vol. 46 (2014), 585.

83 G. Poissonnier and P. Osseland, "À qui appartiennent les îles Senkaku / Diaoyu?," *Journal du Droit International*, Tome 135 (2008), 483.

84 Regarding the invocation of China's acquiescence as the legal basis for Japan's assertion, see C. Ramos-Mrosovsky, "International Law's Unhelpful Role in the Senkaku Islands," *University of Pennsylvania Journal of International Law*, vol. 29 (2008), 923–924.

85 Matsui Yoshirō 松井芳郎, *Kokusaihō Gakusha ga Yomu Senkaku Mondai – Funsō Kaiketsu eno Tenbo o Hiraku* 国際法学者がよむ尖閣問題－紛争解決への展望を拓く [Senkaku Islands Issue from the Perspective of an International Law Scholar: Seeking a Path to Resolve the Dispute] (Tokyo: Nippon Hyoronsha, 2014), 12–13. See also, Y. Matsui, "International Law of Territorial Acquisition and the Dispute over the Senkaku (Diaoyu) Islands," *Japanese Annual of International Law*, no. 40 (1997), 7–8. Furthermore, considering that Japan and China both use the legal status of the Senkaku Islands after the Second World War as the starting point for resolving their opposing claims, the silence of China and Taiwan prior to the critical date is seen as affirming the status quo of the Senkaku Islands during 1945–52. M. H. Loja, "*Status Quo Post Bellum* and the Legal Resolution of the Territorial Dispute between China and Japan over the Senkaku / Diaoyu Islands," *European Journal of International Law*, vol. 27 (2016), 1004. Additionally, regarding the argument that the date of the signing of the Okinawa Reversion Agreement (June 17, 1971), which legally legitimized control of the Senkaku Islands as part of Okinawa, should be set as the critical date, see Serita, *supra* note 62, 157.

86 For an argument that references the Arbitral Award in the Clipperton Island case due to the characteristics of the Senkaku Islands, such as a lack of permanent residents, and considers Chinese acts, such as the use of the Senkaku Islands as navigation markers, prior to 1895 to constitute symbolic acts and evidence that the Senkaku Islands were not *terra nullius* in 1895, see H. Schulte Nordholt, "Delimitation of the Continental Shelf in the East China Sea," *Netherlands International Law Review*, vol. 32 (1985), 147–148.

rights by China and Taiwan are not convincing, and the court is unlikely to accept them as evidence. In particular, the fact that China did not object to or protest Japan's possession of the Senkaku Islands through the 1960s has significant implications.[87]

Furthermore, if, hypothetically, a court does not acknowledge a critical date and takes the position of considering all facts and acts by the parties as evidence, unless it acknowledges the existence of a clearer title, such as a treaty between the relevant parties that recognizes the islands as Chinese territory, or concludes that the actual occupation of the Senkaku Islands was the result of acts that are illegal under international law, the assertions by the Japanese side, which currently occupies the islands, are likely to carry more weight. However, in order to communicate Japan's assertion to the court even more reliably, it is important for Japan to call for a critical date to be designated and for it to have a strict effect, and to undermine the evidentiary value of acts occurring after the critical date.

Additionally, if the historic title asserted by the Chinese side is based on the premodern East Asian normative order,[88] it should be possible to question whether the title has been replaced or supplemented by measures provided for under the modern order based on international law that are capable of confirming the legal relation at the timing of the critical date – effective possession as seen in the "continuous and peaceful display of territorial sovereignty," agreement between the relevant parties, and the transfer or inheritance of

---

87 Miyoshi Masahiro 三好正弘, "Ryōdo Shutoku ni Okeru Kōgi to Mokunin – Senkaku Shoto tono Kanren ni Oite" 領土取得における抗議と黙認—尖閣諸島との関連において [Protest and Acquiescence in Territorial Acquisition: In relation to the Senkaku Islands], *Tōsho Kenkyu Jyānaru* 島嶼研究ジャーナル, vol. 4, no. 2 (2015), 44. International judicial precedents also place emphasis on the fact that the relevant parties did not assert sovereignty over disputed areas. S. P. Sharma, *Territorial Acquisition, Disputes and International Law* (The Hague: Kluwer Law International, 1997), 118. However, there is also a counterargument that even if there was a gap of roughly 70 years from Japan's incorporation measure to China's protest as part of the process of displaying sovereignty, if China had already established the title prior to then, the existence of this 70-year period alone does not negate the title under international law. S. Wei Su, "The Territorial Dispute over the Tiaoyu / Senkaku Islands: An Update," *Ocean Development & International Law*, vol. 36 (2005), 52–53.

88 Regarding the point that the Meiji Government itself linked these uninhabited islands to Chinese sovereignty when it conducted the survey of the Senkaku Islands in November 1885 and was aware that they were "probably under the influence of the fading idea of tribute system," see X. Zhang, "Diaoyu / Senkaku Dilemma: To Be or not to Be?," *Kokusaihō Gaikō Zasshi* 国際法外交雑誌, vol. 113, no. 2 (2014), 34.

sovereignty in the modern sense.[89] An original title itself cannot be the basis for the ability to assert territorial rights under the modern order based on international law. It is the Chinese side that needs to show the existence of a modern replacement or supplementation measure that makes this possible and provide evidence of the replacement or supplementation of historic title resulting therefrom.[90]

4.4 *Meaning of Exemption from Application of Intertemporal Law Principle in the Context of the Decolonization Process*

The above review clarifies that critical date and intertemporal law play important roles in the Takeshima (Dokdo) issue as well as the Senkaku Islands (Diaoyu Islands) issue. Because of this, depending on the content of the assertion, there might be some benefit if, among these two rules, the intertemporal law function in particular is excluded. A notable characteristic of territorial disputes that have emerged since decolonization has been the increase in territorial and border disputes between States that were formerly colonies and had achieved independence. From the standpoint of intertemporal law, there is a tendency to apply it less strictly to territorial disputes between such States than to territorial disputes between European powers. The Advisory Opinion of the ICJ in the Western Sahara case is an example of the application of international law on territory that reflects the evolution of modern international law in view of progress in decolonization. While this could be considered a reformulation based on the second principle of intertemporal law that was formulated by the Arbitral Award in the Island of Palmas case, it could also be an

89 However, there is also the view that since land and maritime space had been legitimately demarcated over many years in relations with adjacent lands as part of the Hua-Yi distinction under the Sinocentric tribute system and there therefore did not exist a clear concept of territorial title held by a single sovereign, it might be possible to argue for the existence of a unique international order in East Asia and make a territorial claim based on such an order, rather than a territorial claim based on Western-centric international law. H. Nasu and D. R. Rothwell, "Re-Evaluating the Role of International Law in Territorial and Maritime Disputes in East Asia," *Asian Journal of International Law*, vol. 4 (2014), 64–65.

90 Matsui Yoshirō, "Between History and International Law: Senkaku / Diaoyu Dispute Revisited," *Kokusaihō Gaikō Zasshi* 国際法外交雑誌, vol. 113, no. 2 (2014), 14–15. In the Minquiers and Ecrehos case, the ICJ explained, "Such an alleged original feudal title of the Kings of France in respect of the Channel Islands could to-day produce no legal effect, unless it had been replaced by another title valid according to the law of the time of replacement. It is for the French Government to establish that it was so replaced." *ICJ Reports 1953*, 56.

indication that the conservative nature of intertemporal law has been coming under fierce criticism.[91]

That is not to say that the territorial issues involving Japan are disputes between newly independent States and their shared former colonizer following the decolonization process. Nevertheless, in the context of linking territorial issues to colonialism, it is necessary to be aware of the possibility of political assertions about history, such as that Japan's colonial control was unjust or that one's territory was invaded by Japan, being made in the trial process. While the question can be asked whether such assertions are valid legal arguments, it should nevertheless be noted that, through differences in the historical perceptions of the parties, there does exist an impetus for legal issues, in the context of modern international law, to be reformulated in favor of the side asserting that it was a colony.[92] However, it should also be noted that the standpoint of criticizing the conservative nature of intertemporal law from the perspective of decolonization has only been expressed as a minority opinion in the ICJ.[93]

Nevertheless, this does not imply a rejection of historical reviews in territorial disputes in general, nor is such a rejection even possible. The degree of

91 *Separate Opinion of Vice-President Ammoun, Western Sahara, ICJ Reports 1975*, 85–87; *Separate Opinion of Judge Forster, ibid.*, 103; *Separate Opinion of Judge Boni, ibid.*, 173–174. The same criticism is seen in Separate Opinions on the Judgment in the *Cameroon-Nigeria* case. *Separate Opinion of Judge Ranjeva, ICJ Reports 2002*, 469–471, paras. 2–6; *Separate Opinion of Judge Al-Khasawneh, ibid.*, 495–496, para. 5.

92 For example, regarding Takeshima (Dokdo), there is the view that the period of Japanese control of the Korean Peninsula during 1905–45 cannot be considered in the current Japan-ROK dispute because "that control is now recognized as having been wrongful and highly injurious to the Koreans" (van Dyke, *supra* note 63, 181). This reflects a stance of assessing past acts in the context of current laws.

93 Although not in the context of a territorial dispute, in its Advisory Opinion on the legal consequences of the separation of the Chagos Archipelago from Mauritius in 1968, the ICJ relied on the first principle of intertemporal law and deemed it necessary to identify, by reference to the period of the decolonization process between the separation in 1965 and Mauritius' independence in 1968, the rules of international law that are applicable to that process. At the same time, however, the ICJ also effectively included content from the second principle of intertemporal law and deemed that it would rely on legal instruments which postdate the period in question in order to confirm or interpret whether the law on self-determination, which has evolved since the adoption of the Charter of the United Nations and of the 1960 resolution entitled "Declaration on the Granting of Independence to Colonial Countries and Peoples," has been established as customary law. *Legal Consequences of the Separation of the Chagos Archipelago from Mauritius in 1965, ICJ Reports 2019*, 130, paras. 140–143. That the ICJ considered the evolution of international law following the decolonization process, while maintaining the existing framework of intertemporal law, is noteworthy.

detail with which history needs to be reviewed in order to find more appropriate solutions to territorial disputes is still unknown.[94]

5 Conclusion

The critical date concept is practical in its content and is used flexibly to achieve resolutions deemed appropriate by the courts and tribunals. In particular, although there is the rule that facts and acts occurring after the critical date should not be considered, it is possible to deviate from this rule in exceptional circumstances, provided doing so does not affect the legal relation at the time of the critical date. Under this formula, depending on the logics of the courts and tribunals in seeking a dispute resolution, it might acknowledge an inverted logical structure of setting the critical date at a time that would have a legal relation suited to a dispute resolution upon with the understanding that it will include facts and acts after the critical date in its considerations. However, in the ruling that it discloses publicly, it will designate the critical date first and seek subsequent facts and acts capable of confirming the legal relation at that time.

On the other hand, from the standpoint of a party, if it deems that it is preferable to obtain the court's acknowledgement of critical date to legitimize its own claims, the party needs to clarify whether it should take the position that, through the designation of the critical date, subsequent facts and acts should not be given any consideration, or if it should take the position that it is only possible to consider subsequent facts and acts for the purpose of confirming the legal relation at the time of the critical date. Furthermore, in the case of an assertion of historic title that depends on the premodern normative order, this must be replaced or supplemented with title under the modern order based on international law or a comparable concept.

However, independent of such intentions of the parties, the court might not designate critical date and instead seek to obtain information that it deems to be appropriate and would be useful for resolving the dispute. In this case, since the timeframe of the applicable laws theoretically widens to the timing

94 In his Separate Opinion regarding the ICJ's Judgment in the Qatar-Bahrain case, Judge Kooijmans criticized the ruling, stating that only by taking into account the full spectrum of the parties' history can their present rights be properly evaluated and that by not giving the full historical context its due, the ICJ had unnecessarily curtailed its scope for settling the dispute in a legally convincing way. *Separate Opinion of Judge Kooijmans*, *ICJ Reports 2001*, 226, para. 4.

at which the dispute was referred to the court, it should be noted that the evolution of law is likely to receive consideration in accordance with the second principle of intertemporal law.

Despite limited opportunities to refer territorial disputes to the ICJ, the parties to the dispute should pay attention to the court's precedents and consciously align their own practices with these in the diplomatic process and the international arena. The rules of critical date and intertemporal law addressed in this chapter have evolved in judicial practice, and the underlying foundation of these rules consists of maintaining legal stability and the principle of good faith.[95] Generally speaking, for diplomatic negotiations between the relevant parties to produce some sort of result, it is essential that there be a relation built on mutual trust and respect for related rules of international law. Therefore, the parties should ensure that their acts and assertions outside the court are, as much as possible, consistent with those within the judicial proceedings. This is particularly true of territorial disputes in which critical date and intertemporal law play important roles.[96]

95 The introduction of intertemporal law in the field of international law area arose, to some extent, from the need to stabilize the status quo (V. Z. Blum, *Historic Titles in International Law* (The Hague: Martinus Nijhoff, 1965), 206–207), with the stability thus argued for being legal stability (M. G. Kohen, "L'influence du temps sur les règlements territoriaux," in Société Française pour le Droit International (ed.), *Colloque de Paris, Le Droit international et le Temps* (Paris: Pedone, 2001), 155). Regarding the relation between critical date and the good faith principle, see R. Kolb, *Good Faith in International Law* (Oxford: Hart Publishing, 2017), 156–157.

96 It might be important for a State to maintain continuity of a policy, rather than legal continuity, even if it means sacrificing the latter, and, in such cases, the State might seek to avoid referring the dispute in question to a court so that it is not criticized for a lack of legal continuity. While this type of political expediency runs contrary to the law, it is widely recognized because of the limited role of international law in international relations. R. Kolb, *Réflexions sur les politiques juridiques extérieures* (Paris: Pedone, 2015), 26. However, even if a State's behavior is in fact contradictory, either synchronically or diachronically, depending on the factual nature of the issue that requires legal resolution, it is still important for the State to maintain continuity in its legal positions. In particular, for issues that address geographical features with few changes over time, consistent theory should be considered to be almost automatically required. G. de Lacharrière, *La politique juridique extérieure* (Paris: Economica, 1983), 189.

Bibliography

Primary Sources

Western Language

"Senkaku Islands Q & A." Ministry of Foreign Affairs of Japan. https://www.mofa.go.jp/region/asia-paci/senkaku/qa_1010.html#q1.

"The Korean Government's Basic Position on Dokdo." Ministry of Foreign Affairs of Republic of Korea. https://dokdo.mofa.go.kr/m/eng/dokdo/government_position.jsp.

"Diaoyu Dao, an inherent Territory of China." September 26, 2012. State Council Information Office, The People's Republic of China. https://www.fmprc.gov.cn/mfa_eng/topics_665678/diaodao_665718/t973774.shtml.

Secondary Sources

Japanese

Etō, Junichi 江藤淳一. "Funsō no Sonzai no Kettei o Meguru Kokusai Shihō Saibansho no Hanrei no Tenkai" 紛争の存在の決定をめぐる国際司法裁判所の判例の展開 [Development of International Court of Justice Precedents on Deciding the Existence of Disputes]. In Kokusai Kankei to Hō no Shihai (Owada Kokusai Shihō Saibansho Saibankan Taikan Kinen) 国際関係と法の支配(小和田国際司法裁判所裁判官退官記念), edited by Iwasawa Yūji 岩澤雄司, and Okano Masataka 岡野正敬. Tokyo: Shinzansha, 2021: 97–120.

Fukamachi, Tomoko 深町朋子. "Ryōdo Kizoku Handan ni okeru Kanren Yōso no Kōryo" 領土帰属判断における関連要素の考慮 [Consideration of Related Elements in Territory Attribution Decisions]. *Kokusai Mondai* 国際問, no. 624 (2013): 35–43.

Fukamachi, Tomoko 深町朋子. "Ryōiki ni Kansuru Genshi Kengen – Ryōki Kengenron wa Nani o Dokomade Atsukau noka." 領域に関する原始権原 – 領域権原論は何をどこまで扱うのか [Original Title to Territory: To What and To What Extent Is the Legal Framework of Title to Territory Applied?]. *Hōgaku Seminā* 法学セミナー, no. 765 (2018), 24–30.

Ha, Yonsu 河錬洙. "'Takeshima Funsō' Saikō – Ryōiki Kengen o Meguru Kokusaihō no Kanten Kara" 「竹島紛争」再考 – 領域権原をめぐる国際法の観点から [Rethinking the Takeshima Dispute: From the Standpoint of International Law on Territorial Title]. *Ryūkoku Hōgaku* 龍谷法学 32, no. 2 (1999): 227–286.

Huh, Sookyeon 許淑娟. *Ryōiki Kengen Ron – Ryōiki Shihai no Jikkōsei to Seitōsei* 領域権原論 – 領域支配の実効性と正当性 [The Acquisition of Territory in International Law: The Effectiveness and Legitimacy of Territorial Control]. Tokyo: University of Tokyo Publishing, 2012.

Magosaki, Ukeru 孫崎享, ed. *Kenshō – Senkakumondai* 検証 – 尖閣問題 [Verification: Senkaku Islands Problems]. Tokyo: Iwanami Publishing, 2021.

Matsui, Yoshirō 松井芳郎. *Kokusaihō Gakusha ga Yomu Senkaku Mondai – Funsō Kaiketsu eno Tenbo o Hiraku* 国際法学者がよむ尖閣問題 – 紛争解決への展望を拓く [Senkaku Islands Issue from the Perspective of an International Law Scholar: Seeking a Path to Resolve the Dispute]. Tokyo: Nippon Hyoronsha, 2014.

Minagawa, Takeshi 皆川洸. "Takeshima Funsō to Kokusai Hanrei" 竹島紛争と国際判例 [Takeshima Dispute and International Precedents]. In *Maehara Mitsuo Kyōju Kanreki Kinen Kokusaihōgaku no Shomondai* 前原光雄教授還暦記念 国際法学の諸問題 [Festschrift for Professor Maehara Mitsuo in Commemoration of His 60th Birthday: Problems in International Law]. Tokyo: Keiō Tsūshin, 1963.

Miyoshi, Masahiro 三好正弘. "Takeshima Mondai to Kuritikaru Dēto" 竹島問題とクリティカル・デート [Takeshima Issue and Critical Date]. *Tōsho Kenkyu Jyānaru* 島嶼研究ジャーナル 3, no. 2 (2014): 28–49.

Miyoshi, Masahiro 三好正弘. "Ryōdo Shutoku ni Okeru Kōgi to Mokunin – Senkaku Shoto tono Kanren ni Oite" 領土取得における抗議と黙認 – 尖閣諸島との関連において [Protest and Acquiescence in Territorial Acquisition: In relation to the Senkaku Islands]. *Tōsho Kenkyu Jyānaru* 島嶼研究ジャーナル 4, no. 2 (2015): 25–46.

Nakatani, Kazuhiro 中谷和弘. "Nihon no Ryōdo Kanren Mondai to Kokusai Saiban Taiō" 日本の領土関連問題と国際裁判対応 [Japan's Territorial Issues and International Court Responses]. *Tōsho Kenkyu Jyānaru* 島嶼研究ジャーナル 7, no. 1 (2017): 20–30.

Nakano, Tetsuya 中野徹也. "Takeshima no Kizoku ni Kansuru Ichi Kōsatsu" 竹島の帰属に関する一考察 [Thoughts on Takeshima's Attribution]. *Kansai Daigaku Hōgaku Ronshū* 関西大学法学論集 60, no. 5 (2011): 103–134.

Nakano, Tetsuya 中野徹也. "1905 Nen Nihon ni yoru Takeshima Ryōdo Hen'nyū Sochi no Hōteki Seishitsu" 1905年日本による竹島領土編入措置の法的性質 [Legal Nature of Japan's Measure to Incorporate Takeshima as Territory in 1905]. *Kansai Daigaku Hōgaku Ronshū* 関ヨ西大学法学論集 61, no. 5 (2012): 113–166.

Nakano, Tetsuya 中野徹也. *Takeshima Mondai to Kokusaihō* 竹島問題と国際法 [Takeshima Issue and International Law]. Shimane: Harvest Publishing, 2019.

Park, Pae Keun 朴培根. "Nihon ni yoru Tosho Sensen no Sho-Senrei –Takeshima / Dokuto ni taisuru Tyoiki Kengen wo Chushin to shite–" 日本による島嶼先占の諸先例 – 竹島／独島に対する領域権原を中心として – [Some Observations on the Territorial Incorporation of Islands by Japan with Special Reference to the Territorial Title over Liancourt Rocks (Takeshima / Dokdo)]. *Kokusaihō Gaikō Zasshi* 国際法外交雑誌 105, no. 2 (2006): 176–191.

Sakai, Hironobu 酒井啓亘. "Kokusai Saiban ni yoru Ryōiki Funsō no Kaiketsu – Saikin no Kokusai Shihō Saibansho no Hanrei no Dōkō" 国際裁判による領域紛争の解決 – 最近の国際司法裁判所の判例の動向 [Territorial Dispute Solutions by the

International Courts and Tribunals: Trends in Recent ICJ Jurisprudence]. *Kokusai Mondai* 国際問題, no. 624 (2013): 5–19.

Sakai, Hironobu 酒井啓亘. "Ryōiki Funsō ni Okeru 'Ketteiteki Kijitsu' no Igi –Kokusai Shihō Saibansho no Saibanrei o Chūshin ni–" 領域紛争における『決定的期日』の意義 – 国際司法裁判所の裁判例を中心に – [The Significance of 'Critical Dates' in Territorial Disputes: Centering on Precedents of the International Court of Justice]. In *Kokusai Kankei to Hō no Shihai* (*Owada Kokusai Shihō Saibansho Saibankan Taikan Kinen*) 国際関係と法の支配（小和田国際司法裁判所裁判官退官記念）, edited by Iwasawa Yūji 岩澤雄司 and Okano Masataka 岡野正敬. Tokyo: Shinzansha, 202: 147–179.

Sakai, Hironobu 酒井啓亘. "Ryōiki Funsō ni Okeru Jisaihō Gensoku no Yakuwari ni tsuite – Kokusai Hanrei no Dōkō o Chushin ni" 領域紛争における時際法原則の役割について – 国際判例の動向を中心に [The Roles of Intertemporal Law in the International Judicial and Arbitral Settlement of the Territorial Disputes]. *Hōgaku Ronsō* 法学論叢 188, 4–6 (2021), 87–126.

Serita, Kentarō 芹田健太郎. *Nihon no Ryōdo* 日本の領土 [The Territory of Japan]. Tokyo: Chuo Koron Shinsha, 2010.

Sugihara, Takane 杉原高嶺. "Kokusaihō kara mita Hoppō Ryōdo" 国際法から見た北方領土 [Northern Territories from the Standpoint of International Law]. In *Hoppō Ryōdo o Kangaeru* 北方領土を考える [Thinking of the Northern Territories], edited by Kimura Hiroshi 木村汎. Hokkaido: Hokkaido Shimbunsha, 1981.

Taijudo, Kanae 太壽堂鼎. *Ryōdo Kizoku no Kokusaihō* 領土帰属の国際法 [Title to Territory in International Law]. Tokyo: Tōshindō, 1998.

Tomabechi, Masato 苫米地真理. *Senkaku Mondai – Seifu Kenkai wa Dō Hensenshita Noka* 尖閣問題 – 政府見解はどう変遷したのか [Senkaku Islands Issue: How Has the Government Opinion Changed]. Tokyo: Kashiwa Shobō, 2020.

Tsukamoto, Takashi 塚本孝. "Takeshima to Senkaku Shotō" 竹島と尖閣諸島 [Takeshima and Senkaku Islands]. *Tōsho Kenkyū Jyānaru* 島嶼研究ジャーナル 5, no. 1 (2015): 6–33.

Western Languages

Bardonnet, Daniel. "Les faits postérieurs à la date critique dans les différends territoriaux et frontaliers." In *Le droit international au service de la paix, de la justice et du développement*, Mélanges Michel Virally, 53–78. Paris: A. Pedone, 1991.

Bennouna, Mohamed. *Le droit international entre la lettre et l'esprit.* Leiden: Brill, 2017.

Blum, Vehuda Z. *Historic Titles in International Law.* The Hague: Martinus Nijhoff, 1965.

Cheng, Tao. "The Sino-Japanese Dispute Over the Tio-yu-tai (Senkaku) Islands and the Law of Territorial Acquisition." *Virginia Journal of International Law* 14 (1974): 221–266.

Cohn, Georg. "Statut juridique du Groënland oriental." *Revue de droit international et de législation comparée* XIV, no. 4 (1933): 557–571.

De Lacharrière, Guy. *La politique juridique extérieure.* Paris: Economica, 1983.

Distefano, Giovanni. "Time Factor and Territorial Disputes." In *Research Handbook on Territorial Disputes in International Law*, edited by M. G. Kohen and M. Hébié, 397–416. Cheltenham: Edward Elgar, 2018.

Fellmeth, Aaron X., and Maurice Horwitz. *Guide to Latin in International Law, Second Edition*. Oxford: Oxford University Press, 2021.

Fitzmaurice, Sir Gerald. *The Law and Procedure of the International Court of Justice, Vol. 1.* Cambridge: Cambridge University Press, 1993.

Goldie, Louis F. E. "The Critical Date." *International and Comparative Law Quarterly* 12, issue 4 (1963): 1251–1284.

Huh, Sookyeon. "Title to Territory in the Post-Colonial Era: Original Title and Terra Nullius in the ICJ Judgments on Cases Concerning Ligitan / Sipadan (2002) and Pedra Branca (2008)." *European Journal of International Law* 26 (2015): 709–725.

Jennings, Robert Y. *The Acquisition of Territory in International Law.* Manchester: Manchester University Press, 1963.

Jennings, Sir Robert, and Sir Arthur Watts, eds. *Oppenheim's International Law. Ninth Edition. Vol. 1. Peace. Parts 2 to 4.* London: Longman, 1992.

Johnson, David H. N. "The Minquiers and Ecrehos Case." *International and Comparative Law Quarterly* 3, issue 2 (1954): 189–216.

Kohen, Marcelo Gustavo and Mamadou Hébié. "Territory, Acquisition." In *The Max Planck Encyclopedia of Public International Law, Volume IX*, edited by R. Wolfrum. Oxford: Oxford University Press, 2012.

Kohen, Marcelo Gustavo. "Original Title in the Light of the ICJ Judgment on Sovereignty over Pedra Branca / Batu Puteh, Middle Rocks and South Ledge." *Journal of the History of International Law* 15 (2013): 151–171.

Kohen, Marcelo Gustavo. "L'influence du temps sur les règlements territoriaux." In *Le Droit international et le Temps*, edited by Société Française pour le Droit International, 129–157. Paris: A. Pedone, 2001.

Kolb, Robert. *Réflexions sur les politiques juridiques extérieures.* Paris: A. Pedone, 2015.

Kolb, Robert. *Good Faith in International Law*. Oxford: Hart Publishing, 2017.

Lee, Han Key. "Korea's Territorial Rights to Tokdo in History and International Law." *Korea Observer* 29 (1998): 1–91.

Lee, Seokwoo. "Towards a Framework for the Resolution of the Territorial Dispute over the Kurile Islands." *Boundary & Territory Briefing* 3, no. 6 (2001): 1–55.

Lee, Seokwoo. "Intertemporal Law, Recent Judgments and Territorial Disputes in Asia." In *Maritime Boundary Disputes, Settlement Processes, and the Law of the Sea*, edited by S.-Y. Hong and J. M. Van Dyke, 119–136. Leiden: Brill, 2009.

Loja, Melissa H. "Status Quo Post Bellum and the Legal Resolution of the Territorial Dispute between China and Japan over the Senkaku / Diaoyu Islands." *European Journal of International Law* 27 (2016): 979–1004.

Matsui, Yoshiro. "International Law of Territorial Acquisition and the Dispute over the Senkaku (Diaoyu) Islands." *Japanese Annual of International Law* 40 (1997): 3–31.

Matsui, Yoshirō. "Between History and International Law: Senkaku / Diaoyu Dispute Revisited." *Kokusaihō Gaikō Zasshi* 国際法外交雑誌 113, no. 2 (2014): 1–24.

Mayali, Laurent, and John Yoo. "Resolution of Territorial Disputes in East Asia: The Case of Dokdo," *Berkeley Journal of International Law* 36 (2018): 504–550.

Munkman, Athene L. W. "Adjudication and Adjustment – International Judicial Decision and the Settlement of Territorial and Boundary Disputes." *British Year Book of International Law* 46 (1972–1973): 1–116.

Nasu, Hitoshi, and Donald R. Rothwell. "Re-Evaluating the Role of International Law in Territorial and Maritime Disputes in East Asia," *Asian Journal of International Law* 4, issue 1 (2014): 55–79.

Neverova, Evgenia V. "The Southern Kuril Deadlock: Effectiveness v. Protest." *Moscow Journal of International Law* 3 (2019): 47–58.

Onuma, Yasuaki. *International Law in a Transcivilizational World*. Cambridge: Cambridge University Press, 2017.

Poissonnier, Ghislain, and Pierre Osseland, "À qui appartiennent les îles Senkaku / Diaoyu?" *Journal du droit international* 135 (2008): 467–484.

Quillen, Amy B. "The "Kuril Islands" or the "Northern Territories": Who Owns Them Island Territorial Dispute Continues to Hinder Relations Between Russia and Japan." *North Carolina Journal of International & Comparative Regulation* 18 (1993): 633–661.

Ramos-Mrosovsky, Carlos. "International Law's Unhelpful Role in the Senkaku Islands," *University of Pennsylvania Journal of International Law* 29 (2008): 903–946.

Rodríguez, L. I. Sánchez. "L'*uti possidetis* et les effectivités dans les contentieux territoriaux et frontaliers." *Recueil des cours* 263 (1997): 149–382.

Schrijver, Nico J., and Vid Prislan. "Case Concerning Sovereignty over Islands before the International Court of Justice and the Dokdo / Takeshima Issue." *Ocean Development & International Law* 46, issue 4 (2015): 281–314.

Scoville, Ryan M. "A Defense of Japanese Sovereignty over the Senkaku / Diaoyu Islands." *The George Washington International Law Review* 46 (2014): 571–605.

Serita, Kentarō. "Some Legal Aspects of Territorial Disputes over Islands." In *Maritime Boundary Disputes, Settlement Processes, and the Law of the Sea*, edited by S.-Y. Hong and J. M. Van Dyke (Leiden: Brill, 2009): 137–144.

Schulte Nordholt, Henk. "Delimitation of the Continental Shelf in the East China Sea." *Netherlands International Law Review* 32 (1985): 123–160.

Sharma, Surya. P. *Territorial Acquisition, Disputes and International Law*. The Hague: Kluwer Law International, 1997.

Tan, Kevin Y. L. "The Role of History in International Territorial Dispute Settlement: The Pedra Branca Case (Singapore v Malaysia)." In *Asian Approaches to International Law and the Legacy of Colonialism. The Law of the Sea, Territorial Disputes and International Dispute Settlement*, edited by J.-H. Paik, S.-W. Lee, and K. Y. L. Tan, 64–80. New York: Routledge, 2013.

van Dyke, Jon M. "Legal Issues Related to Sovereignty over Dokdo and Its Maritime Boundary." *Ocean Development & International Law* 38, issue 1–2 (2007): 157–224.

Wei Su, Steven. "The Territorial Dispute over the Tiaoyu / Senkaku Islands: An Update." *Ocean Development & International Law* 36, issue 1 (2005): 45–61.

Yanagihara, Masaharu. "Significance of the History of the Law of Nations in Europe and East Asia." *Recueil des cours* 371 (2015): 317–349.

Zhang, Xinjun. "Diaoyu / Senkaku Dilemma: To Be or not to Be?" *Kokusaihō Gaikō Zasshi* 国際法外交雑誌 113, no. 2 (2014): 25–48.

PART 4

Territorial Disputes in International Courts and Tribunals

CHAPTER 8

Application and Evaluation of "Pre-modern/ Non-European Territorial Control" in International Courts and Tribunals

Tomoko Fukamachi

1 Introduction

In territorial issues which Japan is involved with, Japan and Korea in the case of Takeshima, and China in the case of the Senkaku Islands, argue that the respective islands fell under their "territorial control"[1] prior to East Asia's acceptance of modern international law and present this as evidence that the island is attributed to them. For example, China explains in its White Paper released in 2012 that it had already discovered, named, and used the islands by the 14th and 15th centuries, that it placed the islands under its jurisdiction by such measures as incorporating them into the coastal defense zone of the Ming court, and that Chinese and foreign maps from the 16th to 19th century showed the islands as belonging to China.[2] Meanwhile, Japan criticizes this stance, pointing out that China's historical argument has not demonstrated any grounds for territorial sovereignty that are regarded as valid under international law and

1 The term "territorial control" used throughout this chapter, other than in cases in which it is part of a book title, refers to a factual relationship between a political entity or ruler and land in Europe prior to the establishment of the sovereign State system and modern international law, as well as in non-European regions prior to the acceptance or adoption of modern international law, in contrast to the territorial sovereignty which a sovereign State holds over a territory under modern international law. Additionally, "pre-modern/non-European territorial control" refers to "territorial control" in Europe prior to the establishment of the sovereign State system and modern international law and in non-European regions prior to the acceptance or adoption of modern international law. To avoid descriptive complication, subsequent use of "territorial control" and "pre-modern/non-European territorial control" will not include quotation marks. When the term "territory" is utilized independently to mean something different than territory under modern international law, it is shown as "territory" using brackets (other than in actual quotations).

2 State Council Information Office, People's Republic of China, "Diaoyu Dao, an Inherent Territory of China," 26 September 2012, at http://www.diaoyudao.org.cn/en/2015-01/25/content_34649357.htm (as of 30 September 2021).

 | DOI:10.1163/9789004706361_009

that China has merely asserted that the islands are "Chinese territory" based on its own unilateral logic.[3]

Turning to academia, we find Matsui Yoshiro remarks that, in accordance with the first rule of intertemporal law, the validity of China's abovementioned historical argument "should be decided in light of international law from the 16th to 19th centuries when the relevant practice occurred."[4] Such a review leads him to conclude that it is difficult to recognize the Chinese historical claim as presenting valid title under modern international law.[5] At the same time, however, Matsui mentions the necessity of considering the matter from the perspective of "whether it was actually possible to apply international law, which is the product of the European international order, to China, Japan, and the Ryukyus, which belonged to the East Asian world order or the traditional Sino-centric order endowed with an entirely different set of organizing principles from that of the European international order"[6] (i.e., the issue of "the law between different legal systems").[7]

Admittedly, China's abovementioned White Paper does not specify by which norms it is acknowledged that the actions of discovery and naming or "placement under jurisdiction" may constitute a basis for territorial attribution. However, there are theorists who do argue that, in light of the possibility of these being regarded, if judged within the framework of modern international law, as "the obviously ineffective display of sovereignty," it is necessary to bring to the fore "China's approaches to displaying its sovereignty"[8] or the existence of the "different requirements and means of displaying title over a

3 Office of Policy Planning and Coordination on Territory and Sovereignty, Cabinet Secretariat, "The Senkaku Islands: Let's see China's Argument," at https://www.cas.go.jp/jp/ryodo_eg/taiou/senkaku/senkaku01-05.html (as of 30 September 2021).

4 Matsui Yoshirō 松井芳郎, *Kokusaihō Gakusha ga Yomu Senkaku Mondai – Funsō Kaiketsu eno Tenbō o Hiraku* 国際法学者がよむ尖閣問題 – 紛争解決への展望を拓く [Senkaku Islands Issue from the Perspective of an International Law Scholar: Seeking a Path to Resolve the Dispute] (Tokyo: Nippon Hyōronsha, 2014), 19.

5 *Ibid.*, 78–89.

6 *Ibid.*, 113.

7 Nevertheless, Matsui's conclusion is that since title deemed to have been obtained under the framework of an order that differs from modern international law needed to be replaced with "effective control of the territory" as part of the process of joining the European international order, efforts to make such a replacement and the provision of proof thereof are important. Regarding the Senkaku Islands ("Diaoyutai Islands"), Matsui's assessment is that China did not engage in such replacement efforts. *Ibid.*, 123–127.

8 Steven W. Su, "The Territorial Dispute over the Tiaoyu/Senkaku Islands: An Update," *Ocean Development & International Law*, vol. 36, issue 1 (2005), 52.

given territory"[9] in the East Asian World Order from those in modern international law.[10] As noted by Lee Keun-Gwan, these arguments take the position that "it would be highly inappropriate to apply the yardstick of modern international law in appreciating the facts that took place under a substantially different normative order"[11] and, in doing so, present one viewpoint on "the law between different legal systems" constructed by Matsui.

Claims of historical attribution prior to the acceptance of modern international law are also made in relation to the Paracel Islands and Spratly Islands, and Fry and Loja examine the validity of such assertions presented by China and Vietnam.[12] Their paper considers, in accordance with the two segments of intertemporal law, (1) the extent to which, regarding the creation of title, international judicial proceedings have acknowledged the existence of non-Western pre-colonial normative systems and applied their rules of territorial acquisition and (2) to the maintenance of created historic title, how rules of territorial acquisition under modern international law apply. What is notable is that in terms of (1) they admit there are two cases that confirmed the existence of title to territory (territorial title) with roots in non-Western normative systems,[13] and conclude that both are cases where "a state or similar central authority exercised territorial sovereignty over the disputed territory."[14] If this is intended to suggest that territorial control in a world with a different normative order from modern international law should, under the first rule of intertemporal law, be evaluated based on the local normative order of that period,

9 Han-yi Shaw, "Revisiting the Diaoyutai/Senkaku Islands Dispute: Examining Legal Claims and New Historical Evidence under International Law and the Traditional East Asian World Order," *Chinese (Taiwan) Yearbook of International Law and Affairs*, vol. 26 (2008), 148.

10 For a work that raised awareness of this issue at an early stage, see Tao Cheng, "The Sino-Japanese Dispute over the Tiao-yu-tai (Senkaku) Islands and the Law of Territorial Acquisition," *Virginia Journal of International Law*, vol. 14 (1974), 253.

11 Keun-Gwan Lee, "An Enquiry into the Palimpsestic Nature of Territorial Sovereignty in East Asia – with Particular Reference to the Senkaku/Diaoyudao Question," in Christine Chinkin and Freya Baetens (eds.), *Sovereignty, Statehood and State Responsibility: Essays in Honour of James Crawford* (Cambridge: Cambridge University Press, 2015), 132–133.

12 James D. Fry and Melissa H. Loja, "The Roots of Historic Title: Non-Western Pre-Colonial Normative Systems and Legal Resolution of Territorial Disputes," *Leiden Journal of International Law*, vol. 27, issue 3 (2014), 727–754.

13 The two cases are *Minquiers and Ecrehos* and *Pedra Branca/Pulau Batu Puteh* but then the term "non-Western normative systems" is misleading because of the inclusion of the *Minquiers and Ecrehos* case. A more appropriate expression would be "normative systems predating colonialism and modern international law," which can be formulated by making use of the expression "non-Western normative systems predating colonialism and modern international law," which appeared elsewhere in the article.

14 Fry and Loja, *supra* note 12, 753–754.

rather than the modern international law contemporary to it, this would show a different orientation from the conventional and prevailing understanding. Alternatively, if this means to require the actual exercise of territorial sovereignty by a local political entity and such an exercise is literally construed as that of modern international law, it greatly diminishes the significance of the purported evaluation based on the local normative order, even though it introduces the "novelty" of applying the territorial sovereignty concept to a local political entity.

Thus, there is still confusion in academic doctrine regarding the question of whether or not territorial control implemented prior to the acceptance or adoption of modern international law under a normative order that differs from modern international law, as well as said order itself, may have any relevance to decisions of territorial attribution based on modern international law, and, if they may, the question of which legal principles or framework they should adhere to. Efforts to clarify these points are essential to legally assessing the historical arguments presented with regard to territorial issues in East Asia. As part of such efforts, this chapter considers the significance of pre-modern/non-European territorial control in relation to the first rule of intertemporal law on the creation of title by means of research into judicial and arbitral cases.[15] The shift from a world in which a normative order that differs from modern international law applies to one in which modern international law applies occurred not only in non-European regions but also within Europe itself in the form of a shift from the pre-modern normative order. From the perspective of "the law between different legal systems," both instances present the same type of problematic circumstances. This chapter will survey two cases related to territorial control in pre-modern Europe and eight cases related to non-European territorial control in the chronological order of the decisions (2.1–2.10), and clarify the contexts in which the assertions of territorial control were made in the proceedings with a focus on the intent and/or purpose of the parties (3.1) and on the concept of title invoked (3.2). Then it will look into how courts and tribunals have treated the assertions of the parties, that is to say, whether or not they reviewed and legally assessed pre-modern/non-European territorial control, and consider the possible factors which led to such treatment, while paying attention to their relation to the contexts clarified in the preceding Subsections (3.3).

15 The maintenance of title, to which the second rule of intertemporal law applies, is outside the scope of this chapter.

2 International Judicial and Arbitral Cases Involving Pre-modern/ Non-European Territorial Control

2.1 *Eastern Greenland*

In this case, it was Denmark that made assertions related to pre-modern/ non-European territorial control. It contradicted the occupation of Eastern Greenland by Norway based on two propositions: (1) Denmark's sovereignty over all of Greenland had been continuously and peacefully exercised for a long time and had not been contested by any power, and (2) Norway had by treaty or otherwise itself recognized Danish sovereignty.[16] In doing so, regarding (1), Denmark invoked, as evidence of Denmark's exercise of sovereignty, a pre-modern background of two settlements, built on the western coast in the 10th century, existing as an independent State and subsequently becoming a tributary to the Kingdom of Norway in the 13th century.[17]

The Permanent Court of International Justice (PCIJ) acknowledged that, because the Danish claim was not founded upon any particular act of occupation but "a title 'founded on the peaceful and continuous display of State authority over the island'," both the existence and the extent of the rights enjoyed by the King of Denmark and Norway must be considered.[18] The specific act cited by the Court was the undertaking in the latter half of the 13th century with regard to fines for murders, recorded by historian or saga writer Sturla Thordarson. According to this, fines had to be paid to the King of Norway by the men of Greenland who had committed murders, whether the victim was a Norwegian or a Greenlander and whether killed in the settlement or outside it. The Court concluded that although "the modern notions as to territorial sovereignty had not come into being" in the period in which the settlements had been in existence, "[s]o far as it is possible to apply modern terminology to the rights and pretensions of the kings of Norway in Greenland in the XIIIth and XIVth centuries, the Court holds that at that date these rights amounted to sovereignty and that they were not limited to the two settlements."[19] This means that, in this case, the Court considered pre-modern territorial control

16 *Legal Status of Eastern Greenland (Denmark v. Norway), PCIJ, Series A/B*, no. 53, 44.

17 Both settlements disappeared by 1500. The rights of the Kingdom of Norway from that time were inherited by Denmark. *Ibid.*, 27, 30–31.

18 However, the Court also explained that even if the material submitted to the Court might be insufficient to establish the existence of sovereignty so far in the past, it is sufficient for a valid title to have been established in the period immediately preceding the critical date. In this way, the Court reserved the view that proof and evaluations dating back through past periods are not necessarily essential. *Ibid.*, 45.

19 *Ibid.*, 27 and 46.

as an element forming "a title founded on the peaceful and continuous display of State authority" by Denmark prior to 1931.[20] However, it did not specify any particular pre-modern normative order or concepts by which the significance of territorial control could have been internally judged.

2.2 *Minquiers and Ecrehos*

Next is the case before the International Court of Justice (ICJ) concerning attribution of the islets and rocks of the Minquiers and Ecrehos groups located between the British Channel Island of Jersey and the coast of France. Both parties, the United Kingdom and France, asserted an ancient title or original title derived from events in pre-modern Europe and invoked, as evidence of effective exercise of sovereignty based on the said title,[21] the exercise of modern State functions[22] as well as pre-modern charters and laws.

The ancient title and original title were claimed as relating to the Channel Islands at large. The Court accepted the United Kingdom's argument and acknowledged the validity of the presumption that the Minquiers and Ecrehos groups had always been distinct from Continental Normandy as a part of the Channel Islands and been attributed to the Kings of England. However, since this was still only a presumption, considerations and assessment relating directly to the Minquiers and Ecrehos groups were of decisive importance.[23] Meanwhile, regarding the original feudal title of the Kings of France to the Channel Islands, even if such a title had existed, the Court deemed that "it must have lapsed" as a consequence of the recovery of Normandy in 1204 and

20 Fry and Loja referred to this case as one in which the Court did not consider pre-modern territorial control. Their evidence is that the Court indicated that the building of settlements in the 10th century occurred before the modern notions of territorial sovereignty came into being and that it is unlikely for either the chief or the settlers to have drawn distinctions between territory which was and which was not subject to them. However, they did not mention that immediately afterwards, the judgment also cited the 13th century undertaking in the manner explained in this chapter. Fry and Loja, *supra* note 12, 733.

21 Besides its claim of the ancient title, the United Kingdom also asserted attribution based on having established title by long continued effective possession alone. Long-term effective possession serves as evidence of title in the former case and as the source of title or the vestitive fact as such in the latter case. *The Minquiers and Ecrehos Case (France/United Kingdom)*, *ICJ Reports 1953*, 50.

22 The United Kingdom invoked the following acts from the 19th and 20th centuries as examples of the exercise of State authority and received Court recognition of their relevance: judicial proceedings by the Court of Jersey regarding criminal offences committed on the Ecrehos; acts of local administration conducted by the Jersey authorities in respect of the Minquiers and Ecrehos such as inquests on corpses, levying of taxes on property, and the taking of censuses surveys; and a treasury warrant that mentions the Ecrehos.

23 *Ibid.*, 53–55.

various subsequent events. The Court stated that it "could to-day produce no legal effect, unless it had been replaced by another title valid according to the law of the time of replacement." France additionally alleged that if the United Kingdom could not establish its claims to the Minquiers and Ecrehos groups, the Court should consider the title as having remained with France since 1204. The Court also denied the validity of this argument based on the fact that further development had occurred as to the territorial position of the Channel Islands and Normandy since 1204. It explained, "What is of decisive importance, in the opinion of the Court, is not indirect presumptions deduced from events in the Middle Ages, but the evidence which relates directly to the possession of the Ecrehos and Minquiers groups."[24] Thus, the word "replacement" and the phrase "not indirect presumptions deduced from events in the Middle Ages," which are the particularly well-known portions of this judgment, were referred to in the Court's assessment of the French argument. The United Kingdom's original title was not rejected. It follows that the significance of examining pre-modern territorial control in making a judgment about territorial attribution in a modern international judicial proceeding was not denied.

Rather, the Court did not only consider facts of pre-modern territorial control regarding the Ecrehos of the 13th and 14th centuries and the Minquiers of the 17th century as "evidence which relates directly to the possession of these groups," but also made its decisions in accordance with the law of the time. For example, in the case of the Ecrehos, the Court cited facts such as the granting, by Piers des Préaux, who had received the fief of the Channel Islands from the English King, of the Ecrehos in frankalmoign to an abbey in Normandy in 1203 and the *Quo Warranto* proceedings to enquire into the property and revenue of the English King in the early 14th century. Then, in deciding whether these were evidence of the English King's control of the Ecrehos, the Court made a reference to the *Grand Coutumier de Normandie*.[25] Also, for the Minquiers, the Court relied on the said *Coutumier* to confirm the legal significance of the fact that the Manorial Court of the fief of Noirmont in Jersey had dealt with two cases of shipwreck found at the Minquiers in the early 17th century.[26] Thus, in this case, the significance and content of actions and facts related to pre-modern territorial control were assessed within the context of the normative order of the time, which differed from modern international law, and were treated as elements in forming a decision on attribution by the Court.

24 *Ibid.*, 56–57.
25 *Ibid.*, 60–63.
26 *Ibid.*, 67–69.

The remaining issue is whether the Court made a reference to Britain's long-term possession, including in pre-modern times, as evidence of title to confirm the presumption that the groups were within the scope of England's ancient title or it viewed this as a source of title itself or, in other words, a vestitive fact. The judgment in this case is generally regarded as a precedent for decisions on attribution that treat the exercise of State authority from modern times as vestitive facts.[27] Such an interpretation of the judgment often seems to accompany an understanding that title based on long-term effective possession replaced England's ancient title. However, in relation to England's title, the Court did not mention the title to have "lapsed" or its "replacement" at any point in the judgment, which shows a clear contrast with its treatment of France's alleged title. In other words, it is quite difficult to find any statement in the judgment which could squarely deny the understanding that what the Court did was to ascertain the Minquiers and the Ecrehos as being within the scope of the ancient title based on various facts spanning the pre-modern era to the modern era. In fact, the ICJ itself, in a 1992 judgment, adopted this interpretation that the Court referenced long-term effective control as evidence of title.[28]

2.3 *Western Sahara*

In this case, the ICJ delivered an advisory opinion on the following questions in response to a request from the General Assembly of the United Nations: (1) Had the Western Sahara been at the time of colonization by Spain at the end of the 19th century a territory belonging to no one (*terra nullius*) and (2) If it had not been *terra nullius*, what had been the legal ties between this territory and the Kingdom of Morocco and the Mauritanian entity at the end of the 19th century.[29]

The argument concerning a pre-modern/non-European order appears in Morocco's allegations for (2). To begin with, in defining legal ties between Western Sahara and itself as ties of sovereignty on the ground of "immemorial possession … based … on the public display of sovereignty, uninterrupted

---

27 One example is Malcolm N. Shaw, *International Law, 9th ed.* (Cambridge: Cambridge University Press, 2021), 426.

28 *Land, Island and Maritime Frontier Dispute (El Salvador/Honduras: Nicaragua intervening)*, *ICJ Reports 1992*, 564–565. For criticism, see Huh Sookyeon 許淑娟, *Ryōiki Kengen Ron – Ryōiki Shihai no Jikkōsei to Seitōsei* 領域権原論 - 領域支配の実効性と正当性 [The Acquisition of Territory in International Law: The Effectiveness and Legitimacy of Territorial Control] (Tokyo: University of Tokyo Press, 2012), 245–246.

29 *Sahara occidental, avis consultatif, CIJ Recueil 1975*, 13–14, para. 1. The Court responded in the negative to the first inquiry.

and uncontested, for centuries," Morocco invoked pre-modern/non-European events dating back to the 7th century as evidence of possession, based mainly on descriptions in historical works.[30] Morocco viewed its assertion as being similar to Denmark's position in *Eastern Greenland*. However, while making reference to special characteristics of Western Sahara in terms of its geography and political organization at the time of colonialization, which had been noted at the start of the review of (2),[31] the Court pointed out that "the paucity of evidence of actual display of authority unambiguously relating to Western Sahara renders it difficult to consider the Moroccan claim as on all fours with that of Denmark in the *Eastern Greenland* case,"[32] and hence did not acknowledge that Morocco had displayed the exercise of authority to support immemorial possession.

The second argument is related to Morocco's exercise of authority over Western Sahara at the end of the 19th century. Morocco's exercise of authority, which it invoked as evidence of its display of sovereignty, consisted mainly of various actions based on a pre-modern/non-European order whereby tribal chiefs had shown allegiance to the Sultan.[33] Therefore, Morocco maintained that in appreciating the evidence, the Court should take account of the special structure of the Sherifian State. In response, the Court first acknowledged that no rule of international law required the structure of a State to follow any particular pattern and deemed that, where sovereignty over territory was claimed, the particular structure of a State might be a relevant element in appreciating the reality or otherwise of a display of State activity adduced as evidence of that sovereignty.[34] Next, the Court confirmed that the Sherifian State had been a special type of State founded on the common religious bond of Islam and on the allegiance of various tribes to the Sultan, rather than a notion of territory.

---

30 *Ibid.*, 42, para. 90.

31 The ICJ noted the following points. (1) It was part of a large desert with low and spasmodic rainfall and was therefore exploited almost exclusively by nomads. (2) The right of pasture was enjoyed in common by the nomadic tribes, while the rights to areas suitable for cultivation were held by individual tribes. (3) Perennial water-holes were the property of the tribe which put them into commission, though their use was open to all. (4) Each tribe had its own burial grounds. (5) Inter-tribal conflict was not infrequent. (6) Nomadic routes extended outside of Western Sahara. (7) All the tribes were of the Islamic faith and the whole territory lay within the Dar al-Islam. (8) A sheikh controlled the tribe, subject to the assent of the "Juma'a," an assembly of its leading members. (9) The tribe was governed by Koranic law and its own customary law. (10) The dependencies or alliances among tribes were ties of allegiance or vassalage and not territorial. *Ibid.*, 41–42, paras. 87–88.

32 *Ibid.*, 43, para. 92.

33 *Ibid.*, 45, para. 99.

34 *Ibid.*, 43–44, para. 94.

Then, regarding the former, the Court rejected its relevance to an appreciation of claims of sovereignty by pointing out the fact that, around the world, common religious links had existed without signifying legal ties. Regarding the latter, meanwhile, the Court conceded that the political ties of allegiance could be an element in the composition of a State, but also stated, "Such an allegiance, however, if it is to afford indications of the ruler's sovereignty, must clearly be real and manifested in acts evidencing acceptance of his political authority."[35] It was from this perspective that the Court evaluated the evidence invoked by Morocco. In its conclusion, the Court rejected the existence of effective and exclusive State activity by Morocco in Western Sahara on such grounds as lack of evidence concerning the imposition of Moroccan taxes and its failure to prove any connection which might have justified the identification of the activities of the sheikhs with the exercise of the Sultan's authority, and hence did not accept Morocco's assertion of territorial sovereignty.[36]

Thus, in this case, while the Court acknowledged a difference between a form of pre-modern/non-European territorial control and that based on modern international law, what it consistently applied in terms of its decision framework for territorial sovereignty were concepts and norms of modern international law, such as "immemorial possession ... based ... on the public display of sovereignty, uninterrupted and uncontested" and "effective and exclusive State activity" displaying the exercise of territorial sovereignty. As a result, the issue of the different nature of its territorial control that Morocco relied upon did not have any substantive significance. However, it is important to recognize that a possible cause for such a decision might be that Morocco itself had not in fact argued for a decision to be made based on a pre-modern/non-European normative order and concepts, but only sought consideration of special and unique circumstances within the context of the application of modern international law.

2.4 *Libya/Chad*

In this ICJ case involving a dispute over the boundary between Libya and Chad, it was Libya, who lost the case, that made assertions based on a pre-modern/non-European order claiming the existence of concepts of "sovereignty" and "State" unique to the Islamic world. According to Libya, title to the territory in question was, at all relevant times, vested in the Libyan peoples inhabiting the disputed area who owed allegiance to the Islamic Senoussi Order, and, on the

35 *Ibid.*, 44, para. 95.

36 *Ibid.*, 47–49, paras. 103–107.

international plane, there had existed a community of title between the title of the indigenous peoples and the titles of the Ottoman Empire, which was passed on to Italy and succeeded by Libya.[37] The foundation of Libya's assertion lay on the idea that, due to the special nature of the Islamic principles of State composition, the Islamic world had fundamentally not been concerned with concepts such as boundaries and territorial sovereignty.[38]

Chad, meanwhile, claimed that a treaty concluded between Libya and France in 1955 had determined the boundary line. As an alternative argument, it alleged that the boundary of a French sphere of influence, which had been defined by various treaties concluded prior to the abovementioned treaty, had acquired the character of boundaries through France's *effectivités*, or that it was possible to make a claim on account of those *effectivités* regardless of the treaty. Furthermore, it challenged Libya's claims based on the following points: (1) The Ottoman Empire had never had title to the disputed territory, neither on the basis of the exercise of effective control nor on any other basis, (2) The Senoussi Order had never been more than a source of religious influence, (3) The failure of the Ottomans and the Senoussi Order to establish an independent source of title was not retrieved by claiming joint sovereignty, and (4) The indigenous peoples had been the bearers of rights over the territory but had been insufficiently organized to possess territorial sovereignty under international law.[39]

In contrast to Libya's approach of emphasizing the relevance of the pre-modern/non-European normative order and territorial control, Chad, which dismissed control by the Ottomans and the Senoussi Order as merely being of a religious nature and asserted that the treaties concluded with colonial powers were of decisive importance, can be said to have maintained a stance of being faithful to modern international law. Eventually it was these arguments of Chad that the Court accepted.[40] To wit, the judgment was fully based on the

37 *Différend territorial (Jamahiriya arabe libyenne/Tchad)*, CIJ *Recueil 1994*, 13, para. 17.

38 Memorial of Libyan Arab Jamahiriya, *Libya/Chad*, vol. I, 31, para. 3.14.

39 Oral Proceedings, *Libya/Chad*, CR 1993/23, 29 June 1993, Chad, Professor Shaw, 63.

40 Burgis, focusing on the "postcolonial paradox," whereby States newly established through independence from their former colonizers had to make their assertions using international law, which enabled their decolonization yet simultaneously supported colonization, explains that, for this case, Chad, which was confronted by said paradox, opted for the logic of the colonial side, which would be familiar to the Court, and hence not surprisingly gained the Court's assent to its argument. Michelle L. Burgis, *Boundaries of Discourse in the International Court of Justice: Mapping Arguments in Arab Territorial Disputes* (Leiden: Martinus Nijhoff Publishers, 2009), 139.

1955 treaty and the Court did not enter into other discussions, not even any specific account of the individual assertions.[41]

2.5 *Eritrea/Yemen*

This was an arbitration between Eritrea and Yemen regarding the attribution of islands in the Red Sea and the delimitation of the maritime boundary between the two parties. The award in the first stage handled the attribution of islands. The two parties did not contest that the Red Sea islands had belonged to the Ottoman Empire, so the issue concerned the consequences of the Ottoman Empire's renunciation of title under Article 16 of the Treaty of Lausanne. In this regard, Yemen asserted the reversion of the Imam's historic or "ancient title" that could be traced back to the *Bilad el-Yemen* (realm of Yemen), which had supposedly existed in the 6th century.[42] As a result, territorial control under a pre-modern/non-European order on the Arabian Peninsula was brought into the Tribunal's considerations in at least two contexts.

The first is where the Tribunal, after confirming the loss of "continuity" of the Imam's title, which was a prerequisite for the claim of reversion, due to the existence of Ottoman sovereignty over the islands, discussed whether the long-standing common use of fishery resources and islands in the southern part of the Red Sea from the two opposite coasts might have any legal significance.[43] The Tribunal admitted that these socio-economic and cultural patterns had been "perfectly in harmony with classical Islamic law concepts" and positioned them as having had no relation to "the principle of 'territorial sovereignty' as it developed among the European powers and became a basic feature of 19th Century western international law." Nevertheless, the Tribunal concluded that, in as much as the Ottomans had "started to abandon the communal aspects of the Islamic system of international law" in the latter half of the 19th century, which had resulted in the adoption of modern international law, and as the concept of territorial sovereignty had become a bedrock for most States, "the situation in the Red Sea could no longer escape the juridical consequences" thereof.[44]

---

41 *Libye/Tchad*, *supra* note 37, 38–39, paras. 75–76.

42 *The Eritrea-Yemen Arbitration, First Stage: Territorial Sovereignty and Scope of the Dispute (Eritrea/Yemen)*, *Reports of International Arbitral Awards*, vol. XXII, 222, paras. 31–32 and 241, para. 116.

43 *Ibid.*, 244–245, paras. 127–131.

44 In this way, the Tribunal clearly denied the relevance of the traditional system in determining attribution of territory. At the same time, however, while citing the strangeness of ideas of territorial sovereignty to peoples brought up in the Islamic tradition and the need for "an appreciation of regional legal traditions" for the reestablishment and development

The second is where the Tribunal recited problems of ancient historic title itself, whose reversion was claimed.[45] To wit, it rejected the existence of ancient historic title for Yemen by highlighting the geographical reality that the area traditionally controlled by the Imam had been that of mountains with almost no coastline or islands, as well as the fact that pre-modern Yemen had not known the concept of territorial sovereignty. According to the Tribunal, "there is a problem of the sheer anachronism of attempting to attribute to such a tribal, mountain and Muslim medieval society the modern Western concept of a sovereignty title."[46]

2.6 *Kasikili/Sedudu Island*

This case before the ICJ involved a dispute over the location of the boundary and the attribution of an island in the boundary river between Botswana and Namibia. The Court reached a decision based on its interpretation of a treaty that had been concluded in 1890 by Great Britain and Germany to delimit their respective spheres of influence, while also engaging in a level of discussion regarding acquisitive prescription, which was put forth as an alternative argument by Namibia. In doing so, the Court reviewed the longstanding and unopposed use of the island by the Masubia people of Caprivi from the standpoint of (1) whether it represented subsequent practice in the application of the 1890 treaty and (2) whether it constituted possession as a requirement for prescription.

According to the Court, in order for (1) to be affirmed, said use needed to be linked to a belief on the part of the Caprivi authorities regarding the boundary laid down by the 1890 treaty, while the silence of Bechuanaland authorities on the other side of the river also needed to be based on its acceptance of the treaty boundary. Yet, the Court found that these criteria were not satisfied. One reason was that it had not been uncommon for the inhabitants of border regions in Africa to traverse such borders for purposes of agriculture and grazing, without raising concern on the part of the authorities on either side

of cooperation between the two parties via the award, the Tribunal ruled that the sovereignty over the islands recognized by the award entailed the perpetuation of the traditional fishing regime in the region and called on Yemen to realize this in the *dispositif* under (vi). *Ibid.*, 329–330, paras. 525–526. Antunes favorably assessed this as demonstrating the possibility of filling the gap between regional legal traditions and contemporary international law. Nuno S. M. Antunes, "The Eritrea-Yemen Arbitration: First Stage – The Law of Title to Territory Re-averred," *International and Comparative Law Quarterly*, vol. 48, issue 2 (1999), 385–386.

45 *Eritrea/Yemen, supra* note 42, 247–248, para. 143.

46 *Ibid.*, 311, para. 446.

of the border.[47] As for (2), relying on the concept of "indirect rule," Namibia maintained that the use by the Masubia people constituted a "continuous and peaceful display of the functions of state" that satisfied the requirement for prescription.[48] In response, the Court explained that even if links of allegiance might have existed between the Masubia and the Caprivi authorities, it had not been established that the members of this tribe had occupied the island *à titre de souverain*, i.e., that they had been exercising functions of State authority there on behalf of those authorities. The Court also pointed out that the Masubia had used the island intermittently for agricultural purposes, which had continued without change before and after the establishment of colonial administration in Caprivi. On the basis of these, it was concluded that the requirement for prescription was not satisfied.[49] Although Namibia provided detailed explanations of the nature and roles of the chiefs and organization of the Masubia, the Court did not delve into these matters.

2.7 *Qatar v. Bahrain*

This was an ICJ case in which Qatar and Bahrain disputed attribution of Zubarah on the west coast of the Qatar Peninsula and multiple islands located between the Qatar Peninsula and the main island of Bahrain. Both parties invoked pre-modern/non-European orders and concepts in their assertions.

Bahrain first presented this kind of argument regarding the attribution of Zubarah. More specifically, it cited, as norms which would substantiate its possession of full and internationally recognized title to the region from 1783 until 1937, "the regional standard of the fealty of the inhabitants of Zubarah to the Ruler of Bahrain," in line with "the international standard of contextually proportionate effective occupation." On this basis, Bahrain alleged that its control had extended to Zubarah through a tribal confederation led by the Naim people, who had remained faithful to the Bahrain's ruling Sheikhs not only before but also after they had moved their seat of government from Zubarah to the main island of Bahrain.[50] As for attribution of the Hawar Islands, Bahrain presented an alternative argument, in case its assertion based on the 1939 decision of Great Britain was not approved, relying on the "exercise of sovereign authority in the Hawar Islands" and "recognition of the title of Bahrain by the inhabitants of the islands." In doing so, it emphasized the relationship of

47 *Kasikili/Sedudu Island (Botswana/Namibia)*, *ICJ Reports 1999*, 1094–1095, paras. 73–75.

48 Memorial of the Republic of Namibia, *Botswana/Namibia*, vol. 1, paras. 218–232.

49 *Kasikili/Sedudu Island*, *supra* note 47, 1105–1106, paras. 98–99.

50 *Délimitation maritime et questions territoriales entre Qatar et Bahreïn (Qatar c. Bahreïn), fond*, *CIJ Recueil 2001*, 64–65, paras. 73–74.

allegiance between the resident Dowasir tribe and the Rulers of Bahrain from about 1800.[51] Qatar rebutted these theses with a citation of the *Western Sahara* advisory opinion, saying that "tribal allegiances, to support any claim for sovereignty, must be real and evidenced by acts manifesting acceptance of political authority."[52]

Conversely, Qatar itself relied on a pre-modern/non-European order and concepts in making a counterargument to Bahrain's assertion, apparently adhering to modern international law, that the handling, by its courts (Qadi), of cases related to land rights and fishing traps in the Hawar Islands constituted evidence of its display of authority.[53] According to Qatar, the duties of a Qadi consist of deciding disputes when two Muslims approach him for the purpose, and it was common for Qadis in one Muslim country to settle disputes between Muslim subjects of another country or in regard to property located in another country, so these did not constitute evidence to support Bahrain's sovereignty.[54]

In spite of the existence of the abovementioned points, the Court once again chose hardly to delve into them. Regarding the Hawar Islands, the Court rendered its ruling based solely on Great Britain's 1939 decision without entering into any other points of argument. In like manner, the conclusion that the rulers of Bahrain had never been in a position to engage in direct acts of authority in Zubarah was reached chiefly through the reflection on the content of the agreement between Bahrain and Great Britain. On the other hand, the claim of the exercise of control over Zubarah through the Naim tribe was rejected point-blank because there was no evidence that members of the Naim had exercised sovereign authority on behalf of the Sheikh of Bahrain within Zubarah, and moreover because "they came under the jurisdiction of the local territorial sovereign."[55] By what standards it made this assessment was not, however, indicated.

51 *Ibid.*, 71, para. 101; Memorial of the State of Bahrain, *Qatar v. Bahrain* (*Merits*), vol. I, 156–158, paras. 344–351.

52 Reply of the State of Qatar, *Qatar v. Bahrain* (*Merits*), Chapter IV, para. 4.160.

53 Memorial of Bahrain, *supra* note 51, 193, para. 433; *Qatar c. Bahreïn*, *supra* note 50, 71, para. 101.

54 Reply of Qatar, *supra* note 52, Chapter IV, para. 4.159 and para. 4.186.

55 *Qatar c. Bahreïn*, *supra* note 50, 67, paras. 83–86. Also, in determining that the attribution of Zubarah was to Qatar, the Court emphasized recognition by Great Britain and the Ottoman Empire of Qatar's control over the territory with little concern for specifying exactly what such control consisted of.

2.8 *Cameroon v. Nigeria*

In this case, the arguments related to a pre-modern/non-European order were posed regarding the attribution of the Bakassi Peninsula. Specifically, whereas Cameroon based its claims on the Anglo-German Treaty of 1913, Nigeria asserted the succession of the original title that had lain with the Kings and Chiefs of Old Calabar (hereinafter, "Old Calabar").[56] In order to establish said succession, Old Calabar had to be a subject which retained the title even after it had concluded the "Treaty of Protection" with Great Britain in 1884. In other words, Nigeria needed to prove that "protection" in the treaty had been that of an international protectorate established between sovereign States and not a "colonial protectorate" in which the side providing protection acquired sovereignty. Therefore, Nigeria asserted that Old Calabar at the time of the conclusion of the treaty had had – and had been recognized by European powers as having – effective territorial control equivalent to territorial sovereignty, even if its system of government had differed from that of European States existing within fixed boundaries. Furthermore, it stated that, in considering the status of local rulers in West Africa in the 19th century, it was important not to uncritically apply present-day terms and concepts so that those circumstances must be evaluated in light of the law as it had stood at the time.[57]

In response, the ICJ noted that in sub-Saharan Africa, "treaties of protection" had been entered into with local rulers who had not been States and that the side providing protection had acquired sovereignty, before citing numerous factors demonstrating that the 1884 treaty came under this category. Specifically, it mentioned, among other factors, the lack of evidence of a central federal power in Old Calabar, the existence of evidence indicating Britain had regarded itself as administering the territories not just protecting them, the absence of records of meetings that were characteristic of international protectorates, and the lack of reference to Old Calabar in various public documents listing Britain's protectorate countries and territories.[58] It should be noted that other than the absence of evidence of a central federal power, these factors refer to circumstances after the conclusion of the treaty. In other words, the Court dismissed Nigeria's assertion of the original title not by examining

56 *Frontière terrestre et maritime entre le Cameroun et le Nigéria* (*Cameroun c. Nigéria: Guinée équatoriale* (*intervenant*)), CIJ *Recueil 2002*, 400, para. 194.

57 Counter-Memorial of the Federal Republic of Nigeria, *Cameroon v. Nigeria*, vol. 1, 87–90. In response, Cameroon provided a detailed account of the international status and territorial scope of Old Calabar and refuted Nigeria's assertion as being mistaken. Réplique de la République du Cameroun, *Cameroun c. Nigéria*, Livre 1, 245–275.

58 *Cameroun c. Nigéria*, *supra* note 56, 404–407, paras. 203–209.

what kind of entity Old Calabar had been regarded as at the time of the conclusion of the treaty but by proving that the concluded treaty had not been a treaty of protection that had established an international protectorate. This enabled the Court to avoid getting into the nature of the pre-colonial territorial control and normative order in Africa and the status of African political entities in modern international law.

2.9 *Pulau Ligitan and Pulau Sipadan*

In this case involving a dispute between Indonesia and Malaysia over the attribution of the islands of Ligitan and Sipadan located in the Celebes Sea, both parties asserted original title with roots in a pre-modern/non-European normative order, the same as in *Minquiers and Ecrehos*. They respectively claimed attribution of the disputed islands to the Sultan of Bulungan (Indonesia) and the Sultan of Sulu (Malaysia).[59] Indonesia explained in detail how the nature of political power and territory, as well as the relationship between the two, in a kingdom ruled by a Sultan had differed from those of Europe and modern international law,[60] and asserted that the Sultan of Bulungan, who had controlled northern Borneo, had deemed the small uninhabited islands off the coast as his property based on this unique conception of territory.[61] Malaysia, meanwhile, maintained that the coastal territory of Borneo and its adjacent islands had been dependencies or dominions of the Sulu Kingdom from the 18th century until 1878 and that the control of these areas had resulted from the allegiance of the local people like the Bajau Laut as well as from the appointment of their local chiefs by the Sultan. It further stated that the islands in question had been used by the Bajau Laut. According to Malaysia, these factors formed the basis for the original title of the Sultan of Sulu.[62]

Remarkably, however, the ICJ's approach turned out to be different from that in *Minquiers and Ecrehos*. For Indonesia, the Court did not see any need to examine the existence or lack of original title and did not even mention the content of Indonesia's argument in the judgment. This is because the Court ruled out the very possibility of Indonesia's succession of title from the

59 *Sovereignty over Pulau Ligitan and Pulau Sipadan (Indonesia/Malaysia)*, *ICJ Reports 2002*, 643, paras. 32–33.

60 Memorial Submitted by the Government of the Republic of Indonesia, *Indonesia/Malaysia*, vol. I, 38–44.

61 Oral Proceedings, *Indonesia/Malaysia*, CR 2002/27, 3 June 2002, Indonesia, M. Pellet, 48–49.

62 Memorial of Malaysia, *Indonesia/Malaysia*, vol. I, 29–34, 61–65; Reply of Malaysia, *Indonesia/Malaysia*, 9–10; *Pulau Ligitan and Pulau Sipadan*, *supra* note 59, 669–670, paras. 97–98.

Netherlands by reviewing multiple contracts of vassalage concluded between the Sultan of Bulungan and the Netherlands so as to confirm that the islands in question had not been among those attributed to the Sultan through the contracts.[63] Regarding Malaysia's assertion, on the other hand, the Court acknowledged that "Malaysia relies on the ties of allegiance which allegedly existed between the Sultan of Sulu and the Bajau Laut who inhabited the islands off the coast of North Borneo and who from time to time may have made use of the two uninhabited islands." Nevertheless, it plainly dismissed the assertion by saying "that such ties may well have existed but that they are in themselves not sufficient to provide evidence that the Sultan of Sulu claimed territorial title to these two small islands or considered them part of his possessions. Nor is there any evidence that the Sultan actually exercised authority over Ligitan and Sipadan."[64]

2.10 *Pedra Branca/Pulau Batu Puteh*

In this case involving a dispute over the attribution of Pedra Branca/Pulau Batu Puteh (hereinafter, Pedra Branca), Middle Rocks, and South Ledge located near the eastern entrance of the Singapore Straits, Singapore claimed attribution to itself based on Britain's occupation of *terra nullius* in the mid-19th century and the succession of said title, while Malaysia once again asserted that it had succeeded original title, just like in the preceding case.[65]

Here, Malaysia relied on original title of the Sultanate of Johor established in the 16th century. However, in contrast to *Pulau Ligitan and Pulau Sipadan*, it did not attempt to prove territorial control by Johor, a pre-modern/non-European political entity, according to a pre-modern/non-European normative order. Instead, Malaysia offered proof based on Johor's relationship with European modern sovereign States and geographical features as follows.[66] First, Johor was recognized as an independent State by Europe in the 16th century as demonstrated by Hugo Grotius' record of Johor as "a sovereign principality" and Johor's conclusion of treaties with the Dutch East India Company. Second, the Crawfurd Treaty of 1824, other legal instruments and official British acts clearly demonstrated British recognition of Johor as an independent State. Third, Johor's protest against the seizure of junk ships by the Dutch in the mid-17th century, British internal documents from the beginning of the

63 *Ibid.*, 669, para. 96.

64 *Ibid.*, 675, para. 110.

65 *Sovereignty over Pedra Branca/Pulau Batu Puteh, Middle Rocks and South Ledge (Malaysia/Singapore)*, *ICJ Reports 2008*, 29–30, paras. 37–42.

66 Memorial of Malaysia, *Malaysia/Singapore*, vol. 1, 15–51.

19th century, Johor's taxation of Orang Laut who lived off the sea, and other evidence of control confirmed that all islands in the Straits were included in the territorial extent of Johor as a Sultanate extending to both coasts and that there were no islands regarded as *terra nullius* in the Straits. Finally, based upon a detailed examination of each of these points relating to Pedra Branca, Malaysia rejected the possibility of it having been *terra nullius* because it had been a well-known island and Johor had displayed its sovereignty over the island in accordance with the circumstances.

In response, Singapore countered with an assertion based around discussion of the differences between "traditional Malay notions of 'sovereignty'" and the European concept of territorial sovereignty, and comparison of the pre-modern/non-European normative order and modern international law, as follows.[67] (1) Traditional Malay notions of "sovereignty" were based on personal allegiance of inhabitants rather than territorial control. (2) Malaysia itself put forth the same assertion in *Pulau Ligitan and Pulau Sipadan*. (3) Malaysia did not mention (1) in this case because it would lead to the conclusion that as Pedra Branca was uninhabited, there were no people on it from whom allegiance could be sought by any ruler. (4) If Malaysia was to show that Pedra Branca had been under Johor sovereignty in accordance with modern international law, it had to demonstrate any intention or will to act as sovereign or any actual exercise or display of State authority over Pedra Branca, but it failed to do so. Therefore, "[w]hether examined within the local context of allegiance or under classical international law principles, Malaysia's claim to original title completely fails."[68]

The Court's decision was largely in line with Malaysia's arguments. First, it recognized the status of Johor as a sovereign State and confirmed the existence of a general acknowledgement until early in the 19th century that Johor's territorial and maritime domain had included the Singapore Straits and all islands in the area of the Straits. Then, having noted the reasonableness of the presumption that Pedra Branca, a known island, had been within Johor territory, it considered that Johor had satisfied the condition of "continuous and peaceful display of territorial sovereignty (peaceful in relation to other States)" over all islands in the Straits, and therefore affirmed that Johor had held original title to Pedra Branca.[69] As evidence of Johor being a "sovereign State," it only mentioned Grotius's description invoked by Malaysia. For the general acknowledgement of Johor's territorial extent, it relied on the junk ship seizures and

67 Counter-Memorial of Singapore, *Malaysia/Singapore*, 18–24, paras. 3.4–3.12.

68 *Ibid.*, 23, para. 3.11.

69 *Pedra Branca/Pulau Batu Puteh*, *supra* note 65, 33–37, paras. 52–68.

the perception of the British Resident in Singapore presented in three letters in 1824, as well as newspaper articles from 1834 as supplemental evidence. The Court inferred that Johor met the requirement of the display of sovereignty based on the two points that Pedra Branca had not been "*terra incognita*" and that there had been no claims from other States, without specifying any particular exercise of State authority. The Court accepted the Sultan's authority over the Orang Laut people as evidence of the exercise of sovereignty based on original title and did not examine the discussion about traditional Malay notions of "sovereignty." To conclude, in this case, the Court did acknowledge the existence of territorial control by a pre-modern/non-European political entity, Johor, and the relevance thereof to its decision of attribution but did not refer to the pre-modern/non-European normative order that should have been the foundation of said territorial control.

3 Decisions on Territorial Attribution and Pre-modern/Non-European Territorial Control

3.1 *Purpose and/or Intent of Parties Invoking Pre-modern/Non-European Territorial Control*

The judicial and arbitral cases covered in the preceding section show that in relation to modern international law, there are at least three types of purpose and/or intent when parties highlight the facts of pre-modern/non-European territorial control and uniqueness of the normative orders in proceedings concerning territorial attribution. First is to exclude an evaluation of the legal significance or effect of territorial control invoked by the party being made in accordance with the principles of modern international law. For example, in *Pulau Ligitan and Pulau Sipadan*, Indonesia made assertions bearing such an intent with respect to original title of the Sultan of Bulungan. Secondly, assuming that modern international law will serve as the evaluation standard, parties may assert the uniqueness of a particular pre-modern/non-European order and territorial control with the aim of seeking special consideration in the concrete application of modern international law. Morocco's allegation in *Western Saharan* is an example of this.

The third category puts forth the pre-modern/non-European order from a reverse perspective compared to the two abovementioned types. To elaborate, for cases in which the other party is claiming territorial sovereignty according to modern international law, this approach aims to derail the argument based on modern international law by demonstrating that the facts and factors used in said argument actually adhered to a pre-modern/non-European order. Qatar's counterargument regarding the "Qadi" cited by Bahrain as evidence of its exercise of sovereignty over Hawar Island in *Qatar v. Bahrain* and Singapore's assertion regarding traditional Malay notions of "sovereignty" in *Pedra Branca/Pulau Batu Puteh* are considered to have been made with this purpose in mind.

It is difficult to determine whether the arguments of Nigeria for Old Calabar's original title in *Cameroon v. Nigeria* and of Bahrain for original title related to Zubarah in *Qatar v. Bahrain* belong to the first or second type. In *Libya/Chad*, Libya could be said to have held both the first and second types of intent when it compared the "shared sovereignty of local tribes, Senoussi and Ottoman Empire" to the dividing or sharing of sovereignty under modern international law, for example in a condominium, while asserting the existence of concepts of sovereignty and State unique to the Islamic world.[70]

3.2 *Historic Title and Original Title*

Next, this section will make clear in relation to what sort of title the parties of the cases covered above did present the arguments of the uniqueness of facts of pre-modern/non-European territorial control and normative orders.

Title to territory is generally defined as the facts that provide the basis for a particular State to have territorial sovereignty over a particular land (i.e., vestitive facts). This definition might seem to call into question what territorial title States hold with regard to all of their territory. However, traditionally, the concept of title to territory has only been used for territory that an existing State is to newly acquire or lose.[71] Vestitive facts in traditional academic doctrine have been standardized as "modes of acquisition of territorial sovereignty," such as cession, occupation, and annexation. Among these "modes of acquisition," it is acquisitive prescription that deems long-term possession to be a component of a vestitive fact. There are two types of acquisitive prescription: acquisition of another State's territory through adverse possession against prior title and establishment of territorial title through possession over a long enough period

70 Reply submitted by the Great Socialist People's Libyan Arab Jamahiriya, *Libya/Chad*, vol. I, 224–225.

71 The territory of modern European States, which were taken as a given for the establishment of modern international law, or the territory forming a part of the qualification elements of statehood, fulfillment of which is required to establish a new State, are considered to be outside the scope of the legal framework of title to territory. Yanagihara Masaharu 柳原正治, "Kyōiki, Hanto, Hōdo, Soshite Ryōiki" 疆域、版図、邦土、そして領域 [Kyōiki, Hanto, Hōdo (Chinese and Japanese Notions of Territory), and Ryōiki (European Notion of Territory)], *Kokusai Mondai* 国際問題, no. 642 (2013), 1.

that it is no longer possible to confirm whether prior title existed. The latter type has been termed "immemorial possession."[72]

Meanwhile, considering the difficulty of applying traditional modes of acquisition to dispute resolution, courts and tribunals, based on the formula used in the *Island of Palmas* case, have come to recognize acquisition of territorial sovereignty on the basis of "continuous and peaceful display of State authority" or "display of sovereignty."[73] Here, title to territory differs from the traditional concept with its elements of dynamism, relativity, and non-uniformity.[74] Furthermore, the judgment in the *Fisheries* case presented the concept of historic title as determined based on the attitude of other States in response to the continuous exercise of State authority[75] or title obtained from historical consolidation as an "aggregation of various interests and relationships."[76] As suggested by the existence of a view that connects title based on the display of sovereignty to historical consolidation[77] and various understandings of the relationship between historic title and acquisitive prescription,[78] it is important to exercise caution in specifying concepts from terminology. Nevertheless, these concepts, including acquisitive prescription, can be characterized as title for the acquisition of territory that deem the long-term continuous exercise of State authority as a vestitive fact or a component thereof. This chapter refers to these as historic title (in a broad sense) for convenience.

72 See, e.g., David H. N. Johnson, "Acquisitive Prescription in International Law," *British Year Book of International Law*, vol. 27 (1950), 334–340; Randall Lesaffer, "Argument from Roman Law in Current International Law: Occupation and Acquisitive Prescription," *European Journal of International Law*, vol. 16, no. 1 (2005), 46–49.

73 Huh Sookyeon 許淑娟, "Ryōdo Kizoku Hōri no Kōzō – Kengen to *effectivités* o Meguru Gokai mo Fukumete" 領土帰属法理の構造 – 権原と *effectivités* をめぐる誤解も含めて [Structure of the Legal Doctrine of Territorial Attribution: Including Misunderstandings around Title and *Effectivités*], *Kokusai Mondai* 国際問題, no. 624 (2013), 22–26.

74 Huh, *supra* note 28, 138–141.

75 See, e.g., *Judicial Regime of Historic Waters, Including Historic Bays: Study Prepared by the Secretariat*, UN Doc. A/CN.4/143 (9 March 1962), 13, para. 80; Yefuda Z. Blum, *Historic Titles in International Law* (The Hague: Martinus Nijhoff, 1965), 99–192.

76 Charles de Visscher, *Théories et réalités en droit international public* (Paris: A. Pedone, 1953), 244–245.

77 For an overview of this opinion, see Huh, *supra* note 28, 181–185.

78 For example, while affirming the similarity of historic title and immemorial possession, some reject the adversary nature of historic title, while others accept historic title as a type of adverse title. For examples of the former and latter, respectively, see Judicial Regime, *supra* note 75, 11–12, paras. 62–68 and Marcelo G. Kohen, "Original Title in the Light of the ICJ Judgment on Sovereignty over Pedra Branca/Pulau Batu Puteh, Middle Rocks and South Ledge," *Journal of the History of International Law*, vol. 15 (2013), 154–155.

In the cases covered above, acquisitive prescription was asserted by Namibia in *Kasikili/Sedudu Island*; immemorial possession by Morocco in *Western Sahara*; and title based on the display of sovereignty by Denmark in *Eastern Greenland*, the United Kingdom in *Minquiers and Ecrehos*,[79] and Morocco in *Western Sahara*. Pre-modern/non-European territorial control was invoked within these respective frameworks.

Incidentally, if title to territory is considered to be title to acquire territory, territories deemed to have existed from the time of the establishment of a State should fall outside the scope of the legal framework of title to territory. It is notable, however, that recent academic discourse[80] has started using the concept of title as it discusses original title to such territories.[81] In this regard, whereas conventional title to territory is purported, in the setting of acquiring territory, to designate vestitive facts that legitimized acquisition, in the case of territory deemed to exist from the time of the establishment of a State, the vestitive facts are nothing but the very establishment of the State. Therefore, it is not correct to consider vestitive facts analogous to those respecting conventional territorial title as applicable also to original title, nor to perceive the judgment on existence or not of original title as being subject to identification of such vestitive facts.[82] Simply put, recognition of statehood invaluably accompanies the presence of original title. Hence, the primary issue regarding original title is existence or not of statehood, and if the answer is in the affirmative, the task of confirming the original title arises as the secondary issue. In this way, it becomes unnecessary to specify or apply the "norms regulating

79 See note 21.

80 *Ibid.*, 151–171; Sookyeon Huh, "Title to Territory in the Post-Colonial Era: Original Title and *Terra Nullius* in the ICJ Judgments on Cases Concerning Ligitan/Sipadan (2002) and Pedra Branca (2008)," *European Journal of International Law*, vol. 26 (2015), 709–725. As seen in the previous section, while the concept of original title already appeared in *Minquiers and Ecrehos*, the cases of *Ligitan and Sipadan* and *Pedra Branca/Pulau Batu Puteh* served as the catalysts for a full-fledged review in academic doctrine.

81 "Original title" in this context differs from previous use to distinguish between original acquisition and derivative acquisition of title. For more details, see Fukamachi Tomoko 深町朋子, "Ryōiki ni Kansuru Genshi Kengen – Ryōiki Kengen Ron wa Nani o Dokomade Atsukaunoka" 領域に関する原始権原 – 領域権原論は何をどこまで扱うのか [Original Title to Territory: To What and To What Extent Is the Legal Framework of Title to Territory Applied?], *Hōgaku Seminā* 法学セミナー, no. 765 (2018), 24–30.

82 For example, Judge Torres Bernárdez, who discussed the concept of original title in the dissenting opinion in *Qatar v. Bahrain*, seemed to consider there to be a mode of establishing original title to territory by a new State that differed from cases of the acquisition or loss of territory by an already existing State. Dissenting Opinion of Judge Torres Bernárdez, *Qatar v. Bahrain*, *ICJ Reports 2001*, 281–282, paras. 59–63.

'territorial' attribution" effective in the pre-modern/non-European order for the sake of deciding attribution. Another point to bear in mind is that when the exercise of State authority is invoked as evidence under the secondary issue, it looks similar to proving historic title (in the broad sense), such as title based on the display of sovereignty. A difference does exist, however, in that, while the exercise of State authority forms a vestitive fact that serves as the source of territorial title in the case of historic title, the exercise of State authority invoked as evidence of original title does not have such a function.

In the cases reviewed in the previous section, France and Britain in *Minquiers and Ecrehos*, Libya in *Libya/Chad*,[83] Malaysia and Indonesia in *Pulau Ligitan and Pulau Sipadan* and Malaysia in *Pedra Branca/Pulau Batu Puteh* made arguments employing the concept of original title. In *Minquiers and Ecrehos*, Britain adopted the term "an ancient title," which is deemed to be conceptually synonymous with original title. In *Eritrea/Yemen*, Yemen also invoked "an ancient title" or "an ancient historic title." Fry and Loja interpret this as being the same as immemorial possession,[84] but it should rather be understood as being comparable to original title. The reason is that the "ancient title" in this case was said to require nothing but proof of common repute,[85] which cannot be a vestitive fact but evidence employed to confirm the existence of title. Nigeria in *Cameroon v. Nigeria* can be regarded as claiming original title of a pre-modern/non-European political entity, but in principle did not use this terminology or concept.

3.3 *Responses of Courts and Tribunals – Is Pre-modern/Non-European Territorial Control Reviewed and/or Assessed?*

Now let us ask how the manner in which courts and tribunals handled the parties' assertions concerning pre-modern/non-European territorial control, with their respective intents, purposes and concepts of title described above, can be categorized.

As explained earlier, perhaps partly because of several well-known phrases from the judgment of *Minquiers and Ecrehos*, there seems to be a widely shared impression that "courts are unsympathetic towards invocations of normative orders or concepts that are different from modern international law." There are certainly examples, such as with Indonesia's assertion in *Pulau Ligitan and*

83 Among Libya's documents, it only used the expression "original title shared between the Senoussi and the Ottoman Empire" once, in its reply. Reply of Libyan Arab Jamahiriya, *Libya/Chad*, vol. 1, 244, para. 9.18.

84 Fry and Loja, *supra* note 12, 728.

85 *Eritrea/Yemen*, *supra* note 42, 239, para. 106.

Pulau Sipadan, in which the Court was extremely "unsympathetic" and did not even mention the existence of a party's argument regarding pre-modern/non-European territorial control in its judgment. In other instances, as with Libya's assertion in *Libya/Chad*, the portion of the judgment related to Hawar Islands in *Qatar v. Bahrain*, and the case of Singapore in *Pedra Branca/Pulau Batu Puteh*, a simple acknowledgement of the existence and content of allegations concerning the pre-modern/non-European territorial control was indeed provided. However, this was immediately followed by the indication that an in-depth review of such arguments was not necessary because a decision was made possible based on some other argument which had already been considered. In these cases, while the Courts surely rendered neither positive nor negative appraisals over the historical argument itself, the possibility cannot be denied that their reason for the very attitude of concentrating on other arguments might have lain in an intention to avoid delving into the issue of pre-modern/non-European territorial control distinct from that under international law. Yet again, a court or tribunal may address concepts and facts related to pre-modern/non-European territorial control only to dismiss them based on an evaluation from a modern international law perspective without considering the pre-modern/non-European normative order. This happened with Morocco in *Western Sahara*.[86]

All those cases notwithstanding, one must not overlook the fact that there are also cases in which a court or tribunal not only considered pre-modern/non-European territorial control but also concluded that this could lead to territorial sovereignty under modern international law. These cases can be divided into two types based on what was referred to in making a decision about pre-modern/non-European territorial control. The first is instances where pre-modern/non-European normative orders were referenced, as is seen in *Minquiers and Ecrehos*. The second is instances in which the existence of pre-modern/non-European territorial control was acknowledged and connected to territorial sovereignty under modern international law without explicit reference to the pre-modern/non-European normative order or direct application of principles and standards of modern international law, as is seen in *Eastern Greenland* and *Pedra Branca/Pulau Batu Puteh*. Then, the question to be asked here is what factors could lead a court or tribunal to review pre-modern/non-European territorial control and to incorporate the results into the decision on territorial sovereignty under modern international law.

86 However, as already noted, Morocco itself presented an argument based on concepts and rules of modern international law in this case.

The fact that, among the ten cases, the two concerning pre-modern Europe are both included in examples where a court or tribunal assessed pre-modern/non-European territorial control and connected it to territorial sovereignty suggests a possibility that whether the dispute concerns Europe or somewhere other than Europe affects the decision. It goes without saying that there is a vast difference in the extent to which European pre-modern orders and non-European ones differ from modern international law. The decision that "[s]o far as it is possible to apply modern terminology to the rights and pretensions of the kings of Norway in Greenland in the XIIIth and XIVth centuries, the Court holds that at that date these rights amounted to sovereignty and that they were not limited to the two settlements" should be understood as one made based on the assumption of fundamental continuity and "possib[ility] to apply modern terminology."

Furthermore, considering the cases of *Minquiers and Ecrehos* and *Pedra Branca/Pulau Batu Puteh*, the key to connecting pre-modern/non-European territorial control to a decision of territorial sovereignty might be adoption of the concept of original title. As demonstrated in *Western Sahara*, reliance on historic title (in the broad sense) would require the concrete existence of the exercise of modern State authority as a vestitive fact. In contrast, the review of original title in *Pedra Branca/Pulau Batu Puteh*, though it cited "continuous and peaceful display of territorial sovereignty (peaceful in relation to other States)" as a requirement, recognized such display without specifically identifying the particular exercise of State authority as already mentioned. Besides, owing to the characterization as confirmation of an already existing title, it was no longer necessary to reach a decision on the very existence or not of title through the identification and application of norms of territorial attribution under a pre-modern/non-European order.

Admittedly, in *Pedra Branca/Pulau Batu Puteh*, display of sovereignty appears to be playing the role of a vestitive fact for original title because the Court discussed the requirement of "continuous and peaceful display of territorial sovereignty (peaceful in relation to other States)" with reference to cases such as *Island of Palmas* and *Eastern Greenland*, which had affirmed establishment of title based on the display of sovereignty.[87] Such an understanding seems to be shared by the author who contrasts occupation of *terra nullius* and original title and argues that *Pedra Branca/Pulau Batu Puteh* has demonstrated that "a lower degree of evidence of *effectivités* is required" for the latter than the former. He regards this case as one that "is a concrete contribution

87 *Pedra Branca/Pulau Batu Puteh*, *supra* note 65, 35–37, paras. 62–67.

to the clarification of the territorial situation in Eastern Asia during the nineteenth century and a reaffirmation of the existence of longstanding States in that region which held original title over the territories located therein."[88] However, one cannot but doubt whether it could be treated as "a matter of degree" when no specific exercise of State authority has even been identified. In fact, theorists who properly understand that the judgment affirmed original title without a review of "display of sovereignty" have voiced concern about this type of attribution decision being "fragile."[89] Thus, opinions remain split on original title, both in terms of the content of the concept itself and in terms of its utility and applicability.

4 Conclusion

It has become apparent that, in many territorial disputes submitted to international courts and tribunals, as more than recorded in their decisions' texts, the parties did invoke as important argumentative points, and delivered detailed explanations on, pre-modern/non-European territorial control, while supposing a certain relationship to modern international law. Among them, for those that relied directly on the pre-modern/non-European order to claim pre-modern/non-European territorial control, in almost all cases, courts rejected its relevance or completely ignored it. On the other hand, as case study showed, the courts acknowledged the existence of pre-modern/non-European territorial control and its potential as a basis for decisions on territorial attribution in (1) cases involving pre-modern European territorial control and (2) cases involving non-European territorial control that use a concept of original title and do not attempt to prove territorial control based on a non-European order. The method utilized to prove original title in (2) was to confirm that the disputed area was within the scope of the territorial domain controlled by a non-European political entity as a "State" based on documents and other evidence from which the territorial perception of the time could be reconstructed. It is admitted that the "continuous and peaceful display of territorial sovereignty (peaceful in relation to other States)" was referred to as a requirement, but this was not accompanied by any substantiation with the concrete exercise of State authority.

88 Kohen, *supra* note 78, 170–171.
89 Huh, *supra* note 80, 724–725.

In the end, it becomes clear that the point that distinguished *Pedra Branca/ Pulau Batu Puteh*, in which original title of a pre-modern/non-European political entity was recognized, from the cases of *Eritrea/Yemen* and *Cameroon v. Nigeria*, in which it was rejected, was whether the Court recognized the "statehood" of the pre-modern/non-European political entity. From this point should arise the next task for finally ascertaining the significance of pre-modern/non-European territorial control in today's decisions on territorial attribution: to clarify what concept of "Statehood" the courts assume and with what decision standards and methods they assess the correspondence of a pre-modern/non-European political entity to the concept assumed.

Bibliography

Primary Sources

Western Language

"Diaoyu Dao, an Inherent Territory of China." State Council Information Office, People's Republic of China. http://www.diaoyudao.org.cn/en/2015-01/25/content_34649357.htm.

"The Senkaku Islands: Let's see China's Argument." Office of Policy Planning and Coordination on Territory and Sovereignty, Cabinet Secretariat. https://www.cas.go.jp/jp/ryodo_eg/taiou/senkaku/senkaku01-05.html.

Secondary Sources

Japanese

Fukamachi, Tomoko 深町朋子. "Ryōiki ni Kansuru Genshi Kengen – Ryōiki Kengen Ron wa Nani o Dokomade Atsukaunoka" 領域に関する原始権原 – 領域権原論は何をどこまで扱うのか [Original Title to Territory: To What and To What Extent Is the Legal Framework of Title to Territory Applied?]. *Hōgaku Seminā* 法学セミナー, no. 765 (2018), 24–30.

Huh, Sookyeon 許淑娟. *Ryōiki Kengen Ron – Ryōiki Shihai no Jikkōsei to Seitōsei* 領域権原論 – 領域支配の実効性と正当性 [The Acquisition of Territory in International Law: The Effectiveness and Legitimacy of Territorial Control]. Tokyo: University of Tokyo Press, 2012.

Huh, Sookyeon 許淑娟. "Ryōdo Kizoku Hōri no Kōzō – Kengen to *effectivités* o Meguru Gokai mo Fukumete" 領土帰属法理の構造 － 権原と *effectivités* をめぐる誤解も含めて [Structure of the Legal Doctrine of Territorial Attribution: Including Misunderstandings around Title and *Effectivités*]. Kokusai Mondai 国際問題, no. 624 (2013): 20–34.

Matsui Yoshirō 松井芳郎. *Kokusaihō Gakusha ga Yomu Senkaku Mondai – Funsō Kaiketsu eno Tenbō o Hiraku* 国際法学者がよむ尖閣問題 – 紛争解決への展望を拓く [Senkaku Islands Issue from the Perspective of an International Law Scholar: Seeking a Path to Resolve the Dispute]. Tokyo: Nippon Hyōronsha, 2014.

Yanagihara Masaharu 柳原正治. "Kyōiki, Hanto, Hōdo, Soshite Ryōiki" 疆域、版図、邦土、そして領域 [Kyōiki, Hanto, Hōdo (Chinese and Japanese Notions of Territory), and Ryōiki (European Notion of Territory)]. *Kokusai Mondai* 国際問題, no. 642 (2013): 1–4.

Western Languages

Antunes, Nuno S. M. "The Eritrea-Yemen Arbitration: First Stage – The Law of Title to Territory Re-averred." *International and Comparative Law Quarterly* 48, issue 2 (1999): 362–386.

Blum, Yehuda Z. *Historic Titles in International Law.* The Hague: Martinus Nijhoff, 1965.

Burgis, Michelle L. *Boundaries of Discourse in the International Court of Justice: Mapping Arguments in Arab Territorial Disputes.* Leiden: Martinus Nijhoff Publishers, 2009.

Cheng, Tao. "The Sino-Japanese Dispute Over the Tiao-yu-tai (Senkaku) Islands and the Law of Territorial Acquisition." *Virginia Journal of International Law* 14 (1974): 221–266.

de Visscher, Charles. *Théories et réalités en droit international public.* Paris: A. Pedone 1953.

Fry, James D., and Melissa H. Loja. "The Roots of Historic Title: Non-Western Pre-Colonial Normative Systems and Legal Resolution of Territorial Disputes." *Leiden Journal of International Law* 27, issue 3 (2014): 727–754.

Huh, Sookyeon. "Title to Territory in the Post-Colonial Era: Original Title and *Terra Nullius* in the ICJ Judgments on Cases Concerning Ligitan/Sipadan (2002) and Pedra Branca (2008)." *European Journal of International Law* 26 (2015): 709–725.

Johnson, David H. N. "Acquisitive Prescription in International Law." *British Year Book of International Law* 27 (1950): 332–354.

Judicial Regime of Historic Waters, Including Historic Bays: Study Prepared by the Secretariat. UN Doc. A/CN.4/143, March 9, 1962.

Kohen, Marcelo G. "Original Title in the Light of the ICJ Judgment on Sovereignty over Pedra Branca/Pulau Batu Puteh, Middle Rocks and South Ledge." *Journal of the History of International Law* 15 (2013): 151–171.

Lee, Keun-Gwan. "An Enquiry into the Palimpsestic Nature of Territorial Sovereignty in East Asia – with Particular Reference to the Senkaku/Diaoyudao Question." In *Sovereignty, Statehood and State Responsibility: Essays in Honour of James Crawford,* edited by Christine Chinkin and Freya Baetens, 126–143. Cambridge: Cambridge University Press, 2015.

Lesaffer, Randall. "Argument from Roman Law in Current International Law: Occupation and Acquisitive Prescription." *European Journal of International Law* 16, no. 1 (2005): 25–58.

Shaw, Han-yi. "Revisiting the Diaoyutai/Senkaku Islands Dispute: Examining Legal Claims and New Historical Evidence under International Law and the Traditional East Asian World Order." *Chinese (Taiwan) Yearbook of International Law and Affairs* 26 (2008): 95–168.

Shaw, Malcolm N. *International Law, 9th ed.* Cambridge: Cambridge University Press, 2021.

Su, Steven W. "The Territorial Dispute over the Tiaoyu/Senkaku Islands: An Update." *Ocean Development & International Law* 36, issue 1 (2005): 45–61.

CHAPTER 9

Recognition of the Existence of Territorial Sovereignty Disputes in International Courts and Tribunals

The Use of the Coastal State Litigation before the Annex VII Arbitration of the UN Convention on the Law of the Sea

Dai Tamada

1 Introduction

This chapter clarifies the method for obtaining recognition of the existence of territorial sovereignty disputes (territorial disputes)[1] in international courts and tribunals. For example, in the case of Takeshima (known as Dokdo in the Republic of Korea (ROK)), there is a method for *forcibly* (i.e., even if the ROK protests) obtaining *objective recognition* (i.e., by international courts and tribunals) of the existence of a territorial sovereignty dispute between Japan and the ROK. Why is it necessary to obtain *recognition* even though (it appears that) a territorial sovereignty dispute regarding Takeshima exists? The answer is that the first and most significant hurdle to settle territorial sovereignty disputes is a conflict of views on *whether a territorial sovereignty dispute exists*. For Takeshima, the Japanese Government asserts that the existence of a territorial sovereignty dispute is an "objective fact"[2] (though this is Japan's subjective opinion). The ROK, meanwhile, asserts that "Dokdo *is not subject to territorial dispute*, and there is no reason for the Republic of Korea to prove its sovereignty

1 This chapter refers to disputes regarding the existence of territorial sovereignty as "territorial sovereignty disputes" or "sovereignty disputes."

2 In response to a question by Diet Member Asano Takahiro about whether there is agreement between the Japanese and ROK Governments that there exists a territorial issue regarding Takeshima, the Japanese Government explained that "The Government thinks the existence of a *territorial issue* regarding Takeshima that needs to be settled with the ROK is an *objective fact*" (emphasis added). This can be found in the written answer to a resubmitted question by Diet Member Asano Takahiro requesting the Ministry of Foreign Affairs' opinion on Japanese citizens visiting Takeshima while adhering to ROK legal procedures. (August 23, 2011: Prime Minister Kan Naoto) at http://www.shugiin.go.jp/internet/itdb_shitsumon_pdf_t.nsf/html/shitsumon/pdfT/b177395.pdf/$File/b177395.pdf.

 DOI:10.1163/9789004706361_010

over Dokdo before international courts" (emphasis added).[3] (This is also a subjective opinion.) The key point here is the two-tiered structure of the ROK Government's assertion that (1) since there is no territorial sovereignty "dispute" over Dokdo, (2) there is no reason to use "dispute" settlement procedures (including diplomatic negotiations and the International Court of Justice (ICJ) referral). In fact, the Japanese Government has proposed the joint referral of the matter to the ICJ three times,[4] but the ROK Government has rejected these proposals *on the basis of the non-existence of* a territorial sovereignty *dispute*.[5] As this shows, when exploring the use of "dispute" settlement procedures (including negotiations), the first issue to be overcome is the assertion denying the existence of a territorial sovereignty dispute ((1) above). As long as the other State does not recognize the existence of a "dispute," there is no chance of utilizing a "dispute" settlement procedure.[6] Conversely, if, hypothetically,

3 "Position of the Government of Korea on Dokdo" at http://overseas.mofa.go.kr/jp-sendai-ja/brd/m_623/view.do?seq=683039&srchFr=&srchTo=&srchWord=&srchTp=&multi_itm_seq=0&itm_seq_1=0&itm_seq_2=0&company_cd=&company_nm=&page=24. The ROK Government also makes the following assertion. "Dokdo is an integral part of Korean territory, historically, geographically and under international law. *No territorial dispute exists* regarding Dokdo, and therefore Dokdo is not a matter to be dealt with through diplomatic negotiations or judicial settlement" (emphasis added). "The Korean Government's Basic Position on Dokdo" at http://dokdo.mofa.go.kr/jp/dokdo/government_position.jsp.

4 Ministry of Foreign Affairs "Proposal of Referral to the International Court of Justice" at https://www.mofa.go.jp/mofaj/area/takeshima/g_teiso.html. In past proposals, Japan has proposed joint referral of the matter through the conclusion of a special agreement.

5 When Japan proposed referral to the ICJ in a note verbale dated September 12, 1954, the ROK rejected the proposal and provided the following explanation in a memorandum on October 28, 1954. "The proposal of the Japanese Government to have the matter be taken to the International Court of Justice is nothing but another attempt at the false claim in judicial disguise. The ROK has the territorial rights *ab initio* over Dokdo and sees no reason why she should seek the verification of her rights before the International Court of Justice. It is Japan who conjures up a quasi territorial dispute where *none should exist*" (emphasis added). Serita Kentaro 芹田健太郎, *Shima no Ryōyū to Keizai Suiiki no Kyōkai Kakutei* 島の領有と経済水域の境界画定 [Island Possession and Economic Zone Delimitation] (Tokyo: Yushindo Kobunsha, 1999), 237–238.

6 Sakamoto Shigeki offers the following explanation. "It has to be said that there is almost no possibility of the ROK, which has taken the position that there is no dispute regarding Takeshima, concluding a special agreement to entrust the dispute to the ICJ." Sakamoto Shigeki 坂元茂樹, "Kaiyō Kyōkai Kakutei to Ryōdo Funsō –Takeshima to Senkakushotō no Kage–" 海洋境界画定と領土紛争—竹島と尖閣諸島の影— [Maritime Boundary Delimitation and Territorial Disputes: Shadow of Takeshima and the Senkaku Islands], *Kokusai Mondai* 国際問題, no. 565 (2007), 25. While there is the option of unilateral referral relying on *forum prorogatum*, there is almost no possibility of the ROK actually appearing before the ICJ. Tamada Dai 玉田大, "Takeshima Funsō wa Kokusai Shihō Saibansho ni

the existence of a territorial sovereignty dispute over Takeshima is *objectively* and *forcibly* recognized, this would eliminate the basis for the ROK's assertion that "there is no territorial sovereignty dispute over Takeshima (Dokdo)" ((1) above) and therefore also the basis for rejecting use of a "dispute" settlement procedure (negotiations or ICJ proceedings; (2) above). The contribution of this chapter concerns this point. It will ultimately conclude that it is indeed possible to obtain recognition of the existence of a territorial sovereignty dispute through the "coastal State litigation" before the Annex VII Arbitration of the United Nations Convention on the Law of the Sea (UNCLOS).

2 Criteria for the Existence of Disputes under International Law

2.1 *Definition of "Dispute"*

The ROK asserts that "there is no territorial sovereignty dispute over Takeshima," but is such an assertion actually even accepted? Since the establishment of the Permanent Court of International Justice (PCIJ), there have been many international precedents regarding the concept of "dispute" in international law and today, "case law" on the subject has been established.[7] The foundation is the formula presented by the PCIJ in the Mavrommatis Palestine Concession case (1924): "a dispute is a disagreement on a point of law or fact, a conflict of legal views or of interests."[8] This formula uses an extremely broad definition of the "dispute" concept and has been subjected to substantial criticism. Nevertheless, it continues to be applied in ICJ judgments today.[9] The threshold

Mochikomenai?" 竹島紛争は国際司法裁判所に持ち込めない？ [Is It Possible to Bring the Takeshima Dispute to the International Court of Justice?], in Morikawa Koichi 森川幸一, et al. (eds.), *Kokusaihō de Sekai ga Wakaru* 国際法で世界がわかる (Tokyo: Iwanami Publishing, 2016), 245–253.

7 The ICJ used the expression "the established case law of the Court" in the case on obligations in nuclear disarmament negotiations (2016). *Obligations concerning Negotiations Relating to Cessation of the Nuclear Arms Race and to Nuclear Disarmament* (*Marshall Islands v. United Kingdom*), *Preliminary Objections*, Judgement of 5 October 2016, *I.C.J. Reports 2016*, 849, para. 37.

8 *Mavrommatis Palestine Concessions* (*Greece v. the United Kingdom*), Judgment of 30 August 1924, *P.C.I.J., Series A, no.* 2, 11.

9 Refer to the following sources on the definition of "dispute" in case law. Tamada Dai 玉田大, "'Funsō' no Sonzai – Kakugunshuku Kōshō Gimu Jiken (Māsharu Shotō Tai Igirisu)"『紛争』の存在—核軍縮交渉義務事件（マーシャル諸島対イギリス） [Existence of "Dispute": Case on Obligations concerning Nuclear Disarmament Negotiations (Marshall Islands vs. the United Kingdom)], in Morikawa Koichi 森川幸一, et al. (eds.), *Kokusaihō Hanrei Hyakusen* 国際法判例百選, 3rd Edition (Tokyo: Yuhikaku Publishing, 2021), 188–189.

for the existence of a "dispute" is thus set quite low. If there is a conflict of views between two States regarding where territorial sovereignty lies, a territorial sovereignty "dispute" exists.

2.2 *Standard for the Denial of a Dispute*

On the other hand, when the broad definition of "dispute" cited above is used, it risks generating a "dispute" even in cases in which State A makes an assertion against State B without any basis and State B refutes that assertion. For example (as an imaginary case), if the Japanese Government claimed territorial sovereignty over all of the United States (US) and the US rejected this claim, a territorial sovereignty "dispute" would exist between the two countries. To eliminate this type of extreme assertion, it has been generally thought that "mere assertions" are not enough to give rise to a dispute.[10] While details of the ROK Government's position on Takeshima are still unclear, it can be understood as taking a position that the Japanese Government's opinion (assertion of territorial sovereignty over Takeshima) is just a "mere assertion" and hence a "dispute" does not exist between the two countries. The following section considers the "mere assertion" concept in international judicial precedents.

2.2.1 The South West Africa Cases (1962)

The ICJ offers the following explanation in the South West Africa cases (Preliminary Objections Judgment, 1962). "[For the existence of a dispute] it is not sufficient for one State to a contentious case to assert that a dispute exists with the other State. *A mere assertion is not sufficient* to prove the existence of a dispute any more than a mere denial of the existence of the dispute proves its non-existence" (emphasis added).[11] In this way, for a "dispute" to exist, the claim by one State must, to some extent, be convincing and have an actual basis, and not be a "mere assertion." The next question, hence, is the standard for deciding whether a certain assertion is a "mere assertion" or not.

10 Kotera Akira 小寺彰, "Ryōdo Mondai no Shori Isoguna" 領土問題の処理急ぐな [Avoid Rushing Handling of Territorial Issues], *Nihon Keizai Shimbun* 日本経済新聞 (available on the Research Institute of Economy, Trade and Industry website) at https://www.rieti.go.jp/jp/papers/contribution/kotera/09.html.

11 *South West Africa Cases* (*Ethiopia v. South Africa; Liberia v. South Africa*), *Preliminary Objections*, Judgment, *I.C.J. Reports 1962*, 319, 328.

2.2.2 The Coastal State Rights Case (2020)

The backdrop to the Coastal State Rights case (Annex VII Arbitration of UNCLOS, 2020)[12] is a territorial sovereignty dispute over the Crimean Peninsula, but deserving of attention is the content of the assertions by the parties in the case. The applicant, Ukraine, asserted that Crimea was clearly part of its territory and therefore that a sovereignty "dispute" could not exist between the two countries.[13] This stance means that there is absolutely no basis for Russia's assertion on the territorial sovereignty over Crimea and hence a "dispute" has not occurred. Meanwhile, the respondent, Russia, asserted that the Tribunal had no jurisdiction because of the existence of a sovereignty "dispute" over Crimea, which went beyond the jurisdiction of the Tribunal. The Tribunal rejected Ukraine's assertion that Russia's sovereignty assertion was implausible,[14] but issued the following comment on the standard for recognition of a sovereign dispute. "Jurisprudence of international courts or tribunals also shows that the threshold for establishing the existence of a dispute is rather low. Certainly a mere assertion would be insufficient in proving the existence of a dispute. However, it does not follow that the validity or strength of the assertion should be put to a plausibility or other test in order to verify the existence of a dispute."[15] As this indicates, the Tribunal confirms that a "dispute" does not exist just from a "mere assertion" by one State but makes it clear that plausibility should not be the standard for the existence of a dispute. Furthermore, as shown below, the Tribunal concluded that a sovereignty "dispute" existed between the two countries regarding Crimea.

> The Arbitral Tribunal does not consider that the Russian Federation's claim of sovereignty is a mere assertion or one which was fabricated solely to defeat its jurisdiction. The Arbitral Tribunal notes that since March 2014, both States have held opposite views on the status of Crimea, and this situation persists today. The States have engaged in the controversy regarding sovereignty before and outside these proceedings, including in various international fora such as in debates at the UNGA. Even if the

---

12 *Dispute Concerning Coastal State Rights in the Black Sea, Sea of Azov, and Kerch Strait* (*Ukraine v. The Russian Federation*), PCA Case no. 2017–06, in the matter of an Arbitration before an Arbitral Tribunal constituted under Annex VII to the 1982 United Nations Convention on the Law of the Sea, Award concerning the Preliminary Objections of the Russian Federation, 21 February 2020, at https://pca-cpa.org/en/cases/149/.

13 In this case, Ukraine asserted that Russia's sovereignty argument was implausible. *Ibid.*, para. 183.

14 *Ibid.*, para. 187.

15 *Ibid.*, para. 188.

> Arbitral Tribunal applied an additional element of [the awareness of the respondent],[16] the Arbitral Tribunal's finding on the existence of a sovereignty dispute over Crimea would not change.[17]

Hence, regarding Crimea's territorial attribution, even though the United Nations General Assembly (UNGA) resolution confirmed Ukraine's sovereignty over Crimea, the Tribunal recognized the existence of a "dispute" based on the opposite views between the two States on Crimea's territorial sovereignty.

2.2.3 The Indian Ocean Maritime Boundary Delimitation Case (2021)

In the Indian Ocean Maritime Boundary Delimitation case (ITLOS Special Chamber, 2021),[18] in contrast to the Coastal State Rights case described above, the ITLOS Chamber denied the existence of a territorial sovereignty "dispute." While the case involved the delimitation of the boundary between Mauritius and the Maldives, the hidden point of contention at the preliminary objections stage was the location of the base line used for the boundary delimitation (in other words, whether territorial sovereignty over the Chagos Archipelago should be attributed to Mauritius or the United Kingdom). The following two decisions are important in this case. First, the Annex VII Arbitral Tribunal had recognized the existence of a territorial sovereignty dispute between Mauritius and the United Kingdom in the Chagos Marine Protected Area (MPA) case (Annex VII Arbitration of UNCLOS, 2015 Judgment)[19] and concluded that it did not have jurisdiction to decide which State is the "coastal State" (explained

---

16 In the Nuclear Arms and Disarmament case, the ICJ required the respondent to be "aware" of the conflict of views as a requirement for the existence of a dispute. ICJ Precedent Study Group 国際司法裁判所判例研究会, "Kakugunbi Kyōsō no Teishi to Kakugunbi no Shukushō ni Kansuru Kōshōgimu Jiken (Māsharu Shotō Tai Eikoku) (Senketsuteki Koben Hanketsu 2016 Nen 10 Gatsu 5 Ka)" 核軍備競争の停止と核軍備の縮小に関する交渉義務事件（マーシャル諸島対英国）（先決的抗弁判決・2016年 10月 5日） [*Obligations concerning Negotiations Relating to Cessation of the Nuclear Arms Race and to Nuclear Disarmament* (*Marshall Islands v. United Kingdom*) (Preliminary Objections Judgment, October 5, 2016)], *Kokusaihō Gaikō Zasshi* 国際法外交雑誌, vol. 116, no. 2 (2017), 97–114.

17 Award of 21 February 2020, para. 189.

18 *Delimitation of the maritime boundary between Mauritius and Maldives in the Indian Ocean (Mauritius/Maldives)*, Preliminary Objections, Judgment of 28 January 2021, at https://www.itlos.org/en/main/cases/list-of-cases/dispute-concerning-delimitation-of-the-maritime-boundary-between-mauritius-and-maldives-in-the-indian-ocean-mauritius/maldives-2/.

19 In the Matter of the Chagos Marine Protected Area Arbitration before an Arbitral Tribunal Constituted under Annex VII of the United Nations Convention on the Law of the Sea between the Republic of Mauritius and the United Kingdom of Great Britain and

below). Second, in the Legal Consequences of the Separation of the Chagos Archipelago from Mauritius case (Advisory Opinion, 2019), the ICJ decided that separation of the Chagos Archipelago from Mauritius infringed Mauritius' right to self-determination and concluded that the United Kingdom had an obligation to bring to an end its administration of the Chagos Archipelago as rapidly as possible.[20]

In this case (the Indian Ocean Maritime Boundary Delimitation case), the Maldives submitted preliminary objections to assert that the ITLOS Special Chamber lacked jurisdiction because of the existence of a territorial sovereignty dispute over the Chagos Archipelago between the United Kingdom and Mauritius (i.e., application of the Monetary Gold Principle). Meanwhile, Mauritius countered that the "dispute" between the United Kingdom and Mauritius no longer existed following the ICJ's Advisory Opinion in 2019. Regarding this point, the Special Chamber confirmed that the ICJ Advisory Opinion was not legally binding but did have considerable implications for the sovereignty claim of Mauritius and "could be interpreted as suggesting" Mauritius' sovereignty over the Chagos Archipelago.[21] Furthermore, the Chamber referred to the "dispute" between the United Kingdom and Mauritius in the following manner. "If, indeed, the ICJ has determined that the Chagos Archipelago is a part of the territory of Mauritius, as Mauritius asserts, the continued claim of the United Kingdom to sovereignty over the Chagos Archipelago cannot be considered anything more than 'a mere assertion'. However, such assertion *does not prove the existence of a dispute*" (emphasis added).[22] As explained above, because the ICJ rendered an opinion (Advisory Opinion) suggesting the attribution of the Chagos Archipelago's sovereignty, the United Kingdom's claim of territorial sovereignty over the Chagos Archipelago became a "mere assertion." Since this means that there is not a territorial sovereignty "dispute" between the two countries, the Special Chamber concluded that "Mauritius can be regarded as the coastal State in respect of the Chagos Archipelago."[23]

The judicial and arbitral precedents mentioned above clarify the following points. First, according to the definition of "dispute" in precedents, a conflict

Northern Ireland, PCA Case no. 2011–03, Award of 18 March 2015, at https://pca-cpa.org/en/cases/11/.

20 *Legal Consequences of the Separation of the Chagos Archipelago from Mauritius in 1965*, Advisory Opinion of 25 February 2019, *I.C.J. Reports 2019*, 140, para. 183.

21 Judgment of 28 January 2021, *supra* note 18, para. 174.

22 *Ibid.*, para. 243.

23 *Ibid.*, para. 249.

of views between two countries immediately generates a "dispute." However, for the existence of a "dispute," there needs to be a certain degree of validity or strength on a claim (without requiring the plausibility of the content of the claim). Second, when a claim of a State is a "mere assertion," there can be no "dispute." Two standards apply in deciding whether a claim is a "mere assertion." (1) Even when an UNGA resolution rejects a claim of territorial sovereignty of a State, if there has been controversy regarding sovereignty inside and outside the proceedings, including in various international fora, and the States have participated in this, then the claim of one of the States does not constitute a "mere assertion." Hence, a "dispute" exists (the Coastal State Rights case).[24] Conversely, (2) if an ICJ decision (even if it is an Advisory Opinion and not a Judgment) rejects a claim of territorial sovereignty by a State, the claim is treated as a "mere assertion" and the existence of a "dispute" cannot be recognized (the Indian Ocean Maritime Boundary Delimitation case). As this shows, the "mere assertion" concept is handled quite restrictively, and denial of the existence of a "dispute" is limited to exceptional circumstances. Taking Takeshima as an example, the Japanese Government's assertion of territorial sovereignty over Takeshima has not been rejected by an "authoritative determination" from a judicial body such as the ICJ, and there is no possibility of it being treated as a "mere assertion." Hence, the ROK Government's assertion that Dokdo "is not subject to dispute" cannot be accepted. The next question is how to obtain an objective recognition of the existence of a dispute by a judicial or arbitral body, when a State denies the existence of a dispute.

3 The Coastal State Litigation under UNCLOS

3.1 *Characteristics of the Annex VII Arbitration*

The method of obtaining recognition of the existence of a territorial sovereignty dispute in international courts and tribunals is to use the coastal State

24 The ITLOS Special Chamber gave the following explanation for why a claim that has been rejected by UNGA would still not be treated as a "mere assertion." "The Annex VII Arbitral Tribunal did not have the benefit of prior authoritative determination of the main issues relating to sovereignty claims to Crimea by any judicial body." *Ibid.*, para. 244. In other words, since an UNGA resolution is not an "authoritative determination" by a "judicial body," a claim rejected by such a resolution is not treated as a "mere assertion."

litigation within the Annex VII Arbitration of UNCLOS. The procedural characteristics of this Arbitration can be summarized as follows.[25]

Firstly, the jurisdiction of the Annex VII Arbitration can be compulsorily established (in cases between UNCLOS States Parties). According to UNCLOS, a State Party shall be free to choose the means for the settlement of disputes (Article 287), and if the disputing Parties have accepted the same procedure, the dispute may be submitted only to that procedure (Article 287, Paragraph 4). However, if the disputing States have not accepted the same procedure for the settlement of the dispute, it may be submitted only to arbitration in accordance with Annex VII (Article 287, Paragraph 5). This means that Annex VII Arbitration has de facto compulsory jurisdiction. For example, since neither Japan nor the ROK have selected a procedure (Article 287),[26] jurisdiction is automatically assigned to Annex VII Arbitration. Secondly, similar to ICJ judgements, awards by Annex VII Arbitration are also legally binding.[27] While there have been some cases of non-compliance with arbitral awards in recent years (for example, Russia in the Arctic Sunrise case and China in the South China Sea case), such non-compliance is not legally permissible.[28]

3.2 *Structure of the Coastal State Litigation*

The jurisdiction *ratione materiae* of Annex VII Arbitration is limited to "any dispute concerning the interpretation or application of this Convention [UNCLOS]" (Article 288, Paragraph 1). Regarding territorial sovereignty itself, UNCLOS does not provide any specific provisions[29] or define any

25 Tamada Dai 玉田大, "UNCLOS Dispute Settlement Mechanism: Contribution to the Integrity of UNCLOS," *Japanese Yearbook of International Law*, vol. 61 (2018) [March 2019], 132–166.

26 Refer to the ITLOS website regarding individual States Parties' choices of procedure (Article 287); https://www.itlos.org/en/main/jurisdiction/declarations-of-states-parties/declarations-made-by-states-parties-under-article-287/.

27 UNCLOS Article 296 Paragraph 1 stipulates, "Any decision rendered by a court or tribunal having jurisdiction under this section shall be final and shall be complied with by all the parties to the dispute," and Paragraph 2 stipulates, "Any such decision shall have no binding force except between the parties and in respect of that particular dispute." While there is a procedure for enforcement in the case of non-compliance with an ICJ judgment (United Nations Charter, Article 94, Paragraph 2), there is no such procedure under UNCLOS.

28 Regarding China's refusal to comply with the arbitral award in the South China Sea case, see Tamada Dai, *supra* note 25, 163–164.

29 Robert W. Smith and Bradford L. Thomas, "Island Disputes and the Law of the Sea: An Examination of Sovereignty and Delimitation Disputes," *Maritime Briefing*, vol. 2, no. 4 (1998), 16; Géraldine Giraudeau, "A Slight Revenge and a Growing Hope for Mauritius and the Chagossians: The UNCLOS Arbitral Tribunal's Award of 18 March 2015 on Chagos

terminology.[30] Hence, Annex VII Arbitration does not have jurisdiction *ratione materiae* over a territorial sovereignty dispute *itself*. Nevertheless, scholars argue that UNCLOS dispute settlement procedures (ITLOS and Annex VII Arbitration) do have jurisdiction *ratione materiae* over territorial sovereignty disputes. The reasons given for this are a contrario implication of UNCLOS Article 298 Paragraph 1(a)(i) or implied power of the UNCLOS Tribunal.[31] However, these theories do not recognize jurisdiction *ratione materiae* for a territorial sovereignty dispute *itself* but recognize jurisdiction *ratione materiae* in regard to a mixed dispute[32] only.[33] The coastal State litigation is a type of litigation related to mixed disputes.

UNCLOS uses the term "coastal State" as a concept similar to territorial sovereignty and defines sea areas that occur from coastal baselines (territorial sea,

Marine Protected Area (Mauritius v. United Kingdom)," *Brazilian Journal of International Law*, vol. 12, no. 2 (2015), 717. While UNCLOS applies to the sovereignty of a coastal State over its land territory, internal waters, and territorial sea (Article 2), it does not provide definitions for any of them.

30 UNCLOS Article 298, Paragraph 1(a)(i) excludes unsettled disputes concerning "sovereignty or other rights over continental or insular land territory" from compulsory conciliation under Annex V, indirectly mentioning territorial sovereignty. However, UNCLOS does not offer any definitions or decision-making methods regarding territorial sovereignty.

31 Irina Buga, "Territorial Sovereignty Issues in Maritime Disputes: A Jurisdictional Dilemma for Law of the Sea Tribunal," *The International Journal of Marine and Coastal Law*, vol. 27 (2012), 77–79. Refer to the following for a broad discussion of supplemental jurisdiction towards non-UNCLOS disputes, including other reasons. Peter Tzeng, "Supplemental Jurisdiction under UNCLOS," *Houston Journal of International Law*, vol. 38, no. 2 (2016), 499–576.

32 "Mixed dispute" refers to disputes that simultaneously have elements of both territorial sovereignty disputes (non-UNCLOS disputes) and UNCLOS disputes. In particular, it envisions the former as ancillary to the latter. For a view that criticizes the structuring of points of dispute that deviate from the actual substance of the dispute in mixed disputes, refer to Kanehara Atsuko 兼原敦子, "Saiban Kankatsuken to Tekiyōhō no Kankei: Kokuren Kaiyōhō Jyoyaku ni Okeru Shihō Saiban to Chūsai Saiban" 裁判管轄権と適用法の関係：国連海洋法条約における司法裁判と仲裁裁判 [Relation between Judicial Jurisdiction Rights and Applicable Laws: Judicial Decisions and Arbitral Decisions in UNCLOS], Serita Kentaro 芹田健太郎, et al. (eds.), *Jisshō no Kokusaihō Gaku no Keishō* 実証の国際法学の継承 (Tokyo: Shinzansha, 2019), 544 and 578.

33 President Wolfrum offered the following comments. "Issues of sovereignty or other rights over continental or insular land territory, which are *closely linked or ancillary to maritime delimitation*, concern the interpretation or application of the Convention and therefore fall within its scope" (emphasis added). ITLOS, Statement by H. E. Judge Rüdiger Wolfrum, President of the International Tribunal for the Law of the Sea, to the Informal Meeting of Legal Advisers of Ministries of Foreign Affairs, New York, 23 October 2006, 6, at https://www.itlos.org/en/main/press-media/statements-of-the-president/statements-of-president-wolfrum/.

contiguous zone, exclusive economic zone (EEZ), and continental shelf) as falling under coastal State rights. The coastal State litigation, aimed at presenting disputes related to coastal States as UNCLOS disputes, have therefore been attempted. Specific examples are (1) requesting determination of a coastal State itself, (2) requesting confirmation of the rights of a State as a coastal State, and (3) claiming infringement of coastal State rights by another State. The coastal State litigation cases are mixed dispute cases involving an aspect of determining coastal States under UNCLOS (i.e., UNCLOS disputes) and an aspect of deciding where the territorial sovereignty of designated maritime features and land lies (non-UNCLOS disputes).

3.3 *Examples of the Coastal State Litigation*

3.3.1 The Chagos Archipelago Marine Protected Area (MPA) Case (2015)

Mauritius and the United Kingdom were in opposition over many years regarding the territorial sovereignty of the Chagos Archipelago in the Indian Ocean. Mauritius brought litigation before the Annex VII Arbitration of UNCLOS with the assertion that the Maritime Protected Area (MPA) established by the United Kingdom around the Chagos Archipelago violated its obligations under UNCLOS. Mauritius contended that the United Kingdom was not entitled to declare an MPA because it was not the "coastal State" of the Chagos Archipelago.[34] Meanwhile, the United Kingdom treated the Mauritius assertion as a "sovereignty claim" and argued that sovereignty was "the real issue in the case" and that this type of dispute fell outside the dispute settlement provisions of UNCLOS.[35] In the United Kingdom's view, "Mauritius is requesting the Tribunal to permit 'an artificial re-characterization of the long-standing sovereignty dispute as a "who is the coastal State" dispute'."[36] The Annex VII Arbitral Tribunal confirmed the existence of a sovereignty dispute between the two countries and then rejected its jurisdiction related to the First and Second Submissions by Mauritius. The following describes the reason for this conclusion.

---

34 According to Mauritius' argument, "The United Kingdom is not entitled to declare an 'MPA' or other maritime zones because it is not the 'coastal State' within the meaning of, *inter alia*, Articles 2, 55, 56 and 76 of the Convention" (First Submission) and "having regard to the commitments that it has made to Mauritius in relation to the Chagos Archipelago, the United Kingdom is not entitled unilaterally to declare an 'MPA' or other maritime zones because Mauritius has rights as a coastal State' within the meaning of *inter alia* Articles 56(1)(b)(iii) and 76(8) of the Convention" (Second Submission). Award of 18 March 2015, *supra* note 19, para. 158.

35 *Ibid.*, paras. 164 and 170.

36 *Ibid.*, para. 172.

First, according to the Tribunal, while the First Submission requests interpretation and application of the term "coastal State," it is not defined in UNCLOS, and UNCLOS does not have guidelines to designate a "coastal State" in the cases where sovereignty over a land territory is disputed.[37] Second, in the Tribunal's view, "the record (see paragraphs 101–107 above)[38] clearly indicates that *a dispute between the Parties exists with respect to sovereignty* over the Chagos Archipelago" (emphasis added).[39] Third, distinct from the dispute over territorial sovereignty, a dispute also exists between the Parties with respect to the manner in which the MPA was declared and the implications of the MPA for the Lancaster House Undertakings.[40] Fourth, the Parties clearly differ regarding the identity of the "coastal State" and the Tribunal must evaluate where the relative weight of the dispute lies.[41] The Tribunal continues, "[a]ccordingly, the Tribunal concludes that the Parties' dispute with respect to Mauritius' First Submission is properly characterized as relating to land sovereignty over the Chagos Archipelago. The Parties' differing views on the "coastal State" for the purposes of the Convention are *simply one aspect* of this larger dispute [i.e., sovereignty dispute]" (emphasis added).[42] Fifth, the Tribunal similarly evaluated the relative weight of the disputes for the Second Submission and found that the Parties' underlying dispute regarding sovereignty over the Archipelago was predominant and the question of the "coastal State" remained merely an aspect of this larger dispute.[43]

As explained above, the Tribunal finally rejected Mauritius' assertion ("coastal State" designation). The following points are worth noting from the decision. First, the Tribunal confirmed the existence of a territorial sovereignty dispute between the two States quite easily. This seems to have been the result of there being no disagreement between the two States regarding the existence of a "dispute" about the territorial sovereignty of the Chagos Archipelago. Second, regarding Mauritius' assertion (First Submission), despite the existence of a sovereignty dispute and an UNCLOS dispute, the Tribunal found that the former was "predominant" and the latter was simply one aspect of the larger dispute (hereinafter, called the "Chagos Formula A"). According to

---

37 *Ibid.*, para. 203.
38 The record cited by the Tribunal (paras. 101–107) summarizes the differences of opinion of the Parties regarding sovereignty over the Chagos Archipelago and past objections.
39 Award of 18 March 2015, *supra* note 19, para. 209.
40 *Ibid.*, para. 210.
41 *Ibid.*, para. 211.
42 *Ibid.*, para. 212.
43 *Ibid.*, para. 229.

this interpretation, it is necessary to review which aspect (sovereignty dispute or UNCLOS dispute) should be given more weight.[44] Third, in contrast to the Chagos Formula A, described above, the Tribunal indicated that the sovereignty dispute accords the Tribunal jurisdiction when that dispute touched in some ancillary manner on an UNCLOS dispute.[45] The Tribunal offered the following explanation of this point.

> The jurisdiction of [the Tribunal] pursuant to Article 288(1) extends to making such findings of fact or ancillary determinations of law as are necessary to resolve the dispute presented to it. ... The Tribunal does not categorically exclude that in some instances a minor issue of territorial sovereignty could indeed be ancillary to a dispute concerning the interpretation or application of the Convention. That, however, is not this case.[46]

Hence, in cases in which a minor issue of territorial sovereignty (non-UNCLOS dispute) *is ancillary* to an UNCLOS dispute, it might sometimes be possible to exercise jurisdiction (hereinafter, called the "Chagos Formula B").

Because the Tribunal did not cite any precedent, it is difficult to envision a scenario to which the Chagos Formula B applies.[47] However, looking at the United Kingdom's assertion in this case,[48] it seems that the Tribunal was considering the ICJ's decision regarding South Ledge in the Pedra Branca case.[49] In that case, Malaysia and Singapore had a territorial dispute regarding South Ledge. The ICJ deemed South Ledge to be a low-tide elevation,[50] but since international law is silent on the question of whether low-tide elevations can be considered to be "territory,"[51] it was difficult to make an independent assessment of territorial sovereignty. (If it were located in the territorial sea, attribution would be to the coastal State of the territorial sea.) In sea areas

44 *Ibid.*, para. 229.

45 *Ibid.*, para. 213.

46 *Ibid.*, paras. 220–221.

47 Typically, since coastal State rights follow the confirmation of the sovereignty of maritime features ("the land dominates the sea"), there can be considered to be no rule that prescribes sovereignty on the basis of making a maritime claim ("the sea dominates the land"). Robert W. Smith and Bradford L. Thomas, *supra* note 29, 16.

48 Award of 18 March 2015, paras. 194–196.

49 *Sovereignty over Pedra Branca / Pulau Batu Puteh, Middle Rocks and South Ledge* (*Malaysia/ Singapore*), Judgment of 23 May 2008, *I.C.J. Reports 2008*, 2.

50 *Ibid.*, para. 291.

51 *Ibid.*, para. 296.

where the territorial seas have yet to be delimited, since low-tide elevations could potentially be located in the territorial seas of either State,[52] attribution becomes an issue. In the Pedra Branca case, however, since the ICJ was not empowered to draw the line of delimitation with respect to territorial seas,[53] it concluded that "South Ledge, as a low-tide elevation, belongs to the State in the territorial sea of which it is located."[54] In this way, the delimitation of the territorial seas, excluding the low-tide elevation, took place first, and the outcome thereof decided which State's territorial seas included South Ledge and hence the attribution (State with territorial sovereignty). In exceptional cases, there can exist a sovereignty dispute (territorial sovereignty dispute related to a low-tide elevation) ancillary to a dispute on the delimitation of a maritime boundary (territorial sea delimitation dispute, i.e., UNCLOS dispute). This is an exceptional case where the Chagos Formula B is supposed to be applied.

3.3.2 The Coastal State Rights Case (2020)

After Russia annexed the Ukrainian territory of Crimea in 2014, Ukraine brought a case to the Annex VII Arbitration of UNCLOS (2016) and asserted that Russia violated UNCLOS. A key point is that Ukraine did not assert that "Ukraine is Crimea's coastal State" but stated that *there is no* dispute regarding sovereignty between the two States. It asserted that Ukraine's sovereignty over Crimea was simply "a matter of background and context."[55] The respondent, Russia, submitted preliminary objections against Ukraine's submission and asserted that "this Arbitral Tribunal lacks jurisdiction" due to the existence of a territorial sovereignty dispute over Crimea.[56] In other words, a territorial sovereignty dispute exists between the two countries (rather than an UNCLOS dispute)[57] and the territorial sovereignty issue was "the front and centre" of the matter before the Tribunal.[58] A point-by-point analysis of the Tribunal's decision is set out below.

First is the matter of whether there is a territorial sovereignty dispute regarding Crimea. On this point, the Tribunal recognized the existence of the dispute in the following way, (1) "[T]he Parties therefore hold clearly opposite views[.] … [I]t is clear that the Parties are in disagreement on various points of law and

52 *Ibid.*, para. 297.
53 *Ibid.*, para. 298.
54 *Ibid.*, para. 299.
55 Award of 21 February 2020, *supra* note 12, paras. 85 and 161.
56 *Ibid.*, paras. 78–79.
57 *Ibid.*, paras. 132 and 161.
58 *Ibid.*, para. 192.

facts relating to the question as to which State is sovereign over Crimea[.]"[59] As this shows, the Tribunal recognized the existence of a territorial sovereignty dispute between the two States. (2) Next is the issue of Ukraine's assertion. Ukraine asserted that there is not a territorial sovereignty dispute between the two States and that Russia's claim of territorial sovereignty was inadmissible and lacked plausibility. The Tribunal rejected these Ukrainian assertions.[60] Based on (1) and (2), the Tribunal reached a conclusion that a dispute regarding the territorial sovereignty of Crimea exists between the two States. In making this decision, the Tribunal (as explained above), determined that it did not consider that Russia's claim of sovereignty was a "mere assertion."[61]

The second issue is the relative weight of the territorial sovereignty dispute and the UNCLOS dispute. Regarding this point, the Tribunal noted the Award in the Chagos Archipelago MPA case that "implied a possibility that its jurisdiction could be extended to ruling upon an ancillary issue of territorial sovereignty."[62] It hence recognized that the Chagos Formula B could be valid. Nevertheless, the Tribunal rejected the notion that the sovereignty dispute was an ancillary issue in the case and provided the following explanation.

> In the view of the Arbitral Tribunal, the key question it should address, therefore, is whether a sovereignty dispute over Crimea in the present case is an issue ancillary to a dispute concerning the interpretation or application of the Convention. The [former dispute] is not a minor issue ancillary to the [latter dispute]. On the contrary, the question of sovereignty is a *prerequisite* to the Arbitral Tribunal's decision on a number of claims submitted by Ukraine under the Convention [UNCLOS]. Those claims simply cannot be addressed without deciding which State is sovereign over Crimea and thus the 'coastal State' within the meaning of provisions of the Convention invoked by Ukraine. (emphasis added)[63]

---

59 *Ibid.*, para. 165.

60 Key points of the Tribunal's award are presented below. (1) Regarding the admissibility of Russia's claims, the Tribunal was unable to accept Ukraine's argument because the UNGA resolutions were framed in hortatory language (Award, para. 175) and estoppel did not operate in the case (Award, para. 181). (2) Regarding the plausibility of Russia's claim, while a unilateral assertion would be insufficient in proving the existence of a dispute, "it does not follow that the validity or strength of the assertion should be put to a plausibility or other test" (Award, para. 188).

61 *Ibid.*, para. 189.

62 *Ibid.*, para. 193.

63 *Ibid.*, paras. 194–195.

As explained above, the Annex VII Arbitration recognized the existence of a territorial sovereignty dispute between the two States over Crimea and decided that settlement of this dispute was "prerequisite" to settling the UNCLOS dispute. The Tribunal hence could not rule on any claims of Ukraine which were dependent on the premise of Ukraine being sovereign over Crimea.[64]

3.4 *Types of Formulas*

The above explanation identifies three types of formulas to address the relation between UNCLOS and non-UNCLOS disputes in a mixed dispute – the Chagos Formula A (i.e., "predominant"), the Chagos Formula B (i.e., "ancillary"), and the Crimea Formula (i.e., "prerequisite"). This section will review the content of each formula and then clarify their relationships.

First, the Chagos Formula B is an approach that envisions an exceptional situation, and it is doubtful that it can be generally applied. The Tribunal initially considered the Chagos Formula B in the Coastal State Rights case, but this was only done because the assertions of both States were in agreement on this point. Second, whereas the Chagos Formula A involves a *quantitative* comparison of the territorial sovereignty dispute and UNCLOS dispute ("predominant" or an "aspect"), the Crimea Formula seems to address the *qualitative* relationship ("prerequisite"). In the latter case, even if the sovereignty dispute is relatively modest and the UNCLOS dispute is relatively large, the Tribunal does not have jurisdiction when the former is a "prerequisite" of the latter. As a result, reliance on the Crimea Formula makes it difficult to establish jurisdiction in many coastal State disputes (UNCLOS disputes). Third, the scope of the dispute (fixed by the submission), which is subject to review, differs between the Chagos Formula A and the Crimea Formula. In the Chagos Formula A, the scope of the dispute is extremely narrow, and in fact, regarding a limited submission such as "whether the United Kingdom is the coastal Sate or not." In such a circumstance, since the "territorial sovereignty dispute is predominant," the submission is characterized as a territorial sovereignty dispute. In contrast, under the Crimea Formula, it was difficult for the Tribunal to uniformly characterize the multiple UNCLOS submissions by Ukraine as "either a sovereignty dispute or an UNCLOS dispute," and it therefore positioned the territorial sovereignty dispute as a "prerequisite" of the UNCLOS disputes.

Based on the above analysis, the formulas follow two patterns. (1) If the claimant State independently makes a submission requesting the Tribunal to confirm that it is the "coastal State" under UNCLOS, the jurisdiction of the

64 *Ibid.*, paras. 197–198.

Tribunal over the dispute, involved in the submission, is rejected in accordance with the Chagos Formula A on the basis that the territorial sovereignty dispute is "predominant." On the other hand, (2) if the applicant State *avoids* a request for designation along the lines of (1) and submits multiple claims of UNCLOS violations, the jurisdiction of the Tribunal over the submission, which positions the settlement of the sovereignty dispute as a "prerequisite," is rejected in accordance with the Crimea Formula.

3.5 *Logical Structure of the Recognition of a Territorial Sovereignty Dispute*

As explained above, despite the difference in formulas for determining jurisdiction depending on the case, the Tribunals recognized the existence of a sovereignty dispute in all cases. In terms of the logical structure by which this recognition is reached, the following points can be made. First, the threshold for the occurrence of a "dispute," including a territorial sovereignty dispute, is extremely low. As indicated earlier (Section 2 of this chapter), other than in exceptional cases in which one State's claim is a "mere assertion," if there is a conflict of views between two States, the Tribunal readily recognizes the existence of a territorial sovereignty dispute. Second, in the Chagos Archipelago MPA case, there was no difficulty to find a difference of views between the two States regarding the existence of a territorial sovereignty dispute. The situation in the Coastal State Rights case, however, was different. That is because there was a difference of views between Ukraine (that no territorial sovereignty dispute exists) and Russia (that a territorial sovereignty dispute exists). In this case, Russia's submission of preliminary objections can be said to be the reason for the Tribunal's recognition of the existence of a territorial sovereignty dispute. The respondent, Russia, submitted preliminary objections against Ukraine's submission and asserted that "this Arbitral Tribunal lacks jurisdiction" due to the existence of a territorial sovereignty dispute over Crimea.[65] Since the relative weight of the territorial sovereignty dispute and UNCLOS dispute is subject to review as part of the hearing of the preliminary objections as explained above, recognition of the existence of a territorial sovereignty dispute was inevitably required.[66] Third, in both cases, the respondents (the

65 *Ibid.*, paras. 78–79.

66 It is of course possible that, when rejecting jurisdiction, the Tribunal under UNCLOS might have a different basis than the existence of a territorial sovereignty dispute (for example, the obligation to exchange views (UNCLOS Article 283), etc.). It must be noted that the review in this chapter assumes that these other jurisdictional requirements have been met.

United Kingdom and Russia) recognized the existence of a territorial sovereignty dispute and submitted objections over the Tribunal's jurisdiction based on this point. However, in the Coastal State Rights case, since the applicant, Ukraine, denied the existence of a territorial sovereignty dispute, the Tribunal carefully reviewed whether or not such a dispute existed and concluded that it in fact did. That being said, it is worth noting that even though Ukraine and Russia had a difference of views on whether or not a territorial sovereignty dispute existed, the existence of such a dispute was nevertheless recognized by the Tribunal.

Considering the points covered above, recognition of the existence of a territorial sovereignty dispute relating to Takeshima requires the following special considerations. Since the claimant (Japan) *asserts the existence of* a territorial sovereignty dispute while the respondent (ROK) *denies the existence* of a territorial sovereignty dispute, there is unlikely to be an objection to jurisdiction along the lines that "the Annex VII Tribunal does not have jurisdiction due to the existence of a territorial sovereignty dispute." Nevertheless, even in a case such as this in which the respondent State does not submit any preliminary objection, as the Tribunal cannot ignore the existence of a territorial sovereignty dispute, the Tribunal will be required to exercise its own power (competence-competence) in assessing whether a territorial sovereignty dispute exists.[67]

4 Recognition of the Existence of a Territorial Sovereignty Dispute over Takeshima

4.1 *Potential UNCLOS Dispute*

When initiating the coastal State litigation before the Annex VII Arbitration, it is firstly premised on the existence of an UNCLOS dispute. The various sea areas in the waters around Takeshima will be considered below.

---

67 Assessment of relative weight in mixed disputes takes place in the context of the characterization of dispute by the Tribunal. Through its exercise of dispute characterization power, the Tribunal decides an important factor in mixed disputes. The right to determine jurisdiction serves as the basis for dispute characterization power. Irina Buga, *supra* note 31, 89–90. The Tribunal in the Coastal State Rights case presented "Nature or Characterisation of the Dispute" as an item and cites the ICJ's Nuclear Tests case (*Nuclear Tests* (*Australia v. France*), Judgment, *I.C.J. Reports 1974*, 253, 262, para. 29) in explaining that "it is ultimately for the Arbitral Tribunal itself to determine ... the nature of the dispute[.]" Award of 21 February 2020, para. 151.

First, regarding the EEZ, the Japan-ROK Fisheries Agreement (1998) delimits the areas other than the provisional waters (Article 7, Paragraphs 1 and 2). However, it does not delimit the provisional waters that include Takeshima.[68] Additionally, in the provisional waters, Japan and the ROK both agreed to "not apply its own fisheries-related laws to citizens and fishing vessels of the other Party" (Annex I, Article 2, Paragraph 1). Thus, there has been no delimitation of an EEZ around Takeshima, and since Japan has not established an EEZ, even if it asserted that "the ROK infringed Japan's sovereign rights in the Japanese EEZ," this would not be treated as an UNCLOS dispute.

Second, regarding the continental shelf, the Agreement between Japan and the Republic of Korea concerning the Establishment of Boundary in the Northern Part of the Continental Shelf Adjacent to the Two Countries (1974), the northernmost point of the boundary line is the part that touches the above-mentioned provisional waters and the Agreement therefore does not establish a continental shelf boundary around Takeshima. Prior to UNCLOS taking effect, the Japanese Government determined that there is no continental shelf in the area around Takeshima.[69] After it entered into force, however, Japan changed its position and recognized the existence of a continental shelf.[70] Therefore, Japan can claim the existence of an UNCLOS dispute by arguing, for example, that "the actions by the ROK infringed the sovereign rights of its continental shelf around Takeshima."

Third, Japan can claim infringement of its sovereignty and sovereign rights in its territorial sea and the contiguous zone around Takeshima. For example, (1) the ROK is infringing Japan's territorial sea by implementing military exercises in Takeshima's territorial sea. (2) Interference with or prevention

---

68 Regarding the provisional waters, the Agreement stipulates, "The Parties shall continue negotiations in good faith aimed at the early delimitation of the provisional waters" (Annex I, Article 1).

69 Minister of Foreign Affairs Hatoyama Ichiro responded to a question at the Diet (80th National Diet, House of Representatives Foreign Affairs Committee no. 18 on May 18, 1977) as follows. "Minister Hatoyama: Regarding Takeshima, the seafloor in the surrounding area becomes deeper at a steep incline and our view is that this is not a continental shelf as defined by current international law" at https://kokkai.ndl.go.jp/#/detail?minId=108003968X01819770518&spkNum=102&single.

70 In response to the question "Is Takeshima an island or a rock under UNCLOS?" at the National Diet, Yachi Shotaro replied, "We think it is an island with a continental shelf and an economic zone" (136th National Diet, House of Councilors' Special Committee on UNCLOS no. 3 on June 4, 1996) at https://kokkai.ndl.go.jp/#/detail?minId=113613938X00319960604&spkNum=232&single.

of Japanese fishing vessels from approaching Takeshima's territorial sea[71] infringes the sovereignty of Japan's territorial sea. (3) Implementation of ocean surveys without prior consent from Japan in Takeshima's territorial sea (2017,[72] 2019)[73] infringes the sovereignty of Japan's territorial sea. (4) If Japan carries out its own ocean survey[74] and faces interference from the ROK, Japan can similarly assert infringement of the sovereignty of its territorial sea. As shown above, based on the assumption that Japan possesses territorial sovereignty over Takeshima, it can initiate instances of the infringement of its various UNCLOS rights (in other words, infringements of Japan's sovereignty and sovereign rights as the coastal State) as UNCLOS disputes before the Annex VII Arbitration.

4.2 *Prospective Submissions and Ruling*

If Japan brings the coastal State litigation against the ROK, the following submissions and ruling by the Arbitral Tribunal are conceivable.

Submission A: "Japan is the coastal State of Takeshima, and the sea areas referred to in the following submissions B–W are all attributed to Japan." In response to the submission, the Annex VII Tribunal is likely to *recognize the existence of a territorial sovereignty dispute over Takeshima*, deem that the dispute is a non-UNCLOS dispute because the territorial sovereignty dispute is "predominant" relative to the UNCLOS dispute in accordance with the Chagos Formula A, and reject jurisdiction on submission A.

71 190th National Diet, House of Representatives' Budget Committee Third Sub-Committee no. 1 on February 25, 2016 (Yamada Kenji), "ROK authorities are currently sending warnings to fishing vessels when they get close to 12 nautical miles out from Takeshima" at https://kokkai.ndl.go.jp/#/detail?minId=119005268X00120160225&spkNum=313&single.

72 193rd National Diet, House of Representatives Foreign Affairs Committee no. 16 on May 31, 2017 (Shindō Yoshitaka) "This is an example from the ROK. A ROK marine survey vessel, without prior consent from Japan, inserted a wire into waters within the EEZ around Takeshima on May 17, 2017. It *entered Japan's territorial sea* and navigated around within them. This has happened four times in the past two years" (emphasis added) at https://kokkai.ndl.go.jp/#/detail?minId=119303968X01620170531&spkNum=10&single.

73 198th National Diet, House of Representatives Environment Committee no. 4 on April 2, 2019 (Nagao Hideki), "In February this year [2019], there was an incident in which the ROK conducted *seafloor survey activities*, such as sediment collection, without Japan's consent, in *Takeshima's territorial sea and contiguous zone*" (emphasis added) at https://kokkai.ndl.go.jp/#/detail?minId=119804006X00420190402&spkNum=56&single.

74 193rd National Diet, House of Representatives Foreign Affairs Committee no. 16 on May 31, 2017 (Shindō Yoshitaka) at https://kokkai.ndl.go.jp/#/detail?minId=119303968X01620170531&spkNum=14&single.

Submissions B–W: "The ROK's XX actions in Japan's YY sea areas (e.g., territorial sea, continental shelf) infringe Japan's rights as the coastal State under UNCLOS." In response to these submissions, the Annex VII Tribunal is likely to *recognize the existence of a territorial sovereignty dispute over Takeshima* and reject jurisdiction on submissions B–W in accordance with the Crimea Formula on the ground that the territorial dispute is a "prerequisite" to settling the UNCLOS dispute.

Submission X is a submission that requires recognition of the facts. Submission Y: "Regardless of whether this is Japan's maritime zone or the ROK's maritime zone, the ROK is violating the duty to protect and preserve the marine environment under UNCLOS." Submission Z: "The ROK has an obligation to provide reparation and remedy for the abovementioned UNCLOS violation." If Japan only submits submissions A and B–W as described above, it is certain to lose the litigation without any progress towards a decision on the merits, due to all the submissions being rejected based on the Tribunal's lack of jurisdiction. To avoid this outcome, Japan needs to include several UNCLOS disputes in the submission as well as submissions that are highly likely to make it to a review of the merits (submissions X, Y, and Z).

As explained above, if Japan submits the coastal State litigation regarding Takeshima, the Tribunal is likely to reject jurisdiction for the core portion of the lawsuit (submission A and submissions B–W). No past cases of the coastal State litigation have made it to the stage of identification as the "coastal State," and the possibility of this happening in the future is almost non-existent.[75]

Nevertheless, the most important point is that when jurisdiction is rejected by the Tribunal, *recognition of the existence of a territorial sovereignty dispute* will inevitably take place. In other words, the Annex VII Tribunal (1) *recognizes the existence of a territorial sovereignty dispute*, (2) evaluates the relative weight of the territorial sovereignty dispute and the UNCLOS dispute, and (3) rejects its jurisdiction over the submitted dispute as the outcome of its evaluation. The Tribunal will hereby inevitably make a decision regarding (1) as the underlying assumption for decisions regarding (2) and (3).

As shown above, the benefit of the coastal State litigation is that Japan potentially can be recognized as the coastal State (having territorial sovereignty) if the litigation makes it to a decision on the merits, and *even if this fails*

75 If there is a possibility of the Annex VII Tribunal deciding Takeshima's "coastal State," it would be in response to a coastal State litigation brought by Japan whereby the Tribunal decides that "because the ROK's claim of territorial sovereignty over Takeshima is a 'mere assertion', no territorial sovereignty 'dispute' exists between Japan and the ROK and the maritime feature is no doubt attributed to Japan's territorial sovereignty."

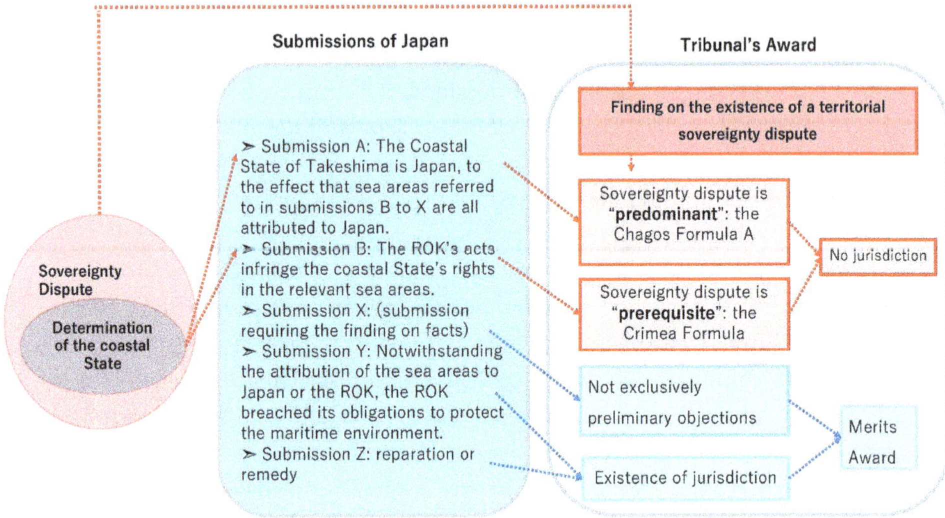

FIGURE 9.1 Japan's coastal State litigation
CREATOR: DAI TAMADA

(i.e., rejection of the Tribunal's jurisdiction), at the minimum, a decision on (1) (i.e., recognition of the existence of a territorial sovereignty dispute) would be made.

4.3 *Other Matters for Consideration*

Attention should also be given to the following points related to the coastal State litigation. First, recognition of the existence of a territorial sovereignty dispute does not immediately enable referral of a case to the ICJ for a judicial decision on the territorial sovereignty of Takeshima. Even though recognition would mean that the ROK could not deny the existence of a territorial sovereignty dispute itself, it would not create any obligation to proceed with a joint referral to the ICJ. The ROK could present a different reason for rejecting a joint referral to the ICJ. Additionally, as seen in the negotiations regarding the Northern Territories with Russia, even if two States agree on the existence of a territorial sovereignty dispute, this alone does not ensure smooth progress in negotiations on the territorial dispute. Recognition of the existence of a territorial sovereignty dispute is simply a prerequisite and first step for starting negotiations between two States. A separate detailed analysis and strategy of the subsequent path towards the settlement of the dispute (including negotiations and referral to the ICJ) is needed.

Second, all UNCLOS States Parties can utilize the UNCLOS coastal State litigation. This means that China, if it is so willing, could utilize it to obtain recognition of the existence of a territorial sovereignty dispute over the Senkaku

Islands. For Japan to maintain its position, it needs to structure its assertion along the line that "the Chinese claim is a 'mere assertion' and no dispute exists on Senkaku," as shown in Section 2 (Criteria for Occurrence of Disputes under International Law) of this chapter.

Third, there is leeway to consider the possibility of the coastal State litigation against Russia regarding the Northern Territories. Although Japan and Russia had differed in their stances on whether a territorial sovereignty dispute existed during the Cold War,[76] Russia has recognized the existence, itself, of a territorial sovereignty dispute after the Cold War.[77] The Japanese-Soviet Union Joint Communiqué (1991) used the phrase "taking into consideration the positions of both sides on the attribution"[78] and the Tokyo Declaration (1993) referred, in Paragraph 2, to agreement "on the issue of where [the islands belong]" to work towards a "solution ... based on ... the principles of law and justice."[79] In other words, since Japan and Russia are not in disagreement over the existence

76 "In 1960, in connection with the conclusion of the new Japanese-US Security Treaty, the Soviet Union stated that the return of the islands of Habomai and Shikotan to Japan would be conditional upon the withdrawal of all foreign troops from Japanese territory. In response, the Government of Japan raised the objection that the terms of the Joint Declaration between Japan and the USSR could not be changed unilaterally, because it was an international agreement that had been ratified by the Parliaments of both countries. The Soviet side later asserted that the territorial issue in Japanese-Soviet relations had been resolved as a result of World War II and such an issue did not exist." Ministry of Foreign Affairs of Japan and Ministry of Foreign Affairs of the Russian Federation, "Joint Compendium of Documents on the History of Territorial Issue between Japan and Russia" (1992 version) at https://www.mofa.go.jp/mofaj/area/hoppo/1992.pdf.

77 "[A]s the Cold War drew to a close, Russia *acknowledged the existence of the territorial issue* and again confirmed that the Japan-Soviet Joint Declaration remained valid between Japan and Russia" (emphasis added). Ministry of Foreign Affairs "Northern Territories Issue Q&A" at https://www.mofa.go.jp/mofaj/area/hoppo/mondai_qa.html.

78 "... held an in-depth and thorough negotiations on a whole range of issues relating to the preparation and conclusion of a peace treaty between Japan and the Union of Soviet Socialist Republics, including the issue of territorial demarcation, taking into consideration the positions of both sides on the attribution of the islands of Habomai, Shikotan, Kunashiri, and Etorofu. The joint work done previously – particularly the negotiations at the highest level – has made it possible to confirm a series of conceptual understandings: that the peace treaty should be the document marking the *final resolution* of war-related issues, *including the territorial issue*" (emphasis added). Japanese-Soviet Joint Communiqué at https://www8.cao.go.jp/hoppo/shiryou/pdf/gaikou35.pdf.

79 "[Japan and Russia] have undertaken serious negotiations on the issue of where Etorofu, Kunashiri, Shikotan and the Habomai Islands belong. They agree that negotiations towards an early conclusion of a peace treaty through the solution of this issue on the basis of historical and legal facts and based on the documents produced with the two countries' agreement as well as on the principles of law and justice should continue, and that the relations between the two countries should thus be fully normalized." Tokyo

of a territorial sovereignty dispute regarding the Northern Territories, it is not necessary to use the UNCLOS coastal State litigation. However, considering Russia's attitude of rejecting the existence of a dispute between the two sides in recent years,[80] the conclusions reached in this chapter could also be applied to the Northern Territories.

Fourth, as precedents of the UNCLOS coastal State litigation have been rapidly established in recent years, some observers have criticized the abusive use of the arbitration procedure under UNCLOS Annex VII.[81] If such criticism spreads in response to the expanded use of the coastal State litigation, it is not impossible that precedents may change going forward. If Japan is considering the use of the coastal State litigation, it would be better to initiate it prior to any major changes to precedents.

5 Conclusion

As explained in this chapter, it is possible to obtain recognition of the existence of a territorial sovereignty dispute (for example, related to Takeshima) using the coastal State litigation before the Annex VII Tribunal of UNCLOS. An important point is the possibility for Japan to *forcibly* obtain (i.e., despite opposition by the respondent State) *objective* recognition of the existence of a territorial sovereignty dispute in an international tribunal (i.e., Annex VII Tribunal of UNCLOS). Here, it is not necessary to reemphasize the significance and importance of obtaining recognition of the existence of a territorial sovereignty "dispute" (refer to the "Introduction" of this chapter). Thus far, the Japanese Government has always envisioned litigation before the ICJ and actually proposed such a joint referral to the ICJ. However, in the case of ICJ litigation (whether it is joint referral or unilateral referral), the ROK can reject it outright by replying that "there is no reason to respond because no dispute exists." No matter how much Japan strategizes about a referral to the ICJ, there are no hopes of it making any progress towards settling the dispute. Understanding the situation to be thus, the Japanese Government should

Declaration on Japan-Russia Relations at https://www8.cao.go.jp/hoppo/shiryou/pdf/gaikou46.pdf.

80 For example, Russian Foreign Minister Lavrov called on the Japanese side "to recognize all of the results of the Second World War" (January 14, 2019 press conference) at https://www.huffingtonpost.jp/2019/01/14/meeting-taro-kono-sergey-lavrov_a_23642564/.

81 Award of 18 March 2015, *supra* note 19, para. 198.

seriously consider using the coastal State litigation before the Annex VII Tribunal of UNCLOS as explained in this chapter.

Bibliography

Primary Sources

Japanese

"Hoppō Ryōdo Mondai ni Kansuru Q ando A" 北方領土問題に関するQ&A [Northern Territories Issue Q&A]. Ministry of Foreign Affairs of Japan. https://www.mofa.go.jp/mofaj/area/hoppo/mondai_qa.html.

Kan, Naoto 菅直人. "Tōben Dai 395 Gō" 答弁第三九五号 [Written Answer no.395]. House of Representatives of Japan. August 23, 2011. http://www.shugiin.go.jp/internet/itdb_shitsumon_pdf_t.nsf/html/shitsumon/pdfT/b177395.pdf/$File/b177395.pdf.

"Kokusai Shihō Saibansho eno Teiso no Teian" 国際司法裁判所への提訴の提案 [Proposal of Referral to the International Court of Justice]. Ministry of Foreign Affairs of Japan. https://www.mofa.go.jp/mofaj/area/takeshima/g_teiso.html.

National Diet Library. "80th National Diet, House of Representatives Foreign Affairs Committee no. 18 on May 18, 1977 (102 Minister of Foreign Affairs Hatoyama Iichiro)." Full-text Database System for the Minutes of the Diets. https://kokkai.ndl.go.jp/#/detail?minId=108003968X01819770518&spkNum=102&single.

National Diet Library. "136th National Diet, House of Councillors' Special Committee on UNCLOS no. 3 on June 4, 1996 (232 Yachi Shōtaro)." Full-text Database System for the Minutes of the Diets. https://kokkai.ndl.go.jp/#/detail?minId=113613938X00319960604&spkNum=232&single.

National Diet Library. "190th National Diet, House of Representatives' Budget Committee Third Sub-Committee no. 1 on February 25, 2016 (313 Yamada Kenji)." Full-text Database System for the Minutes of the Diets. https://kokkai.ndl.go.jp/#/detail?minId=119005268X00120160225&spkNum=313&single.

National Diet Library. "193rd National Diet, House of Representatives Foreign Affairs Committee no. 16 on May 31, 2017 (010, 014 Shindō Yoshitaka)." Full-text Database System for the Minutes of the Diets. https://kokkai.ndl.go.jp/#/detail?minId=119303968X01620170531&spkNum=10&single, and https://kokkai.ndl.go.jp/#/detail?minId=119303968X01620170531&spkNum=14&single.

National Diet Library. "198th National Diet, House of Representatives Environment Committee no. 4 on April 2, 2019 (056 Nagao Hideki)." Full-text Database System for the Minutes of the Diets. https://kokkai.ndl.go.jp/#/detail?minId=119804006X00420190402&spkNum=56&single.

"Nichiro Kan Ryōdo Mondai no Rekishi ni Kansuru Kyōdō Sakusei Shiryōshū" 日露間領土問題の歴史に関する共同作成資料集 [Joint Compendium of Documents on the History of Territorial Issue between Japan and Russia]. Ministry of Foreign Affairs of Japan. September 1992. https://www.mofa.go.jp/mofaj/area/hoppo/1992.pdf.

"Nichiro Kankei ni Kansuru Tokyo Sengen" 日露関係に関する東京宣言 [Tokyo Declaration on Japan-Russia Relations]. Cabinet Office of Japan. October 13, 1993. https://www8.cao.go.jp/hoppo/shiryou/pdf/gaikou46.pdf.

"Nisso Kyōdō Seimei" 日ソ共同声明 [Japanese-Soviet Joint Communiqué]. Cabinet Office of Japan. April 18, 1991. https://www8.cao.go.jp/hoppo/shiryou/pdf/gaikou35.pdf.

Western Language

"Declarations made by States Parties under article 287." ITLOS. https://www.itlos.org/en/main/jurisdiction/declarations-of-states-parties/declarations-made-by-states-parties-under-article-287/.

"Position of the Government of Korea on Dokdo." Ministry of Foreign Affairs of Republic of Korea. http://overseas.mofa.go.kr/jp-sendai-ja/brd/m_623/view.do?seq=683039&srchFr=&srchTo=&srchWord=&srchTp=&multi_itm_seq=0&itm_seq_1=0&itm_seq_2=0&company_cd=&company_nm=&page=24.

"The Korean Government's Basic Position on Dokdo." Ministry of Foreign Affairs of Republic of Korea. http://dokdo.mofa.go.kr/jp/dokdo/government_position.jsp.

Wolfrum, Rüdiger. "Statement given to the Informal Meeting of Legal Advisers of Ministries of Foreign Affairs." ITLOS. October 23, 2006. https://www.itlos.org/en/main/press-media/statements-of-the-president/statements-of-president-wolfrum/.

Secondary Sources

Japanese

ICJ Precedent Study Group 国際司法裁判所判例研究会. "Kakugunbi Kyōsō no Teishi to Kakugunbi no Shukushō ni Kansuru Kōshōgimu Jiken (Māsharu Shotō Tai Eikoku) (Senketsuteki Koben Hanketsu 2016 Nen 10 Gatsu 5 Ka)" 核軍備競争の停止と核軍備の縮小に関する交渉義務事件（マーシャル諸島対英国）（先決的抗弁判決・2016年 10月 5日）[*Obligations concerning Negotiations Relating to Cessation of the Nuclear Arms Race and to Nuclear Disarmament* (*Marshall Islands v. United Kingdom*) (Preliminary Objections Judgment, October 5, 2016)]. *Kokusaihō Gaikō Zasshi* 国際法外交雑誌 116, no. 2 (2017): 97–114.

Kanehara, Atsuko 兼原敦子. "Saiban Kankatsuken to Tekiyōhō no Kankei: Kokuren Kaiyōhō Jyoyaku ni Okeru Shihō Saiban to Chūsai Saiban" 裁判管轄権と適用法の関係：国連海洋法条約における司法裁判と仲裁裁判 [Relation between Judicial

Jurisdiction Rights and Applicable Laws: Judicial Decisions and Arbitral Decisions in UNCLOS]. In *Jisshō no Kokusaihō Gaku no Keishō* 実証の国際法学の継承 [Succession of Positivism in International Law], edited by Serita Kentaro 芹田健太郎, et al., 543–582. Tokyo: Shinzansha, 2019.

Kotera Akira 小寺彰. "Ryōdo Mondai no Shori Isoguna" 領土問題の処理急ぐな [Avoid Rushing Handling of Territorial Issues]. *Nihon Keizai Shimbun* 日本経済新聞, October 9, 2012.

Sakamoto, Shigeki 坂元茂樹. Kaiyō Kyōkai Kakutei to Ryōdo Funsō –Takeshima to Senkakushotō no Kage– 海洋境界画定と領土紛争—竹島と尖閣諸島の影— [Maritime Boundary Delimitation and Territorial Disputes: Shadow of Takeshima and the Senkaku Islands]. *Kokusai Mondai* 国際問題, no. 565 (2007): 15–29.

Sekine, Kazuhiro 関根和弘. "'Hoppō Ryōdo wa Subete Rosia no Shuken dato Mitomeyo' Rosia no Raburohu Gaisō ga Kōno Tarō Gaisō ni Semaru (Kaiken Zenbun)" 「北方領土はすべてロシアの主権だと認めよ」ロシアのラブロフ外相が河野太郎外相に迫る（会見全文）[Russian Foreign Minister Lavrov called on the Japanese side "to recognize all of the results of the Second World War" (Full Text of the Interview)]. *Huffingtonpost*, January 15, 2019. https://www.huffingtonpost.jp/2019/01/14/meeting-taro-kono-sergey-lavrov_a_23642564/.

Serita, Kentaro 芹田健太郎. *Shima no Ryōyū to Keizai Suiiki no Kyōkai Kakutei* 島の領有と経済水域の境界画定 [Island Possession and Economic Zone Delimitation]. Tokyo: Yūshindō Kōbunsha, 1999.

Tamada, Dai 玉田大. "Takeshima Funsō wa Kokusai Shihō Saibansho ni Mochikomenai?" 竹島紛争は国際司法裁判所に持ち込めない？ [Is It Possible to Bring the Takeshima Dispute to the International Court of Justice?]. In *Kokusaihō de Sekai ga Wakaru* [Understand the World with International Law], edited by Morikawa Koichi 森川幸一, et al., 245–253. Tokyo: Iwanami Publishing, 2016.

Tamada, Dai 玉田大. "'Funsō' no Sonzai – Kakugunshuku Kōshō Gimu Jiken (Māsharu Shotō Tai Igirisu)" 『紛争』の存在 – 核軍縮交渉義務事件（マーシャル諸島対イギリス）[Existence of "Dispute": Case on Obligations concerning Nuclear Disarmament Negotiations (Marshall Islands vs. the United Kingdom)]. In *Kokusaihō Hanrei Hyakusen Dai 3 Ban* 国際法判例百選（第3版）[100 Cases on International Law (3rd Edition)], edited by Morikawa Koichi 森川幸一, et al., 188–189. Tokyo: Yūhikaku Publishing, 2021.

Western Language

Buga, Irina. "Territorial Sovereignty Issues in Maritime Disputes: A Jurisdictional Dilemma for Law of the Sea Tribunal." *The international Journal of Marine and Coastal Law* 27, no. 1 (2012), 59–95.

Giraudeau, Géraldine. "A Slight Revenge and a Growing Hope for Mauritius and the Chagossians: The UNCLOS Arbitral Tribunal's Award of 18 March 2015 on Chagos

Marine Protected Area (Mauritius v. United Kingdom)." *Brazilian Journal of International Law* 12, no. 2 (2015), 705–727.

Smith, Robert W., and Bradford L. Thomas. "Island Disputes and the Law of the Sea: An Examination of Sovereignty and Delimitation Disputes." *Maritime Briefing* 2, no. 4 (1998): 1–27.

Tamada Dai 玉田大. "UNCLOS Dispute Settlement Mechanism: Contribution to the Integrity of UNCLOS." *Japanese Yearbook of International Law* 61 (2018) [March 2019]: 132–166.

Tzeng, Peter. "Supplemental Jurisdiction under UNCLOS." *Houston Journal of International Law* 38, no. 2 (2016): 499–576.

Conclusion

Atsuko Kanehara

As indicated in the Foreword, this book contains chapters that address two questions. These are: 1) the historical evolution of the concept of "territory" and 2) methods for resolving territorial disputes. Each chapter is a complete and independent work and the Foreword therefore introduced the essence of each. It demonstrates the mutual connections, albeit of a relatively loose nature, of these individual papers. However, their mutual connections do not end there. As the final section of this book, the Conclusion aims to provide further clarification of the cross-cutting connections across these nine chapters. These are in large part due to the research framework formed as part of preparations for publishing this collection.

As part of the research project explained in the Foreword, two study groups were set up to conduct research on the two questions, and the two editors of this book each served as the directors for their respective study groups. The authors of the papers in Part 1 and Part 2 of the book were members of the "Study Group on the Historical Evolution of the Concept of 'Territory'," and authors of the papers in Part 3 and Part 4 of the book were members of the "Study Group on Methods for Resolving Territorial Disputes." Besides the roundtable meeting held once a year when all of the members assembled, the two study groups held their own meetings from 2018, and each author had four opportunities to present their work through 2021. The project also encouraged interaction and exchange, whereby members of each study group could freely attend the other. However, this was not always easy because some members had to travel long distances in order to participate.

The COVID-19 pandemic, meanwhile, actually contributed "positively" to this situation. It meant that all meetings for the two study groups in the final year took place virtually. Although this may have made it more difficult to engage in the same kind of detailed discussion as during in-person meetings, the online format nevertheless helped members based far away to participate more easily and also promoted interaction and exchange by these members as well. This research framework and the way in which it was implemented encouraged cross-cutting connections across all the papers at a variety of levels. Needless to say, the discussions within the respective study groups also have mutual connections.

Regarding the result of each group, as stated in the Foreword, the "Study Group on the Historical Evolution of the Concept of 'Territory'" had a shared

 | DOI:10.1163/9789004706361_011

awareness of examining the concept and the actual situation of "the spatial order in East Asia before the establishment of modern international law relations" and laying out "a discussion of the issues in relation to Japan's contemporary territorial issues" in light of "how territory in modern international law was established and changed." The entire research of this group eloquently demonstrates the synergistic effect of reviewing studies on the concept of "territory" itself and the concept of territorial extensions, based on a shared focus on modern Japan, which offers historical insight into the territorial issues of modern Japan.

Similarly, as explained in the Foreword, the "Study Group on Methods for Resolving Territorial Disputes" had a shared research purpose of looking at "the latest developments in international jurisprudence and other territorial dispute resolution cases as well as at changes in the usage and significance of international law concepts that are related to territory, taking up existing articles and commentaries on judicial precedents and, in particular, examining their points with Japan's territorial issues in mind." Based on this common purpose, the research of the study group came to provide a perspective on multiple specific issues regarding concepts and principles of international law related to territory that, combined, form a comprehensive whole. This notably extended to general observations of international law, covering not only international law related to territorial disputes, but also the validity of international law, assessment of the intent of sovereign States, and the mutual interaction between the jurisdiction of courts and tribunals and the concept of territorial disputes.

Turning to the cross-cutting connections between the two study groups, as discussed in the Foreword, all chapters in this book have a consistent and shared awareness of looking at Japan's territorial issues. This aspect clearly and jointly defines the research conducted by the two study groups. Furthermore, reviewing suitable legal principles for resolving territorial disputes is meaningless unless it is premised on the definition of the concept of "territory."

In this way, the research of the two study groups obviously has mutual and cross-cutting connections. Looking at this in greater depth reveals that the research of the two study groups has multiple mutual connections, which brought synergy effect of the research by each group, as follows. First, question of how to treat an act of the State and the acts of Japan as a State forms a consistent theme across the respective perspectives and is covered by the authors of both study groups.

In trying to understand the acts of the State of modern Japan and the evidence thereof, authors from the "Study Group on the Historical Evolution of the Concept of 'Territory'" had different focuses and emphases regarding the question whether to seek out the views expressed in public fora such as the Japanese Diet by policymakers and government officials or whether to also seek out the theories and opinions of private individuals, such as scholars who were influential at the time. This resulted in a broad assessment of the acts of the State of modern Japan.

The study group also conducted complementary, that is to say indirect, examination of the state of affairs, in other words the "context" by which policymakers and government officials more broadly, as well as scholars with influence at the time, formed their respective views. Specific focuses lay on the opinions of foreign diplomats (such as Ernest Satow) and political elements, such as Diet tactics and factional strife within the Government at the time.

Considering this shared awareness regarding "the acts of the State" by the "Study Group on the Historical Evolution of the Concept of 'Territory'," the "Study Group on Methods for Resolving Territorial Disputes" reviewed the acts of the State in relation to the requirement for territorial acquisition of "continuous and peaceful display of territorial sovereignty." Display of territorial sovereignty must take place as an act of the State. Indeed, with regard to the Senkaku Islands and Takeshima, the questions of whether the acts of assertion by Japan, China, and the Republic of Korea (ROK) are acts of the State and whether the intent of possessing the territory has been displayed by these States are important ones. Furthermore, there is also the question of whereupon acts of the State depend, and its consideration leads to an examination of the elements of intent related to territorial acquisition, such as acquiescence, approval, and protest by the relevant States.

The second element that connects the research across the two study groups is comparison of modern European international law and the East Asian spatial order. Modern European international law was formed based upon the modern European sovereign State system mainly from the 15th to 18th century and further developed in the 19th and 20th century. In this approach, the issue of "whereupon acts of the State depend" cited in the first point is a specific area of study. In other words, to understand the acts of the State, the research returned to the reality that notions of State differed in modern Europe and East Asia.

Obviously, the issue of mutual comparison of modern European international law and the East Asian spatial order was an essential subject for the two study groups to review. Mutual comparison of modern European international law and the East Asian spatial order was one of the most important bases of research for the "Study Group on the Historical Evolution of the Concept of 'Territory'." This point also applies to the "Study Group on Methods for Resolving Territorial Disputes" in the following way. Territorial issues related to Japan have existed over a very long period of time spanning multiple centuries. Therefore, the various related issues, such as which legal order could serve as the basis of Japan's claims of territorial sovereignty in the period in which Japan belonged to the East Asian spatial order, in the period when it accepted modern European international law, and in the period thereafter, how courts and tribunals have treated this issue centered mainly on intertemporal law, and which legal order would be appropriate for making assertions in bilateral negotiations, as opposed to courts and tribunals, with Asian countries such as China and the ROK, can only be meaningfully examined within the framework of a mutual comparison of modern European international law and the East Asian spatial order.

Furthermore, looking at the issue of applicable laws for resolving territorial disputes, the issues of intertemporal law and critical date, which are procedural theories related to time, when placed in the unique context of Japan's territorial issues, concern more than procedural principles and bring the discussion back to the fundamental problem of the legal order of the international community, specifically the relation between modern European international law and the East Asian spatial order.

The third element is the way in which the two study groups expanded their research scope related to the concept of "territory." The "Study Group on the Historical Evolution of the Concept of 'Territory'" dealt with concepts related to territory (*hankoku*: domain State; *hanpō*: domain territory; *zokkoku*: client state; *hanto*: territory; *hōdo*: realm; *kyōiki*: territory; etc.) and concepts related to the extension of territory (*gaichi*: overseas territory; leased territory; etc.). Furthermore, the "Study Group on Methods for Resolving Territorial Disputes" pursued research on whether historic titles can serve as territorial titles, the types of premodern/non-European titles related to territorial control, and the types of relationships between disputes regarding territory (i.e., territorial sovereignty) and coastal State litigation under the United Nations Convention on the Law of the Sea.

The three points discussed above are just some examples of the shared awareness and research topics of the authors in this book. The research framework comprising two study groups clearly facilitated meaningful cross-cutting connections, not only between the study groups but also among the respective papers. In this respect, this book is the result of a collaborative effort by all of the authors. The two editors served as the main reviewers of the study groups based on this understanding and communicated shared comments that they considered to be appropriate to the authors after reading the drafts.

Nevertheless, each author ultimately had complete freedom to make decisions about how to handle the comments. This is because all papers compiled in this book are also considered to be the results of completely independent research by the authors. This independence is reflected in the bibliography listed for each Part. Different from this, references to judicial and arbitral precedents are provided in an integrated index. The bulk of these references is included in Part 3 and Part 4, due to the subjects that they deal with.

Thus, this book is the result of both the independent research and the collaborative works by all the authors and those who were engaged in its publication.

Index of Cases

International Court of Justice

Permanent Court of International Justice

International Tribunal for the Law of the Sea

The Annex VII Arbitral Tribunals of the United Nations Convention on the Law of the Sea

Other Courts and Tribunals

www.ingramcontent.com/pod-product-compliance
Lightning Source LLC
Chambersburg PA
CBHW071326230926
51849CB00002B/322
* 9 7 8 9 0 0 4 7 0 6 3 5 4 *